COMPUTER ORGANIZATION AND DESIGN FUNDAMENTALS

Examining Computer Hardware from the Bottom to the Top

David Tarnoff

Revised First Edition

Computer Organization and Design Fundamentals
by David Tarnoff

Copyright © 2005-2007 by David L. Tarnoff. All rights reserved.
Published with the assistance of Lulu.com

This book was written by David L. Tarnoff who is also responsible for the creation of all figures contained herein.

Cover design by David L. Tarnoff
Cover cartoons created by Neal Kegley

Printing History:
   July 2005:   First edition.
   January 2006:   Minor corrections to first edition.
   July 2007:   Added text on Gray code, DRAM technologies, Mealy machines, XOR boolean rules, signed BCD, and hard drive access times. Also made minor corrections.

Legal Notice:
The 3Com® name is a registered trademark of the 3Com Corporation.
The Apple® name and iTunes® name are registered trademarks of Apple Computer, Inc.
The Dell® name is a registered trademark of Dell, Inc.
The Intel® name, Pentium® 4 Processor Extreme Edition, Hyper-Threading Technology™, and Hyper-Pipelined Technology™ are registered trademarks of the Intel Corporation.
PowerPC® is a registered trademark of International Business Machines Corporation.
The Microsoft® name is a registered trademark of the Microsoft Corporation.

While every precaution has been taken to ensure that the material contained in this book is accurate, the author assumes no responsibility for errors or omissions, or for damage incurred as a result of using the information contained in this book.

Please report any errors found to the author at tarnoff@etsu.edu. In addition, suggestions concerning improvements or additions to the text are encouraged. Please direct such correspondence to the author.

*This book is dedicated to
my wife and our son.
I love you both with all my heart.*

TABLE OF CONTENTS

Preface xxi

Chapter One: Digital Signals and Systems 1
    1.1 Should Software Engineers Worry About Hardware? 1
    1.2 Non-Digital Signals 3
    1.3 Digital Signals 4
    1.4 Conversion Systems 6
    1.5 Representation of Digital Signals 7
    1.6 Types of Digital Signals 9
        1.6.1 Edges 9
        1.6.2 Pulses 9
        1.6.3 Non-Periodic Pulse Trains 10
        1.6.4 Periodic Pulse Trains 11
        1.6.5 Pulse-Width Modulation 13
    1.7 Unit Prefixes 15
    1.8 What's Next? 16
    Problems 16

Chapter Two: Numbering Systems 17
    2.1 Unsigned Binary Counting 17
    2.2 Binary Terminology 20
    2.3 Unsigned Binary to Decimal Conversion 20
    2.4 Decimal to Unsigned Binary Conversion 23
    2.5 Binary Representation of Analog Values 25
    2.6 Sampling Theory 31
    2.7 Hexadecimal Representation 34
    2.8 Binary Coded Decimal 36
    2.9 Gray Codes 37
    2.10 What's Next? 40
    Problems 41

Chapter Three: Binary Math and Signed Representations 43
    3.1 Binary Addition 43
    3.2 Binary Subtraction 45
    3.3 Binary Complements 46
        3.3.1 One's Complement 46
        3.3.2 Two's Complement 47
        3.3.3 Most Significant Bit as a Sign Indicator 50
        3.3.4 Signed Magnitude 51

3.3.5 MSB and Number of Bits 51
3.3.6 Issues Surrounding the Conversion of Binary Numbers. 52
3.3.7 Minimums and Maximums 55
3.4 Floating Point Binary 57
3.5 Hexadecimal Addition 61
3.6 BCD Addition 64
3.7 Multiplication and Division by Powers of Two 65
3.8 Easy Decimal to Binary Conversion Trick 67
3.9 Arithmetic Overflow 67
3.10 What's Next? 69
Problems 69

Chapter Four: Logic Functions and Gates 71
4.1 Logic Gate Basics 71
    4.1.1 NOT Gate 72
    4.1.2 AND Gate 72
    4.1.3 OR Gate 73
    4.1.4 Exclusive-OR (XOR) Gate 74
4.2 Truth Tables 75
4.3 Timing Diagrams for Gates 79
4.4 Combinational Logic 80
4.5 Truth Tables for Combinational Logic 83
4.6 What's Next? 86
Problems 87

Chapter Five: Boolean Algebra 89
5.1 Need for Boolean Expressions 89
5.2 Symbols of Boolean Algebra 90
5.3 Boolean Expressions of Combinational Logic 92
5.4 Laws of Boolean Algebra 95
5.5 Rules of Boolean Algebra 96
    5.5.1 NOT Rule 96
    5.5.2 OR Rules 96
    5.5.3 AND Rules 97
    5.5.4 XOR Rules 98
    5.5.5 Derivation of Other Rules 99
5.6 Simplification 101
5.7 DeMorgan's Theorem 103
5.8 What's Next? 106
Problems 107

Chapter Six: Standard Boolean Expression Formats 109
6.1 Sum-of-Products 109
6.2 Converting an SOP Expression to a Truth Table 110
6.3 Converting a Truth Table to an SOP Expression 112
6.4 Product-of-Sums 114
6.5 Converting POS to Truth Table 115
6.6 Converting a Truth Table to a POS Expression 118
6.7 NAND-NAND Logic 119
6.8 What's Next? 122
Problems 123

Chapter Seven: Karnaugh Maps 125
7.1 The Karnaugh Map 125
7.2 Using Karnaugh Maps 129
7.3 "Don't Care" Conditions in a Karnaugh Map 137
7.4 What's Next? 138
Problems 139

Chapter Eight: Combinational Logic Applications 141
8.1 Adders 141
8.2 Seven-Segment Displays 147
8.3 Active-Low Signals 151
8.4 Decoders 152
8.5 Multiplexers 155
8.6 Demultiplexers 157
8.7 Integrated Circuits 159
8.8 What's Next? 163
Problems 164

Chapter Nine: Binary Operation Applications 165
9.1 Bitwise Operations 165
   9.1.1 Clearing/Masking Bits 167
   9.1.2 Setting Bits 171
   9.1.3 Toggling Bits 171
9.2 Comparing Bits with XOR 173
9.3 Parity 174
9.4 Checksum 175
9.5 Cyclic Redundancy Check 179
   9.5.1 CRC Process 185
   9.5.2 CRC Implementation 187
9.6 Hamming Code 188

9.7 What's Next? 199
Problems 199

Chapter Ten: Memory Cells 203
10.1 New Truth Table Symbols 203
    10.1.1 Edges/Transitions 203
    10.1.2 Previously Stored Values 204
    10.1.3 Undefined Values 204
10.2 The S-R Latch 205
10.3 The D Latch 209
10.4 Divide-By-Two Circuit 212
10.5 Counter 213
10.6 Parallel Data Output 214
10.7 What's Next? 215
Problems 216

Chapter Eleven: State Machines 217
11.1 Introduction to State Machines 217
    11.1.1 States 217
    11.1.2 State Diagrams 218
    11.1.3 Errors in State Diagrams 222
    11.1.4 Basic Circuit Organization 222
11.2 State Machine Design Process 225
11.3 Another State Machine Design: Pattern Detection 234
11.4 Mealy Versus Moore State Machines 237
11.5 What's Next? 238
Problems 239

Chapter Twelve: Memory Organization 241
12.1 Early Memory 241
12.2 Organization of Memory Device 242
12.3 Interfacing Memory to a Processor 244
    12.3.1 Buses 244
    12.3.2 Memory Maps 248
    12.3.3 Address Decoding 250
    12.3.4 Chip Select Hardware 255
12.4 Memory Mapped Input/Output 259
12.5 Memory Terminology 260
    12.5.1 Random Access Memory 260
    12.5.2 Read Only Memory 261
    12.5.3 Static RAM versus Dynamic RAM 261

12.5.4 Types of DRAM and Their Timing 263
12.5.5 Asynchronous vs. Synchronous Memory 266
12.6 What's Next? 267
Problems.. 267

Chapter Thirteen: Memory Hierarchy 269
13.1 Characteristics of the Memory Hierarchy 269
13.2 Physical Characteristics of a Hard Drive 269
    13.2.1 Hard Drive Read/Write Head 270
    13.2.2 Data Encoding 272
    13.2.3 Hard Drive Access Time 275
    13.2.4 S.M.A.R.T. 278
13.3 Organization of Data on a Hard Drive 279
13.4 Cache RAM... 284
    13.4.1 Cache Organization 286
    13.4.2 Dividing Memory into Blocks 287
    13.4.3 Cache Operation 289
    13.4.4 Cache Characteristics 290
    13.4.5 Cache Mapping Functions... 290
    13.4.6 Cache Write Policy 299
13.5 Registers.. 300
13.6 What's Next? 300
Problems.. 301

Chapter Fourteen: Serial Protocol Basics..................................... 303
14.1 OSI Seven-Layer Network Model 303
14.2 Serial versus Parallel Data Transmission........................... 304
14.3 Anatomy of a Frame or Packet 306
14.4 Sample Protocol: IEEE 802.3 Ethernet............................... 308
14.5 Sample Protocol: Internet Protocol 310
14.6 Sample Protocol: Transmission Control Protocol.............. 313
14.7 Dissecting a Frame 317
14.8 Additional Resources 320
14.9 What's Next? 322
Problems.. 322

Chapter Fifteen: Introduction to Processor Architecture............ 325
15.1 Organization versus Architecture.. 325
15.2 Components 325
    15.2.1 Bus.. 325
    15.2.2 Registers... 326

15.2.3 Flags 327
15.2.4 Buffers 328
15.2.5 The Stack 329
15.2.6 I/O Ports 331
15.3 Processor Level 332
15.4 CPU Level 333
15.5 Simple Example of CPU Operation 334
15.6 Assembly and Machine Language 338
15.7 Big-Endian/Little-Endian 345
15.8 Pipelined Architectures 346
15.9 Passing Data To and From Peripherals 350
    15.9.1 Memory-Mapped I/O 351
    15.9.2 Polling 353
    15.9.3 Interrupts 354
    15.9.4 Direct Memory Access 355
    15.9.5 I/O Channels and Processors 356
15.10 What's Next? 357
Problems 357

Chapter Sixteen: Intel 80x86 Base Architecture 359
16.1 Why Study the 80x86? 359
16.2 Execution Unit 360
    16.2.1 General Purpose Registers 361
    16.2.2 Address Registers 362
    16.2.3 Flags 363
    16.2.4 Internal Buses 365
16.3 Bus Interface Unit 365
    16.3.1 Segment Addressing 366
    16.3.2 Instruction Queue 370
16.4 Memory versus I/O Ports 371
16.5 What's Next? 372
Problems 373

Chapter Seventeen: Intel 80x86 Assembly Language 375
17.1 Assemblers versus Compilers 375
17.2 Components of a Line of Assembly Language 376
17.3 Assembly Language Directives 378
    17.3.1 SEGMENT Directive 378
    17.3.2 .MODEL, .STACK, .DATA, and .CODE Directives . 380
    17.3.3 PROC Directive 381

17.3.4 END Directive..382
17.3.5 Data Definition Directives 382
17.3.6 EQU Directive..383
17.4 80x86 Opcodes..385
17.4.1 Data Transfer..385
17.4.2 Data Manipulation..386
17.4.3 Program Control...387
17.4.4 Special Operations 390
17.5 Addressing Modes...391
17.5.1 Register Addressing 391
17.5.2 Immediate Addressing..392
17.5.3 Pointer Addressing 392
17.6 Sample 80x86 Assembly Language Programs....................393
17.7 Additional 80x86 Programming Resources 397
17.8 What's Next? 398
Problems...398

Index..**401**

TABLE OF FIGURES

1-1	Sample Digital System.. 3
1-2	Continuous Analog Signal with Infinite Resolution 4
1-3	Sample of Discrete Measurements Taken Every 0.1 Sec.......... 4
1-4	Samples Taken of an Analog Signal 5
1-5	Slow Sampling Rate Missed an Anomaly............................... 5
1-6	Poor Resolution Resulting in an Inaccurate Measurement 5
1-7	Block Diagram of a System to Capture Analog Data 6
1-8	Representation of a Single Binary Signal 8
1-9	Representation of Multiple Digital Signals.............................. 8
1-10	Alternate Representation of Multiple Digital Signals............... 9
1-11	Digital Transition Definitions 10
1-12	Pulse Waveforms 10
1-13	Non-Periodic Pulse Train 10
1-14	Periodic Pulse Train 11
1-15	Periodic Pulse Train with Different Pulse Widths 11
1-16	Periodic Pulse Train with 25% Duty Cycle 13
2-1	Counting in Decimal 17

2-2	Counting in Binary	18
2-3	Binary-Decimal Equivalents from 0 to 17	19
2-4	Values Represented By Each of the First 8 Bit Positions	21
2-5	Sample Conversion of 10110100_2 to Decimal	21
2-6	Decimal to Unsigned Binary Conversion Flow Chart	24
2-7	Sample Analog Signal of Sound	26
2-8	Effects of Number of Bits on Roundoff Error	32
2-9	Aliasing Effects Due to Slow Sampling Rate	33
2-10	Eight Binary Values Identifying Rotating Shaft Position	38
2-11	Example of a Position Encoder	38
2-12	Conversion from Unsigned Binary to Gray Code	39
3-1	Four Possible Results of Adding Two Bits	44
3-2	Four Possible Results of Adding Two Bits with Carry	44
3-3	Two's Complement Short-Cut	49
3-4	Converting a Two's Complement Number to a Decimal	53
3-5	IEEE Standard 754 Floating-Point Formats	59
3-6	Duplicate MSB for Right Shift of 2's Complement Values	66
4-1	Basic Format of a Logic Gate	71
4-2	Basic Logic Symbols	72
4-3	Operation of the NOT Gate	72
4-4	Operation of a Two-Input AND Gate	73
4-5	Operation of a Two-Input OR Gate	74
4-6	Operation of a Two-Input XOR Gate	74
4-7	Sample Three-Input Truth Table	75
4-8	Listing All Bit Patterns for a Four-Input Truth Table	76
4-9	Inverter Truth Table	77
4-10	Two-Input AND Gate Truth Table	77
4-11	Two-Input OR Gate Truth Table	77
4-12	Two-Input XOR Gate Truth Table	78
4-13	Three-Input AND Gate Truth Table With Don't Cares	78
4-14	Sample Timing Diagram for a Three-Input AND Gate	79
4-15	Sample Timing Diagram for a Three-Input OR Gate	79
4-16	Sample Timing Diagram for a Three-Input XOR Gate	79
4-17	Sample Combinational Logic	80
4-18	Combinational Logic for a Simple Security System	80
4-19	Truth Table for Simple Security System of Figure 4-18	81
4-20	"NOT" Circuits	82
4-21	Schematic "Short-Hand" for Inverted Inputs	82

Table of Contents   xiii

4-22	Sample of Multi-Level Combinational Logic	83
4-23	Process of Passing Inputs Through Combinational Logic	83
4-24	Steps That Inputs Pass Through in Combinational Logic	84
4-25	All Combinations of Ones and Zeros for Three Inputs	84
4-26	Step (a) in Sample Truth Table Creation	85
4-27	Step (b) in Sample Truth Table Creation	85
4-28	Step (c) in Sample Truth Table Creation	86
4-29	Step (d) in Sample Truth Table Creation	86
5-1	Schematic and Truth Table of Combinational Logic	89
5-2	Boolean Expression for the AND Function	90
5-3	Boolean Expression for the OR Function	91
5-4	Boolean Expression for the NOT Function	91
5-5	Circuit Representation of the Boolean Expression 1+0+1	91
5-6	Sample of Multi-Level Combinational Logic	92
5-7	Creating Boolean Expression from Combinational Logic	93
5-8	Examples of the Precedence of the NOT Function	93
5-9	Example of a Conversion from a Boolean Expression	94
5-10	Commutative Law for Two Variables OR'ed Together	95
5-11	Schematic Form of NOT Rule	96
5-12	Rules of Boolean Algebra	101
5-13	Application of DeMorgan's Theorem	105
5-14	Schematic Application of DeMorgan's Theorem	106
6-1	Sample Sum-of-Products Binary Circuit	110
6-2	Samples of Single Product (AND) Truth Tables	111
6-3	Sample of a Sum-of-Products Truth Table	111
6-4	Conversion of an SOP Expression to a Truth Table	112
6-5	Sample Product-of-Sums Binary Circuit	115
6-6	Samples of Single Sum (OR) Truth Tables	115
6-7	Sample of a Product-of-Sums Truth Table	116
6-8	Sample Sums With Multiple Zero Outputs	117
6-9	Conversion of a POS Expression to a Truth Table	118
6-10	Circuit Depiction of DeMorgan's Theorem	120
6-11	OR Gate Equals a NAND Gate With Inverted Inputs	120
6-12	OR-to-NAND Equivalency Expanded to Four Inputs	120
6-13	Sample SOP Circuit	121
6-14	Sample SOP Circuit with Output OR Gate Replaced	121
6-15	Sample SOP Circuit Implemented With NAND Gates	122
7-1	2-by-2 Karnaugh Map Used with Two Inputs	126

7-2	Mapping a 2-Input Truth Table to Its Karnaugh Map	126
7-3	Three-Input Karnaugh Map	127
7-4	Four-Input Karnaugh Map	127
7-5	Identifying the Products in a Karnaugh Map	130
7-6	Karnaugh Map with Four Adjacent Cells Containing '1'	130
7-7	Sample Rectangle in a Three-Input Karnaugh Map	133
7-8	Karnaugh Map with a "Don't Care" Elements	138
7-9	Karnaugh Map with a "Don't Care" Elements Assigned	138
8-1	Four Possible Results of Adding Two Bits	141
8-2	Block Diagram of a Half Adder	142
8-3	Four Possible States of a Half Adder	142
8-4	Logic Circuit for a Half Adder	143
8-5	Block Diagram of a Multi-bit Adder	144
8-6	Block Diagram of a Full Adder	144
8-7	Sum and Carryout Karnaugh Maps for a Full Adder	145
8-8	Logic Circuit for a Full Adder	146
8-9	Seven-Segment Display	147
8-10	Displaying a '1' with a 7-Segment Display	147
8-11	A Seven-Segment Display Displaying a Decimal '2'	148
8-12	Block Diagram of a Seven-Segment Display Driver	148
8-13	Segment Patterns for all Hexadecimal Digits	149
8-14	Seven Segment Display Truth Table	149
8-15	Karnaugh Map for Segment 'e'	150
8-16	Karnaugh Map for Segment 'e' with Rectangles	150
8-17	Logic Circuit for Segment e of 7-Segment Display	151
8-18	Labeling Conventions for Active-Low Signals	152
8-19	Sample Circuit for Enabling a Microwave	153
8-20	Sample Circuit for Delivering a Soda	153
8-21	Truth Table to Enable a Device for A=1, B=1, & C=0	154
8-22	Digital Circuit for a 1-of-4 Decoder	154
8-23	Digital Circuit for an Active-Low 1-of-4 Decoder	155
8-24	Truth Table for an Active-Low 1-of-8 Decoder	155
8-25	Block Diagram of an Eight Channel Multiplexer	156
8-26	Truth Table for an Eight Channel Multiplexer	156
8-27	Logic Circuit for a 1-Line-to-4-Line Demultiplexer	158
8-28	Truth Table for a 1-Line-to-4-Line Demultiplexer	159
8-29	Examples of Integrated Circuits	159
8-30	Pin-out of a Quad Dual-Input NAND Gate IC (7400)	160
8-31	Sample Pin 1 Identifications	160

8-32	Generic Protoboard	161
8-33	Generic Protoboard Internal Connections	161
8-34	Sample Circuit Wired on a Protoboard	162
8-35	Schematic Symbol of a Light-Emitting Diode (LED)	162
8-36	LED Circuit	163
8-37	Switch Circuit	163
9-1	Graphic of a Bitwise Operation Performed on LSB	166
9-2	Bitwise AND of 01101011_2 and 11011010_2	166
9-3	Three Sample Bitwise ANDs	168
9-4	Possible Output from a Motion Detector	173
9-5	A Difference in Output Indicates an Error	173
9-6	Simple Error Detection with an XOR Gate	174
9-7	Sample Block of Data with Accompanying Datasums	176
9-8	Small Changes in Data Canceling in Checksum	179
9-9	Example of Long Division in Binary	181
9-10	Example of Long Division Using XOR Subtraction	182
9-11	Sample Code for Calculating CRC Checksums	189
9-12	Venn Diagram Representation of Hamming Code	192
9-13	Example Single-Bit Errors in Venn Diagram	192
9-14	Example of a Two-Bit Error	193
9-15	Using Parity to Check for Double-Bit Errors	194
10-1	Symbols for Rising Edge and Falling Edge Transitions	204
10-2	Sample Truth Table Using Undefined Output	204
10-3	Primitive Feedback Circuit using Inverters	205
10-4	Operation of a NAND Gate with One Input Tied High	206
10-5	Primitive Feedback Circuit Redrawn with NAND Gates	206
10-6	Only Two Possible States of Circuit in Figure 10-5	206
10-7	Operation of a Simple Memory Cell	207
10-8	Operation of a Simple Memory Cell (continued)	208
10-9	S-R Latch	209
10-10	S-R Latch Truth Table	209
10-11	Block Diagram of the D Latch	209
10-12	Edge-Triggered D Latch Truth Tables	211
10-13	Transparent D Latch Truth Tables	211
10-14	Divide-By-Two Circuit	212
10-15	Clock and Output Timing in a Divide-By-Two Circuit	212
10-16	Cascading Four Divide-By-Two Circuits	213
10-17	Counter Implemented with Divide-By-Two Circuits	213

10-18   Output of Binary Counter Circuit 214
10-19   Output Port Data Latch Circuitry 215

11-1   Adding Memory to a Digital Logic Circuit 217
11-2   States of a Traffic Signal System 218
11-3   States of a Light Bulb 218
11-4   State Diagram for Light Bulb State Machine 218
11-5   Complete State Diagram for Light Bulb State Machine 219
11-6   Block Diagram of an Up-Down Binary Counter 220
11-7   State Diagram for a 3-Bit Up-Down Binary Counter 221
11-8   Sample of a Reset Indication in a State Diagram 221
11-9   Block Diagram of a State Machine 223
11-10   Initial State of the Push Button Light Control 226
11-11   Transitions from State 0 of Push Button Circuit 226
11-12   B=0 Transition from State 0 of Push Button Circuit 227
11-13   B=1 Transition from State 0 of Push Button Circuit 227
11-14   B=0 Transition from State 1 of Push Button Circuit 227
11-15   B=1 Transition from State 1 of Push Button Circuit 228
11-16   Transitions from State 2 of Push Button Circuit 228
11-17   Final State Diagram for Push Button Circuit 229
11-18   Block Diagram for Push Button Circuit 230
11-19   K-Maps for S_1', S_0', and L of Push Button Circuit 232
11-20   Finished Push Button Circuit 232
11-21   Revised Truth Table and K Map for Push Button Circuit 233
11-22   Identifying the Bit Pattern "101" in a Bit Stream 234
11-23   State Diagram for Identifying the Bit Pattern "101" 235
11-24   Next State and Output Truth Tables for Pattern Detect 236
11-25   K-Maps for S_1', S_0', and P of Pattern Detect Circuit 237
11-26   Final Circuit to Identify the Bit Pattern "101" 237
11-27   Basic Configuration of a Mealy Machine 238
11-28   Sample State Diagram of a Mealy Machine 238
11-29   Output Truth Table for Sample Mealy Machine 239

12-1   Diagram of a Section of Core Memory 241
12-2   Basic Organization of a Memory Device 243
12-3   Basic Processor to Memory Device Interface 245
12-4   Two Memory Devices Sharing a Bus 246
12-5   Three Buffers Trying to Drive the Same Output 248
12-6   Sample Memory Maps 249
12-7   Full Address with Enable Bits and Device Address Bits 251

12-8	IPv4 Address Divided into Subnet and Host IDs	254
12-9	Sample Chip Select Circuit for a Memory Device	256
12-10	Some Types of Memory Mapped I/O Configurations	260
12-11	Basic Addressing Process for a DRAM	264
12-12	Organization of DRAM	265
12-13	Example of an FPM Transfer	265
12-14	Example of an EDO Transfer	266
13-1	Block Diagram of a Standard Memory Hierarchy	269
13-2	Configuration of a Hard Drive Write Head	271
13-3	Sample FM Magnetic Encoding	273
13-4	Sample MFM Magnetic Encoding	274
13-5	RLL Relation between Bit Patterns and Polarity Changes	274
13-6	Sample RLL Magnetic Encoding	275
13-7	Components of Disk Access Time	277
13-8	Relation between Read/Write Head and Tracks	279
13-9	Organization of Hard Disk Platter	280
13-10	Illustration of a Hard Drive Cylinder	281
13-11	Equal Number of Bits per Track versus Equal Sized Bits	282
13-12	Comparison of Sector Organizations	282
13-13	Cache Placement between Main Memory and Processor	285
13-14	L1 and L2 Cache Placement	285
13-15	Split Cache Organization	286
13-16	Organization of Cache into Lines	287
13-17	Division of Memory into Blocks	288
13-18	Organization of Address Identifying Block and Offset	289
13-19	Direct Mapping of Main Memory to Cache	291
13-20	Direct Mapping Partitioning of Memory Address	292
13-21	Fully Associative Partitioning of Memory Address	295
13-22	Set Associative Mapping of Main Memory to Cache	297
13-23	Effect of Cache Set Size on Address Partitioning	298
14-1	Sample Protocol Stack using TCP, IP, and Ethernet	307
14-2	Layout of an IEEE 802.3 Ethernet Frame	308
14-3	Layout of an IP Packet Header	311
14-4	Layout of a TCP Packet Header	314
14-5	Position and Purpose of TCP Control Flags	315
14-6	Layout of a TCP Pseudo Header	316
14-7	Simulated Raw Data Capture of an Ethernet Frame	317
15-1	Sample Code Using Conditional Statements	328

xviii Computer Organization and Design Fundamentals

15-2   Block Diagram of a System Incorporating a Buffer 329
15-3   Generic Block Diagram of a Processor System 332
15-4   Generic Block Diagram of Processor Internals 333
15-5   Generic Block Diagram of a Typical CPU 334
15-6   Decoded Assembly Language from Table 15-6 343
15-7   Non-Pipelined Execution of Five Instructions 348
15-8   Pipelined Execution of Five Instructions 348
15-9   Sample Memory Mapped Device Circuit 352
15-10 Basic Operation of an ISR 355

16-1   Block Diagram of 80x86 Execution Unit (EU) 360
16-2   Block Diagram of 80x86 Bus Interface Unit (BIU) 366
16-3   Segment/Pointer Relation in the 80x86 Memory Map 368

17-1   Format of a Line of Assembly Language Code 377
17-2   Format and Parameters Used to Define a Segment 379
17-3   Format of the .MODEL Directive 380
17-4   Format and Parameters Used to Define a Procedure 381
17-5   Format and Parameters of Some Define Directives 383
17-6   Example Uses of Define Directives 384
17-7   Format and Parameters of the EQU Directive 384
17-8   Sample Code with and without the EQU Directive 384
17-9   Format and Parameters of the MOV Opcode 385
17-10 Format and Parameters of the IN and OUT Opcodes 385
17-11 Format and Parameters of the ADD Opcode 386
17-12 Format and Parameters of NEG, NOT, DEC, and INC 386
17-13 Format and Parameters of SAR, SHR, SAL, and SHL 387
17-14 Example of a JMP Instruction 387
17-15 Example of a LOOP Instruction 389
17-16 Sample Organization of a Procedure Call 390
17-17 Examples of Register Addressing 392
17-18 Examples of Immediate Addressing 392
17-19 Examples of an Address being used as an Operand 393
17-20 Skeleton Code for a Simple Assembly Program 393
17-21 Code to Assign Data Segment Address to DS Register 394
17-22 Code to Inform O/S that Program is Terminated 395
17-23 Skeleton Code with Code Added for O/S Support 395
17-24 Data Defining Directives for Example Code 396
17-25 Step-by-Step Example Operation Converted to Code 396
17-26 Final Code for Example Assembly Language Program 397

TABLE OF TABLES

1-1	Unit Prefixes	15
2-1	Converting Binary to Decimal and Hexadecimal	35
2-2	Converting BCD to Decimal	36
2-3	Derivation of the Four-Bit Gray Code	40
3-1	Representation Comparison for 8-bit Binary Numbers	57
3-2	Hexadecimal to Decimal Conversion Table	62
3-3	Multiplying the Binary Value 1001_2 by Powers of Two	65
8-1	Addition Results Based on Inputs of a Full Adder	144
8-2	Sum and Carryout Truth Tables for a Full Adder	145
9-1	Truth Table for a Two-Input XOR Gate	172
9-2	Addition and Subtraction Without Carries or Borrows	181
9-3	Reconstructing the Dividend Using XORs	183
9-4	Second Example of Reconstructing the Dividend	184
9-5	Data Groupings and Parity for the Nibble 1011_2	190
9-6	Data Groupings with a Data Bit in Error	190
9-7	Data Groupings with a Parity Bit in Error	191
9-8	Identifying Errors in a Nibble with Three Parity Bits	191
9-9	Parity Bits Required for a Specific Number of Data Bits	195
9-10	Membership of Data and Parity Bits in Parity Groups	197
11-1	List of States for Push Button Circuit	230
11-2	Next State Truth Table for Push Button Circuit	231
11-3	Output Truth Table for Push Button Circuit	231
11-4	Revised List of States for Push Button Circuit	233
11-5	List of States for Bit Pattern Detection Circuit	236
12-1	The Allowable Settings of Four Chip Selects	247
12-2	Sample Memory Sizes versus Required Address Lines	251
15-1	Conditional Jumps to be Placed After a Compare	337
15-2	Conditional Jumps to be Placed After an Operation	338
15-3	Numbered Instructions for Imaginary Processor	340
15-4	Assembly Language for Imaginary Processor	340
15-5	Operand Requirements for Imaginary Processor	341
15-6	A Simple Program Stored at Memory Address 1000_{16}	342
15-7	Signal Values for Sample I/O Device	351
15-8	Control Signal Levels for I/O and Memory Transactions	353

16-1 Summary of Intel 80x86 Bus Characteristics 360
16-2 Summary of the 80x86 Read and Write Control Signals 372
17-1 Memory Models Available for use with .MODEL 381
17-2 Summary of 80x86 Conditional Jumps 388
17-3 80x86 Instructions for Modifying Flags 390

PREFACE

When I first taught computer organization to computer science majors here at East Tennessee State University, I was not sure where to begin. My training as an electrical engineer provided me with a background in DC and AC electrical theory, electronics, and circuit design. Was this where I needed to start? Do computer science majors really need to understand computers at the transistor level?

The textbook used by my predecessors assumed the reader had had some experience with electronics. The author went so far as to use screen captures from oscilloscopes and other test equipment to describe circuit properties. I soon found that this was a bad assumption to make when it came to students of computer science.

To provide a lifeline to my floundering students, I began writing supplementary notes and posting them to my course web site. Over the years, the notes matured until eventually students stopped buying the course textbook. When the on-line notes were discovered by search engines, I began receiving messages from other instructors asking if they could link to my notes. The answer was obvious: of course!

The on-line notes provided a wonderful opportunity. Instead of requiring a textbook for my course, I could ask my students to purchase hardware or software to supplement the university's laboratory equipment. This could include anything from external hard drives to circuit components. By enhancing the hands-on portion of the course, I hope that I have improved each student's chance to learn and retain the material.[1]

In April of 2004, I became aware of recent advances in self-publishing with services such as Lulu.com. In an effort to reduce the costs paid by students who were printing the course notes from the web, I decided to compile my web notes into a book. For years, I had been receiving comments from students about dried up printer cartridges. I once found a student searching the recycled paper bin for scrap paper on which to print my notes. Even our campus technology group had begun to suggest I was one of the causes for the overuse of campus printers.

---

[1] Korwin, Anthony R., Jones, Ronald E., "Do Hands-On, Technology-Based Activities Enhance Learning by Reinforcing Cognitive Knowledge and Retention?" Journal of Technology Education, Vol. 1, No. 2, Spring 1990. Online. Internet. Available WWW: http://scholar.lib.vt.edu/ejournals/JTE/v1n2/pdf/jones.pdf

So here it is, a textbook open to anyone with a simple desire to learn about the digital concepts of a computer. I've tried to address topics such as analog to digital conversion, CRC's, and memory organization using practical terms and examples instead of the purely theoretical or technical approaches favored by engineers. Hopefully I've succeeded.

I do not pretend to believe that this book alone will provide the reader with the background necessary to begin designing and building contemporary computer circuits. I do, however, believe that reading it will give people the tools to become better developers of software and computer systems by understanding the tools for logic design and the organization of the computer's internals.

The design concepts used for hardware are just as applicable to software. In addition, an understanding of hardware can be applied to software design allowing for improved system performance. This book can be used as a springboard to topics such as advanced computer architecture, embedded system design, network design, compiler design, or microprocessor design. The possibilities are endless.

Organization of This Book

The material in this book is presented in three stages. The first stage, Chapters 1 through 7, discusses the mathematical foundation and design tools that address the digital nature of computers. The discussion begins in Chapters 1, 2, and 3 where the reader is introduced to the differences between the physical world and the digital world. These chapters show how the differences affect the way the computer represents and manipulates data. Chapter 4 introduces digital logic and logic gates followed by Chapters 5, 6, and 7 where the tools of design are introduced.

The second stage, Chapters 8 through 11, applies the fundamentals of the first seven chapters to standard digital designs such as binary adders and counters, checksums and cyclic redundancy checks, network addressing, storage devices, and state machines.

The last stage, Chapters 12 through 17, presents the top-level view of the computer. It begins with the organization of addressable memory in Chapter 12. This is followed in Chapter 13 with a discussion of the memory hierarchy starting with the physical construction of hard drives and ending with the organization of cache memory and processor registers. Chapter 14 brings the reader through the concepts of serial protocols ending with descriptions of the IEEE 802.3 Ethernet, TCP, and IP protocols. Chapter 15 presents the theories of computer architecture while Chapters 16 and 17 use the Intel 80x86 family as a means of example.

Each chapter concludes with a short section titled "What's Next?" describing where the next chapter will take the reader. This is followed by a set of questions that the reader may use to evaluate his or her understanding of the topic.

Acknowledgments

I would like to begin by thanking my department chair, Dr. Terry Countermine, for the support and guidance with which he provided me. At first I thought that this project would simply be a matter of converting my existing web notes into a refined manuscript. This was not the case, and Dr. Countermine's support and understanding were critical to my success.

I would also like to thank my computer organization students who tolerated being the test bed of this textbook. Many of them provided suggestions that strengthened the book, and I am grateful to them all.

Most of all, I would like to thank my wife, Karen, who has always encouraged and supported me in each of my endeavors. You provide the foundation of my success.

Lastly, even self-published books cannot be realized without some support. I would like to thank those who participate as contributors and moderators on the Lulu.com forums. In addition, I would like to thank Lulu.com directly for providing me with a quality outlet for my work.

Disclaimer

The information in this book is based on the personal knowledge collected by David Tarnoff through years of study in the field of electrical engineering and his work as an embedded system designer. While he believes this information is correct, he accepts no responsibility or liability whatsoever with regard to the application of any of the material presented in this book.

In addition, the design tools presented here are meant to act as a foundation to future learning. David Tarnoff offers no warranty or guarantee toward products used or developed with material from this book. He also denies any liability arising out of the application of any tool or product discussed in this book. If the reader chooses to use the material in this book to implement a product, he or she shall indemnify and hold the author and any party involved in the publication of this book harmless against all claims, costs, or damages arising out of the direct or indirect application of the material.

David L. Tarnoff
Johnson City, Tennessee
USA
May 11, 2005
tarnoff@etsu.edu

Note About Third Printing

Over the past two years, a number of small issues have been revealed to me about this work. A few topics needed elaboration and a few errors that had slipped through the self-editing process needed correction. There were not enough issues to require the release of a second edition, but readers of this book should be aware that changes have been made in this the third printing of the book.

The new topics now included in this book are Gray codes, signed BCD, XOR boolean rules, Mealy state machines (the first printing only addressed Moore state machines), DRAM technologies, and hard drive access times. If any reader feels that additional topics should be included in future printings or editions, please feel free to e-mail me at tarnoff@etsu.edu.

David L. Tarnoff
July 6, 2007

CHAPTER ONE

Digital Signals and Systems

1.1 Should Software Engineers Worry About Hardware?

Some students of computer and information sciences look at computer hardware the same way many drivers look at their cars: the use of a car doesn't require the knowledge of how to build one. Knowing how to design and build a computer may not be vital to the computer professional, but it goes a long way toward improving their skills, i.e., making them better drivers. For anyone going into a career involving computer programming, computer system design, or the installation and maintenance of computer systems, the principles of computer organization provide tools to create better designs. These include:

- *System design tools* – The same design theories used at the lowest level of system design are also applied at higher levels. For example, the same methods a circuit board designer uses to create the interface between a processor and its memory chips are used to design the addressing scheme of an IP network.
- *Software design tools* – The same procedures used to optimize digital circuits can be used for the logic portions of software. Complex blocks of if-statements, for example, can be simplified or made to run faster using these tools.
- *Improved troubleshooting skills* – A clear understanding of the inner workings of a computer gives the technician servicing it the tools to isolate a problem quicker and with greater accuracy.
- *Interconnectivity* – Hardware is needed to connect the real world to a computer's inputs and outputs. Writing software to control a system such as an automotive air bag could produce catastrophic results without a clear understanding of the architecture and hardware of a microprocessor.
- *Marketability* – *Embedded system design* puts microprocessors into task-specific applications such as manufacturing, communications, and automotive control. As processors become cheaper and more powerful, the same tools used for desktop software design are being applied to embedded system design. This means that the software

engineer with experience in hardware design has a significant advantage over hardware engineers in this market.

If that doesn't convince you, take a look at what Shigeki Ishizuka, the head of Sony's digital camera division, says about understanding hardware. "When you control parts design, you can integrate the whole package much more elegantly." In other words, today's business environment of low cost and rapid market response, success may depend on how well you control the hardware of your system.

Think of the myriad of systems around you such as your car, cell phone, and PlayStation® that rely on a programmer's understanding of hardware. A computer mouse, for example, sends digital information into the computer's mouse port. In order for the software to respond properly to the movement or button presses of the mouse, the software designer must be able to interpret the digital signal.

On a much greater scale, consider a construction company with projects scattered across a large region that wants to monitor its equipment from a central location such as its corporate offices. A system such as this could be used for inventory control allowing a remote user to locate each piece of equipment from their Internet-enabled desktop computer. E-mail alerts could be sent predicting possible failures when conditions such as overheating or excessive vibration are detected. The system could deliver e-mails or messages to pagers in cases of theft or notify maintenance that periodic service is needed. Here again, the link between software and hardware is critical.

An embedded processor inside the equipment communicates with sensors that monitor conditions such as temperature, vibration, or oil pressure. The processor is capable of transmitting this information to the remote user via a cellular link either when prompted or as an emergency notification. In addition, the processor may be capable of using GPS to determine its geographic location. If the equipment is moved outside of a specified range, a message can be sent indicating a possible theft.

The design of a system such as this raises many questions including:

- What physical values do the digital values that are read from the sensors represent in the real world?
- How can useful information be pulled from the data stream being received by the processors?

- How should the data be formatted for optimal storage, searching, and retrieval?
- Is it possible that using a slower data rate might actually mean shorter connect times over expensive cellular links?

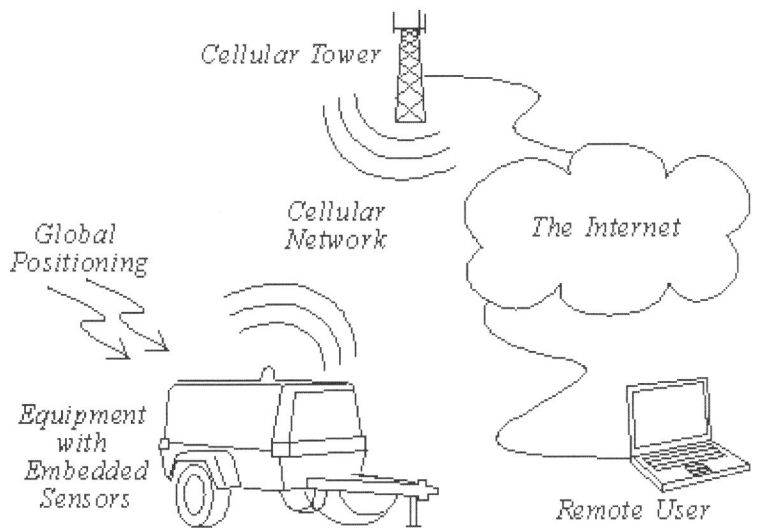

Figure 1-1 Sample Digital System

Computer organization theories answer these and many other questions.

1.2 Non-Digital Signals

The real world is analog. What does that mean? Well, an analog value is equivalent to a floating-point number with an infinite number of places to the right of the decimal point. For example, temperatures do not take on distinct values such as 75°, 76°, 77°, 78°, etc. They take values like 75.434535... In fact, between the temperatures 75.435° and 75.436°, there are an infinite number of possible values. A man doesn't weigh exactly 178 pounds. Add an atom, and his weight changes.

When values such as temperature or weight change over time, they follow what is called a continuous curve. Between any two values on the curve, an infinite number of values take place over an infinite number of points in time.

Okay, so these are ridiculous examples. We can get by without knowing the weight of a man plus or minus an atom. Heck, if we measured to that level of accuracy, his weight would be changing every second. (Time is also an analog value.) It is sufficient to say that analog values represent a continuous signal with infinitesimal resolution.

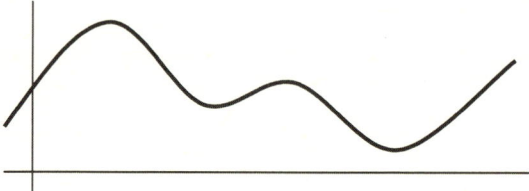

Figure 1-2 Continuous Analog Signal with Infinite Resolution

1.3 Digital Signals

There is such a thing as an analog computer, a computer that processes information using analog levels of electricity or the positions of mechanical devices. The overwhelming majority of today's computers do not do this, however. Instead, they represent an analog value by converting it to a number with a fixed resolution, i.e., a fixed number of digits to the right of the decimal point. This measurement is referred to as a ***digital value***. If the value is changing with respect to time, then a sequence of measurements can be taken, the period between the measurements typically remaining fixed.

Time (seconds)	Measurement
0.00	0.1987
0.10	0.2955
0.20	0.3894
0.30	0.4794
0.40	0.5646

Figure 1-3 Sample of Discrete Measurements Taken Every 0.1 Sec

Since computers look at the world with a fixed resolution in both time and magnitude, when the computer records an analog signal such as the sound waves from music, it does it by taking a sequence of snapshots. For example, assume Figure 1-2 is an analog "real world" signal such as a sound wave. The computer can only measure the signal at intervals. Each measurement is called a *sample*. The rate at which these samples are taken is called the *sampling rate*. The X's in Figure 1-4 represent these measurements.

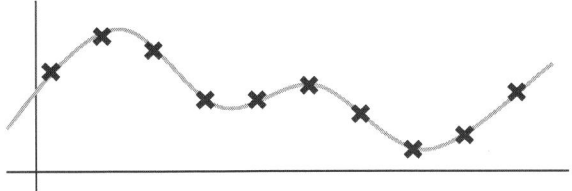

Figure 1-4   Samples Taken of an Analog Signal

Two problems arise from this process: information can be lost *between* the measurements and information can be lost due to the *rounding* of the measurement. First, if the sampling rate is too slow, then some details of the signal may be missed.

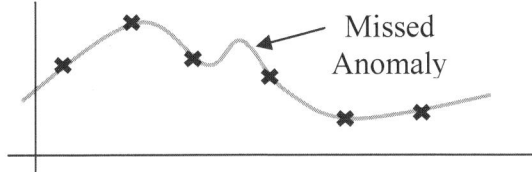

Figure 1-5   Slow Sampling Rate Missed an Anomaly

Second, if the computer does not record with enough accuracy (i.e., enough digits after the decimal point) an error may be introduced between the actual measurement and the recorded value.

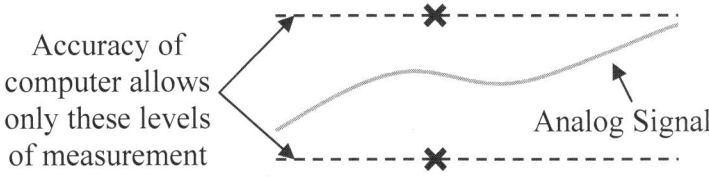

Figure 1-6   Poor Resolution Resulting in an Inaccurate Measurement

6 *Computer Organization and Design Fundamentals*

These effects can be reduced by increasing the resolution of the measurement and increasing the sampling rate. A discussion of this can be found in Chapter 2 in the section titled "Sampling Theory".

1.4 Conversion Systems

The typical system used to convert an external condition such as pressure, temperature, or light intensity to a format usable by a digital system is shown in the block diagram in Figure 1-7.

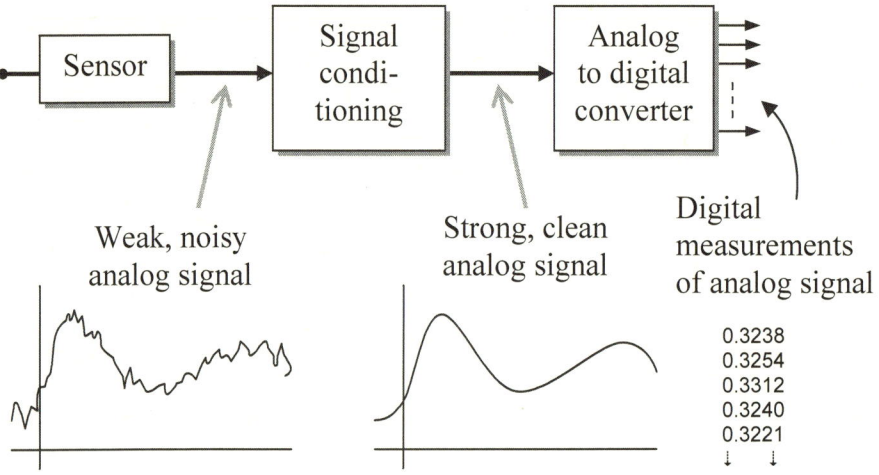

Figure 1-7 Block Diagram of a System to Capture Analog Data

The interface between the external condition and the electronics of the system is the sensor. This device converts the environmental conditions into a signal readable by analog electronics. Often, this signal is weak and is easily distorted by noise. Therefore, the output of the sensor is usually amplified and cleaned up before being converted to digital values by the Analog-to-Digital Converter (ADC). Continuous operation of this system results in a sequence of digital measurements or samples that are stored in the computer where it can be viewed much like the table of numbers in a spreadsheet.

There are benefits to using data in a digital format rather than analog. First, if an analog signal is transmitted over long distances, noise attaches itself to the signal. To keep the signal strong enough to reach its destination, it must be amplified. All of the noise that attached itself to the signal, however, is amplified along with the original signal resulting in distortion. For example, before the advent of digital phone networks, long distance phone calls over analog lines were often full of static and interference that made understanding people who were physically farther away more difficult.

Noise cannot attach itself to a digital signal. Once an analog signal has been converted to a sequence of numbers, the signal's characteristics remain the same as long as the numbers don't change. Therefore, digital systems such as the contemporary long-distance phone system do not suffer from degradation over long distances.

A second benefit is that once a signal is turned into a sequence of numbers, mathematical algorithms can be used to operate on the data. Disciplines such as Digital Signal Processing (DSP) and the study of wavelets allow for much more accurate processing of signals than analog systems were ever able to achieve.

A sequence of digital numbers can also be stored more compactly than an analog signal. The data compression behind the MP3 technology is not remotely possible with analog technology. In addition, supplementary data can be stored along with the samples for information such as digital watermarking for security or codes for error checking or error correction.

These advantages come at a price, however. As mentioned earlier, if the samples are taken too slowly, details of the analog input are missed. If the resolution of the samples is not fine enough, the signal may not be precisely represented with the digital values. Last of all, additional hardware is required to convert the signal from analog to digital.

1.5 Representation of Digital Signals

Digital systems do not store numbers the way humans do. A human can remember the number 4.5 and understand that it represents a quantity. The digital system does not have this capability. Instead, digital systems work with numbers using millions of tiny switches called *transistors*. Each transistor can remember only one of two possible values, on or off. This is referred to as a *binary system*.

The values represented by the transistors of a binary system can be interpreted as needed by the application. On and off can just as easily mean 1 or 0, yes or no, true or false, up or down, or high or low. At this point, it is immaterial what the two values represent. What matters is that there are only two possible values per transistor. The complexity of the computer comes in how the millions of transistors are designed to

8 *Computer Organization and Design Fundamentals*

work together. For the purpose of this discussion, the two values of a transistor will be referred to as ***logic 1*** and ***logic 0***.

Now let's examine some of the methods used to represent binary data by first looking at a single binary signal. Assume we are recording the binary values present on a single wire controlling a light bulb.

Excluding lights controlled by dimmer switches, a light bulb circuit is a binary system; the light is either on or off, a logic 1 or a logic 0 respectively. Over time, the state of the light bulb changes following the position of the switch. The top portion of Figure 1-8 represents the waveform of the binary signal controlling the light bulb based on the changes in the switch position shown in the lower half of the figure.

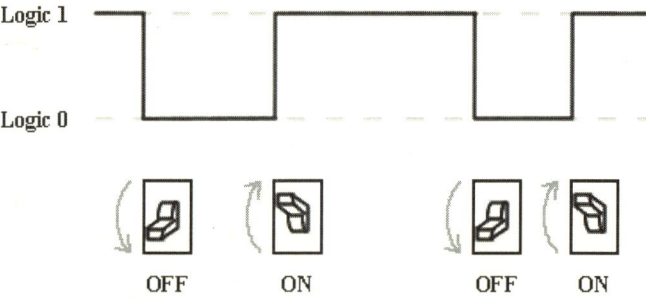

Figure 1-8 Representation of a Single Binary Signal

This representation is much like a mathematical x-y plot where the x-axis represents time and the y-axis identifies either logic 1 or 0.

Sometimes, two or more binary lines are grouped together to perform a single function. For example, the overall lighting in a room may be controlled by three different switches controlling independent banks of lights. This circumstance may be represented with a diagram such as the one shown in Figure 1-9.

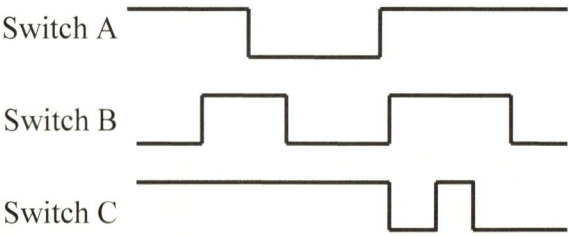

Figure 1-9 Representation of Multiple Digital Signals

Alternatively, multiple lines can be combined into a more abstract representation such as the one shown in Figure 1-10.

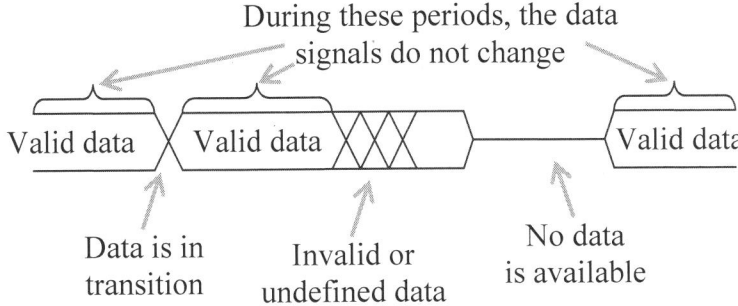

Figure 1-10 Alternate Representation of Multiple Digital Signals

Two horizontal lines, one at a logic 1 level and one at a logic 0 level indicate constant signals from all of the lines represented. A single horizontal line running approximately between logic 1 and logic 0 means that the signals are not sending any data. This is different from an "off" or logic 0 in that a logic 0 indicates a number while no data means that the device transmitting the data is not available. Hash marks indicate invalid or changing data. This could mean that one or all of the signals are changing their values, or that due to the nature of the electronics, the values of the data signals cannot be predicted. In the later case, the system may need to wait to allow the signals to stabilize.

1.6 Types of Digital Signals

1.6.1 Edges

A single binary signal can have one of two possible transitions as shown in Figure 1-11. The first one, a transition from a logic 0 to a logic 1, is called a rising edge transition. The second one, a transition from a logic 1 to a logic 0 is called a falling edge transition.

1.6.2 Pulses

A binary pulse occurs when a signal changes from one value to the other for a short period, then returns to its original value. Examples of this type of signal might be the power-on or reset buttons on a computer (momentarily pressed, then released) or the button used to initialize synchronization between a PDA and a computer.

       a.) Rising Edge   b.) Falling Edge

Figure 1-11 Digital Transition Definitions

There are two types of pulses. The first is called a *positive-going pulse*, and it has an idle state of logic 0 with a short pulse to logic 1. The other one, a *negative-going pulse*, has an idle state of logic 1 with a short pulse to logic 0. Both of these signals are shown in Figure 1-12.

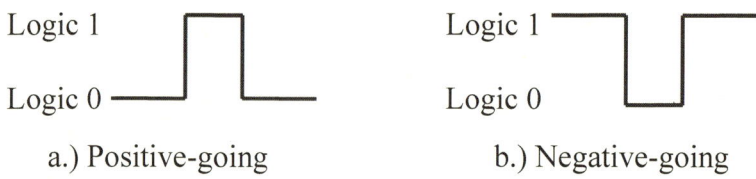

       a.) Positive-going   b.) Negative-going

Figure 1-12 Pulse Waveforms

1.6.3 Non-Periodic Pulse Trains

Some digital signals such as the data wires of an Ethernet link or the data and address lines of a memory interface do not have a characteristic pattern in their changes between logic 1 and logic 0. These are called *non-periodic pulse trains*.

Figure 1-13 Non-Periodic Pulse Train

Like music, the duration of the notes or the spaces between the notes can be longer or shorter. On the page, they do not look meaningful, but once the reader is given the tools to interpret the signal, the data they contain becomes clear.

1.6.4 Periodic Pulse Trains

Some signals act as the heartbeat to a digital system. For example, a signal might tell a system, "Every 1/100th of a second, you need to ____." The output from a car's processor to control the engine's spark plug is such a signal. These signals are referred to as *periodic pulse trains*. Like the drum beat to a song, a periodic pulse train is meant to synchronize events or keep processes moving.

The defining characteristic of this type of waveform is that all measurements between any two subsequent, identical parts of the waveform produce the same value. This value is referred to as the *period, T,* and it has units of seconds/cycle (read seconds per cycle). Figure 1-14 identifies the measurement of a period in a typical periodic Pulse Train.

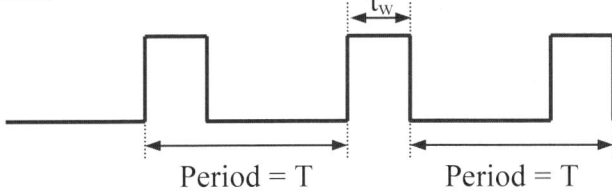

Figure 1-14 Periodic Pulse Train

The measurement of the period does not fully describe a periodic pulse train, however; a second measurement, the width of the pulse, t_w, is needed. For example, the two signals in Figure 1-15 have the same period. Their pulse widths, however, are not the same. In signal a, t_w is about one-fourth of the signal's period while t_w of signal b is about one-half of the signal's period.

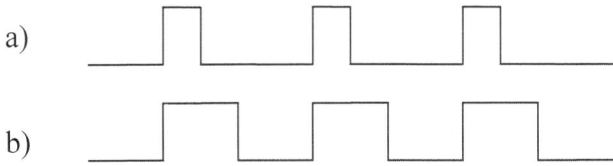

Figure 1-15 Periodic Pulse Train with Different Pulse Widths

The units of t_w is seconds. Its value will always be greater than zero and less than the period. A t_w of zero implies the signal has no pulses, and if t_w equaled the period, then the signal would never go low.

It is also common to represent the rate of the pulses in a periodic pulse train with the inverse measurement of the period. This measurement, called the *frequency* of the periodic pulse train has units of cycles/second, otherwise known as **Hertz** (Hz).

To determine the frequency of a periodic pulse train from the period, invert the measurement for the period.

$$\text{Frequency} = \frac{1}{\text{Period in seconds}} \quad (1.1)$$

Example

If it takes 0.1 seconds for a periodic pulse train to make a complete cycle or period, what is that waveform's frequency?

Solution

$$\text{Frequency} = \frac{1}{\text{Period in seconds}}$$

$$\text{Frequency} = \frac{1}{0.1 \text{ seconds}}$$

$$\text{Frequency} = 10 \text{ Hz}$$

Example

If a computer's system clock is 2 Gigahertz (2,000,000,000 Hz), what is the duration of its system clock's period?

Solution

Inverting Equation 1.1 gives us the equation used to determine the period from the frequency.

$$\text{Period} = \frac{1}{\text{Frequency}}$$

Substituting 2,000,000,000 Hz for the frequency in this new equation gives us the following solution.

$$\text{Period} = \frac{1}{2{,}000{,}000{,}000 \text{ Hz}}$$

Period = 0.0000000005 seconds = 0.5 nanoseconds

1.6.5 Pulse-Width Modulation

The last measurement of a periodic waveform is the *duty cycle*. The duty cycle represents the percentage of time that a periodic signal is a logic '1'. For example, Figure 1-16 represents a periodic pulse train where t_w is about one-quarter or 25% of the duration of the period. Therefore, the duty cycle of this signal is 25%.

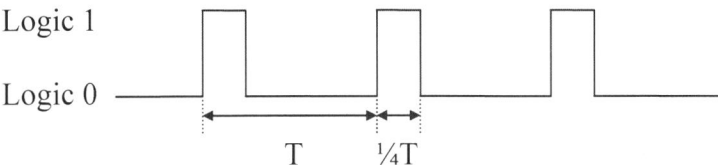

Figure 1-16 Periodic Pulse Train with 25% Duty Cycle

Equation 1.2 represents the formula used to calculate the duty cycle where both t_w and T have units of seconds.

$$\text{Duty Cycle} = \frac{\text{logic 1 pulse duration } (t_w)}{\text{Period (T)}} \times 100\% \quad (1.2)$$

Since the range of t_w is from 0 to T, then the duty cycle has a range from 0% (a constant logic 0) to 100% (a constant logic 1).

Example

The typical human eye cannot detect a light flashing on and off at frequencies above 40 Hz. For example, fluorescent lights flicker at a low frequency, around 60 Hz, which most people cannot see. (Some people can detect higher frequencies and are sensitive to what they correctly perceive as the flashing of fluorescent lights.)

For higher frequencies, a periodic pulse train sent to a light appears to the human eye to simply be dimmer than the same light sent a constant logic 1. This technique can be used to dim light emitting diodes (LEDs), devices that respond to only logic 1's or logic 0's. The brightness of the LED with respect to the full on state is equivalent to the duty cycle. For example, to make an LED shine half as bright as it would with a constant logic 1 sent to it, the duty cycle should be 50%. The frequency is irrelevant as long as it is higher than the human eye can detect.

Example

Assume that a 1 kHz (1,000 Hz) periodic pulse train is sent to an LED. What should the pulse width (t_w) be to make the light emitted from the LED one-third of its full capability?

Solution

Examining equation 1.2 shows that to determine the pulse width, we must first get the values for the period and the duty cycle.

The duty cycle is equal to the level of intensity that the LED is to be lit, i.e., one-third or 33%. The period, T, is equal to one over the frequency.

$$\text{Period} = \frac{1}{\text{Frequency}}$$

$$\text{Period} = \frac{1}{1,000 \text{ Hz}}$$

$$\text{Period} = 0.001 \text{ seconds}$$

To determine the pulse width, solve equation 1.2 for t_w, then substitute the values for the period and the duty cycle.

$$\text{Duty Cycle} = \frac{t_w}{T} \times 100\%$$

$$t_w = \frac{T \times (\text{Duty Cycle})}{100\%}$$

$$t_w = 0.001 \text{ seconds} \times 0.33$$

$$t_w = 0.00033 \text{ seconds} = 330 \text{ microseconds}$$

Chapter 1: Digital Signals and Systems   15

1.7 Unit Prefixes

You may have noticed that in some of our examples, a prefix was used with the units of seconds or Hertz. This is done to reduce the number of leading zeros between a decimal point and a magnitude or to reduce the number of trailing zeros in a very large magnitude.

A prefix replaces a power of 10 multiplier. For example, the measurement 5,000 hertz is equivalent to 5×10^3 hertz. The multiplier 10^3 can be replaced with the prefix "kilo" giving us 5 kilohertz. Each prefix has a single-letter abbreviation that can be used with the abbreviation of the units. For example, to use kilo with the abbreviation Hz, the single letter "k" would be used giving us kHz.

Throughout this book, many prefixes will be used to describe the measurements being discussed. These are presented in the table in Table 1-1. Note that there are prefixes well beyond those presented in this table. They will not be used in this book.

Table 1-1   Unit Prefixes

Prefix	Symbol	Power of 10
zetta	Z	10^{21}
exa	E	10^{18}
peta	P	10^{15}
tera	T	10^{12}
giga	G	10^{9}
mega	M	10^{6}
kilo	k	10^{3}
milli	m	10^{-3}
micro	μ or u	10^{-6}
nano	n	10^{-9}
pico	p	10^{-12}

To use the table, just substitute the prefix for its power of ten. For example, substitute 10^{-6} for the prefix "μ" in the value 15.6 μS. This would give us 15.6×10^{-6} seconds, which in turn equals 0.0000156 seconds.

1.8 What's Next?

In this chapter, we've seen how the methods that a computer uses to store and interpret values are different from the ways in which those values appear in the real world. We've also seen some of the methods used to measure and represent these digital signals.

In Chapter 2 we will see how digital values are used to represent integers. This is the first major step toward understanding some of the idiosyncrasies of computing systems such as why a compiler might restrict the values of a data type from –32,768 to 32,767. In addition, it shows how some bugs occur in programs due to the misuse of data types.

Problems

1. Define the term "sample" as it applies to digital systems.
2. Define the term "sampling rate" as it applies to digital systems.
3. What are the two primary problems that sampling could cause?
4. Name the three parts of the system used to input an analog signal into a digital system and describe their purpose.
5. Name four benefits of a digital system over an analog system.
6. Name three drawbacks of a digital system over an analog system.
7. True or False: Since non-periodic pulse trains do not have a predictable format, there are no defining measurements of the signal.
8. If a computer runs at 12.8 GHz, what is the period of its clock signal?
9. If the period of a periodic pulse train is 125 nanoseconds, what is the signal's frequency?
10. If the period of a periodic pulse train is 50 microseconds, what should the pulse width, t_w, be to achieve a duty cycle of 15%?
11. True or False: A signal's frequency can be calculated from its duty cycle alone.

CHAPTER TWO

Numbering Systems

Chapter one discussed how computers remember numbers using transistors, tiny devices that act like switches with only two positions, on or off. A single transistor, therefore, can only remember one of two possible numbers, a one or a zero. This isn't useful for anything more complex than controlling a light bulb, so for larger values, transistors are grouped together so that their combination of ones and zeros can be used to represent larger numbers.

This chapter discusses some of the methods that are used to represent numbers with groups of transistors or *bits*. The reader will also be given methods for calculating the minimum and maximum values of each representation based on the number of bits in the group.

2.1 Unsigned Binary Counting

The simplest form of numeric representation with bits is *unsigned binary*. When we count upward through the positive integers using decimal, we start with a 0 in the one's place and increment that value until we reach the upper limit of a single digit, i.e., 9. At that point, we've run out of the "symbols" we use to count, and we need to increment the next digit, the ten's place. We then reset the one's place to zero, and start the cycle again.

Ten's place	One's place
	0
	1
	2
	3
	⋮
	8
	9
1	0

Figure 2-1   Counting in Decimal

Since computers do not have an infinite number of transistors, the number of digits that can be used to represent a number is limited. This

17

18   Computer Organization and Design Fundamentals

would be like saying we could only use the hundreds, tens, and ones place when counting in decimal.

This has two results. First, it limits the number of values we can represent. For our example where we are only allowed to count up to the hundreds place in decimal, we would be limited to the range of values from 0 to 999.

Second, we need a way to show others that we are limiting the number of digits. This is usually done by adding leading zeros to the number to fill up any unused places. For example, a decimal 18 would be written 018 if we were limited to three decimal digits.

Counting with bits, hereafter referred to as counting in binary, is subject to these same issues. The only difference is that decimal uses ten symbols (0, 1, 2, 3, 4, 5, 6, 7, 8, and 9) while binary only uses two symbols (0 and 1).

To begin with, Figure 2-2 shows that when counting in binary, we run out of symbols quickly requiring the addition of another "place" after only the second increment.

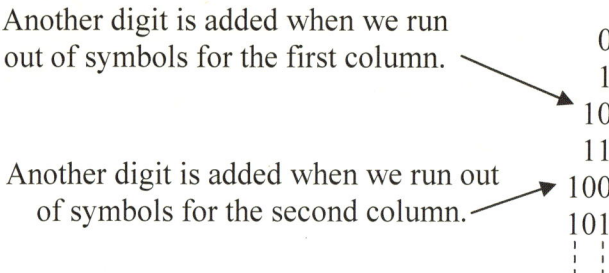

Figure 2-2   Counting in Binary

If we were counting using four bits, then the sequence would look like: 0000, 0001, 0010, 0011, 0100, 0101, 0110, 0111, 1000, 1001, 1010, 1011, 1100, 1101, 1110, and 1111. Notice that when restricted to four bits, we reach our limit at 1111, which happens to be the fifteenth value. It should also be noted that we ended up with 2 x 2 x 2 x 2 = 16 different values. With two symbols for each bit, we have 2^n possible combinations of symbols where n represents the number of bits.

In decimal, we know what each digit represents: ones, tens, hundreds, thousands, etc. How do we figure out what the different digits in binary represent? If we go back to decimal, we see that each place can contain one of ten digits. After the ones digit counts from 0 to

9, we need to increment the tens place. Subsequently, the third place is incremented after 9 tens and 9 ones, i.e., 99 increments, have been counted. This makes it the hundreds place.

In binary, the rightmost place is considered the ones place just like decimal. The next place is incremented after the ones place reaches 1. This means that the second place in binary represents the value after 1, i.e., a decimal 2. The third place is incremented after a 1 is in both the ones place and the twos place, i.e., we've counted to a decimal 3. Therefore, the third place represents a decimal 4. Continuing this process shows us that each place in binary represents a successive power of two.

Figure 2-3 uses 5 bits to count up to a decimal 17. Examine each row where a single one is present in the binary number. This reveals what that position represents. For example, a binary 01000 is shown to be equivalent to a decimal 8. Therefore, the fourth bit position from the right is the 8's position.

Decimal value	Binary value	Decimal value	Binary value
0	00000	9	01001
1	00001	10	01010
2	00010	11	01011
3	00011	12	01100
4	00100	13	01101
5	00101	14	01110
6	00110	15	01111
7	00111	16	10000
8	01000	17	10001

Figure 2-3 Binary-Decimal Equivalents from 0 to 17

This information will help us develop a method for converting unsigned binary numbers to decimal and back to unsigned binary.

Some of you may recognize this as "base-2" math. This gives us a method for indicating which representation is being used when writing a number down on paper. For example, does the number 100 represent a decimal value or a binary value? Since binary is base-2 and decimal is base-10, a subscript "2" is placed at the end of all binary numbers in this book and a subscript "10" is placed at the end of all decimal numbers. This means a binary 100 should be written as 100_2 and a decimal 100 should be written as 100_{10}.

2.2 Binary Terminology

When writing values in decimal, it is common to separate the places or positions of large numbers in groups of three digits separated by commas. For example, 345323745_{10} is typically written $345,323,745_{10}$ showing that there are 345 millions, 323 thousands, and 745 ones. This practice makes it easier to read and comprehend the magnitude of the numbers. Binary numbers are also divided into components depending on their application. Each binary grouping has been given a name.

To begin with, a single place or position in a binary number is called a *bit*, short for binary digit. For example, the binary number 0110_2 is made up of four bits. The rightmost bit, the one that represents the ones place, is called the ***Least Significant Bit or LSB***. The leftmost bit, the one that represents the highest power of two for that number, is called the ***Most Significant Bit or MSB***. Note that the MSB represents a bit position. It doesn't mean that a '1' must exist in that position.

The next four terms describe how bits might be grouped together.

- *Nibble* – A four bit binary number
- *Byte* – A unit of storage for a single character, typically an eight bit (2 nibble) binary number (short for binary term)
- *Word* – Typically a sixteen bit (2 byte) binary number
- *Double Word* – A thirty-two bit (2 word) binary number

The following are some examples of each type of binary number.

Bit	1_2
Nibble	1010_2
Byte	10100101_2
Word	1010010111110000_2
Double Word	$10100101111100001100110111011101_2$

2.3 Unsigned Binary to Decimal Conversion

As shown in section 2.1, each place or position in a binary number corresponds to a specific power of 2 starting with the rightmost bit which represents $2^0=1$. It is through this organization of the bits that we will convert binary numbers to their decimal equivalent. Figure 2-4 shows the bit positions and the corresponding powers of two for each bit in positions 0 through 7.

Numbered bit position	7	6	5	4	3	2	1	0
Corresponding power of 2	2^7	2^6	2^5	2^4	2^3	2^2	2^1	2^0
Decimal equivalent of power of 2	128	64	32	16	8	4	2	1

Figure 2-4 Values Represented By Each of the First 8 Bit Positions

To begin converting an unsigned binary number to decimal, identify each bit position that contains a 1. It is important to note that we number the bit positions starting with 0 identifying the rightmost bit.

Next, add the powers of 2 for each position containing a 1. This sum is the decimal equivalent of the binary value. An example of this process is shown in Figure 2-5 where the binary number 10110100_2 is converted to its decimal equivalent.

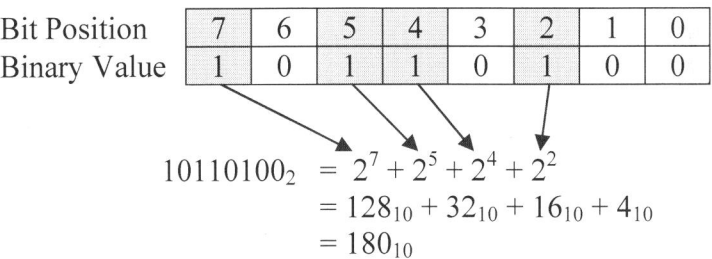

$$10110100_2 = 2^7 + 2^5 + 2^4 + 2^2$$
$$= 128_{10} + 32_{10} + 16_{10} + 4_{10}$$
$$= 180_{10}$$

Figure 2-5 Sample Conversion of 10110100_2 to Decimal

This brings up an important issue when representing numbers with a computer. Note that when a computer stores a number, it uses a limited number of transistors. If, for example, we are limited to eight transistors, each transistor storing a single bit, then we have an upper limit to the size of the decimal value we can store.

The largest unsigned eight bit number we can store has a 1 in all eight positions, i.e., 11111111_2. This number cannot be incremented without forcing an overflow to the next highest bit. Therefore, the largest decimal value that 8 bits can represent in unsigned binary is the sum of all powers of two from 0 to 7.

$$\begin{aligned} 11111111_2 &= 2^7 + 2^6 + 2^5 + 2^4 + 2^3 + 2^2 + 2^1 + 2^0 \\ &= 128 + 64 + 32 + 16 + 8 + 4 + 2 + 1 \\ &= 255_{10} \end{aligned}$$

If you add one to this value, the result is 256 which is 2^8, the power of two for the next bit position. This makes sense because if you add 1 to 11111111_2, then beginning with the first column, 1 is added to 1 giving us a result of 0 with a 1 carry to the next column. This propagates to the MSB where a final carry is passed to the ninth bit. The final value is then $100000000_2 = 256_{10}$.

$$11111111_2 + 1 = 100000000_2 = 256_{10} = 2^8$$

Therefore, the maximum value that can be represented with 8 bits in unsigned binary is $2^8 - 1 = 255$.

It turns out that the same result is found for any number of bits. The maximum value that can be represented with n bits in unsigned binary is $2^n - 1$.

Max unsigned binary value represented with n bits = $2^n - 1$ (2.1)

We can look at this another way. Each digit of a binary number can take on 2 possible values, 0 and 1. Since there are two possible values for the first digit, two possible values for the second digit, two for the third, and so on until you reach the n-th bit, then we can find the total number of possible combinations of 1's and 0's for n-bits by multiplying 2 n-times, i.e., 2^n.

How does this fit with our upper limit of 2^n-1? Where does the "-1" come from? Remember that counting using unsigned binary integers begins at 0, not 1. Giving 0 one of the bit patterns takes one away from the maximum value.

2.4 Decimal to Unsigned Binary Conversion

Converting from decimal to unsigned binary is a little more complicated, but it still isn't too difficult. Once again, there is a well-defined process.

To begin with, it is helpful to remember the powers of 2 that correspond to each bit position in the binary numbering system. These were presented in Figure 2-4 for the powers of 2^0 up to 2^7.

What we need to do is separate the decimal value into its power of 2 components. The easiest way to begin is to find the largest power of 2 that is less than or equal to our decimal value. For example if we were converting 75_{10} to binary, the largest power of 2 less than or equal to 75_{10} is $2^6 = 64$.

The next step is to place a 1 in the location corresponding to that power of 2 to indicate that this power of 2 is a component of our original decimal value.

Next, subtract this first power of 2 from the original decimal value. In our example, that would give us $75_{10} - 64_{10} = 11_{10}$. If the result is not equal to zero, go back to the first step where we found the largest power of 2 less than or equal to the new decimal value. In the case of our example, we would be looking for the largest power of 2 less than or equal to 11_{10} which would be $2^3 = 8$.

When the result of the subtraction reaches zero, and it eventually will, then the conversion is complete. Simply place 0's in the bit positions that do not contain 1's. Figure 2-6 illustrates this process using a flowchart.

If you get all of the way to bit position zero and still have a non-zero result, then one of two things has happened. Either there was an error in one of your subtractions or you did not start off with a large enough number of bits. Remember that a fixed number of bits, n, can only represent an integer value up to $2^n - 1$. For example, if you are trying to convert 312_{10} to unsigned binary, eight bits will not be enough because the highest value eight bits can represent is $2^8 - 1 = 255_{10}$. Nine bits, however, will work because its maximum unsigned value is $2^9 - 1 = 511_{10}$.

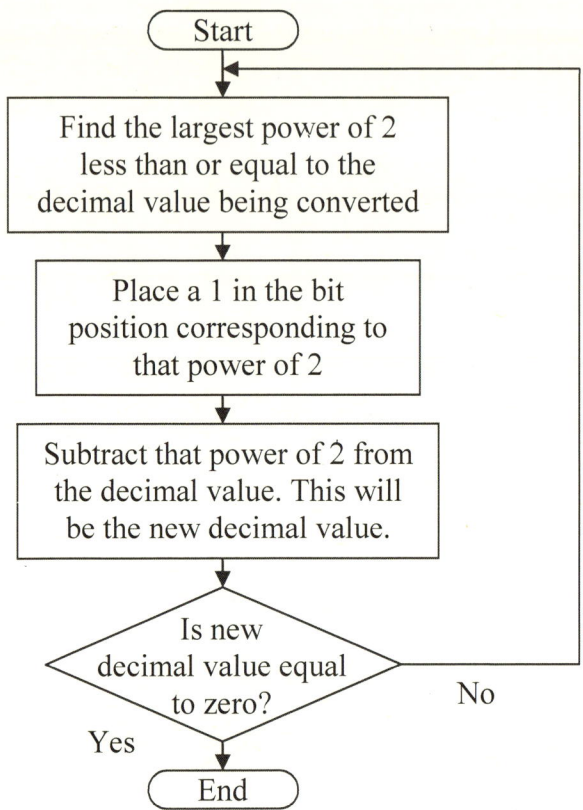

Figure 2-6 Decimal to Unsigned Binary Conversion Flow Chart

Example

Convert the decimal value 133_{10} to an 8 bit unsigned binary number.

Solution

Since 133_{10} is less than $2^8 - 1 = 255$, 8 bits will be sufficient for this conversion. Using Figure 2-4, we see that the largest power of 2 less than or equal to 133_{10} is $2^7 = 128$. Therefore, we place a 1 in bit position 7 and subtract 128 from 133.

Bit position	7	6	5	4	3	2	1	0
	1							

$$133 - 128 = 5$$

Our new decimal value is 5. Since this is a non-zero value, our next step is to find the largest power of 2 less than or equal to 5. That would be $2^2 = 4$. So we place a 1 in the bit position 2 and subtract 4 from 5.

Bit position	7	6	5	4	3	2	1	0
	1					1		

$$5 - 4 = 1$$

Our new decimal value is 1, so find the largest power of 2 less than or equal to 1. That would be $2^0 = 1$. So we place a 1 in the bit position 0 and subtract 1 from 1.

Bit position	7	6	5	4	3	2	1	0
	1					1		1

$$1 - 1 = 0$$

Since the result of our last subtraction is 0, the conversion is complete. Place zeros in the empty bit positions.

Bit position	7	6	5	4	3	2	1	0
	1	0	0	0	0	1	0	1

And the result is:

$$133_{10} = 10000101_2$$

2.5 Binary Representation of Analog Values

Converting unsigned (positive) integers to binary is only one of the many ways that computers represent values using binary bits. This chapter still has two more to cover, and Chapter 3 will cover even more.

This section focuses on the problems and solutions of trying to map real world values such as temperature or weight from a specified range to a binary integer. For example, a computer that uses 8 bits to represent an integer is capable of representing 256 individual values from 0 to 255. Temperature, however, is a floating-point value with unrealistic upper and lower limits. Can we get a computer to represent a temperature using eight bits? The answer is yes, but it will cost us in the areas of resolution and range.

Another example of analog values is the pattern of sound waves such as that from music. Figure 2-7 represents such a signal.

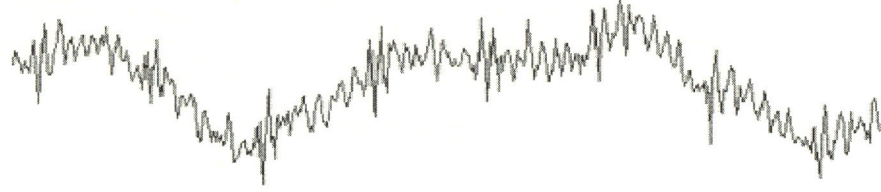

Figure 2-7 Sample Analog Signal of Sound

Remember that a single binary bit can be set to only one of two values: logic 1 or logic 0. Combining many bits together allows for a range of integers, but these are still discrete values. The real world is analog, values represented with floating-point measurements capable of infinite resolution. To use an n-bit binary number to represent analog, we need to put some restrictions on what is being measured.

First, an n-bit binary number has a limited range. We saw this when converting unsigned positive integers to binary. In this case, the lower limit was 0 and the upper limit was 2^n-1. To use n-bits to represent an analog value, we need to restrict the allowable range of analog measurements. This doesn't need to be a problem.

For example, does the typical bathroom scale need to measure values above 400 pounds? If not, then a digital system could use a 10-bit binary number mapped to a range from zero to 400 pounds. A binary 0000000000_2 could represent zero pounds while 1111111111_2 could represent 400 pounds.

What is needed next is a method to map the values inside the range zero to 400 pounds to the binary integers in the range 0000000000_2 to 1111111111_2. To do this, we need a linear function defining a one-to-one mapping between each binary integer and the analog value it represents. To do this, we turn to the basic math expression for a linear function.

$$y = mx + b$$

This function defines m as the rate of the change in y with respect to changes in x and b as the value y is set to when x equals 0. We can use this expression to map a binary integer x to an analog value y.

The slope of this function, m, can be calculated by dividing the range of analog values by the number of intervals defined by the n-bit binary integer. The number of intervals defined by the n-bit binary integer is equal to the upper limit of that binary number if it were being used as an unsigned integer, i.e., 2^n-1.

$$m = \frac{\text{Range of analog values}}{\text{Number of intervals of binary integer}}$$

$$m = \frac{\text{Max analog value - Min analog value}}{2^n - 1} \quad (2.2)$$

Let's go back to our example of the kitchen scale where the maximum analog value is 400 pounds while the minimum is zero pounds. If a 10-bit binary value is used to represent this analog value, then the number of intervals of the binary integer is $2^{10} - 1 = 1023$. This gives us a slope of:

$$m = \frac{400 \text{ pounds} - 0 \text{ pounds}}{1023 \text{ binary increments}} = 0.391 \text{ pounds/binary increment}$$

That means that each time the binary number increments, e.g., 0110110010_2 goes to 0110110011_2, it represents an increment in the analog value of 0.391 pounds. Since a binary value of 0000000000_2 represents an analog value of 0 pounds, then 0000000001_2 represents 0.391 pounds, 0000000010_2 represents $2 \times 0.391 = 0.782$ pounds, 0000000011_2 represents $3 \times 0.391 = 1.173$ pounds, and so on.

In some cases, the lower limit might be something other than 0. This is important especially if better accuracy is required. For example, a kitchen oven may have an upper limit of 600°F. If zero were used as the lower limit, then the temperature range 600°F − 0°F = 600°F would need to be mapped to the 2^n possible binary values of an n-bit binary number. For a 9-bit binary number, this would result in an m of:

$$m = \frac{600°F - 0°F}{2^9 - 1} = 1.1742 \text{ degrees/binary increment}$$

Does an oven really need to measure values below 100°F though? If not, a lower limit of 100°F could be used reducing the size of the analog range to 500°F. This smaller range would improve the accuracy of the system because each change in the binary value would result in a smaller increment in the analog value.

$$m = \frac{600°F - 100°F}{2^9 - 1} = 0.9785 \text{ degrees/binary increment}$$

The smaller increment means that each binary value will be a more accurate representation of the analog value.

This non-zero lower limit is realized as a non-zero value for **b** in the linear expression y=mx + b. Since **y** is equal to **b** when **x** is equal to zero, then b must equal the lower limit of the range.

$$b = \text{Minimum analog value} \qquad 2.3$$

The final expression representing the conversion between an analog value at its binary representation is shown in Equation 2.4.

$$A_{calc} = \left(\frac{A_{max} - A_{min}}{2^n - 1} * X\right) + A_{min} \qquad (2.4)$$

where:

A_{calc} = analog value represented by binary value
A_{max} = maximum analog value
A_{min} = minimum analog value
X = binary value representing analog value
n = number of bits in binary value

Example

Assume that the processor monitoring the temperature of an oven with a temperature range from 100°F to 600°F measures a 9-bit binary value of 011001010_2. What temperature does this represent?

Solution

Earlier, we calculated the rate of change, m, for an oven with a temperature range from 100°F to 600°F is 500°F ÷ 511 binary increments. Substituting this along with our minimum analog value of 100°F into Equation 2.4 gives us:

$$\text{temperature} = \frac{500}{511} °\text{F/binary increment} * \text{binary value} + 100°\text{F}$$

If the processor monitoring the temperature of this oven reads a binary value of 011001010_2, the approximate temperature can be determined by converting 011001010_2 to decimal and inserting it into the equation above.

$$\begin{aligned}011001010_2 &= 2^7 + 2^6 + 2^3 + 2^1 \\ &= 128 + 64 + 8 + 2 \\ &= 202_{10}\end{aligned}$$

$$\text{temperature} = \frac{500°\text{F}}{511} * 202 + 100°\text{F}$$

$$\text{temperature} = 297.65°\text{F}$$

The value from the above example is slightly inaccurate. The binary value 011001010_2 actually represents a range of values 0.9785°F wide centered around or with a lower limit of 297.65°F. Only a binary value with an infinite number of bits would be entirely accurate. Since this is not possible, there will always be a gap or resolution associated with a digital system due to the quantized nature of binary integer values. That gap is equivalent to the increment or rate of change of the linear expression.

$$\text{Resolution} = \frac{\text{Analog range}}{2^n - 1} \qquad (2.5)$$

Example
Assume that the analog range of a system using a 10-bit analog-to-digital converter goes from a lower limit of 5 ounces to an upper limit of 11 ounces. What is the resolution of this system?

Solution
To determine the resolution, we begin with the analog range.

Analog range = Max analog value - Min analog value
= 11 ounces – 5 ounces
= 6 ounces

Substituting this range into equation 2.5 and using n=10 to represent the number of bits, we get:

$$\text{Resolution} = \frac{6 \text{ ounces}}{2^{10} - 1}$$

$$= \frac{6 \text{ ounces}}{1023 \text{ increments}}$$

$$= 0.005865 \text{ oz/inc}$$

If we examine the results of the example above, we see that our system can measure 0 ounces, 0.005865 ounces, 0.011730 ounces, (2 * 0.005865 ounces), 0.017595 (3 * 0.005865 ounces), and so on, but it can never represent the measurement 0.015 ounces. Its resolution is not that good. In order to get that resolution, you would need to increase the number of bits in the binary integer or reduce the analog range.

Example

How many bits would be needed for the example above to improve the resolution to better than 0.001 ounces per increment?

Solution

Each time we increase the number of bits in our binary integer by one, the number of increments in the range is approximately doubled. For example, going from 10 bits to 11 bits increases the number of increments in the range from $2^{10} - 1 = 1023$ to $2^{11} - 1 = 2047$. The question is how high do we have to go to get to a specified resolution? To answer that, let's begin by setting Equation 2.5 to represent the fact that we want a resolution of **better than** 0.001 ounces/increment.

$$0.001 \text{ oz/inc.} > \frac{6 \text{ ounces}}{2^n - 1}$$

Solving for $2^n - 1$ gives us:

$$2^n - 1 > \frac{6 \text{ ounces}}{0.001 \text{ oz/inc.}}$$

$$2^n - 1 > 6{,}000 \text{ increments}$$

By substituting different integers for n into the above equation, we find that n=13 is the lowest value of n for which a resolution better than 0.001 ounces/increment is reached. n=13 results in a resolution of 6 ÷ 8191 = 0.0007325 ounces/increment.

2.6 Sampling Theory

The previous discussion of the integer representation of analog values shows how the number of bits can affect the roundoff error of the representation. In general, an n-bit analog-to-digital converter divides the analog range into $2^n - 1$ increments. Figure 2-8 presents four graphs, each with a different number of bits providing different levels of resolution. The figure shows how the addition of a bit can improve the resolution of the values represented by the binary integers.

Earlier, it was mentioned how a computer can only capture a "snap shot" or sample of an analog voltage. This is sufficient for slowly varying analog values, but if a signal is varying quickly, details might be missed. To improve the signal's digital representation, the rate at which the samples are taken, the *sampling rate*, needs to be increased.

There is also a chance of missing a higher frequency because the sampling rate is too slow. This is called *aliasing*, and there are examples of it in everyday life.

When riding in a car at night, you may have noticed that at times the wheels of an adjacent car appear to be spinning at a different rate than they really are or even appear to spin backwards. (If you have no idea what I'm talking about, watch the wheels of the car next to you the next time you are a passenger riding at night under street lights.)

The effect is caused by the fact that the light from street lamps actually pulses, a fact that is usually not detectable with the human eye. This pulsing provides a sampling rate, and if the sampling rate is not fast enough for the spinning wheel, the wheel appears to be spinning at a different rate than it really is. Street lights are not necessary to see this effect. Your eye has a sampling rate of its own which means that you may experience this phenomenon in the day time.

32   Computer Organization and Design Fundamentals

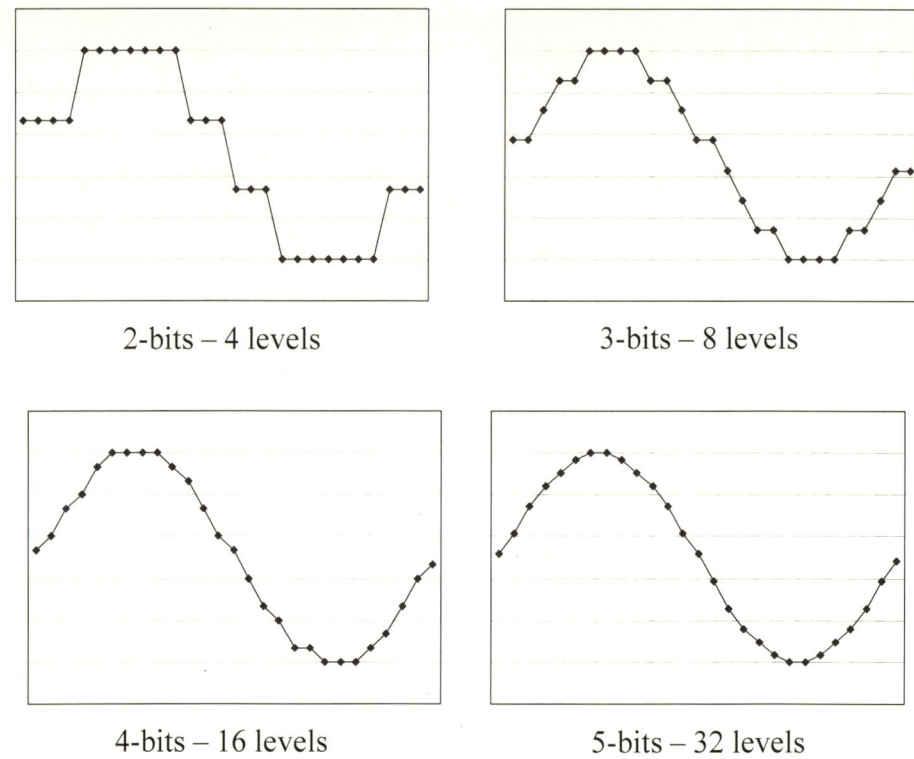

Figure 2-8   Effects of Number of Bits on Roundoff Error

Aliasing is also the reason fluorescent lights are never used in sawmills. Fluorescent lights blink much like a very fast strobe light and can make objects appear as if they are not moving. If the frequency of the fluorescent lights and the speed of a moving saw blade are multiples of each other, it can appear as if the spinning blade is not moving at all.

Both of these examples are situations where aliasing has occurred. If a signal's frequency is faster than the sampling rate, then information will be lost, and the collected data will never be able to duplicate the original.

The graphs in Figure 2-9 show how different sampling rates can result in different interpretations of the collected data, the dark points representing the samples. Note that the bottom-right graph represents a good sampling rate. When the computer reproduces the signal, the choppiness of the reproduction will be removed due to the natural filtering effects of analog circuitry.

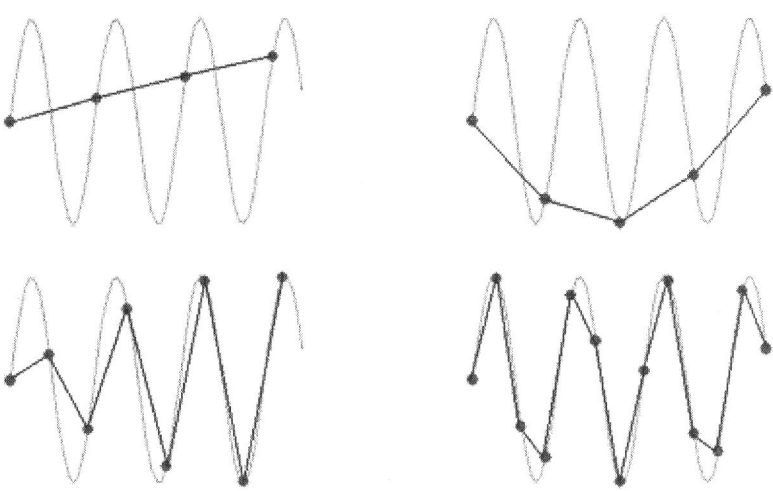

Figure 2-9 Aliasing Effects Due to Slow Sampling Rate

To avoid aliasing, the rate at which samples are taken must be more than twice as fast as the highest frequency you wish to capture. This is called the ***Nyquist Theorem***. For example, the sampling rate for audio CDs is 44,100 samples/second. Dividing this number in half gives us the highest frequency that an audio CD can play back, i.e., 22,050 Hz.

For an analog telephone signal, a single sample is converted to an 8-bit integer. If these samples are transmitted across a single channel of a T1 line which has a data rate of 56 Kbps (kilobits per second), then we can determine the sampling rate.

$$\text{Sampling rate}_{T1} = \frac{56{,}000 \text{ bits/second}}{8 \text{ bits/sample}}$$

$$\text{Sampling rate}_{T1} = 7{,}000 \text{ samples/second}$$

This means that the highest analog frequency that can be transmitted across a telephone line using a single channel of a T1 link is 7,000÷2 = 3,500 Hz. That's why the quality of voices sent over the telephone is poor when compared to CD quality. Although telephone users can still

34 *Computer Organization and Design Fundamentals*

recognize the voice of the caller on the opposite end of the line when the higher frequencies are eliminated, their speech often sounds muted.

2.7 Hexadecimal Representation

It is usually difficult for a person to look at a binary number and instantly recognize its magnitude. Unless you are quite experienced at using binary numbers, recognizing the relative magnitudes of 10101101_2 and 10100101_2 is not immediate (173_{10} is greater than 165_{10}). Nor is it immediately apparent to us that 1001101101_2 equals 621_{10} without going through the process of calculating 512 + 64 + 32 + 8 + 4 + 1.

There is another problem: we are prone to creating errors when writing or typing binary numbers. As a quick exercise, write the binary number $10010111110110100100111_2$ onto a sheet of paper. Did you make a mistake? Most people would have made at least one error.

To make the binary representation of numbers easier on us humans, there is a shorthand representation for binary values. It begins by partitioning a binary number into its nibbles starting at the least significant bit (LSB). An example is shown below:

The number:	10010111101101000100111				
...can be divided into:	10	0101	1110	1101	0010	0111

Next, a symbol is used to represent each of the possible combinations of bits in a nibble. We start by numbering them with the decimal values equivalent to their binary value, i.e.:

$$0000_2 = 0_{10}$$
$$0001_2 = 1_{10}$$
$$0010_2 = 2_{10}$$
$$\vdots \quad \vdots \quad \vdots$$
$$1000_2 = 8_{10}$$
$$1001_2 = 9_{10}$$

At 9, however, we run out of decimal characters. There are six more nibbles to label, so we begin using letters: A, B, C, D, E, and F. These represent the decimal values 10_{10}, 11_{10}, 12_{10}, 13_{10}, 14_{10}, and 15_{10} respectively.

$1010_2 = A$
$1011_2 = B$
: : :
$1111_2 = F$

Table 2-1 presents the mapping between the sixteen patterns of 1's and 0's in a binary nibble and their corresponding decimal and hexadecimal (hex) values.

Table 2-1 Converting Binary to Decimal and Hexadecimal

Binary	Decimal	Hex	Binary	Decimal	Hex
0000	0	0	1000	8	8
0001	1	1	1001	9	9
0010	2	2	1010	10	A
0011	3	3	1011	11	B
0100	4	4	1100	12	C
0101	5	5	1101	13	D
0110	6	6	1110	14	E
0111	7	7	1111	15	F

Another way to look at it is that hexadecimal counting is also similar to decimal except that instead of having 10 numerals, it has sixteen. This is also referred to as a base-16 numbering system.

How do we convert binary to hexadecimal? Begin by dividing the binary number into its nibbles (if the number of bits is not divisible by 4, add leading zeros), then nibble-by-nibble use the table above to find the hexadecimal equivalent to each 4-bit pattern. For example:

The number:	100101110110100100111					
...is divided into:	0010	0101	1110	1101	0010	0111
...which translates to:	2	5	E	D	2	7

Therefore, $100101110110100100111_2 = 25ED27_{16}$. Notice the use of the subscript "16" to denote hexadecimal representation.

Going the other way is just as easy. Translating $5D3F21_{16}$ to binary goes something like this:

The hexadecimal value:	5	D	3	F	2	1
...translates to:	0101	1101	0011	1111	0010	0001

Therefore, $5D3F21_{16} = 010111010011111100100001_2$.

It is vital to note that computers do not use hexadecimal, humans do. Hexadecimal provides humans with a reliable, short-hand method of writing large binary numbers.

2.8 Binary Coded Decimal

When was the last time you multiplied your house number by 5? Or have you ever added 215 to your social security number? These questions seem silly, but they reveal an important fact about numbers. Some numbers do not need to have mathematical operations performed on them, and therefore, do not need to have a mathematically correct representation in binary.

In an effort to afford decimal notation the same convenience of conversion to binary that hex has, Binary Coded Decimal (BCD) was developed. It allows for fast conversion to binary of integers that do not require mathematical operations.

As in hex, each decimal digit represents a nibble of the binary equivalent. Table 2-2 shows the conversion between each decimal digit and the binary equivalent.

Table 2-2 Converting BCD to Decimal

BCD Nibble	Decimal Digit	BCD Nibble	Decimal Digit
0000	0	1000	8
0001	1	1001	9
0010	2	1010	Invalid
0011	3	1011	Invalid
0100	4	1100	Invalid
0101	5	1101	Invalid
0110	6	1110	Invalid
0111	7	1111	Invalid

For example, the BCD value 0001 0110 1001 0010 equals 1692_{10}.

It is important to note that there is no algorithmic conversion between BCD and decimal. BCD is only a method for representing decimal numbers in binary.

Another item of note is that not all binary numbers convert from BCD to decimal. 0101 1011 0101 for example is an illegal BCD value because the second nibble, 1011, does not have a corresponding decimal value.

There are two primary advantages of BCD over binary. First, any mathematical operation based on a factor of ten is simpler in BCD. Multiplication by ten, for example, appends a nibble of zeros to the right side of the number. All it takes to truncate or round a base-10 value in BCD is to zero the appropriate nibbles. Because of this advantage, BCD is used frequently in financial applications due to legal requirements that decimal values be *exactly* represented. Binary cannot do this for fractions as we shall see in Chapter 3.

The second advantage is that conversion between entered or displayed numeric characters and the binary value being stored is fast and does not require much code.

The primary disadvantage is that unless the operation is based on a power of ten, mathematical operations are more complex and require more hardware. In addition, BCD is not as compact as unsigned binary and may require more memory for storage.

BCD can be used to represent signed values too, although there are many implementations. Different processor manufacturers use different methods making it hard to select a standard. One of the easiest ways to represent negative numbers in BCD is to add a nibble at the beginning of the number to act as a plus/minus sign. By using one of the illegal BCD values to represent a negative sign and another to represent a positive sign, BCD values can be made negative or positive. Binary values of 1010, 1100, or 1110 typically mean the number is positive while binary values of 1011 or 1101 mean the number is negative. For example, -1234 in signed BCD would be 1101 0001 0010 0011 0100 while +1234 would be 1100 0001 0010 0011 0100. BCD values preceded with 1111 typically indicate unsigned values.

2.9 Gray Codes

The use of binary counting sequences is common in digital applications. For example, an n-bit binary value can be used to identify the position of a rotating shaft as being within one of 2^n different arcs.

38   Computer Organization and Design Fundamentals

As the shaft turns, a sensor can detect which of the shaft's arcs it is aligned with by reading a digital value and associating it with a specific arc. By remembering the previous position and timing the changes between positions, a processor can also compute speed and direction.

Figure 2-10 shows how a shaft's position might be divided into eight arcs using three bits. This would allow a processor to determine the shaft's position to within $360°/8 = 45°$.

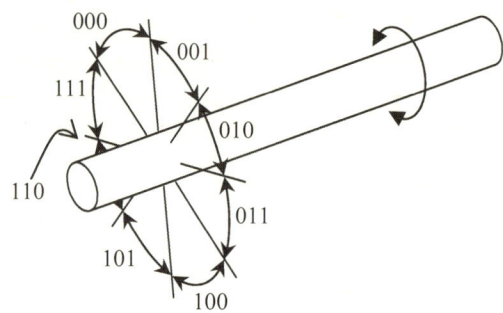

Figure 2-10   Eight Binary Values Identifying Rotating Shaft Position

One type of shaft position sensor uses a disk mounted to the shaft with slots cut into the disk at different radii representing different bits. Light sources are placed on one side of the disk while sensors on the other side of the disk detect when a hole is present, i.e., the sensor is receiving light. Figure 2-11 presents a disk that might be used to identify the shaft positions of the example from Figure 2-10.

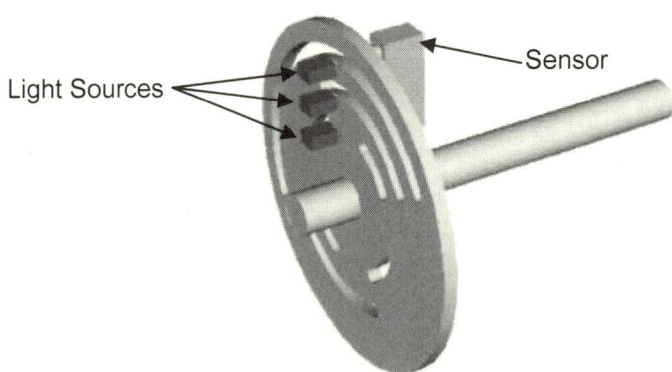

Figure 2-11   Example of a Position Encoder

In its current position in the figure, the slots in the disk are lined up between the second and third light sensors, but not the first. This means that the sensor will read a value of 110 indicating the shaft is in position number $110_2 = 6$.

There is a potential problem with this method of encoding. It is possible to read the sensor at the instant when more than one gap is opening or closing between its light source and sensor. When this happens, some of the bit changes may be detected while others are not. If this happens, an erroneous measurement may occur.

For example, if the shaft shown above turns clockwise toward position $101_2 = 5$, but at the instant when the sensor is read, only the first bit change is detected, then the value read will be $111_2 = 7$ indicating counter-clockwise rotation.

To solve this problem, alternate counting sequences referred to as the *Gray code* are used. These sequences have only one bit change between values. For example, the values assigned to the arcs of the above shaft could follow the sequence 000, 001, 011, 010, 110, 111, 101, 100. This sequence is not correct numerically, but as the shaft turns, only one bit will change as the shaft turns from one position to the next.

There is an algorithm to convert an n-bit unsigned binary value to its corresponding n-bit Gray code. Begin by adding a 0 to the most significant end of the unsigned binary value. There should now be n boundaries between the n+1 bits. For each boundary, write a 0 if the adjacent bits are the same and a 1 if the adjacent bits are different. The resulting value is the corresponding n-bit Gray code value. Figure 2-12 presents an example converting the 6 bit value 100011_2 to Gray code.

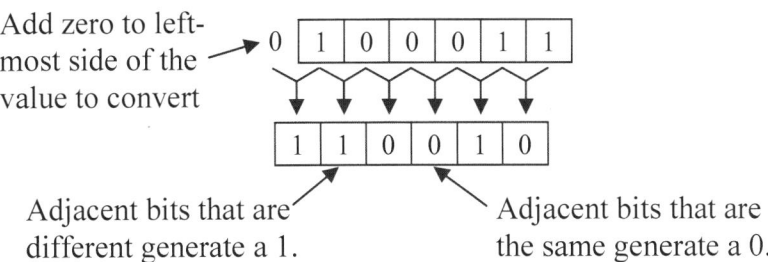

Figure 2-12 Conversion from Unsigned Binary to Gray Code

Using this method, the Gray code for any binary value can be determined. Table 2-3 presents the full Gray code sequence for four bits. The shaded bits in third column are bits that are different then the bit immediately to their left. These are the bits that will become ones in the Gray code sequence while the bits not shaded are the ones that will be zeros. Notice that exactly one bit changes in the Gray code from one row to the next and from the bottom row to the top row.

Table 2-3 Derivation of the Four-Bit Gray Code

Decimal	Binary	Binary w/starting zero	Gray Code
0	0 0 0 0	0 0 0 0 0	0 0 0 0
1	0 0 0 1	0 0 0 0 1	0 0 0 1
2	0 0 1 0	0 0 0 1 0	0 0 1 1
3	0 0 1 1	0 0 0 1 1	0 0 1 0
4	0 1 0 0	0 0 1 0 0	0 1 1 0
5	0 1 0 1	0 0 1 0 1	0 1 1 1
6	0 1 1 0	0 0 1 1 0	0 1 0 1
7	0 1 1 1	0 0 1 1 1	0 1 0 0
8	1 0 0 0	0 1 0 0 0	1 1 0 0
9	1 0 0 1	0 1 0 0 1	1 1 0 1
10	1 0 1 0	0 1 0 1 0	1 1 1 1
11	1 0 1 1	0 1 0 1 1	1 1 1 0
12	1 1 0 0	0 1 1 0 0	1 0 1 0
13	1 1 0 1	0 1 1 0 1	1 0 1 1
14	1 1 1 0	0 1 1 1 0	1 0 0 1
15	1 1 1 1	0 1 1 1 1	1 0 0 0

2.10 What's Next?

In this chapter, we've covered the different methods of representing values, specifically positive integers, using digital circuitry. In addition to counting integers, the issues surrounding the conversion of analog or "real world" values to digital were examined along with some of the problems encountered when sampling. Finally, two methods of binary representation were presented: hexadecimal and BCD.

Chapter 3 examines the special needs surrounding the digital representation of addition, subtraction, and floating-point values. It also introduces the operation of the processor in handling some arithmetic functions.

Problems

1. What is the minimum number of bits needed to represent 768_{10} using unsigned binary representation?

2. What is the largest possible integer that can be represented with a 6-bit unsigned binary number?

3. Convert each of the following values to decimal.
   a) 10011101_2 b) 10101_2 c) 111001101_2 d) 01101001_2

4. Convert each of the following values to an 8-bit unsigned binary value.
   a) 35_{10} b) 100_{10} c) 222_{10} d) 145_{10}

5. If an 8-bit binary number is used to represent an analog value in the range from 0_{10} to 100_{10}, what does the binary value 01100100_2 represent?

6. If an 8-bit binary number is used to represent an analog value in the range from 32 to 212, what is the accuracy of the system? In other words, if the binary number is incremented by one, how much change does it represent in the analog value?

7. Assume a digital to analog conversion system uses a 10-bit integer to represent an analog temperature over a range of -25°F to 125°F. If the actual temperature being read was 65.325°F, what would be the closest possible value that the system could represent?

8. What is the minimum sampling rate needed in order to successfully capture frequencies up to 155 KHz in an analog signal?

9. Convert the following numbers to hexadecimal.
   a) 1010111100101100011_2
   b) 10010101001001101001_2
   c) $0110110100101001100 1_2$
   d) 10101100100010_2

10. Convert each of the following hexadecimal values to binary.
    a) $ABCD_{16}$ b) $1DEF_{16}$ c) 8645_{16} d) $925A_{16}$

11. True or False: A list of numbers to be added would be a good candidate for conversion using BCD.

12. Determine which of the following binary patterns represent valid BCD numbers (signed or unsigned). Convert the valid ones to decimal.
    a.) 1010111100101100011
    b.) 10010101001001101001
    c.) 01101101001010011001
    d.) 11000110010000010000
    e.) 1101100101110010
    f.) 111100010010010101101000
    g.) 10101100100010

13. Convert the decimal number 96404_{10} to BCD.

14. Create the 5-bit Gray code sequence.

CHAPTER THREE

Binary Math and Signed Representations

Representing numbers with bits is one thing. Doing something with them is an entirely different matter. This chapter discusses some of the basic mathematical operations that computers perform on binary numbers along with the binary representations that support those operations. These concepts will help programmers better understand the limitations of doing math with a processor, and thereby allow them to better handle problems such as the upper and lower limits of variable types, mathematical overflow, and type casting.

3.1 Binary Addition

Regardless of the numbering system, the addition of two numbers with multiple digits is performed by adding the corresponding digits of a single column together to produce a single digit result. For example, 3 added to 5 using the decimal numbering system equals 8. The 8 is placed in the same column of the result where the 3 and 5 came from. All of these digits, 3, 5, and 8, exist in the decimal numbering system, and therefore can remain in a single column.

In some cases, the result of the addition in a single column might be more than 9 making it necessary to place a '1' overflow or carry to the column immediately to the left. If we add 6 to 5 for example, we get 11 which is too large to fit in a single decimal digit. Therefore, 10 is subtracted from the result leaving 1 as the new result for that column. The subtraction of 10 is compensated for by placing a carry in the next highest column, the ten's place. Another way of saying this is that 6 added to 5 equals 1 with a carry of 1. It is important to note that the addition of two digits in decimal can never result in a value greater than 18. Therefore, the carry to the next highest position will never be larger than 1.

Binary addition works the same way except that we're limited to two digits. Three of the addition operations, 0+0, 0+1, and 1+0, result in 0 or 1, digits that already exist in the binary numbering system. This means no carry will be needed.

Adding 1 to 1, however, results in a decimal 2, a digit which does not exist in binary. In this case, we need to create a carry or overflow that will go to the next column.

The next highest bit position represents $2^1 = 2$. Just as we did with decimal, we subtract one instance of the next highest bit position from our result. In the case of 1+1=2, we subtract 2 from 2 and get 0. Therefore, 0 is the result that is placed in the current column, and the subtraction of 2 becomes a carry to the next column. Therefore, 1+1 in binary equals 0 with a carry of 1. Each of the possible binary additions of two variables is shown in Figure 3-1.

```
                                                1
     0          0          1          1
   + 0        + 1        + 0        + 1
   ---        ---        ---        ---
     0          1          1         10
```

Figure 3-1 Four Possible Results of Adding Two Bits

The last addition $1_2 + 1_2 = 10_2$ is equivalent to the decimal addition $1_{10} + 1_{10} = 2_{10}$. Converting 2_{10} to binary results in 10_2, the result shown in the last operation of Figure 3-1, which confirms our work.

Now we need to figure out how to handle a carry from a previous column. In decimal, a carry from a previous column is simply added to the next column. This is the same as saying that we are adding three digits where one of the digits, the carry, is always a one.

In binary, accounting for a carry adds four new scenarios to the original four shown in Figure 3-1. Just like decimal, it is much like adding three values together: 1+0+0, 1+0+1, 1+1+0, or 1+1+1. The four additional cases where a carry is added from the previous column are shown in Figure 3-2.

```
Previous              1          1          1
Carry →    1          1          1          1
           0          0          1          1
         + 0        + 1        + 0        + 1
         ---        ---        ---        ---
           1         10         10         11
```

Figure 3-2 Four Possible Results of Adding Two Bits with Carry

Chapter 3: Binary Math and Signed Representations   45

The second and third cases are similar to the last case presented in Figure 3-1 where two 1's are added together to get a result of 0 with a carry. The last case in Figure 3-2, however, has three 1's added together which equals 3_{10}. Subtracting 2 from this result places a new result of 1 in the current column and sends a carry to the next column. And just as in decimal addition, the carry in binary is never greater than 1.

Now let's try to add binary numbers with multiple digits. The example shown below presents the addition of 10010110_2 and 00101011_2. The highlighted values are the carries from the previous column's addition, and just as in decimal addition, they are added to the next most significant digit/bit.

```
      1 1 1 1
    1 0 0 1 0 1 1 0
  + 0 0 1 0 1 0 1 1
    1 1 0 0 0 0 0 1
```

3.2 Binary Subtraction

Just as with addition, we're going to use the decimal numbering system to illustrate the process used in the binary numbering system for subtraction.

There are four possible cases of single-bit binary subtraction: 0 – 0, 0 – 1, 1 – 0, and 1 – 1. As long as the value being subtracted from (the minuend) is greater than or equal to the value subtracted from it (the subtrahend), the process is contained in a single column.

```
Minuend    →       0          1          1
Subtrahend →     - 0        - 0        - 1
                   0          1          0
```

But what happens in the one case when the minuend is less than the subtrahend? As in decimal, a borrow must be taken from the next most significant digit. The same is true for binary.

```
  1 0         A "borrow" is made from
- 1           the next highest bit position
  1
```

46 Computer Organization and Design Fundamentals

Pulling 1 from the next highest column in binary allows us to add 10_2 or a decimal 2 to the current column. For the previous example, 10_2 added to 0 gives us 10_2 or a decimal 2. When we subtract 1 from 2, the result is 1.

Now let's see how this works with a multi-bit example.

```
    0 1          0
    ⎧ ⎧¹0 1 1 ⎧¹0 1 1
  - 0 0 1 0 1 0 1 0 1
    _____
    0 1 1 1 0 0 1 1 0
```

Starting at the rightmost bit, 1 is subtracted from 1 giving us zero. In the next column, 0 is subtracted from 1 resulting in 1. We're okay so far with no borrows required. In the next column, however, 1 is subtracted from 0. Here we need to borrow from the next highest digit.

The next highest digit is a 1, so we subtract 1 from it and add 10 to the digit in the 2^2 column. (This appears as a small "1" placed before the 0 in the minuend's 2^2 position.) This makes our subtraction 10 - 1 which equals 1. Now we go to the 2^3 column. After the borrow, we have $0 - 0$ which equals 0.

We need to make a borrow again in the third column from the left, the 2^6 position, but the 2^7 position of the minuend is zero and does not have anything to borrow. Therefore, the next highest digit of the minuend, the 2^8 position, is borrowed from. The borrow is then cascaded down until it reaches the 2^6 position so that the subtraction may be performed.

3.3 Binary Complements

In decimal arithmetic, every number has an additive complement, i.e., a value that when added to the original number results in a zero. For example, 5 and -5 are additive complements because $5 + (-5) = 0$. This section describes the two primary methods used to calculate the complements of a binary value.

3.3.1 One's Complement

When asked to come up with a pattern of ones and zeros that when added to a binary value would result in zero, most people respond with, "just flip each bit in the original value." This "inverting" of each bit, substituting 1's for all of the 0's and 0's for all of the 1's, results in the ***1's complement*** of the original value. An example is shown below.

Previous value	1	0	0	1	0	1	1	1
1's complement	0	1	1	0	1	0	0	0

The 1's complement of a value is useful for some types of digital functions, but it doesn't provide much of a benefit if you are looking for the additive complement. See what happens when we add a value to its 1's complement.

```
  1 0 0 1 0 1 1 0
+ 0 1 1 0 1 0 0 1
  ─────────────────
  1 1 1 1 1 1 1 1
```

If the two values were additive complements, the result should be zero, right? Well, that takes us to the 2's complement.

3.3.2 Two's Complement

The result of adding an n-bit number to its one's complement is always an n-bit number with ones in every position. If we add 1 to that result, our new value is an n-bit number with zeros in every position and an overflow or carry to the next highest position, the $(n+1)^{th}$ column which corresponding to 2^n. For our 8-bit example above, the result of adding 10010110_2 to 01101001_2 is 11111111_2. Adding 1 to this number gives us 00000000_2 with an overflow carry of 1 to the ninth or 2^8 column. If we restrict ourselves to 8 bits, this overflow carry can be ignored.

This gives us a method for coming up with the additive complement called the ***2's complement*** representation. The 2's complement of a value is found by first taking the 1's complement, then incrementing that result by 1. For example, in the previous section, we determined that the 1's complement of 10010111_2 is 01101000_2. If we add 1 to this value, we get:

```
    0 1 1 0 1 0 0 0
+                 1
    ─────────────────
    0 1 1 0 1 0 0 1
```

Therefore, the 2's complement of 10010111_2 is 01101001_2. Let's see what happens when we try to add the value to its 2's complement.

48   Computer Organization and Design Fundamentals

```
  1 1 1 1 1 1 1
  1 0 0 1 0 1 1 1
+ 0 1 1 0 1 0 0 1
  ─────────────────
  0 0 0 0 0 0 0 0
```

The result is zero! Okay, so most of you caught the fact that I didn't drop down the last carry which would've made the result 100000000_2. This is not a problem, because in the case of signed arithmetic, the carry has a purpose other than that of adding an additional digit representing the next power of two. As long as we make sure that the two numbers being added have the same number of bits, and that we keep the result to that same number of bits too, then any carry that goes beyond that should be discarded.

Actually, discarded is not quite the right term. In some cases we will use the carry as an indication of a possible mathematical error. It should not, however, be included in the result of the addition. This is simply the first of many "anomalies" that must be watched when working with a limited number of bits.

Two more examples of 2's complements are shown below.

Original value (10_{10})	0	0	0	0	1	0	1	0
1's complement	1	1	1	1	0	1	0	1
2's complement (-10_{10})	1	1	1	1	0	1	1	0

Original value (88_{10})	0	1	0	1	1	0	0	0
1's complement	1	0	1	0	0	1	1	1
2's complement (-88_{10})	1	0	1	0	1	0	0	0

Now let's see if the 2's complement representation stands up in the face of addition. If $88_{10} = 01011000_2$ and $-10_{10} = 11110110_2$, then the addition of these two numbers should equal $78_{10} = 01001110_2$.

```
    1 1 1 1
    0 1 0 1 1 0 0 0
+   1 1 1 1 0 1 1 0
  ───────────────────
    0 1 0 0 1 1 1 0
```

Chapter 3: Binary Math and Signed Representations   49

There is also a "short-cut" to calculating the 2's complement of a binary number. This trick can be used if you find the previous way too cumbersome or if you'd like a second method in order to verify the result you got from using the first.

The trick works by copying the zero bit values starting with the least significant bit until you reach your first binary 1. Copy that 1 too. If the least significant bit is a one, then only copy that bit. Next, invert all of the remaining bits. Figure 3-3 presents an example of the short-cut.

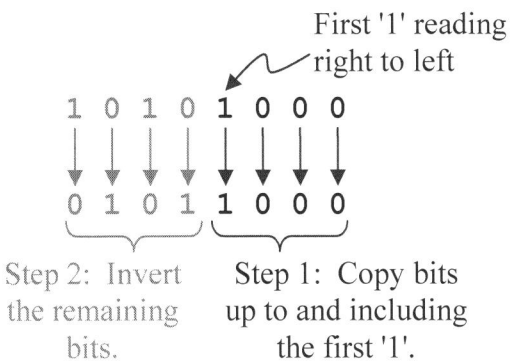

Figure 3-3   Two's Complement Short-Cut

This result matches the result for the previous example.

In decimal, the negative of 5 is -5. If we take the negative a second time, we return to the original value, e.g., the negative of -5 is 5. Is the same true for taking the 2's complement of a 2's complement of a binary number? Well, let's see.

The binary value for 45_{10} is 00101101_2. Watch what happens when we take the 2's complement twice.

Original value = 45	0	0	1	0	1	1	0	1
1's complement of 45	1	1	0	1	0	0	1	0
2's complement of 45 = -45	1	1	0	1	0	0	1	1
1's complement of -45	0	0	1	0	1	1	0	0
2's complement of -45 = 45	0	0	1	0	1	1	0	1

It worked! The second time the 2's complement was taken, the pattern of ones and zeros returned to their original values. It turns out that this is true for any binary number of a fixed number of bits.

3.3.3 Most Significant Bit as a Sign Indicator

As was stated earlier, 2's complement is used to allow the computer to represent the additive complement of a binary number, i.e., negative numbers. But there is a problem. As we showed earlier in this section, taking the 2's complement of $45_{10} = 00101101_2$ gives us $-45_{10} = 11010011_2$. But in Chapter 2, the eight bit value 11010011_2 was shown to be equal to $2^7 + 2^6 + 2^4 + 2^1 + 2^0 = 128 + 64 + 16 + 2 + 1 = 211_{10}$. So did we just prove that -45_{10} is equal to 211_{10}? Or maybe 00101101_2 is actually -211_{10}.

It turns out that when using 2's complement binary representation, half of the binary bit patterns must lose their positive association in order to represent negative numbers. So is 11010011_2 -45_{10} or 211_{10}? It turns out that 11010011_2 is one of the bit patterns meant to represent a negative number, so in 2's complement notation, $11010011_2 = -45_{10}$. But how can we tell whether a binary bit pattern represents a positive or a negative number?

From the earlier description of the 2's complement short-cut, you can see that except for two cases, the MSB of the 2's complement is always the inverse of the original value. The two cases where this isn't true are when all bits of the number except the most significant bit equal 0 and the most significant bit is a 0 or a 1. In both of these cases, the 2's complement equals the original value.

In all other cases, when we apply the shortcut we will always encounter a 1 before we get to the MSB when reading right to left. Since every bit after this one will be inverted, then the most significant bit must be inverted toggling it from its original value. If the original value has a zero in the MSB, then its 2's complement must have a one and vice versa. Because of this characteristic, the MSB of a value can be used to indicate whether a number is positive or negative and is called a ***sign bit***.

A binary value with a 0 in the MSB position is considered positive and a binary value with a 1 in the MSB position is considered negative. This makes it vital to declare the number of bits that a signed binary number uses. If this information is not given, then the computer or the user looking at a binary number will not know which bit is the MSB.

Since the MSB is being used to indicate the sign of a signed binary number, it cannot be used to represent a power of 2, i.e., if a number is said to represent a 2's complement value, only n-1 of its n bits can be used to determine the magnitude since the MSB is used for the sign. This cuts in half the number of positive integers n bits can represent.

And the special cases? Well, a binary number with all zeros is equal to a decimal 0. Taking the negative of zero still gives us zero. The other case is a bit trickier. In the section on minimums and maximums, we will see that an n-bit value with an MSB equal to one and all other bits equal to zero is a negative number, specifically, $-2^{(n-1)}$. The largest positive number represented in 2's complement has an MSB of 0 with all the remaining bits set to one. This value equals $2^{(n-1)} - 1$. Therefore, since $2^{(n-1)} > 2^{(n-1)} - 1$, we can see that there is no positive equivalent to the binary number $100...00_2$.

3.3.4 Signed Magnitude

A second, less useful way to represent positive and negative binary numbers is to take the MSB and use it as a sign bit, much like a plus or minus sign, and leave the remaining bits to represent the magnitude. The representation is called *signed magnitude* representation. For example, –45 and +45 would be identical in binary except for the MSB which would be set to a 1 for –45 and a 0 for +45. This is shown below for an 8-bit representation.

$+45_{10}$ in binary	0	0	1	0	1	1	0	1
-45_{10} using signed magnitude	1	0	1	0	1	1	0	1

3.3.5 MSB and Number of Bits

Since the MSB is necessary to indicate the sign of a binary value, it is vital that we know how many bits a particular number is being represented with so we know exactly where the MSB is. In other words, the leading zeros of a binary value may have been removed making it look like the binary value is negative since it starts with a one.

For example, if the binary value 10010100_2 is assumed to be an 8-bit signed number using 2's complement representation, then converting it to decimal would give us -108_{10}. (We will discuss converting signed values to decimal later in this chapter.) If, however, it was a 10-bit number, then the MSB would be 0 and it would convert to the positive value 148_{10}.

3.3.6 Issues Surrounding the Conversion of Binary Numbers

Since computers don't use an infinite number of bits to represent values, the software must know two things before it can interpret a binary value: the number of bits and the type of binary representation being used. This usually is confusing for the novice.

Identifying 10100110_2 as an 8-bit number isn't enough. Note that the MSB is equal to 1. Therefore, this value represents one number in unsigned binary, another number in 2's complement, and yet a third in signed magnitude.

First, let's do the conversion of 10100110_2 assuming it is an 8-bit, unsigned binary like those described in Chapter 2.

$$10100110_2 = 2^7 + 2^5 + 2^2 + 2^1 = 128 + 32 + 4 + 2 = 166_{10}$$

Now let's do the conversion in 2's complement. Before we do, however, let's examine the process. First, if the MSB is equal to 0, then the value is a positive number. In 2's complement notation, positive numbers look just like unsigned binary and should be treated exactly the same when performing a conversion to decimal.

If, however, the MSB is equal to 1, then the value represented by this pattern of ones and zeros is negative. To turn it into a negative number, someone had to apply the process of taking the 2's complement to the original positive value. Therefore, we must remove the negative sign before we do the conversion.

It was shown earlier how a second application of the 2's complement conversion process returns the number back to its original positive value. If taking the 2's complement of a negative number returns it to its positive value, then the positive value can be converted to decimal using the same process used for an unsigned binary value. Adding a negative sign to the decimal result completes the conversion. Figure 3-4 presents a flow chart showing this process graphically.

A second method of converting an n-bit 2's complement value to decimal is to perform the conversion as you would an unsigned binary value except that the MSB digit is treated as -2^{n-1} instead of 2^{n-1}. For example, the MSB of an 8-bit 2's complement value would represent $-2^7 = -128$.

Chapter 3: Binary Math and Signed Representations   53

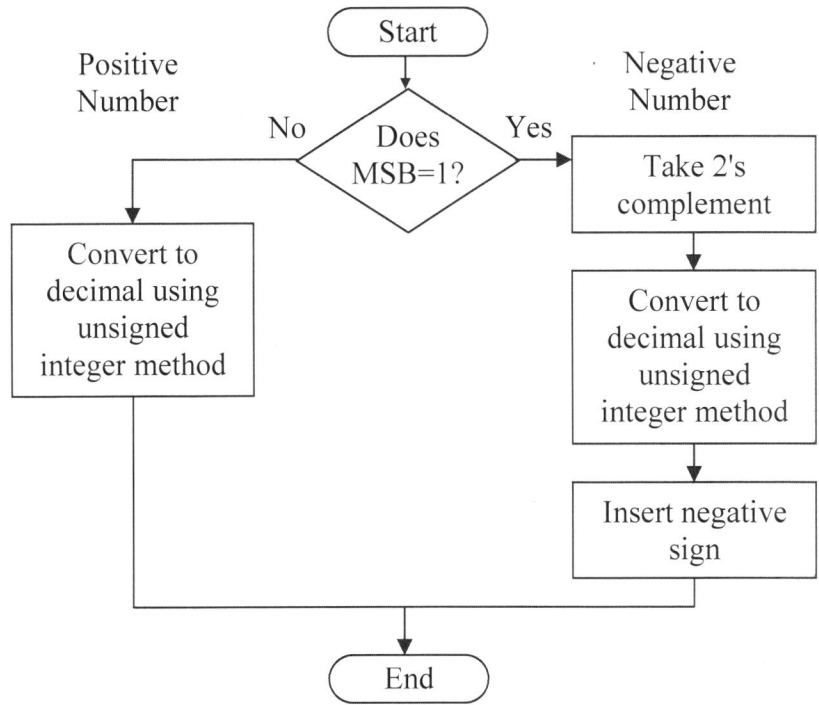

Figure 3-4   Converting a Two's Complement Number to a Decimal

In the case of 10100110_2, the MSB is a 1. Therefore, it is a negative number. By following the right branch of the flowchart in Figure 3-4, we see that we must take the two's complement to find the positive counterpart for our negative number.

Negative value	1	0	1	0	0	1	1	0
1's comp. of negative value	0	1	0	1	1	0	0	1
2's comp. of negative value	0	1	0	1	1	0	1	0

Now that we have the positive counterpart for the 2's complement value of the negative number 10100110_2, we convert it to decimal just as we did with the unsigned binary value.

$$01011010_2 = 2^6 + 2^4 + 2^3 + 2^1 = 64 + 16 + 8 + 2 = 90_{10}$$

Since the original 2's complement value was negative to begin with, the value 10100110_2 in 8-bit, 2's complement form is –90.

54 Computer Organization and Design Fundamentals

We can duplicate this result using the second method of conversion, i.e., converting 10100110_2 using the unsigned binary method while treating the MSB as -2^7. In this case, there is a 1 in the -2^7, 2^5, 2^2, and 2^1 positions.

$$10100110_2 = 2^{-7} + 2^5 + 2^2 + 2^1 = -128 + 32 + 4 + 2 = -90_{10}$$

Next, let's do the conversion assuming 10100110_2 is in 8-bit signed magnitude where the MSB represents the sign bit. As with the 2's complement form, an MSB of 1 means that the number is negative.

The conversion of a signed magnitude binary number to decimal is different than 2's complement. In the case of signed magnitude, remove the MSB and convert the remaining bits using the same methods used to convert unsigned binary to decimal. When done, place a negative sign in front of the decimal result only if the MSB equaled 1.

Meaning of bit position	Sign	2^6	2^5	2^4	2^3	2^2	2^1	2^0
Binary value	1	0	1	0	0	1	1	0

To convert this value to a positive number, remove the sign bit. Next, calculate the magnitude just as we would for the unsigned case.

$$0100110_2 = 2^5 + 2^2 + 2^1 = 32 + 4 + 2 = 38_{10}$$

Since the MSB of the original value equaled 1, the signed magnitude value was a negative number to begin with, and we need to add a negative sign. Therefore, 10100110_2 in 8-bit, signed magnitude representation equals -38_{10}.

But what if this binary number was actually a 10-bit number and not an 8 bit number? Well, if it's a 10 bit number (0010100110_2), the MSB is 0 and therefore it is a positive number. This makes our conversion much easier. *The method for converting a positive binary value to a decimal value is the same for all three representations.* The conversion goes something like this:

Bit position	MSB	2^8	2^7	2^6	2^5	2^4	2^3	2^2	2^1	2^0
Binary value	0	0	1	0	1	0	0	1	1	0

$$0010100110_2 = 2^7 + 2^5 + 2^2 + 2^1 = 128 + 32 + 4 + 2 = 166_{10}$$

Chapter 3: Binary Math and Signed Representations   55

This discussion shows that it is possible for a binary pattern of ones and zeros to have three interpretations. It all depends on how the computer has been told to interpret the value.

In a programming language such as C, the way in which a computer treats a variable depends on how it is declared. Variables declared as *unsigned int* are stored in unsigned binary notation. Variables declared as *int* are treated as either 2's complement or signed magnitude depending on the processor and/or compiler.

3.3.7 Minimums and Maximums

When using a finite number of bit positions to store information, it is vital to be able to determine the minimum and maximum values that each binary representation can handle. Failure to do this might result in bugs in the software you create. This section calculates the minimum and maximum values for each of the three representations discussed in this and the previous chapter using a fixed number of bits, n.

Let's begin with the most basic representation, unsigned binary. The smallest value that can be represented with unsigned binary representation occurs when all the bits equal zero. Conversion from binary to decimal results in $0 + 0 + ... + 0 = 0$. Therefore, for an n bit number:

$$\text{Minimum n-bit unsigned binary number} = 0 \quad (3.1)$$

The largest value that can be represented with unsigned binary representation is reached when all n bits equal one. When we convert this value from binary to decimal, we get $2^{n-1} + 2^{n-2} + ... + 2^0$. As was shown in Chapter 2, adding one to this expression results in 2^n. Therefore, for an n-bit unsigned binary number, the maximum is:

$$\text{Maximum n-bit unsigned binary number} = 2^n - 1 \quad (3.2)$$

Next, let's examine the minimum and maximum values for an n-bit 2's complement representation. Unlike the unsigned case, the lowest decimal value that can be represented with n-bits in 2's complement representation is not obvious. Remember, 2's complement uses the MSB as a sign bit. Since the lowest value will be negative, the MSB should be set to 1 (a negative value). But what is to be done with all of the remaining bits? A natural inclination is to set all the bits after the

56 Computer Organization and Design Fundamentals

MSB to one. This should be a really big negative number, right? Well, converting it to decimal results in something like the 8 bit example below:

2's comp. value	1	1	1	1	1	1	1	1
Intermediate 1's complement	0	0	0	0	0	0	0	0
Positive value of 2's comp.	0	0	0	0	0	0	0	1

This isn't quite what we expected. Using the 2's complement method to convert 11111111_2 to a decimal number results in -1_{10}. This couldn't possibly be the lowest value that can be represented with 2's complement.

It turns out that the lowest possible 2's complement value is an MSB of 1 followed by all zeros as shown in the 8 bit example below. For the conversion to work, you must strictly follow the sequence presented in Figure 3-4 to convert a negative 2's complement value to decimal.

2's comp. value	1	0	0	0	0	0	0	0
Intermediate 1's complement	0	1	1	1	1	1	1	1
Positive value of 2's comp.	1	0	0	0	0	0	0	0

Converting the positive value to decimal using the unsigned method shows that $10000000_2 = -2^7 = -128$. Translating this to n-bits gives us:

$$\text{Minimum n-bit 2's complement number} = -2^{(n-1)} \quad (3.3)$$

The maximum value is a little easier to find. It is a positive number, i.e., an MSB of 0. The remaining n–1 bits are then treated as unsigned magnitude representation. Therefore, for n bits:

$$\text{Maximum n-bit 2's complement number} = 2^{(n-1)} - 1 \quad (3.4)$$

Last of all, we have the signed magnitude representation. To determine the magnitude of a signed magnitude value, ignore the MSB and use the remaining n–1 bits to convert to decimal as if they were in unsigned representation. This means that the largest and smallest values represented with an n-bit signed magnitude number equals the positive and negative values of an (n–1)-bit unsigned binary number.

Chapter 3: Binary Math and Signed Representations 57

Minimum n-bit signed magnitude number = $-(2^{(n-1)} - 1)$ (3.5)

Maximum n-bit signed magnitude number = $(2^{(n-1)} - 1)$ (3.6)

As an example, Table 3-1 compares the minimum and maximum values of an 8-bit number for each of the binary representations. The last column shows the number of distinct integer values possible with each representation. For example, there are 256 integer values between 0 and 255 meaning the 8-bit unsigned binary representation has 256 possible combinations of 1's and 0's, each of which represents a different integer in the range.

Table 3-1 Representation Comparison for 8-bit Binary Numbers

Representation	Minimum	Maximum	Number of integers represented
Unsigned	0	255	256
2's Complement	-128	127	256
Signed Magnitude	-127	127	255

So why can 8-bit signed magnitude only represent 255 possible values instead of 256? It is because in signed magnitude 00000000_2 and 10000000_2 both represent the same number, a decimal 0.

3.4 Floating Point Binary

Binary numbers can also have decimal points, and to show you how, we will once again begin with decimal numbers. For decimal numbers with decimal points, the standard way to represent the digits to the right of the decimal point is to continue the powers of ten in descending order starting with -1 where $10^{-1} = 1/10$th $= 0.1$. That means that the number 6.5342 has 5 increments of 10^{-1} (tenths), 3 increments of 10^{-2} (hundredths), 4 increments of 10^{-3} (thousandths), and 2 increments of 10^{-4} (ten-thousandths). The table below shows this graphically.

Exponent	3	2	1	0	-1	-2	-3	-4
Position value	1000	100	10	1	0.1	0.01	0.001	0.0001
Sample values	0	0	0	6	5	3	4	2

Therefore, our example has the decimal value 6*1 + 5*0.1 + 3*0.01 + 4*0.001 + 2*0.0001 = 6.5342.

Binary representation of real numbers works the same way except that each position represents a power of two, not a power of ten. To convert 10.01101 to decimal for example, use descending negative powers of two to the right of the decimal point.

Exponent	2	1	0	-1	-2	-3	-4	-5
Position value	4	2	1	0.5	0.25	0.125	0.0625	0.03125
Sample values	0	1	0	0	1	1	0	1

Therefore, our example has the decimal value 0*4 + 1*2 + 0*1 +0*0.5 + 1*0.25 + 1*0.125 + 0*0.0625 + 1*0.03125 = 2.40625. This means that the method of conversion is the same for real numbers as it is for integer values; we've simply added positions representing negative powers of two.

Computers, however, use a form of binary more like scientific notation to represent floating-point or real numbers. For example, with scientific notation we can represent the large value 342,370,000 as 3.4237×10^8. This representation consists of a decimal component or mantissa of 3.4237 with an exponent of 8. Both the mantissa and the exponent are signed values allowing for negative numbers and for negative exponents respectively.

Binary works the same way using 1's and 0's for the digits of the mantissa and exponent and using 2 as the multiplier that moves the decimal point left or right. For example, the binary number 100101101.010110 would be represented as:

$$1.00101101010110 * 2^8$$

The decimal point is moved left for negative exponents of two and right for positive exponents of two.

The IEEE Standard 754 is used to represent real numbers on the majority of contemporary computer systems. It utilizes a 32-bit pattern to represent single-precision numbers and a 64-bit pattern to represent double-precision numbers. Each of these bit patterns is divided into three parts, each part representing a different component of the real number being stored. Figure 3-5 shows this partitioning for both single- and double-precision numbers.

Chapter 3: Binary Math and Signed Representations 59

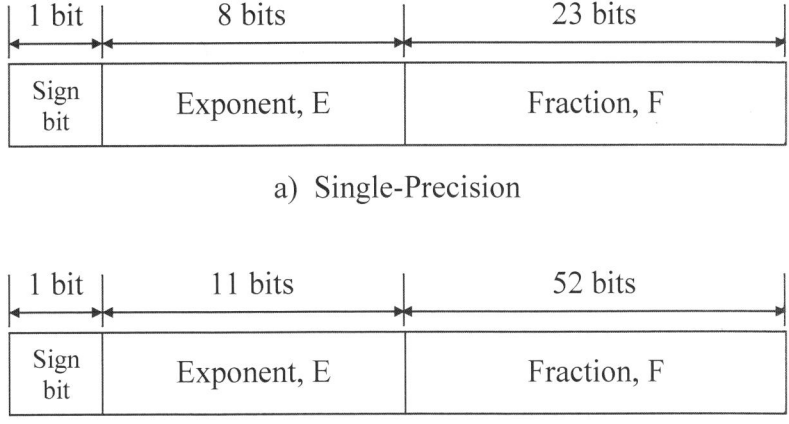

Figure 3-5 IEEE Standard 754 Floating-Point Formats

Both formats work the same differing only by the number of bits used to represent each component of the real number. In general, the components of the single-precision format are substituted into Equation 3.7 where the sign of the value is determined by the sign bit (0 – positive value, 1 – negative value). Note that E is in unsigned binary representation.

$$(\pm)1.F \times 2^{(E-127)} \qquad (3.7)$$

Equation 3.8 is used for the double-precision values.

$$(\pm)1.F \times 2^{(E-1023)} \qquad (3.8)$$

In both cases, F is preceded with an implied '1' and a binary point. There are, however, some special cases. These are as follows:

- Positive, E=255, F=0: represents positive infinite;
- Negative, E=255, F=0: represents negative infinite; and
- Positive or negative, E=0, F=0: represents zero.

Example

Convert the 32-bit single-precision IEEE Standard 754 number shown below into its binary equivalent.

11010110101101101011000000000000

Solution

First, break the 32-bit number into its components.

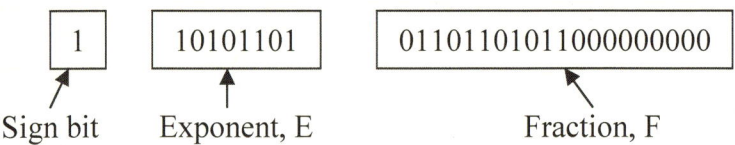

| 1 | 10101101 | 01101101011000000000 |

Sign bit   Exponent, E   Fraction, F

A sign bit of 1 means that this will be a negative number.

The exponent, E, will be used to determine the power of two by which our mantissa will be multiplied. To use it, we must first convert it to a decimal integer using the unsigned method.

$$\begin{aligned} \text{Exponent, E} &= 10101101_2 \\ &= 2^7 + 2^5 + 2^3 + 2^2 + 2^0 \\ &= 128 + 32 + 8 + 4 + 1 \\ &= 173_{10} \end{aligned}$$

Substituting these components into Equation 3.7 gives us:

$$(\pm)1.F \times 2^{(E-127)} = -1.01101101011000000000 \times 2^{(173-127)}$$
$$= -1.01101101011 \times 2^{46}$$

Example

Create the 32-bit single-precision IEEE Standard 754 representation of the binary number 0.000000110110100101.

Solution

Begin by putting the binary number above into the binary form of scientific notation with a single 1 to the left of the decimal point. Note that this is done by moving the decimal point seven positions to the right giving us an exponent of −7.

$0.00000011011010010_1 = 1.10110100101 \times 2^{-7}$

The number is positive, so the sign bit will be 0. The fraction (value *after* the decimal point and not including the leading 1) is 10110100101 with 12 zeros added to the end to make it 23 bits. Lastly, the exponent must satisfy the equation:

$$E - 127 = -7$$
$$E = -7 + 127 = 120$$

Converting 120_{10} to binary gives us the 8-bit unsigned binary value 01111000_2. Substituting all of these components into the IEEE 754 format gives us:

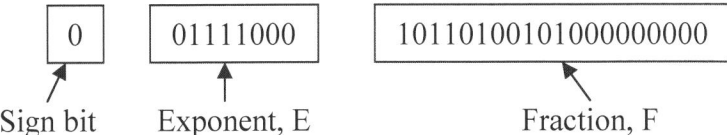

Sign bit   Exponent, E   Fraction, F

Therefore, the answer is 00111100010110100101000000000000.

3.5 Hexadecimal Addition

At the beginning of this chapter, it was shown how binary addition (base 2) with its two digits, 1 and 0, is performed the same way decimal addition (base 10) is with its ten digits, 0, 1, 2, 3, 4, 5, 6, 7, 8 and 9. The only difference is the limitation placed on the addition by the number of digits. In binary, the addition of two or three ones results in a carry since the result goes beyond 1, the largest binary digit. Decimal doesn't require a carry until the result goes beyond 9.

Hexadecimal numbers (base 16) can be added using the same method. The difference is that there are more digits in hexadecimal than there are in decimal. For example, in decimal, adding 5 and 7 results in 2 with a carry to the next highest position. In hexadecimal, however, 5 added to 7 does not go beyond the range of a single digit. In this case, $5 + 7 = C_{16}$ with no carry. It isn't until a result greater than F_{16} is reached (a decimal 15_{10}) that a carry is necessary.

In decimal, if the result of an addition is greater than 9, subtract 10_{10} to get the result for the current column and add a carry to the next column. In binary, when a result is greater than 1, subtract 10_2 (i.e., 2_{10}) to get the result for the current column then add a carry to the next column. In hexadecimal addition, if the result is greater than F_{16} (15_{10}) subtract 10_{16} (16_{10}) to get the result for the current column and add a carry to the next column.

$$D_{16} + 5_{16} = 13_{10} + 5_{10} = 18_{10}$$

By moving a carry to the next highest column, we change the result for the current column by subtracting 16_{10}.

$$18_{10} = 2_{10} + 16_{10}$$
$$= 2_{16} \text{ with a carry to the next column}$$

Therefore, D_{16} added to 5_{16} equals 2_{16} with a carry to the next column.

Just like decimal and binary, the addition of two hexadecimal digits never generates a carry greater than 1. The following shows how adding the largest hexadecimal digit, F_{16}, to itself along with a carry from the previous column still does not require a carry larger than 1 to the next highest column.

$$F_{16} + F_{16} + 1 = 15_{10} + 15_{10} + 1 = 31_{10}$$
$$= 15_{10} + 16_{10}$$
$$= F_{16} \text{ with a 1 carry to the next column}$$

When learning hexadecimal addition, it might help to have a table showing the hexadecimal and decimal equivalents such as that shown in Table 3-2. This way, the addition can be done in decimal, the base with which most people are familiar, and then the result can be converted back to hex.

Table 3-2 Hexadecimal to Decimal Conversion Table

Hex	Dec	Hex	Dec	Hex	Dec	Hex	Dec
0_{16}	0_{10}	4_{16}	4_{10}	8_{16}	8_{10}	C_{16}	12_{10}
1_{16}	1_{10}	5_{16}	5_{10}	9_{16}	9_{10}	D_{16}	13_{10}
2_{16}	2_{10}	6_{16}	6_{10}	A_{16}	10_{10}	E_{16}	14_{10}
3_{16}	3_{10}	7_{16}	7_{10}	B_{16}	11_{10}	F_{16}	15_{10}

Example

Add $3DA32_{16}$ to $4292F_{16}$.

Solution

Just like in binary and decimal, place one of the numbers to be added on top of the other so that the columns line up.

```
    3 D A 3 2
  + 4 2 9 2 F
```

Adding 2_{16} to F_{16} goes beyond the limit of digits hexadecimal can represent. It is equivalent to $2_{10} + 15_{10}$ which equals 17_{10}, a value greater than 16_{10}. Therefore, we need to subtract 10_{16} (16_{10}) giving us a result of 1 with a carry into the next position.

```
              1
    3 D A 3 2
  + 4 2 9 2 F
              1
```

For the next column, the 16^1 position, we have $1 + 3 + 2$ which equals 6. This result is less than 16_{10}, so there is no carry to the next column.

```
              1
    3 D A 3 2
  + 4 2 9 2 F
            6 1
```

The 16^2 position has $A_{16} + 9_{16}$ which in decimal is equivalent to $10_{10} + 9_{10} = 19_{10}$. Since this is greater than 16_{10}, we must subtract 16_{10} to get the result for the 16^2 column and add a carry in the 16^3 column.

```
        1     1
    3 D A 3 2
  + 4 2 9 2 F
          3 6 1
```

For the 16^3 column, we have $1_{16} + D_{16} + 2_{16}$ which is equivalent to $1_{10} + 13_{10} + 2_{10} = 16_{10}$. This gives us a zero for the result in the 16^3 column with a carry.

```
  1 1   1
  3 D A 3 2
+ 4 2 9 2 F
  0 3 6 1
```

Last of all, $1 + 3 + 4 = 8$ which is the same in both decimal and hexadecimal, so the result is $3DA32_{16} + 4292F_{16} = 80361_{16}$:

```
  1 1   1
  3 D A 3 2
+ 4 2 9 2 F
  8 0 3 6 1
```

3.6 BCD Addition

When we introduced Binary Coded Decimal numbers, we said that the purpose of these numbers was to provide a quick conversion to binary that would not be used in mathematical functions. It turns out, however, that BCD numbers can be added too, there's just an additional step that occurs when each column of digits is added.

When two BCD numbers are added, the digits 1010, 1011, 1100, 1101, 1110, and 1111 must be avoided. This is done by adding an additional step anytime the binary addition of two nibbles results in one of these illegal values or if a carry is generated. When this happens, the invalid result is corrected by adding 6 to skip over the illegal values. For example:

```
   BCD        Decimal

   0011          3
  +1000         +8
   1011       Invalid
  +0110         +6
  10001         11
```

Chapter 3: Binary Math and Signed Representations 65

This step is also necessary if a carry results from a BCD addition.

```
BCD       Decimal

1001         9
+1000       +8
10001      Carry
+0110       +6
10111       17
```

3.7 Multiplication and Division by Powers of Two

Due to factors to be examined later in this book, multiplication and division is a time-intensive operation for processors. Therefore, programmers and compilers have a trick they use to divide or multiply binary by powers of two. Examine Table 3-3 to see if you can find a pattern in the multiples of two of the binary number 1001_2.

Table 3-3 Multiplying the Binary Value 1001_2 by Powers of Two

Decimal	2^8	2^7	2^6	2^5	2^4	2^3	2^2	2^1	2^0
9	0	0	0	0	0	1	0	0	1
18	0	0	0	0	1	0	0	1	0
36	0	0	0	1	0	0	1	0	0
72	0	0	1	0	0	1	0	0	0
144	0	1	0	0	1	0	0	0	0
288	1	0	0	1	0	0	0	0	0

(Columns labeled "Binary")

Note that multiplying by two has the same effect as shifting all of the bits one position to the left. Similarly, a division by two is accomplished by a right shift one position. This is similar to moving a decimal point right or left when multiplying or dividing a decimal number by a power of ten.

Since a shift operation is significantly faster than a multiply or divide operation, compilers will always substitute a shift operation when a program calls for a multiply or divide by a power of two. For example, a division by $16_{10} = 2^4$ is equivalent to a right shift by 4 bit positions.

This works for all positive binary representations of integers and real numbers as well as 2's complement representation of negative numbers. Care must be taken in a few instances in order to maintain the data's integrity.

First, carefully watch the bits that are shifted out to verify that data isn't being lost. If during a left shift (multiplication), a one is shifted out of an unsigned binary value or the MSB of a 2's complement number changes, then you've gone beyond the range of values for that number of bits. If during a right shift (division), a one is shifted out of an integer value, then a decimal value has been truncated.

For negative 2's complement values, there is an additional concern. Since the MSB is a sign bit, if we fill in the empty bits coming in from the left with zeros when performing a right shift, then a negative number has been turned into a positive number. To avoid this, always duplicate the sign bit in the MSB for each right shift of a 2's complement value.

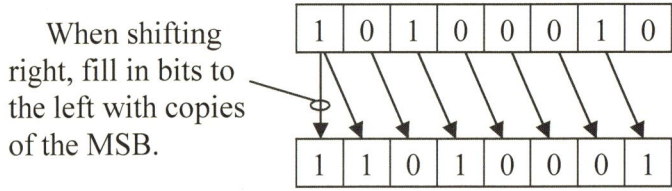

Figure 3-6 Duplicate MSB for Right Shift of 2's Complement Values

This operation can even be used for some multiplications by constants other than powers of two. For example, if a processor needed to multiply a value x by 10, it could first multiply x by 2 (a single left shift), then multiply x by 8 (a left shift by three bit positions), then add the two shifted values together. This would still be a time savings over a multiplication.

A bit shift is easily accomplished in high-level programming languages such as C. In C, the operator used to perform a left shift is '<<' while a right shift is '>>'. Place the variable to be shifted to the left of the operator and to the right of the operator, enter the number of positions to shift. Some sample C code is shown below.

Chapter 3: Binary Math and Signed Representations 67

```
result = iVal << 3;    // Set result equal to iVal
                       // shifted left 3 places
result = iVal >> 4;    // Set result equal to iVal
                       // shifted right 4 places
```

The first line of code shifts *iVal* left three positions before putting the new value into *result*. This is equivalent to multiplying *iVal* by $2^3 = 8$. The second line shifts *iVal* right 4 positions which has the same effect as an integer divide by $2^4 = 16$.

3.8 Easy Decimal to Binary Conversion Trick

The fact that a single shift right is equivalent to a division by two gives us a simple way to convert from decimal integers to unsigned binary. Each 1 that is shifted out because of a right shift is equivalent to a remainder of 1 after a division by two. Therefore, if you record the remainders generated by successive divisions by two, you will find that you've generated the binary equivalent of the original decimal value. For example, let's convert the decimal value 156_{10} to binary.

$$156_{10} \div 2 = 78_{10} \text{ with a remainder of } 0$$
$$78_{10} \div 2 = 39_{10} \text{ with a remainder of } 0$$
$$39_{10} \div 2 = 19_{10} \text{ with a remainder of } 1$$
$$19_{10} \div 2 = 9_{10} \text{ with a remainder of } 1$$
$$9_{10} \div 2 = 4_{10} \text{ with a remainder of } 1$$
$$4_{10} \div 2 = 2_{10} \text{ with a remainder of } 0$$
$$2_{10} \div 2 = 1_{10} \text{ with a remainder of } 0$$
$$1_{10} \div 2 = 0_{10} \text{ with a remainder of } 1$$

Listing the remainders by reversing the order in which they were generated gives us 10011100_2, the binary value for 156_{10}.

3.9 Arithmetic Overflow

In Section 3.3, the carry was ignored when two 2's complement values were added. This is not always the case. For some numbering systems, a carry is an indication that an error has occurred.

An arithmetic overflow error occurs when two numbers are added and the result falls outside the valid range of the binary representation being used. For example, the numbers 200_{10} and 175_{10} can be represented in 8-bit unsigned binary notation. The result of their

68   Computer Organization and Design Fundamentals

addition, however, 375_{10}, is not. Therefore, the following 8-bit binary addition (200_{10} + 175_{10}) results in an error.

```
  1
    1 1 0 0 1 0 0 0
  + 1 0 1 0 1 1 1 1
    ─────────────────
    0 1 1 1 0 1 1 1
```

Remember that the result must have the same bit count as the sources, and in this case, the 8-bit unsigned binary result 01110111_2 equals 119_{10}, not 375_{10}.

When adding unsigned binary values, there is a simple way to determine if an arithmetic overflow has occurred. *In unsigned binary addition, if a carry is produced from the column representing the MSBs thereby requiring another bit for the representation, an overflow has occurred.*

In 2's complement addition, there is a different method for determining when an arithmetic overflow has occurred. To begin with, remember that an arithmetic overflow occurs when the result falls outside the minimum and maximum values of the representation. In the case of 2's complement representation, those limits are defined by Equations 3.3 and 3.4.

The only way that this can happen is if two numbers with the same sign are added together. *It is impossible for the addition of two numbers with different signs to result in a value outside of the range of 2's complement representation.*

When two numbers of the same sign are added together, however, there is a simple way to determine if an error has occurred. If the result of the addition has the opposite sign of the two numbers being added, then the result is in error. In other words, if the addition of two positive numbers resulted in a negative number, or if the addition of two negative numbers resulted in a positive number, there were not enough bits in the representation to hold the result. The example below presents one possible case.

```
   2's complement    Decimal
      01100011          99
     +00110101         +53
      ────────         ────
      10011000        -104
```

If this had been done assuming unsigned notation, the result of 152_{10} would have been fine because no carry was generated. From equation 3.4, however, we see that the largest value that 8-bit 2's complement representation can hold is $2^{(8-1)} - 1 = 127_{10}$. Since 152_{10} is greater than 127_{10}, it is outside the range of 8-bit 2's complement representation. In 2's complement representation, the bit pattern 10011000_2 actually represents -104_{10}.

3.10 What's Next?

Computers use different numeric representations depending on the application. For example, a person's weight may be stored as a 16-bit integer while their house address may be stored in BCD. At this point, five binary representations have been introduced (unsigned binary, signed magnitude, 2's complement, BCD, and floating-point), and hexadecimal representation has been presented as a quick means for writing binary values.

Computers, however, do more with numbers than simply represent them. In Chapter 4, logic gates, the components that computers use to manipulate binary signals, will be presented. They are the lowest-level of computer hardware that we will be examining. We will use them to begin constructing the more complex components of the computer.

Problems

1. True or False: 01101011_2 has the same value in both unsigned and 2's complement form.

2. True or False: The single-precision floating-point number 10011011011010011011001011000010 is negative.

3. What is the lowest possible value for an 8-bit signed magnitude binary number?

4. What is the highest possible value for a 10-bit 2's complement binary number?

5. Convert each of the following decimal values to 8-bit 2's complement binary.
   a) 54_{10} b) -49_{10} c) -128_{10} d) -66_{10} e) -98_{10}

6. Convert each of the following 8-bit 2's complement binary numbers to decimal.
   a) 10011101_2 b) 00010101_2 c) 11100110_2 d) 01101001_2

70   Computer Organization and Design Fundamentals

7. Convert each of the following decimal values to 8-bit signed magnitude binary.
   a) 54_{10} b) -49_{10} c) -127_{10} d) -66_{10} e) -98_{10}

8. Convert each of the following 8-bit signed magnitude binary numbers to decimal.
   a) 10011101_2 b) 00010101_2 c) 11100110_2 d) 01101001_2

9. Convert 1101.0011011_2 to decimal.

10. Convert 10101.11101_2 to decimal.

11. Convert $1.00011011101 \times 2^{34}$ to IEEE Standard 754 for single-precision floating-point values.

12. Convert the IEEE Standard 754 number 11000010100011010100000000000000 to its binary equivalent.

13. Using hexadecimal arithmetic, add $4D231_{16}$ to $A413F_{16}$.

14. Using BCD arithmetic, add 0111010010010110 to 1000001001100001.

15. Why is the method of shifting bits left or right to produce multiplication or division results by a power of 2 preferred?

16. How many positions must the number 000110110_2 be shifted left in order to multiply it by 8?

17. True or False: Adding 01101101_2 to 10100010_2 in 8-bit unsigned binary will cause an overflow.

18. True or False: Adding 01101101_2 to 10100010_2 in 8-bit 2's complement binary will cause an overflow.

19. What would be the best binary representation for each of the following applications?

    - Phone number

    - Age (positive integer)

    - Exam grade

    - Checking account balance

    - Value read from a postal scale

    - Price

CHAPTER FOUR

Logic Functions and Gates

Representing numbers using transistors is one thing, but getting the computer to do something with those numbers is an entirely different matter. Digital circuitry is used to perform operations such as addition or multiplication, manage data, or execute programs. This chapter presents the circuitry that is the foundation of data manipulation and management within a computer.

4.1 Logic Gate Basics

Unless you are an electrical engineer, an understanding of the operation of transistors is unnecessary. One level above the transistors, however, is a set of basic building blocks for digital circuitry. These building blocks are called *logic gates*, and it is at this level that we will begin our discussion.

A logic gate has the basic format shown below in Figure 4-1. It takes one or more binary signals as its inputs, and using a specific algorithm, outputs a single bit as a result. Each time the inputs change, the output bit changes in a predictable fashion.

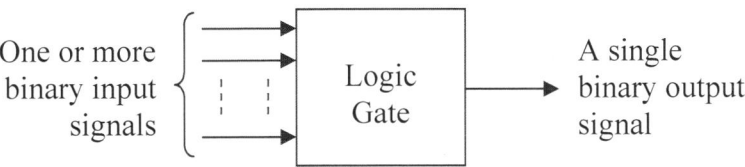

Figure 4-1 Basic Format of a Logic Gate

For example, the algorithm for a specific gate may cause a one to be output if an odd number of ones are present at the gate's input and a zero to be output if an even number of ones is present.

A number of standard gates exist, each one of which has a specific symbol that uniquely identifies its function. Figure 4-2 presents the symbols for the four primary types of gates that are used in digital circuit design.

71

72 Computer Organization and Design Fundamentals

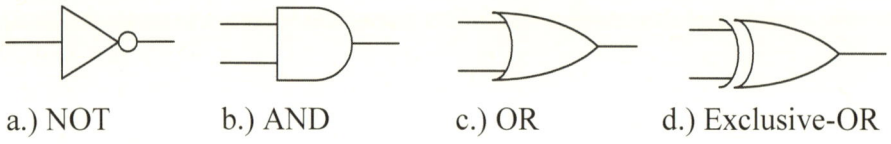

a.) NOT   b.) AND   c.) OR   d.) Exclusive-OR

Figure 4-2 Basic Logic Symbols

4.1.1 NOT Gate

Let's begin with the *NOT gate*. This logic gate, sometimes referred to as an *inverter*, is the only one in Figure 4-2 that has a single input. Its input goes into the left side of a triangle symbol while its output exits the gate through a small circle placed at the tip of the opposite corner. Note that it is the small circle that defines the operation of this gate, so it should not be left out.

The NOT gate is used to flip the value of a digital signal. In other words, it changes a logic 1 input to a logic 0 or it changes a logic 0 input to a logic 1. An example of an inverter might be the light detection circuit used to control the automatic headlights of a car. During the daylight hours, sunshine enters the light detector which is typically installed on the top surface of the car's dashboard. This acts as a logic 1 input. Since it is daytime, the headlights need to be turned off, a logic 0. When the sun goes down and no light enters the light detector, a logic 0, then the headlights must be turned on, a logic 1. Figure 4-3 shows the operation of the NOT gate.

Figure 4-3 Operation of the NOT Gate

Note that with a single input, the NOT gate has only 2 possible states.

4.1.2 AND Gate

The operation of the *AND gate* is such that its output is a logic 1 *only* if all of its inputs are logic 1. Otherwise the output is a logic 0. The AND gate in Figure 4-2 has only two inputs, but an AND gate may have as many inputs as the circuit requires. Regardless of the number of inputs, all inputs must be a logic 1 for the output to be a logic 1.

Chapter 4: Logic Functions and Gates 73

As an example, picture a lamp that is connected to a plug in the wall that is subsequently controlled by the light switch that is protected with a circuit breaker. In order for the lamp to be on (logic 1), the switch at the lamp must be on, the wall switch must be on, and the circuit breaker must be on. If any of the switches turns to off (logic 0), then the lamp will turn off. Another way to describe the operation of this circuit might be to say, "The lamp is on if and only if the lamp switch is on *and* the wall switch is on *and* the circuit breaker is on." This should give you a good idea of when an AND gate is used; just look for the use of the word "and" when describing the operation of the circuit. Figure 4-4 shows all $2^2 = 4$ states for a two-input AND gate.

Figure 4-4 Operation of a Two-Input AND Gate

4.1.3 OR Gate

An **OR gate** outputs a logic 1 if *any* of its inputs are a logic 1. An OR gate only outputs a logic 0 if all of its inputs are logic 0. The OR gate in Figure 4-2 has only two inputs, but just like the AND gate, an OR gate may have as many inputs as the circuit requires. Regardless of the number of inputs, if any input is a logic 1, the output is a logic 1.

A common example of an OR gate circuit is a security system. Assume that a room is protected by a system that watches three inputs: a door open sensor, a glass break sensor, and a motion sensor. If none of these sensors detects a break-in condition, i.e., they all send a logic 0 to the OR gate, the alarm is off (logic 0). If any of the sensors detects a break-in, it will send a logic 1 to the OR gate which in turn will output a logic 1 indicating an alarm condition. It doesn't matter what the other sensors are reading, if any sensor sends a logic 1 to the gate, the alarm should be going off. Another way to describe the operation of this circuit might be to say, "The alarm goes off if the door opens *or* the glass breaks *or* motion is detected." Once again, the use of the word "or" suggests that this circuit should be implemented with an OR gate.

Figure 4-5 shows the $2^2 = 4$ possible states for a two-input OR gate.

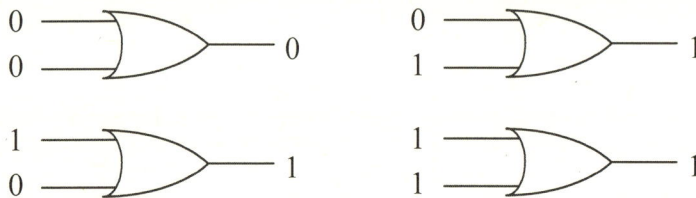

Figure 4-5   Operation of a Two-Input OR Gate

4.1.4 Exclusive-OR (XOR) Gate

An **Exclusive-OR gate** is sometimes called a parity checker. Parity checkers count the number of ones being input to a circuit and output a logic 1 or 0 based on whether the number of ones is odd or even. The Exclusive-OR (XOR) gate counts the number of ones at its input and outputs a logic 1 for an odd count and a logic 0 for an even count.

A common application for XOR gates is in error checking circuits. If two digital signals are compared bit-by-bit, an error free condition means that a logic 0 will be compared to a logic 0 and a logic 1 will be compared with a logic 1. In both of these cases, there is an even number of logic 1's being input to the XOR gate. Therefore, as long as the XOR gate outputs a logic 0, there is no error.

If, however, an error has occurred, then one signal will be logic 1 and the other will be a logic 0. This odd number of logic 1's will cause the XOR gate to output a logic 1 indicating an error condition.

Just as with the AND and OR gates, the XOR gate may have two or more inputs. Figure 4-6 shows all four states for a two-input XOR.

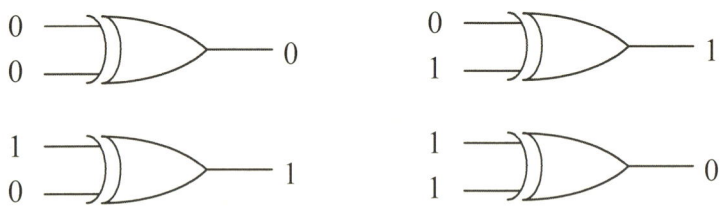

Figure 4-6   Operation of a Two-Input XOR Gate

These representations of logic gates can be an awkward way to describe the operation of a complex circuit. The next section will introduce an easier method for representing the operation of any digital circuit incorporating the NOT, AND, OR, and XOR gates.

4.2 Truth Tables

The previous section described the operation of each logic gate with words. This method isn't efficient and is prone to misinterpretation. What we need is a method to show the output of a digital system based on each of the possible input patterns of ones and zeros.

A *truth table* serves this purpose by making a column for each of the inputs to a digital circuit and a column for the resulting output. A row is added for each of the possible patterns of ones and zeros that could be input to the circuit. For example, a circuit with three inputs, A, B, and C, would have $2^3 = 8$ possible patterns of ones and zeros:

A=0, B=0, C=0   A=0, B=1, C=0   A=1, B=0, C=0   A=1, B=1, C=0
A=0, B=0, C=1   A=0, B=1, C=1   A=1, B=0, C=1   A=1, B=1, C=1

This means that a truth table representing a circuit with three inputs would have 8 rows. Figure 4-7 presents a sample truth table for a digital circuit with three inputs, A, B, and C, and one output, X. Note that the output X doesn't represent anything in particular. It is just added to show how the output might appear in a truth table.

A	B	C	X
0	0	0	1
0	0	1	0
0	1	0	1
0	1	1	1
1	0	0	0
1	0	1	1
1	1	0	0
1	1	1	1

Figure 4-7 Sample Three-Input Truth Table

For the rest of this book, the inputs to a digital circuit will be labeled with capital letters, A, B, C, etc., while the output will be labeled X.

For some, the hardest part of creating a truth table is being able to list all possible patterns of ones and zeros for the inputs. One thing that can help us is that we know that for n inputs, there must be 2^n different patterns of inputs. Therefore, if your truth table doesn't have exactly 2^n rows, then a pattern is either missing or one has been duplicated.

There is also a trick to deriving the combinations. Assume we need to build a truth table with four inputs, A, B, C, and D. Since $2^4 = 16$, we know that there will be sixteen possible combinations of ones and zeros. For half of those combinations, A will equal zero, and for the other half, A will equal one.

When A equals zero, the remaining three inputs, B, C, and D, will go through every possible combination of ones and zeros for three inputs. Three inputs have $2^3 = 8$ patterns, which coincidentally, is half of 16. For half of the 8 combinations, B will equal zero, and for the other half, B will equal one. Repeat this for C and then D.

This gives us a process to create a truth table for four inputs. Begin with the A column and list eight zeros followed by eight ones. Half of eight is four, so in the B column write four zeros followed by four ones in the rows where A equals zero, then write four zeros followed by four ones in the rows where A equals one. Half of four equals two, so the C column will have two zeros followed by two ones followed by two zeros then two ones and so on. The process should end with the last column having alternating ones and zeros. If done properly, the first row should have all zeros and the last row should have all ones.

A	B	C	D	X
0	0	0	0	
0	0	0	1	
0	0	1	0	
0	0	1	1	
0	1	0	0	
0	1	0	1	
0	1	1	0	
0	1	1	1	
1	0	0	0	
1	0	0	1	
1	0	1	0	
1	0	1	1	
1	1	0	0	
1	1	0	1	
1	1	1	0	
1	1	1	1	

Figure 4-8 Listing All Bit Patterns for a Four-Input Truth Table

In addition to verifying that all combinations of ones and zeros have been listed, this method also provides a consistency between all truth tables in the way that their rows are organized.

Now let's use truth tables to describe the functions of the four basic logic gates beginning with the inverter. The inverter has one input and one output. Therefore, there is one column for inputs and one column for outputs. For single input, there are exactly two possible states: logic 1 and logic 0. Therefore, there will be two rows of data for the inverter truth table. That table is shown in Figure 4-9.

A	X
0	1
1	0

Figure 4-9 Inverter Truth Table

Remember that an AND gate outputs a logic 1 *only* if all of its inputs are logic 1. The operation of a two-input AND gate can be represented with the truth table shown in Figure 4-10.

A	B	X
0	0	0
0	1	0
1	0	0
1	1	1

Figure 4-10 Two-Input AND Gate Truth Table

The output of an OR gate is set to logic 1 if any of its inputs equal 1. The OR gate truth table is shown in Figure 4-11.

A	B	X
0	0	0
0	1	1
1	0	1
1	1	1

Figure 4-11 Two-Input OR Gate Truth Table

78   Computer Organization and Design Fundamentals

The XOR gate's output is set to logic 1 if there are an odd number of ones being input to the circuit. Figure 4-12 below shows that for a two-input XOR gate, this occurs twice, once for A=0 and B=1 and once for A=1 and B=0.

A	B	X
0	0	0
0	1	1
1	0	1
1	1	0

Figure 4-12   Two-Input XOR Gate Truth Table

In some cases, the output of a digital circuit can be known without knowing what all of the inputs are. The AND gate, for instance, outputs a zero if *any* of the inputs equal zero. It doesn't matter what the other inputs are. This can be represented in a truth table with a third symbol called a "don't care". The "don't care", written as an 'X' in one of the input columns, indicates that the output does not depend on this input.

Take for example a three-input AND gate. Inputs B and C can take on one of four different values when the input A=0: B=0 and C=0; B=0 and C=1; B=1 and C=0; and B=1 and C=1. Each of these cases has an output of X=0. This can be shown in the truth table by replacing the four rows where A=0 with one row: A=0, B=X, and C=X. Figure 4-13 shows the resulting truth table where "don't cares" are used to reduce the number of rows. In this example, the original eight-row truth table has been replaced with one having only 4 rows.

A	B	C	X
0	X	X	0
X	0	X	0
X	X	0	0
1	1	1	1

Figure 4-13   Three-Input AND Gate Truth Table With Don't Cares

A similar truth table can be made for the OR gate. In this case, if *any* input to an OR gate is one, the output is 1. The only time an OR gate outputs a 0 is when *all* of the inputs are set to 0.

4.3 Timing Diagrams for Gates

The operation of a logic gate can also be represented with a timing diagram. Figures 4-14, 4-15, and 4-16 show the output that results from three binary input signals for an AND gate, OR gate, and XOR gate respectively. Remember that the AND gate outputs a one only if all its inputs equal one, the OR gate outputs a one if any input equals one, and the XOR gate outputs a one if an odd number of ones is present at the input. Use these rules to verify the outputs shown in the figures.

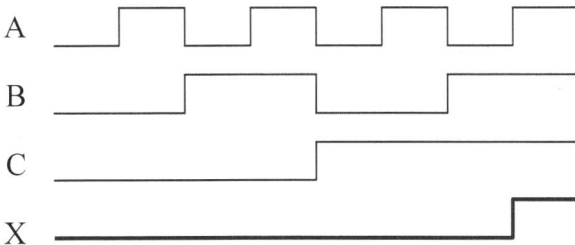

Figure 4-14 Sample Timing Diagram for a Three-Input AND Gate

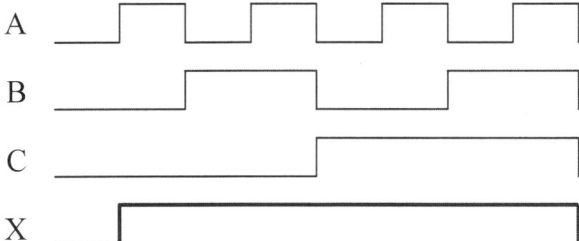

Figure 4-15 Sample Timing Diagram for a Three-Input OR Gate

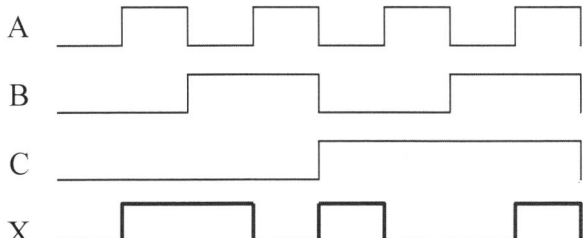

Figure 4-16 Sample Timing Diagram for a Three-Input XOR Gate

4.4 Combinational Logic

By themselves, logic gates are not very practical. Their power comes when you combine them to create *combinational logic*. Combinational logic connects multiple logic gates by using the outputs from some of the gates as the inputs to others. Figure 4-17 presents a sample of combinational logic.

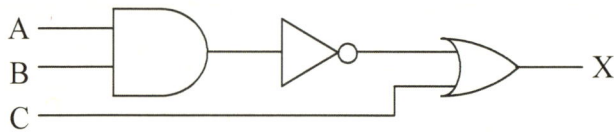

Figure 4-17 Sample Combinational Logic

In an earlier section, a security system was given as an example for an application of an OR gate: the alarm goes off if the door opens *or* the glass breaks *or* motion is detected. This circuit description is incomplete though; it doesn't take into account the fact that security systems can be armed or disarmed. This would extend our system description to: the alarm goes off if the system is armed *and* (the door opens *or* the glass breaks *or* motion is detected). The parentheses are added here to remove any ambiguity in the precedence of the logical operations. Figure 4-18 shows our new security circuit.

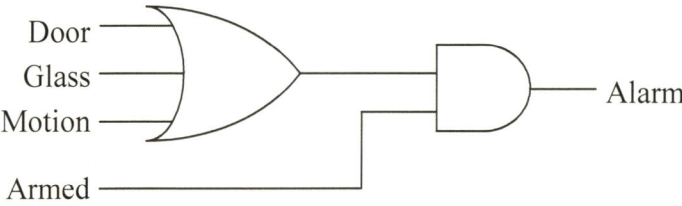

Figure 4-18 Combinational Logic for a Simple Security System

The operation of this circuit can also be represented with a truth table. Figure 4-19 shows how the four inputs, Door, Glass, Motion, and Armed, affect the output Alarm. Note that Alarm never goes high (logic 1) if the system is disarmed, i.e., Armed = logic 0. If the system is armed, Armed = logic 1, but none of the alarm inputs are set to a logic 1, then the alarm stays off. If, however, the system is armed and any one of the other inputs is a logic 1, then the Alarm goes to a logic 1.

Armed	Door	Glass	Motion	Alarm
0	0	0	0	0
0	0	0	1	0
0	0	1	0	0
0	0	1	1	0
0	1	0	0	0
0	1	0	1	0
0	1	1	0	0
0	1	1	1	0
1	0	0	0	0
1	0	0	1	1
1	0	1	0	1
1	0	1	1	1
1	1	0	0	1
1	1	0	1	1
1	1	1	0	1
1	1	1	1	1

Figure 4-19 Truth Table for Simple Security System of Figure 4-18

We determined the pattern of ones and zeros for the output column of the truth table through an understanding of the operation of a security system. We could have also done this by examining the circuit itself. Starting at the output side of Figure 4-18 (the right side) the AND gate will output a one only if *both* inputs are one, i.e., the system is armed and the OR gate is outputting a one.

The next step is to see when the OR gate outputs a one. This happens when *any* of the inputs, Door, Glass, or Motion, equal one. From this information, we can determine the truth table. The output of our circuit is equal to one when Armed=1 AND when either Door OR Glass OR Motion equal 1. For all other input conditions, a zero should be in the output column.

There are three combinational logic circuits that are so common that they are considered gates in themselves. By adding an inverter to the output of each of the three logic gates, AND, OR, and XOR, three new combinational logic circuits are created. Figure 4-20 shows the new logic symbols.

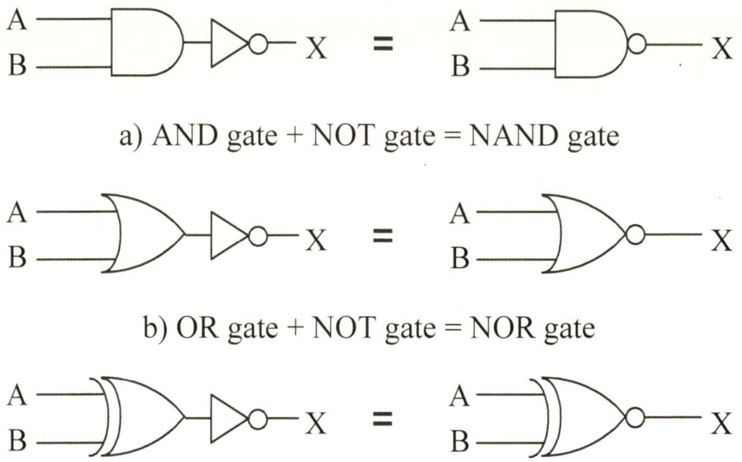

82　Computer Organization and Design Fundamentals

a) AND gate + NOT gate = NAND gate

b) OR gate + NOT gate = NOR gate

c) Exclusive-OR gate + NOT gate = Exclusive NOR gate

Figure 4-20　"NOT" Circuits

The NAND gate outputs a 1 if *any* input is a zero. Later in this book, it will be shown how this gate is in fact a very important gate in the design of digital circuitry. It has two important characteristics: (1) the transistor circuit that realizes the NAND gate is typically one of the fastest circuits and (2) every digital circuit can be realized with combinational logic made entirely of NAND gates.

The NOR gate outputs a 1 *only* if all of the inputs are zero. The Exclusive-NOR gate outputs a 1 as an indication that an even number of ones is being input to the gate.

A similar method is used to represent inverted inputs. Instead of inserting the NOT gate symbol in a line going to the input of a gate, a circle can be placed at the gate's input to show that the signal is inverted before entering the gate. An example of this is shown in the circuit on the right in Figure 4-21.

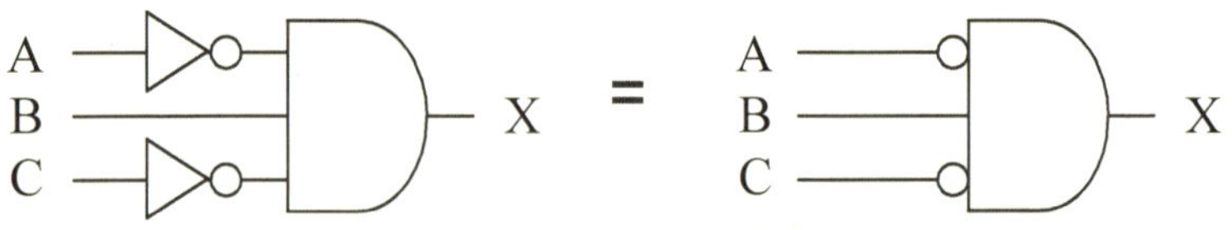

Figure 4-21　Schematic "Short-Hand" for Inverted Inputs

4.5 Truth Tables for Combinational Logic

Not all digital circuits lend themselves to quick conversion to a truth table. For example, input B in the digital circuit shown in Figure 4-22 passes through four logic gates before its effect is seen at the output.

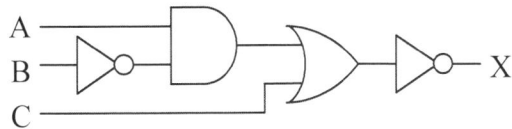

Figure 4-22 Sample of Multi-Level Combinational Logic

So how do we convert this circuit to a truth table? One method is to go through each pattern of ones and zeros at the input and fill in the resulting output in the truth table row by row. Figure 4-23 takes A=0, B=0, and C=0 through each gate to determine its corresponding output.

a.) A 0 is input to the first inverter which outputs a 1.

b.) The 1 coming from the inverter is combined with a 0 in the AND gate to output a 0.

c.) The OR gate receives a 0 from the AND and a 0 from the inputs which makes it output a 0.

d.) The 0 output from the OR gate passes through the inverter output a 1.

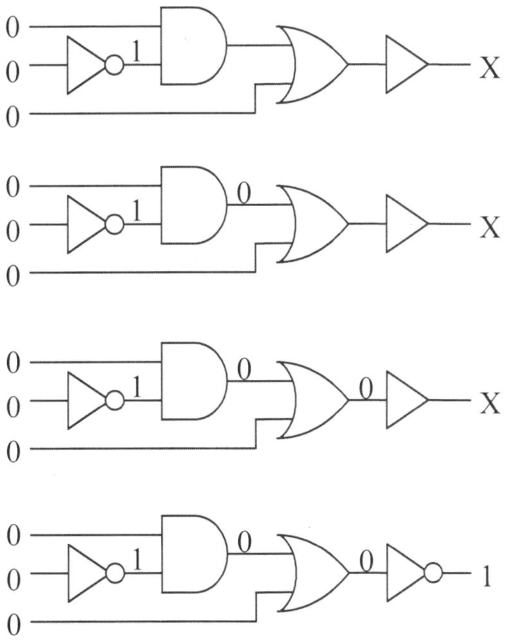

Figure 4-23 Process of Passing Inputs Through Combinational Logic

84   Computer Organization and Design Fundamentals

This process can be rather tedious, especially if there are more than three inputs to the combinational logic. Note that the bit pattern in Figure 4-23 represents only one row of a truth table with eight rows. Add another input and the truth table doubles in size to sixteen rows.

There is another way to determine the truth table. Notice that in Figure 4-23, we took the inputs through a sequence of steps passing it first through the inverter connected to the input B, then through the AND gate, then through the OR gate, and lastly through the inverter connected to the output of the OR gate. These steps are labeled (a), (b), (c), and (d) in Figure 4-24.

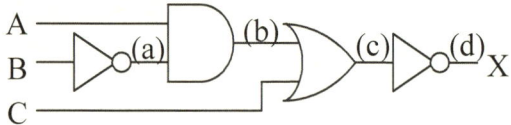

Figure 4-24   Steps That Inputs Pass Through in Combinational Logic

If we apply those same steps to the individual columns of a truth table instead of using the schematic, the process becomes more orderly. Begin by creating the input columns of the truth table listing all of the possible combinations of ones and zeros for the inputs. In the case of our sample circuit, that gives us a truth table with eight rows.

A	B	C
0	0	0
0	0	1
0	1	0
0	1	1
1	0	0
1	0	1
1	1	0
1	1	1

Figure 4-25   All Combinations of Ones and Zeros for Three Inputs

Next, add a column for each layer of logic. Going back to Figure 4-24, we begin by making a column representing the (a) step. Since (a) represents the output of an inverter that has B as its input, fill the (a) column with the opposite or inverse of each condition in the B column.

Chapter 4: Logic Functions and Gates   85

A	B	C	(a) = NOT of B
0	0	0	1
0	0	1	1
0	1	0	0
0	1	1	0
1	0	0	1
1	0	1	1
1	1	0	0
1	1	1	0

Figure 4-26 Step (a) in Sample Truth Table Creation

Next, step (b) is the output of an AND gate that takes as its inputs step (a) and input A. Add another column for step (b) and fill it with the AND of columns A and (a).

A	B	C	(a)	(b) = (a) AND A
0	0	0	1	0
0	0	1	1	0
0	1	0	0	0
0	1	1	0	0
1	0	0	1	1
1	0	1	1	1
1	1	0	0	0
1	1	1	0	0

Figure 4-27 Step (b) in Sample Truth Table Creation

Step (c) is the output from the OR gate that takes as its inputs step (b) and the input C. Add another column for (c) and fill it with the OR of column C and column (b). This is shown in Figure 4-28.

Last of all, Figure 4-29 shows the final output is the inverse of the output of the OR gate of step (c). Make a final column and fill it with the inverse of column (c). This will be the final output column for the truth table.

A	B	C	(a)	(b)	(c) = (b) OR C
0	0	0	1	0	0
0	0	1	1	0	1
0	1	0	0	0	0
0	1	1	0	0	1
1	0	0	1	1	1
1	0	1	1	1	1
1	1	0	0	0	0
1	1	1	0	0	1

Figure 4-28 Step (c) in Sample Truth Table Creation

A	B	C	(a)	(b)	(c)	X = (d) = NOT of (c)
0	0	0	1	0	0	1
0	0	1	1	0	1	0
0	1	0	0	0	0	1
0	1	1	0	0	1	0
1	0	0	1	1	1	0
1	0	1	1	1	1	0
1	1	0	0	0	0	1
1	1	1	0	0	1	0

Figure 4-29 Step (d) in Sample Truth Table Creation

This can be done with any combinational logic circuit. Begin by creating a table from the list of combinations of ones and zeros that are possible at the inputs. Next, determine the order of gates that the signals come to as they pass from the input to the output. As each set of signals passes through a gate, create another column in the truth table for the output of that gate. The final column should be the output of your combinational logic circuit.

4.6 What's Next?

The introduction of logic operations and logic gates opens up the field of computer design. Topics ranging from the mathematical circuitry inside the processor to the creation and delivery of an Ethernet message will no longer remain abstract concepts.

Chapter 5 presents a mathematical-like method for representing logic circuits along with some techniques to manipulate them for faster performance or a lower chip count. These tools can then be used to effectively design the components of a computer system.

Problems

1. Identify a real-world example for an AND gate and one for an OR gate other than those presented in this chapter.

2. How many rows does the truth table for a 4-input logic gate have?

3. Construct the truth table for a four-input OR gate.

4. Construct the truth table for a two-input NAND gate.

5. Construct the truth table for a three-input Exclusive-NOR gate.

6. Construct the truth table for a three-input OR gate using don't cares for the inputs similar to the truth table constructed for the three-input AND gate shown in Figure 4-13.

7. Draw the output X for the pattern of inputs shown in the figure below for a three input NAND gate.

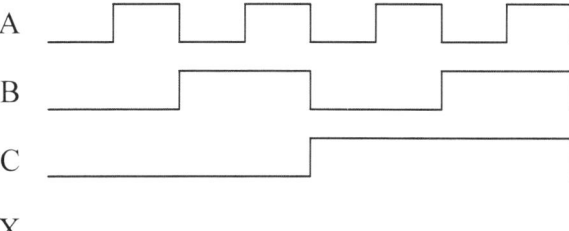

8. Repeat problem 7 for a NOR gate.

88 Computer Organization and Design Fundamentals

9. Show the output waveform of an AND gate with the inputs A, B, and C indicated in the figure below.

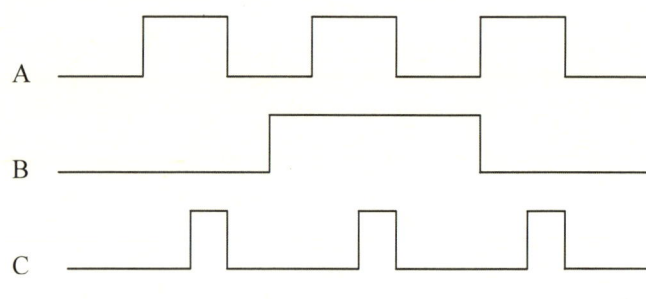

A · B · C

10. Develop the truth table for each of the combinational logic circuits shown below.

a.)

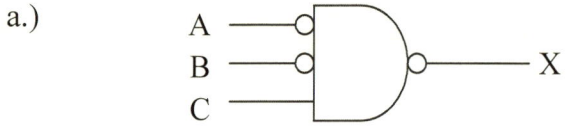

b.)

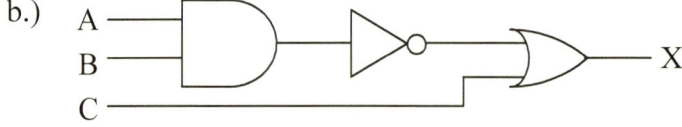

c.)

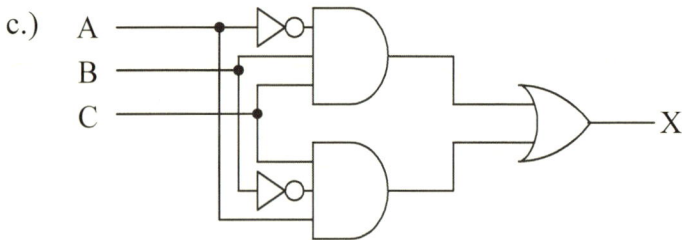

CHAPTER FIVE

Boolean Algebra

5.1 Need for Boolean Expressions

At this point in our study of digital circuits, we have two methods for representing combinational logic: schematics and truth tables.

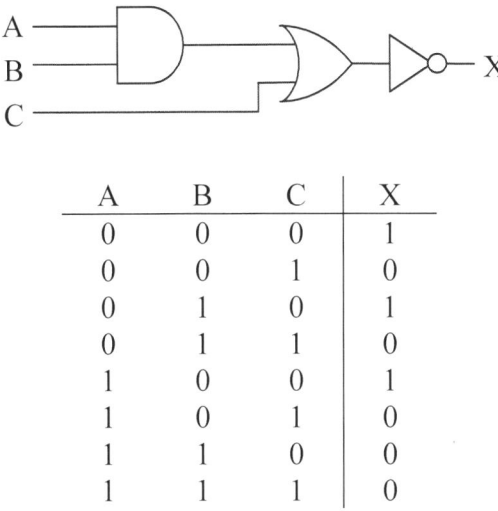

A	B	C	X
0	0	0	1
0	0	1	0
0	1	0	1
0	1	1	0
1	0	0	1
1	0	1	0
1	1	0	0
1	1	1	0

Figure 5-1 Schematic and Truth Table of Combinational Logic

These two methods are inadequate for a number of reasons:

- Both schematics and truth tables take too much space to describe the operation of complex circuits with numerous inputs.
- The truth table "hides" circuit information.
- The schematic diagram is difficult to use when trying to determine output values for each input combination.

To overcome these problems, a discipline much like algebra is practiced that uses expressions to describe digital circuitry. These expressions, which are called *boolean expressions*, use the input variable names, A, B, C, etc., and combine them using symbols representing the AND, OR, and NOT gates. These boolean expressions can be used to describe or evaluate the output of a circuit.

There is an additional benefit. Just like algebra, a set of rules exist that when applied to boolean expressions can dramatically simplify them. A simpler expression that produces the same output can be realized with fewer logic gates. A lower gate count results in cheaper circuitry, smaller circuit boards, and lower power consumption.

If your software uses binary logic, the logic can be represented with boolean expressions. Applying the rules of simplification will make the software run faster or allow it to use less memory.

The next section describes the representation of the three primary logic functions, NOT, AND, and OR, and how to convert combinational logic to a boolean expression.

5.2 Symbols of Boolean Algebra

Analogous behavior can be shown between boolean algebra and mathematical algebra, and as a result, similar symbols and syntax can be used. For example, the following expressions hold true in math.

$0 \cdot 0 = 0$ $0 \cdot 1 = 0$ $1 \cdot 0 = 0$ $1 \cdot 1 = 1$

This looks like the AND function allowing an analogy to be drawn between the mathematical multiply and the boolean AND functions. Therefore, in boolean algebra, A AND'ed with B is written $A \cdot B$.

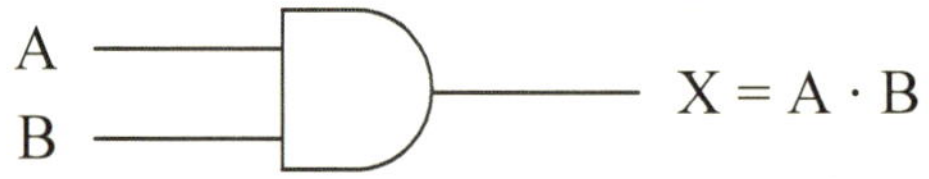

Figure 5-2 Boolean Expression for the AND Function

Mathematical addition has a similar parallel in boolean algebra, although it is not quite as flawless. The following four mathematical expressions hold true for addition.

$0 + 0 = 0$ $0 + 1 = 1$ $1 + 0 = 1$ $1 + 1 = 2$

The first three operations match the OR function, and if the last operation is viewed as having a non-zero result instead of the decimal result of two, it too can be viewed as operating similar to the OR

Chapter 5: Boolean Algebra 91

function. Therefore, the boolean OR function is analogous to the mathematical function of addition.

$$X = A + B$$

Figure 5-3 Boolean Expression for the OR Function

An analogy cannot be made between the boolean NOT and any mathematical operation. Later in this chapter we will see how the NOT function, unlike AND and OR, requires its own special theorems for algebraic manipulation. The NOT is represented with a bar across the inverted element.

$$X = \overline{A}$$

Figure 5-4 Boolean Expression for the NOT Function

The NOT operation may be used to invert the result of a larger expression. For example, the NAND function which places an inverter at the output of an AND gate is written as:

$$X = \overline{A \cdot B}$$

Since the bar goes across A · B, the NOT is performed after the AND.

Let's begin with some simple examples. Can you determine the output of the boolean expression 1 + 0 + 1? Since the plus-sign represents the OR circuit, the expression represents 1 or 0 or 1.

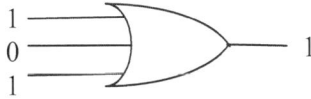

Figure 5-5 Circuit Representation of the Boolean Expression 1+0+1

Since an OR-gate outputs a 1 if any of its inputs equal 1, then 1 + 0 + 1 = 1.

The two-input XOR operation is represented using the symbol ⊕, but it can also be represented using a boolean expression. Basically, the two-input XOR equals one if A = 0 and B = 1 or if A = 1 and B = 0. This gives us the following expression.

$$X = A \oplus B = \overline{A} \cdot B + A \cdot \overline{B}$$

The next section shows how the boolean operators ·, +, ⊕, and the NOT bar may be combined to represent complex combinational logic.

5.3 Boolean Expressions of Combinational Logic

Just as mathematical algebra combines multiplication and addition to create complex expressions, boolean algebra combines AND, OR, and NOT functions to represent complex combinational logic. Our experience with algebra allows us to understand the expression Y = X · (X +5) + 3. The decimal value 5 is added to a copy of X, the result of which is then multiplied by a second copy of X. Lastly, a decimal 3 is added and the final result is assigned to Y.

This example shows us two things. First, each mathematical operation has a priority, e.g., multiplication is performed before addition. This priority is referred to as precedence. Second, variables such X can appear multiple times in an expression, each appearance representing the current value of X.

Boolean algebra allows for the same operation. Take for example the circuit shown in Figure 5-6.

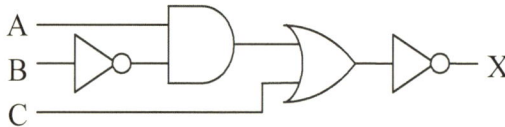

Figure 5-6   Sample of Multi-Level Combinational Logic

In Chapter 4, we determined the truth table for this circuit by taking the input signals A, B, and C from left to right through each gate. As shown in Figure 5-7, we can do the same thing to determine the boolean expression.

Notice the use of parenthesis in step c. Just as in mathematical algebra, parenthesis can be used to force the order in which operations are taken. In the absence of parenthesis, however, the AND, OR, and NOT functions have an order of precedence.

Chapter 5: Boolean Algebra   93

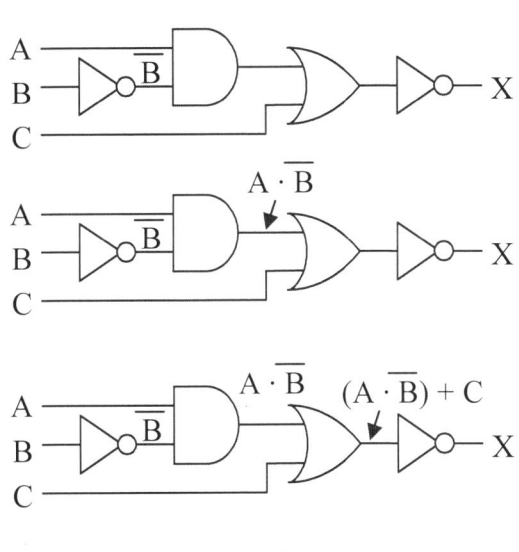

a) B goes through the first inverter which outputs a $\overline{B}$

b) A and $\overline{B}$ go through the AND gate which outputs $A \cdot \overline{B}$.

c) $A \cdot \overline{B}$ and C go through the OR gate which outputs $(A \cdot \overline{B}) + C$.

d) The output of the OR gate goes through a second inverter giving us our result.

Figure 5-7   Creating Boolean Expression from Combinational Logic

To begin with, AND takes precedence over OR unless overridden by parenthesis. NOT is a special case in that it can act like a set of parenthesis. If the bar indicating the NOT function spans a single variable, it takes precedence over AND and OR. If, however, the NOT bar spans an expression, the expression beneath the bar must be evaluated before the NOT is taken. Figure 5-8 presents two examples of handling precedence with the NOT function.

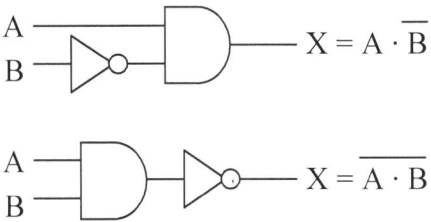

Figure 5-8   Examples of the Precedence of the NOT Function

Understanding this is vital because unlike the mathematical inverse, the two expressions below are *not* equivalent.

$$\overline{A} \cdot \overline{B} \neq \overline{A \cdot B}$$

Let's do an example addressing precedence with a more complex boolean expression. Using parenthesis and the order of precedence, the boolean expression below has a single interpretation.

$$X = A \cdot D + (A + \overline{B + C})$$

The following steps show the order to evaluate the above expression.

1. OR B with C because the operation is contained under a single NOT bar and is contained within the lowest set of parenthesis
2. Invert the result of step 1 because NOT takes precedence over OR
3. OR A with the result of step 2 because of the parenthesis
4. Invert result of step 3
5. AND A and D because AND takes precedence over OR
6. OR the results of steps 4 and 5

We can use this order of operations to convert the expression to its schematic representation. By starting with a list of inputs to the circuit, then passing each input through the correct gates, we can develop the circuit. Figure 5-9 does just this for the previous boolean expression. We list the inputs for the expression, A, B, C, and D, on the left side of the figure. These inputs are then passed through the gates using the same order as the steps shown above. The number inside each gate of the figure corresponds to the order of the steps.

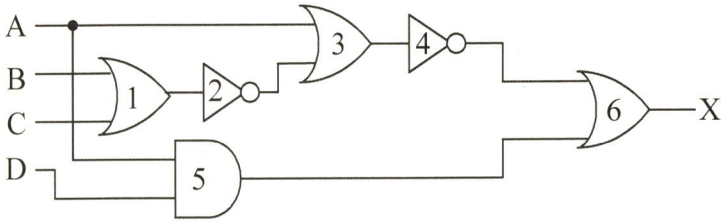

Figure 5-9 Example of a Conversion from a Boolean Expression

Chapter 5: Boolean Algebra 95

The following sections show how boolean expressions can be used to modify combinational logic in order to reduce complexity or otherwise modify its structure.

5.4 Laws of Boolean Algebra

The manipulation of algebraic expressions is based on fundamental laws. Some of these laws extend to the manipulation of boolean expressions. For example, the commutative law of algebra which states that the result of an operation is the same regardless of the order of operands holds true for boolean algebra too. This is shown for the OR function applied to two variables in the truth tables of Figure 5-10.

A	B	A + B	A	B	B + A
0	0	0+0 = 0	0	0	0+0 = 0
0	1	0+1 = 1	0	1	1+0 = 1
1	0	1+0 = 1	1	0	0+1 = 1
1	1	1+1 = 1	1	1	1+1 = 1

Figure 5-10 Commutative Law for Two Variables OR'ed Together

Not only does Figure 5-10 show how the commutative law applies to the OR function, it also shows how truth tables can be used in boolean algebra to prove laws and rules. If a rule states that two boolean expressions are equal, then by developing the truth table for each expression and showing that the output is equal for all combinations of ones and zeros at the input, then the rule is proven true.

Below, the three fundamental laws of boolean algebra are given along with examples.

Commutative Law: The results of the boolean operations AND and OR are the same regardless of the order of their operands.

$$A + B = B + A$$
$$A \cdot B = B \cdot A$$

Associative Law: The results of the boolean operations AND and OR with three or more operands are the same regardless of which pair of elements are operated on first.

$$A + (B + C) = (A + B) + C$$
$$A \cdot (B \cdot C) = (A \cdot B) \cdot C$$

Distributive Law: The AND'ing of an operand with an OR expression is equivalent to OR'ing the results of an AND between the first operand and each operand within the OR expression.

$$A \cdot (B + C) = A \cdot B + A \cdot C$$

The next section uses truth tables and laws to prove twelve rules of boolean algebra.

5.5 Rules of Boolean Algebra

5.5.1 NOT Rule

In algebra, the negative of a negative is a positive and taking the inverse of an inverse returns the original value. Although the NOT gate does not have an equivalent in mathematical algebra, it operates in a similar manner. If the boolean inverse of a boolean inverse is taken, the original value results.

$$\overline{\overline{A}} = A$$

This is proven with a truth table.

A	$\overline{A}$	$\overline{\overline{A}}$
0	1	0
1	0	1

Since the first column and the third column have the same pattern of ones and zeros, they must be equivalent. Figure 5-11 shows this rule in schematic form.

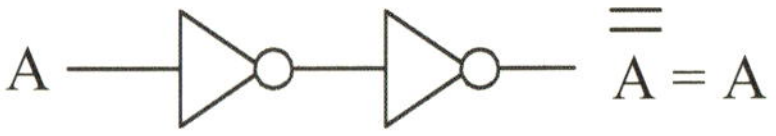

Figure 5-11 Schematic Form of NOT Rule

5.5.2 OR Rules

If an input to a logic gate is a constant 0 or 1 or if the same signal is connected to more than one input of a gate, a simplification of the

Chapter 5: Boolean Algebra   97

expression is almost always possible. This is true for the OR gate as is shown with the following four rules for simplifying the OR function.

First, what happens when one of the inputs to an OR gate is a constant logic 0? It turns out that the logic 0 input drops out leaving the remaining inputs to stand on their own. Notice that the two columns in the truth table below are equivalent thus proving this rule.

Rule: A + 0 = A

A	A + 0
0	0+0 = 0
1	1+0 = 1

What about inputting a logic 1 to an OR gate? In this case, a logic 1 forces the other operands into the OR gate to drop out. Notice that the output column (A + 1) is always equal to 1 regardless of what A equals. Therefore, the output of this gate will always be 1.

Rule: A + 1 = 1

A	A + 1
0	0+1 = 1
1	1+1 = 1

If the same operand is connected to all of the inputs of an OR gate, we find that the OR gate has no effect. Notice that the two columns in the truth table below are equivalent thus proving this rule.

Rule: A + A = A

A	A + A
0	0+0 = 0
1	1+1 = 1

Another case of simplification occurs when an operand is connected to one input of a two-input OR gate and its inverse is connected to the other. In this case, either the operand is equal to a one or its inverse is. There is no other possibility. Therefore, at least one logic 1 is connected to the inputs of the OR gate. This gives us an output of logic 1 regardless of the inputs.

Rule: A + $\overline{A}$ = 1

A	A + $\overline{A}$
0	0+1 = 1
1	1+0 = 1

5.5.3 AND Rules

Just as with the OR gate, if either of the inputs to an AND gate is a constant (logic 0 or logic 1) or if the two inputs are the same or inverses of each other, a simplification can be performed. Let's begin with the case where one of the inputs to the AND gate is a logic 0. Remember that an AND gate must have all ones at its inputs to output a one. In this case, one of the inputs will always be zero forcing this AND to always output zero. The truth table below shows this.

Rule: A · 0 = 0

A	A · 0
0	0 · 0 = 0
1	1 · 0 = 0

If one input of a two-input AND gate is connected to a logic 1, then it only takes the other input going to a one to get all ones on the inputs. If the other input goes to zero, the output becomes zero. This means that the output follows the input that is not connected to the logic 1.

Rule: A · 1 = A

A	A · 1
0	0 · 1 = 0
1	1 · 1 = 1

If the same operand is connected to all of the inputs of an AND gate, we get a simplification similar to that of the OR gate. Notice that the two columns in the truth table below are equivalent proving this rule.

Rule: A · A = A

A	A · A
0	0 · 0 = 0
1	1 · 1 = 1

Last of all, when an operand is connected to one input of a two-input AND gate and its inverse is connected to the other, either the operand is equal to a zero or its inverse is equal to zero. There is no other possibility. Therefore, at least one logic 0 is connected to the inputs of the AND gate giving us an output of logic 0 regardless of the inputs.

Rule: A · $\overline{A}$ = 0

A	A · $\overline{A}$
0	0 · 1 = 0
1	1 · 0 = 0

5.5.4 XOR Rules

Now let's see what happens when we apply these same input conditions to a two-input XOR gate. Remember that a two-input XOR gate outputs a 1 if its inputs are different and a zero if its inputs are the same.

If one of the inputs to a two-input XOR gate is connected to a logic 0, then the gate's output follows the value at the second input. In other words, if the second input is a zero, the inputs are the same forcing the output to be zero and if the second input is a one, the inputs are different and the output equals one.

Rule: $A \oplus 0 = A$

A	$A \oplus 0$
0	$0 \oplus 0 = 0$
1	$1 \oplus 0 = 1$

If one input of a two-input XOR gate is connected to a logic 1, then the XOR gate acts as an inverter as shown in the table below.

Rule: $A \oplus 1 = \overline{A}$

A	$A \oplus 1$
0	$0 \oplus 1 = 1$
1	$1 \oplus 1 = 0$

If the same operand is connected to both inputs of a two-input XOR gate, then the inputs are always the same and the gate outputs a 0.

Rule: $A \oplus A = 0$

A	$A \oplus A$
0	$0 \oplus 0 = 0$
1	$1 \oplus 1 = 0$

Lastly, if the inputs of a two-input XOR gate are inverses of each other, then the inputs are always different and the output is 1.

Rule: $A \oplus \overline{A} = 1$

A	$A \oplus \overline{A}$
0	$0 \oplus 1 = 1$
1	$1 \oplus 0 = 1$

5.5.5 Derivation of Other Rules

If we combine the NOT, OR, and AND rules with the commutative, associative, and distributive laws, we can derive other rules for boolean algebra. This can be shown with the following example.

Example

Prove that $A + A \cdot B = A$

Solution

A + A·B	= A·1 + A·B	Rule: A · 1 = A
	= A·(1 + B)	Distributive Law
	= A·(B + 1)	Commutative Law
	= A·1	Rule: A + 1 = 1
	= A	Rule: A · 1 = A

Remember also that rules of boolean algebra can be proven using a truth table. The example below uses a truth table to derive another rule.

Example

Prove $A + \overline{A} \cdot B = A + B$

Solution

The truth table below goes step-by-step through both sides of the expression to prove that $A + \overline{A} \cdot B = A + B$.

A	B	$\overline{A}$	$\overline{A}$·B	A + $\overline{A}$·B	A + B
0	0	1	0	0	0
0	1	1	1	1	1
1	0	0	0	1	1
1	1	0	0	1	1

The mathematical "F-O-I-L" principle, based on the distributive law, works in boolean algebra too. FOIL is a memory aid referring to the multiplication pattern for multiplying quadratic equations. It stands for:

F – AND the first terms from each OR expression
O – AND the outside terms (the first term from the first OR expression and the last term from the last OR expression)
I – AND the inside terms (the last term from the first OR expression and the first term from the last OR expression)
L – AND the last terms from each OR expression

Example

Prove $(A + B) \cdot (A + C) = A + B \cdot C$

Solution

$(A + B) \cdot (A + C)$	$= (A + B) \cdot A + (A + B) \cdot C$	Distributive Law
	$= A \cdot A + B \cdot A + A \cdot C + B \cdot C$	Distributive Law
	$= A + B \cdot A + A \cdot C + B \cdot C$	Rule: $A \cdot A = A$
	$= A + A \cdot B + A \cdot C + B \cdot C$	Commutative Law
	$= A + A \cdot C + B \cdot C$	Rule: $A + A \cdot B = A$
	$= A + B \cdot C$	Rule: $A + A \cdot B = A$

Now that you have a taste for the manipulation of boolean expressions, the next section will show examples of how complex expressions can be simplified.

5.6 Simplification

Many students of algebra are frustrated by problems requiring simplification. Sometimes it feels as if extrasensory perception is required to see where the best path to simplification lies. Unfortunately, boolean algebra is no exception. There is no substitute for practice. Therefore, this section provides a number of examples of simplification in the hope that seeing them presented in detail will give you the tools you need to simplify the problems on your own.

The rules of the previous section are summarized in Figure 5-12.

1. $\overline{\overline{A}} = A$
2. $A + 0 = A$
3. $A + 1 = 1$
4. $A + A = A$
5. $A + \overline{A} = 1$
6. $A \cdot 0 = 0$
7. $A \cdot 1 = A$
8. $A \cdot A = A$
9. $A \cdot \overline{A} = 0$
10. $A \oplus 0 = A$
11. $A \oplus 1 = \overline{A}$
12. $A \oplus A = 0$
13. $A \oplus \overline{A} = 1$
14. $A + A \cdot B = A$
15. $A + \overline{A} \cdot B = A + B$
16. $(A + B) \cdot (A + C) = A + B \cdot C$

Figure 5-12 Rules of Boolean Algebra

Example

Simplify $(A \cdot B + C)(A \cdot B + D)$

Solution

From the rules of boolean algebra, we know that $(A + B)(A + C) = A + BC$. Substitute A·B for A, C for B, and D for C and we get:

$$(A \cdot B + C)(A \cdot B + D) = A \cdot B + C \cdot D$$

Example

Simplify $(A + B) \cdot (\overline{B} + B)$

Solution

$(A + B) \cdot 1$	Anything OR'ed with its inverse is 1
$(A + B)$	Anything AND'ed with 1 is itself

Example

Simplify $\overline{B} \cdot (A + \overline{A} \cdot B)$

Solution

$\overline{B} \cdot A + \overline{B} \cdot \overline{A} \cdot B$	Distributive Law
$\overline{B} \cdot A + \overline{A} \cdot \overline{B} \cdot B$	Associative Law
$\overline{B} \cdot A + \overline{A} \cdot 0$	Anything AND'ed with its inverse is 0
$\overline{B} \cdot A + 0$	Anything AND'ed with 0 is 0
$\overline{B} \cdot A$	Anything OR'ed with 0 is itself
$A \cdot \overline{B}$	Associative Law

Example

Simplify $(\overline{A} + B) \cdot (A + \overline{B})$

Solution

$\bar{A} \cdot A + \bar{A} \cdot \bar{B} + B \cdot A + B \cdot \bar{B}$ Use FOIL to distribute terms

$0 + \bar{A} \cdot \bar{B} + B \cdot A + 0$ Anything AND'ed with its inverse is 0

$\bar{A} \cdot \bar{B} + B \cdot A$ Anything OR'ed with 0 is itself

Example

Simplify $\bar{A} \cdot \bar{B} \cdot \bar{C} + \bar{A} \cdot \bar{B} \cdot C + \bar{A} \cdot B \cdot \bar{C} + \bar{A} \cdot B \cdot C$

Solution

$\bar{A} \cdot (\bar{B} \cdot \bar{C} + \bar{B} \cdot C + B \cdot \bar{C} + B \cdot C)$ Distributive Law

$\bar{A} \cdot (\bar{B} \cdot (\bar{C} + C) + B \cdot (\bar{C} + C))$ Distributive Law

$\bar{A} \cdot (\bar{B} \cdot 1 + B \cdot 1)$ Anything OR'ed with its inverse is 1

$\bar{A} \cdot (\bar{B} + B)$ Anything AND'ed with 1 is itself

$\bar{A} \cdot 1$ Anything OR'ed with its inverse is 1

$\bar{A}$ Anything AND'ed with 1 is itself

5.7 DeMorgan's Theorem

Some of you may have noticed that the truth tables for the AND and OR gates are similar. Below is a comparison of the two operations.

AND

A	B	X = A·B
0	0	0
0	1	0
1	0	0
1	1	1

OR

A	B	X = A+B
0	0	0
0	1	1
1	0	1
1	1	1

Okay, so maybe they're not exactly the same, but notice that the output for each gate is the same for three rows and different for the fourth. For the AND gate, the row that is different occurs when all of the inputs are ones, and for the OR gate, the different row occurs when all of the inputs are zeros. What would happen if we inverted the inputs of the AND truth table?

AND of inverted inputs

A	B	$X = \overline{A} \cdot \overline{B}$
0	0	1
0	1	0
1	0	0
1	1	0

OR

A	B	$X = A+B$
0	0	0
0	1	1
1	0	1
1	1	1

The two truth tables are still not quite the same, but they are quite close. The two truth tables are now inverses of one another. Let's take the inverse of the output of the OR gate and see what happens.

AND of inverted inputs

A	B	$X = \overline{A} \cdot \overline{B}$
0	0	1
0	1	0
1	0	0
1	1	0

OR with inverted output

A	B	$X = \overline{(A+B)}$
0	0	1
0	1	0
1	0	0
1	1	0

So the output of an AND gate with inverted inputs is equal to the inverted output of an OR gate with non-inverted inputs. A similar proof can be used to show that the output of an OR gate with inverted inputs is equal to the inverted output of an AND gate with non-inverted inputs. This resolves our earlier discussion where we showed that the NOT gate cannot be distributed to the inputs of an AND or an OR gate.

This brings us to DeMorgan's Theorem, the last Boolean law presented in this chapter.

$$\overline{A + B} = \overline{A} \cdot \overline{B} \qquad \overline{A} + \overline{B} = \overline{A \cdot B}$$

The purpose of DeMorgan's Theorem is to allow us to distribute an inverter from the output of an AND or OR gate to the gate's inputs. In doing so, an AND gate is switched to an OR gate and an OR gate is switched to an AND gate. Figure 5-13 shows how pushing the inverter from the output of a gate to its inputs.

a.) Pushing an inverter through an AND gate flips it to an OR gate

b.) Pushing an inverter through an OR gate flips it to an AND gate

Figure 5-13 Application of DeMorgan's Theorem

DeMorgan's Theorem applies to gates with three or more inputs too.

$$\overline{A + B + C + D} = \overline{(A + B) \cdot (C + D)}$$
$$= (\overline{A \cdot B}) \cdot (\overline{C \cdot D})$$
$$= \overline{A} \cdot \overline{B} \cdot \overline{C} \cdot \overline{D}$$

One of the main purposes of DeMorgan's Theorem is to distribute any inverters in a digital circuit back to the inputs. This typically improves the circuit's performance by removing layers of logic and can be done either with the boolean expression or the schematic. Either way, the inverters are pushed from the output side to the input side one gate at a time. The sequence of steps in Figure 5-14 shows this process using a schematic.

It is a little more difficult to apply DeMorgan's Theorem to a boolean expression. To guarantee that the inverters are being distributed properly, it is a good idea to apply DeMorgan's Theorem in the reverse order of precedence for the expression.

$\overline{A \cdot B + C}$ Step 1: The AND takes precedence over the OR, so distribute inverter across the OR gate first.

$\overline{A \cdot B} \cdot \overline{C}$ Step 2: Now distribute the inverter across the A·B term.

$(\overline{A} + \overline{B}) \cdot \overline{C}$ Step 3: In this final case, the use of parenthesis is vital.

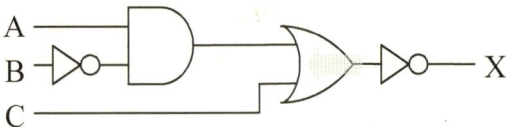

a.) Push inverter through the OR gate distributing it to the inputs

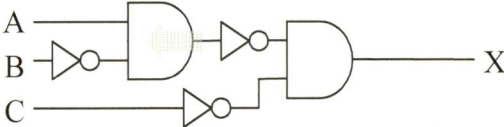

b.) Push inverter through the AND gate distributing it to the inputs

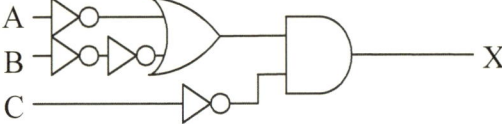

c.) Two inverters at B input cancel each other

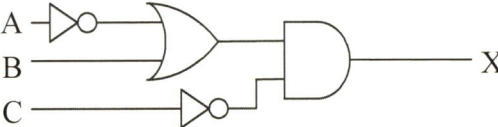

Figure 5-14 Schematic Application of DeMorgan's Theorem

5.8 What's Next?

Using the methods presented in this chapter, a boolean expression can be manipulated into whatever form best suits the needs of the computer system. As far as the binary operation is concerned, two circuits are the same if their truth tables are equivalent. The circuits, however, may not be the same when measuring performance or when counting the number of gates it took to implement the circuit. The

Chapter 5: Boolean Algebra 107

optimum circuit for a specific application can be designed using the tools presented in this chapter.

In Chapter 6, we will show how the rules presented in this chapter are used to take any boolean expression and put it into one of two standard formats. The standard formats allow for quicker operation and support the use of programmable hardware components. Chapter 6 also presents some methods to convert truth tables into circuitry. It will be our first foray into designing circuitry based on a system specification.

Problems

1. List three drawbacks of using truth tables or schematics for describing a digital circuit.

2. List three benefits of a digital circuit that uses fewer gates.

3. True or False: Boolean expressions can be used to optimize the logic functions in software.

4. Convert the following boolean expressions to their schematic equivalents. Do not modify the original expression

   a.) $\overline{A \cdot B} + C$

   b.) $A \cdot \overline{B} \cdot C + \overline{A} \cdot B + \overline{A \cdot C}$

   c.) $\overline{(A + B \cdot C)} + A \cdot \overline{D}$

   d.) $A \cdot \overline{B} + \overline{A} \cdot B$

5. Convert each of the digital circuits shown below to their corresponding boolean expressions without simplification.

   a.) 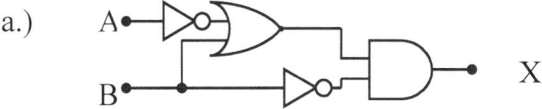   X b.)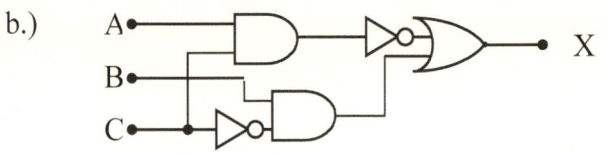

c.)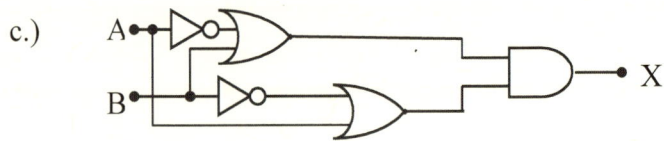

6. Apply DeMorgan's Theorem to each of the following expressions so that the NOT bars do not span more than a single variable.

   a.) $\overline{A \cdot C} + B$

   b.) $\overline{D(C + B)(A + B)}$

   c.) $\overline{A + \overline{B} + C + \overline{(AB)}}$

7. Simplify each of the following expressions.

   a.) $B \cdot A + B \cdot \overline{A}$

   b.) $(A + B)(B + \overline{A})$

   c.) $A + \overline{B} + C + \overline{(AB)}$

   d.) $\overline{B}(A + A \cdot B)$

   e.) $(\overline{A} + B)(A + \overline{B})$

   f.) $\overline{B} + \overline{(AB)} + \overline{C}$

CHAPTER SIX

Standard Boolean Expression Formats

The development of standards is important to the computer industry for a number of reasons. It allows independently developed systems and subsystems to be connected, it provides reliability through well-tested design methods, and it shortens the design time by providing off-the-shelf tools and components for quick development.

In the design of digital systems, there are some standards that are regularly applied to combinational logic. Over time, design tools and programmable hardware have been developed to support these standards allowing for quick implementation of digital logic.

This chapter outlines two standard representations of combinational logic: Sum-of-Products and Product-of-Sums. Both of these formats represent the fastest possible digital circuitry since, aside from a possible inverter, all of the signals pass through exactly two layers of logic gates. This also opens the door for the development of programmable hardware where a single computer chip can be programmed to handle any logic circuit.

6.1 Sum-of-Products

A sum-of-products (SOP) expression is a boolean expression in a specific format. The term sum-of-products comes from the expression's form: a sum (OR) of one or more products (AND). As a digital circuit, an SOP expression takes the output of one or more AND gates and OR's them together to create the final output.

The inputs to the AND gates are either inverted or non-inverted input signals. This limits the number of gates that any input signal passes through before reaching the output to an inverter, an AND gate, and an OR gate. Since each gate causes a delay in the transition from input to output, and since the SOP format forces all signals to go through exactly two gates (not counting the inverters), an SOP expression gives us predictable performance regardless of which input in a combinational logic circuit changes.

Below is an example of an SOP expression:

$$\overline{A}BC\overline{D} + A\overline{B}D + C\overline{D} + A\overline{D}$$

110 Computer Organization and Design Fundamentals

There are no parentheses in an SOP expression since they would necessitate additional levels of logic. This also means that an SOP expression cannot have more than one variable combined in a term with an inversion bar. The following is *not* an SOP expression:

$$(\overline{AB})\overline{CD} + A\overline{B}D + \overline{CD} + A\overline{D}$$

This is because the first term has A and B passing through a NAND gate before being AND'ed with C and D thereby creating a third level of logic. To fix this problem, we need to break up the NAND using DeMorgan's Theorem.

$$(\overline{AB})\overline{CD} + A\overline{B}D + \overline{CD} + A\overline{D}$$

$$(\overline{A} + \overline{B})\overline{CD} + A\overline{B}D + \overline{CD} + A\overline{D}$$

$$\overline{A}\overline{CD} + \overline{B}\overline{CD} + A\overline{B}D + \overline{CD} + A\overline{D}$$

This expression is now considered to be in SOP format.

As far as the implementation of an SOP expression is concerned, combinations of non-inverted and inverted signals are input to one or more AND gates. The outputs from these gates are all input to a single OR gate. Figure 6-1 shows a sample SOP binary circuit.

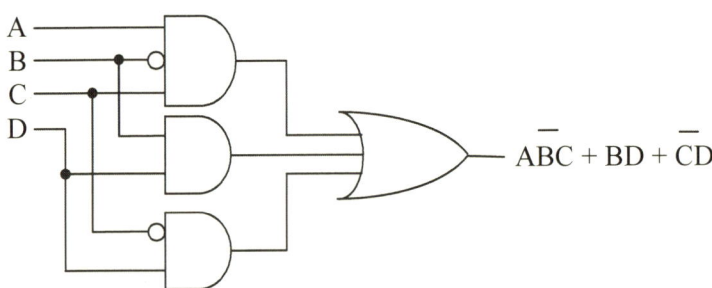

Figure 6-1 Sample Sum-of-Products Binary Circuit

6.2 Converting an SOP Expression to a Truth Table

Examining the truth table for an AND gate reveals that exactly one row has a one for its output. All of the other rows have a zero output. If we invert one of the inputs, this simply moves the row with the one

Chapter 6: Standard Boolean Expression Formats 111

output to another position. There is still only one row outputting a one. Figure 6-2 shows some examples of this behavior.

A	B	C	A·B·C	A	B	C	A·B̄·C	A	B	C	Ā·B·C̄
0	0	0	0	0	0	0	0	0	0	0	0
0	0	1	0	0	0	1	0	0	0	1	0
0	1	0	0	0	1	0	0	0	1	0	1
0	1	1	0	0	1	1	0	0	1	1	0
1	0	0	0	1	0	0	0	1	0	0	0
1	0	1	0	1	0	1	1	1	0	1	0
1	1	0	0	1	1	0	0	1	1	0	0
1	1	1	1	1	1	1	0	1	1	1	0

Figure 6-2 Samples of Single Product (AND) Truth Tables

The output of an OR gate is a one if any of the inputs is a one. Therefore, when the products are OR'ed together, a one appears in the output column for each of the products. For example, if we OR'ed together each of the products from Figure 6-2, a one would be output in the rows corresponding to A=1, B=1, and C=1; A=1, B=0, and C=1; and A=0, B=1, and C=0. This is shown in Figure 6-3.

A	B	C	A·B·C	A·B̄·C	Ā·B·C̄	ABC + AB̄C + ĀBC̄
0	0	0	0	0	0	0
0	0	1	0	0	0	0
0	1	0	0	0	1	1
0	1	1	0	0	0	0
1	0	0	0	0	0	0
1	0	1	0	1	0	1
1	1	0	0	0	0	0
1	1	1	1	0	0	1

Figure 6-3 Sample of a Sum-of-Products Truth Table

Therefore, to convert an SOP expression to a truth table, examine each product to determine when it is equal to a one. Where that product is a one, a one will also be outputted from the OR gate.

Each of the products in the above example contains all of the input variables for the SOP expression. What if one of the products doesn't do this? For example, what if an SOP expression has inputs A, B, and C, but one of its products only depends on A and B?

112 Computer Organization and Design Fundamentals

This is not a problem if we remember that we are looking to see when that product is equal to a one. For a product containing only A and B in an SOP expression containing inputs A, B, and C, the product has ones in *two rows*, one for C=0 and one for C=1. As an example, let's convert the following SOP expression to a truth table.

$$\overline{A}B\overline{C} + A\overline{B} + ABC$$

The first step is to determine where each product equals a one. Beginning with the first term, the different input conditions resulting in the output of a logic one from the AND gates are listed below.

$\overline{A}B\overline{C}$ = 1 when $\overline{A}$=1, B=1, and $\overline{C}$=1,
which means when A=0, B=1, and C=0.

$A\overline{B}$ = 1 when A=1, $\overline{B}$=1, and C=1 or 0,
which means when A=1, B=0, and C=0 or 1, i.e., two rows will have a one output due to this term.

ABC = 1 when A=1, B=1, and C=1.

Placing a one in each row identified above should result in the truth table for the corresponding SOP expression. Remember to set the remaining row outputs to zero to complete the table.

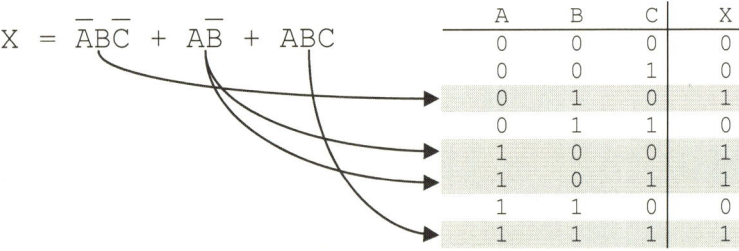

A	B	C	X
0	0	0	0
0	0	1	0
0	1	0	1
0	1	1	0
1	0	0	1
1	0	1	1
1	1	0	0
1	1	1	1

Figure 6-4 Conversion of an SOP Expression to a Truth Table

6.3 Converting a Truth Table to an SOP Expression

Any truth table can be converted to an SOP expression. The conversion process goes like this: identify the rows with ones as the output, and then come up with the unique product to put a one in that row. Note that this will give us an SOP expression where all of the

Chapter 6: Standard Boolean Expression Formats

products use all of the variables for inputs. This usually gives us an expression that can be simplified using the tools from Chapter 5.

Example

Derive the SOP expression for the following truth table.

A	B	C	X
0	0	0	0
0	0	1	1
0	1	0	0
0	1	1	1
1	0	0	1
1	0	1	0
1	1	0	1
1	1	1	0

Solution

First, identify each row that contains a one as the output.

A	B	C	X	
0	0	0	0	
0	0	1	1	A = 0, B = 0, and C = 1
0	1	0	0	
0	1	1	1	A = 0, B = 1, and C = 1
1	0	0	1	A = 1, B = 0, and C = 0
1	0	1	0	
1	1	0	1	A = 1, B = 1, and C = 0
1	1	1	0	

Now we need to make a product for each of these rows. The product that outputs a one for the row where A=0, B=0, and C=1 must invert A and B in order to have a product of 1·1·1 = 1. Therefore, our product is:

$$\overline{A} \cdot \overline{B} \cdot C$$

The product that outputs a one for the row where A=0, B=1, and C=1 must invert A in order to have a product of 1·1·1 = 1. This gives us our second product:

$$\overline{A} \cdot B \cdot C$$

The third product outputs a one for the row where A=1, B=0, and C=0. Therefore, we must invert B and C in order to have a product of 1·1·1 = 1.

$$A \cdot \overline{B} \cdot \overline{C}$$

The final product outputs a one for the row where A=1, B=1, and C=0. This time only C must be inverted.

$$A \cdot B \cdot \overline{C}$$

OR'ing all of these products together gives us our SOP expression.

$$\overline{A} \cdot \overline{B} \cdot C + \overline{A} \cdot B \cdot C + A \cdot \overline{B} \cdot \overline{C} + A \cdot B \cdot \overline{C}$$

The next three sections parallel the first three for a second standard boolean expression format: the product-of-sums.

6.4 Product-of-Sums

The product-of-sums (POS) format of a boolean expression is much like the SOP format with its two levels of logic (not counting inverters). The difference is that the outputs of multiple OR gates are combined with a single AND gate which outputs the final result. The expression below adheres to the format of a POS expression.

$$(\overline{A}+B+C+\overline{D})\ (A+\overline{B}+D)\ (C+\overline{D})\ (A+\overline{D})$$

As with SOP expressions, a POS expression cannot have more than one variable combined in a term with an inversion bar. For example, the following is not a POS expression:

$$\overline{(A+B+C+D)}\ (A+\overline{B}+D)\ (C+\overline{D})\ (A+\overline{D})$$

In this example, the sum (OR) of A, B, and C is inverted thereby adding a third level of logic: A, B, and C are OR'ed together then inverted and then OR'ed with D before going to the AND gate. Getting this expression to adhere to the proper POS format where the NOT is distributed to the individual terms is not as easy as it was with the SOP. Often times it is easier to determine the truth table for the function and then convert that truth table to the correct POS format. This will be shown in a later section in this chapter.

Chapter 6: Standard Boolean Expression Formats 115

As far as hardware is concerned, POS expressions take the output of OR gates and connect them to the inputs of a single AND gate. The sample circuit shown in Figure 6-5 adheres to this format.

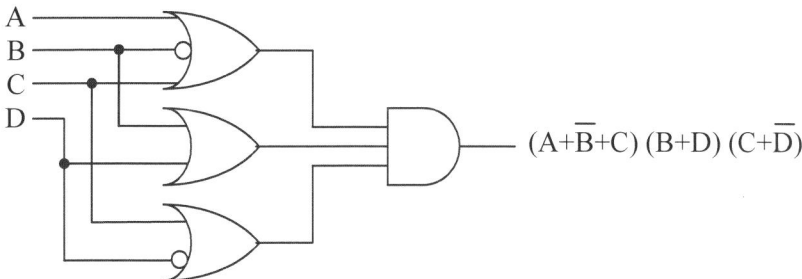

$(A+\overline{B}+C)(B+D)(C+\overline{D})$

Figure 6-5 Sample Product-of-Sums Binary Circuit

6.5 Converting POS to Truth Table

Converting a POS expression to a truth table follows a similar process as the one used to convert an SOP expression to a truth table. The difference is this: where the SOP conversion focuses on rows with a one output, the POS conversion focuses on rows with a zero output.

We do this because the OR gate has an output of zero on exactly one row while all of the other rows have an output of one. If we invert one of the inputs, this moves the row with the zero output to another position. There is still only one row outputting a zero.

The row with the zero output is the row where all of the inputs equal zero. If one of the inputs is inverted, then its non-inverted value must be one for the OR gate to output a zero. Figure 6-6 shows a few examples of this behavior.

A	B	C	A+B+C	A	B	C	A+$\overline{B}$+C	A	B	C	$\overline{A}$+B+$\overline{C}$
0	0	0	0	0	0	0	1	0	0	0	1
0	0	1	1	0	0	1	1	0	0	1	1
0	1	0	1	0	1	0	0	0	1	0	1
0	1	1	1	0	1	1	1	0	1	1	1
1	0	0	1	1	0	0	1	1	0	0	1
1	0	1	1	1	0	1	1	1	0	1	0
1	1	0	1	1	1	0	1	1	1	0	1
1	1	1	1	1	1	1	1	1	1	1	1

Figure 6-6 Samples of Single Sum (OR) Truth Tables

116 Computer Organization and Design Fundamentals

By AND'ing the output from these OR gates together, then the final output will be zero anytime one of the OR gates outputs a zero. Therefore, AND'ing the three sums in Figure 6-6 together will produce a zero output on the following conditions:

$$A=0, B=0, \text{ and } C=0$$
$$A=0, B=1, \text{ and } C=0$$
$$A=1, B=0, \text{ and } C=1$$

This is shown in Figure 6-7.

A	B	C	A+B+C	A+B+$\overline{C}$	$\overline{A}$+B+$\overline{C}$	(A+B+C)(A+$\overline{B}$+C)($\overline{A}$+B+$\overline{C}$)
0	0	0	0	1	1	0
0	0	1	1	1	1	1
0	1	0	1	0	1	0
0	1	1	1	1	1	1
1	0	0	1	1	1	1
1	0	1	1	1	0	0
1	1	0	1	1	1	1
1	1	1	1	1	1	1

Figure 6-7 Sample of a Product-of-Sums Truth Table

Therefore, to convert a POS expression to a truth table, examine each of the sums to determine where the sum is equal to zero. When that sum is equal to a zero, a zero will also be present at the final output of the circuit.

When a sum does not contain all of the circuit's inputs, then more than one row will get a zero output from the OR gate. Every time an input drops out of a sum, the number of rows with a zero output from that OR gate is doubled.

For example, if a POS expression uses as its inputs A, B, C, and D, then a sum within that expression that uses only B, C, and D as inputs will have two rows with zero outputs and a sum using only A and C as inputs will have four rows with zero outputs.

The output of the first sum is equal to zero only when all of the inputs, A, B and the inverse of D, are equal to zero. This occurs in two places, once for C=0 and once for C=1. Therefore, the output of a product-of-sums circuit with this OR expression in it will have a zero in the rows where A=0, B=0, C=0, and D=1 and where A=0, B=0, C=1, and D=1.

Chapter 6: Standard Boolean Expression Formats 117

The next sum uses only B and C from the four inputs. Therefore, there must be four rows with outputs of zero. This is because A and D have no effect on this sum and can have any of the four states: A=0 and D=0; A=0 and D=1; A=1 and D=0; or A=1 and D=1.

A single variable sum as shown in the last column of the truth table in Figure 6-8 will force zeros to be output for half of the input conditions. In the case of this truth table, the inverse of A equals zero when A equals 1.

A	B	C	D	A+B+$\overline{\text{D}}$	B+$\overline{\text{C}}$	$\overline{\text{A}}$
0	0	0	0	1	1	1
0	0	0	1	0	1	1
0	0	1	0	1	0	1
0	0	1	1	0	0	1
0	1	0	0	1	1	1
0	1	0	1	1	1	1
0	1	1	0	1	1	1
0	1	1	1	1	1	1
1	0	0	0	1	1	0
1	0	0	1	1	1	0
1	0	1	0	1	0	0
1	0	1	1	1	0	0
1	1	0	0	1	1	0
1	1	0	1	1	1	0
1	1	1	0	1	1	0
1	1	1	1	1	1	0

Figure 6-8 Sample Sums With Multiple Zero Outputs

Example

Convert the following POS expression to a truth table.

$$(\overline{A}+B+\overline{C})(A+\overline{B})(A+B+C)$$

Solution

The first step is to determine where each sum equals zero. Beginning with the first term, the three different conditions for a zero output are listed below.

$\overline{A}+B+\overline{C} = 0$ when $\overline{A}=0$, $B=0$, and $\overline{C}=0$,
which means when A=1, B=0, and C=1.

$\overline{A}+\overline{B} = 0$ when A=0, $\overline{B}$=0, and C=1 or 0, which means when A=0, B=1, and C=0 or 1, i.e., two rows will have a zero output due to this term.

A+B+C = 0 when A=0, B=0, and C=0.

Placing a zero in each row identified above should result in the truth table for the corresponding POS expression. Remember to set the remaining row outputs to zero to complete the table.

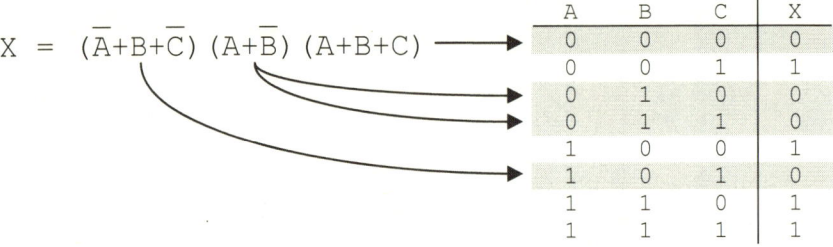

X = (Ā+B+C̄) (A+B̄) (A+B+C)

A	B	C	X
0	0	0	0
0	0	1	1
0	1	0	0
0	1	1	0
1	0	0	1
1	0	1	0
1	1	0	1
1	1	1	1

Figure 6-9 Conversion of a POS Expression to a Truth Table

6.6 Converting a Truth Table to a POS Expression

Just as with SOP expressions, any truth table can be converted to a POS expression. The conversion process goes like this: identify the rows with zeros as the output, and then come up with the unique sum to put a zero in that row. The final group of sums can then be AND'ed together producing the POS expression.

Let's go through the process by deriving the POS expression for the following truth table.

A	B	C	X
0	0	0	0
0	0	1	1
0	1	0	0
0	1	1	1
1	0	0	1
1	0	1	0
1	1	0	1
1	1	1	0

First, identify each row that contains a zero as the output.

Chapter 6: Standard Boolean Expression Formats 119

A	B	C	X	
0	0	0	0	A = 0, B = 0, and C = 0
0	0	1	1	
0	1	0	0	A = 0, B = 1, and C = 0
0	1	1	1	
1	0	0	1	
1	0	1	0	A = 1, B = 0, and C = 1
1	1	0	1	
1	1	1	0	A = 1, B = 1, and C = 1

Next, make a sum for each of these rows. Remember that a sum outputs a zero when all of its inputs equal zero. Therefore, to make a sum for a row equal to zero, the inputs equal to one must be inverted. For the first row, a zero is output when A=0, B=0, and C=0. Since for this case, all of the inputs are already zero, simply OR the non-inverted inputs together.

$$A+B+C$$

The sum that outputs a zero for the row where A=0, B=1, and C=0 must invert B in order to have a sum of 0+0+0=0. This gives us our second sum:

$$A+\overline{B}+C$$

The third sum outputs a zero for the row where A=1, B=0, and C=1. Therefore, we must invert A and C in order to have a sum of 0+0+0=0.

$$\overline{A}+B+\overline{C}$$

The final sum outputs a zero for the row where A=1, B=1, and C=1. In this case, all of the inputs must be inverted to get the sum 0+0+0=0.

$$\overline{A}+\overline{B}+\overline{C}$$

AND'ing all of these sums together gives us our POS expression.

$$(A+B+C)\ (A+\overline{B}+C)\ (\overline{A}+B+\overline{C})\ (\overline{A}+\overline{B}+\overline{C})$$

6.7 NAND-NAND Logic

Chapter 5 presented DeMorgan's Theorem and its application to Boolean expressions. The theorem is repeated below for convenience.

$$\overline{A+B} = \overline{A} \cdot \overline{B}$$
$$\overline{A} + \overline{B} = \overline{A \cdot B}$$

Figure 6-10 depicts DeMorgan's Theorem with circuit diagrams.

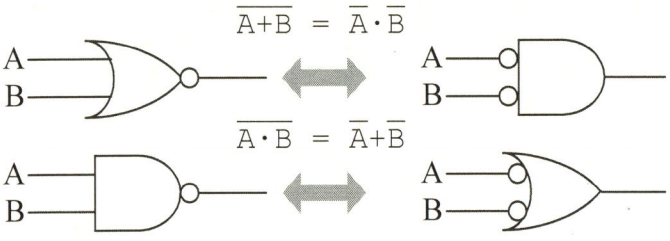

Figure 6-10 Circuit Depiction of DeMorgan's Theorem

If we invert both sides of the first expression where the inverse of the sum is equal to the product of the inverses, then we get the new circuit equivalents shown in Figure 6-11. Note that the double inverse over the OR cancels.

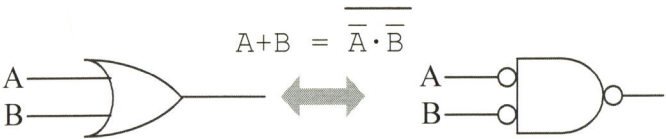

Figure 6-11 OR Gate Equals a NAND Gate With Inverted Inputs

This means that an OR gate operates identically to a NAND gate with inverted inputs. This is also true for OR gates with three or more inputs.

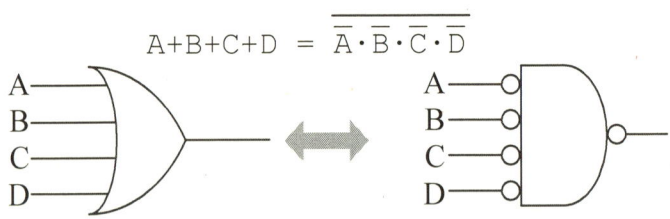

Figure 6-12 OR-to-NAND Equivalency Expanded to Four Inputs

Chapter 6: Standard Boolean Expression Formats 121

Now let's turn our attention to SOP expressions. Assume we have an equation like the one below.

$$X = (\overline{A} \cdot B \cdot \overline{C}) + (\overline{A} \cdot \overline{B} \cdot C) + (A \cdot B \cdot \overline{C})$$

Figure 6-13 shows the logic circuit equivalent of this expression.

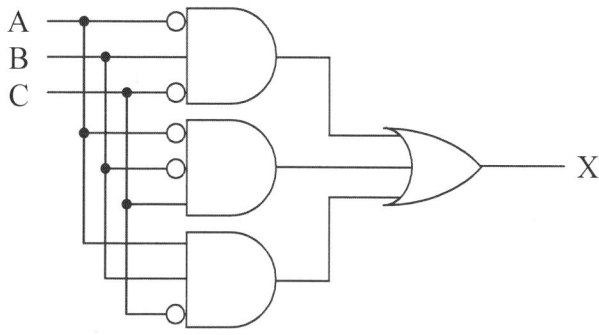

Figure 6-13   Sample SOP Circuit

If we substitute the OR gate with a NAND gate with inverted inputs, we get the circuit shown in Figure 6-14.

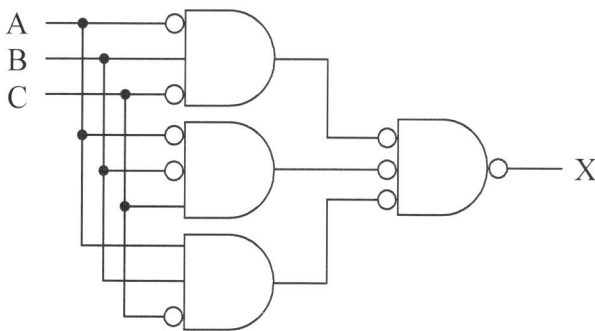

Figure 6-14   Sample SOP Circuit with Output OR Gate Replaced

If we take each of the inverter circles at the inputs to the rightmost gate (the NAND gate that replaced the OR gate), and move them to the outputs of the AND gates, we get the circuit shown in Figure 6-15.

This example shows that all of the gates of a sum-of-products expression, both the AND gates and the OR gate, can be replaced with

NAND gates. Though this doesn't appear at first to be significant, it is important to the implementation of digital logic.

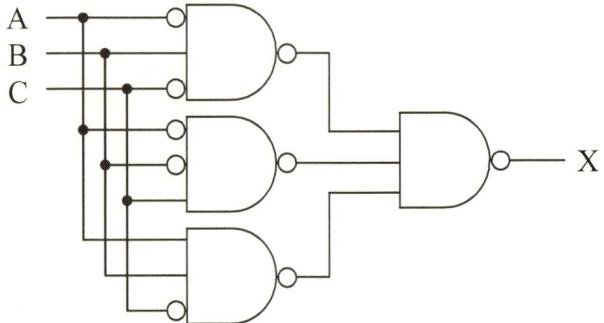

Figure 6-15 Sample SOP Circuit Implemented With NAND Gates

Since an SOP expression can be created for any truth table, then any truth table can be implemented entirely with NAND gates. This allows a designer to create an entire digital system from a single type of gate resulting in a more efficient use of the hardware.

There is an additional benefit to this observation. For most of the technologies used to implement digital logic, the NAND gate is the fastest available gate. Therefore, if a circuit can maintain the same structure while using the fastest possible gate, the overall circuit will be faster.

Another way to make digital circuits faster is to reduce the number of gates in the circuit or to reduce the number of inputs to each of the circuit's gates. This will not only benefit hardware, but also any software that uses logic processes in its operation. Chapter 7 presents a graphical method for generating optimally reduced SOP expressions without using the laws and rules of boolean algebra.

6.8 What's Next?

At this point, we should be able to convert any truth table to a boolean expression and finally to digital circuitry. It should also be clear that no truth table is represented by a unique circuit.

Chapter 7 introduces a simple graphical tool that uses the distributive law to generate the most reduced form of the SOP circuit for a given truth table. As long as the user can follow a set of rules used to generate the products for the circuit, it is a fail-safe tool to make simplified hardware.

Problems

1. Which of the following boolean expressions are in proper sum-of-products form?

   a.) $\overline{A} \cdot B \cdot \overline{D} \cdot \overline{E} + \overline{B} \cdot \overline{C} \cdot D$

   b.) $A \cdot B \cdot C + A \cdot \overline{B} \cdot \overline{C} + \overline{A}(\overline{B} \cdot \overline{C} + B \cdot C)$

   c.) $A + \overline{B} \cdot C \cdot E + D \cdot \overline{E}$

   d.) $A \cdot D + A \cdot \overline{C} + \overline{A \cdot B \cdot C \cdot D}$

   e.) $\overline{B} \cdot C + B \cdot D + \overline{B} \cdot (E + \overline{F})$

2. If a POS expression uses five input variables and has a sum within it that uses only three variables, how many rows in the POS expression's truth table have zeros as a result of that sum?

3. Draw the digital circuit corresponding to the following SOP expressions.

   a.) $\overline{A} \cdot B \cdot \overline{D} \cdot \overline{E} + A \cdot \overline{B} \cdot \overline{C} \cdot D$

   b.) $A \cdot B \cdot C + A \cdot \overline{B} \cdot \overline{C} + \overline{A} \cdot \overline{B} \cdot \overline{C} + \overline{A} \cdot B \cdot C$

   c.) $A \cdot \overline{C} + \overline{B} \cdot C \cdot E + D \cdot \overline{E}$

4. Draw the NAND-NAND digital logic circuit for each of the SOP expressions shown in problem 3.

5. List the two reasons why the NAND-NAND implementation of an SOP expression is preferred over an AND-OR implementation.

6. Put the following boolean expression into the proper SOP format.

   $$\overline{\overline{A} \cdot B \cdot C} + \overline{A} \cdot B \cdot \overline{C} + \overline{A \cdot B \cdot C}$$

7. Which form of boolean expression, SOP or POS, would best be used to implement the following truth table?

A	B	C	X
0	0	0	1
0	0	1	1
0	1	0	0
0	1	1	1
1	0	0	1
1	0	1	0
1	1	0	1
1	1	1	0

8. Derive the SOP and POS expressions for each of the truth tables shown below.

a.)

A	B	C	X
0	0	0	0
0	0	1	1
0	1	0	0
0	1	1	0
1	0	0	0
1	0	1	0
1	1	0	1
1	1	1	1

b.)

A	B	C	X
0	0	0	0
0	0	1	1
0	1	0	0
0	1	1	1
1	0	0	1
1	0	1	0
1	1	0	0
1	1	1	1

c.)

A	B	C	X
0	0	0	1
0	0	1	0
0	1	0	1
0	1	1	1
1	0	0	1
1	0	1	0
1	1	0	1
1	1	1	0

9. Derive the truth table for each of the following SOP expressions.

a.) $\overline{A} \cdot B \cdot \overline{C} + A \cdot \overline{B} \cdot C + \overline{A} \cdot \overline{B} \cdot C$

b.) $\overline{A} + A \cdot \overline{B} \cdot \overline{C} + A \cdot B \cdot \overline{C}$

c.) $A \cdot \overline{C} + \overline{A} \cdot B \cdot C + \overline{A} \cdot \overline{B} \cdot \overline{C}$

10. Derive the truth table for each of the following POS expressions.

a.) $(\overline{A}+B+\overline{C}) \cdot (A+\overline{B}+C) \cdot (\overline{A}+\overline{B}+C)$

b.) $(A + B) \cdot (\overline{A} + \overline{C})$

c.) $(A+\overline{C}) \cdot (\overline{A}+B+C) \cdot (\overline{A}+\overline{B}+\overline{C})$

CHAPTER SEVEN

Karnaugh Maps

7.1 The Karnaugh Map

With the introduction of SOP and POS functions in Chapter 6, we learned how to convert a truth table to a boolean expression, and if necessary, a digital circuit. Recall that in the SOP form of a boolean expression, each row with an output of one corresponded to a product. The OR of all of the products produced an expression that satisfied the truth table, but not necessarily one that was reduced to its simplest form. For example, the truth table below has four rows, each of which corresponds to a one output.

A	B	C	X	
0	0	0	1	A = 0, B = 0, and C = 0
0	0	1	1	A = 0, B = 0, and C = 1
0	1	0	0	
0	1	1	0	
1	0	0	1	A = 1, B = 0, and C = 0
1	0	1	0	
1	1	0	1	A = 1, B = 1, and C = 0
1	1	1	0	

The resulting boolean expression will produce the correct output satisfying the truth table, but it can be simplified.

$\overline{A}\cdot\overline{B}\cdot\overline{C} + \overline{A}\cdot\overline{B}\cdot C + A\cdot\overline{B}\cdot\overline{C} + A\cdot B\cdot\overline{C}$

$\overline{A}\cdot\overline{B}\cdot(\overline{C} + C) + A\cdot\overline{C}\cdot(\overline{B} + B)$ Distributive Law

$\overline{A}\cdot\overline{B}\cdot 1 + A\cdot\overline{C}\cdot 1$ OR'ing anything with its inverse is 1

$\overline{A}\cdot\overline{B} + A\cdot\overline{C}$ AND'ing anything with 1 is itself

The application of the rule stating that OR'ing anything with its inverse results in a one (the third line in the above simplification) is the most common way to simplify an SOP expression. This chapter presents a graphical method to quickly pair up products where this rule can be applied in order to drop out as many terms as possible.

126 Computer Organization and Design Fundamentals

Karnaugh Maps are graphical representations of truth tables. They consist of a grid with one cell for each row of the truth table. The grid shown below in Figure 7-1 is the two-by-two Karnaugh map used to represent a truth table with two input variables.

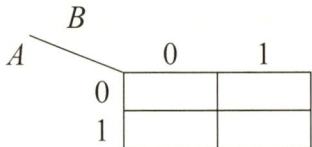

Figure 7-1 2-by-2 Karnaugh Map Used with Two Inputs

The intersection of each row and column corresponds to a unique set of input values. For example, the left column of the Karnaugh map in Figure 7-1 represents the outputs when the input B equals zero and the right column represents the outputs when the input B equals one. The top row represents the outputs when A equals zero and the bottom row represents the outputs when A equals one. Therefore, the left, top cell corresponds to A=0 and B=0, the right, top cell corresponds to A=0 and B=1, and so on. Figure 7-2 shows how the rows of a two-input truth table map to the cells of the Karnaugh map. The variables labeled S_n in the figure represent the binary output values.

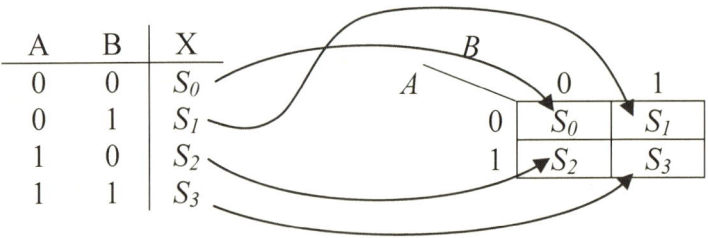

Figure 7-2 Mapping a 2-Input Truth Table to Its Karnaugh Map

The purpose of Karnaugh maps is to rearrange truth tables so that adjacent cells can be represented with a single product using the simplification described above where OR'ing anything with its inverse equals one. This requires adjacent cells to differ by exactly one of their input values thereby identifying the input that will drop out. When four rows or columns are needed as with a 3- or 4-input Karnaugh map, the

2-bit Gray code must be used to ensure that only one input differs between neighboring cells. Take for example the three-input Karnaugh map shown in Figure 7-3. The four rows are each identified with one of the potential values for A and B. This requires them to be numbered 00-01-11-10 in order to have only one input change from row to row.

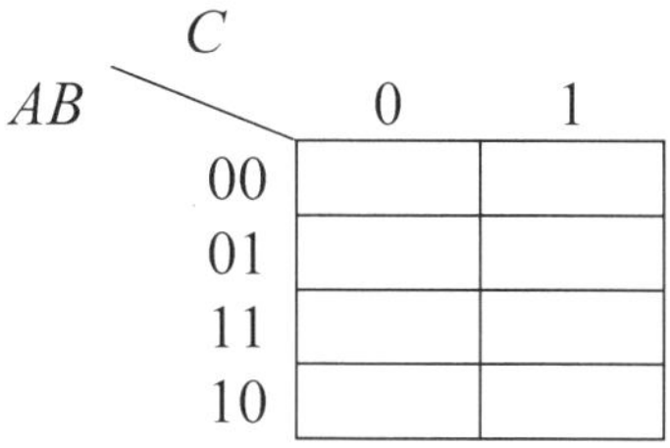

AB \ C	0	1
00		
01		
11		
10		

Figure 7-3 Three-Input Karnaugh Map

If we were to use the normal convention for binary counting to number the four rows, they would be numbered 00-01-10-11. In this case, moving from the second to the third row would result in A changing from 0 to 1 and B changing from 1 to 0. This means *two* inputs would change with a vertical movement between two cells and we would lose the simplification benefit we get using Karnaugh maps.

Figure 7-4 shows a four-input Karnaugh map. Notice that the Gray code had to be used for both the rows and the columns.

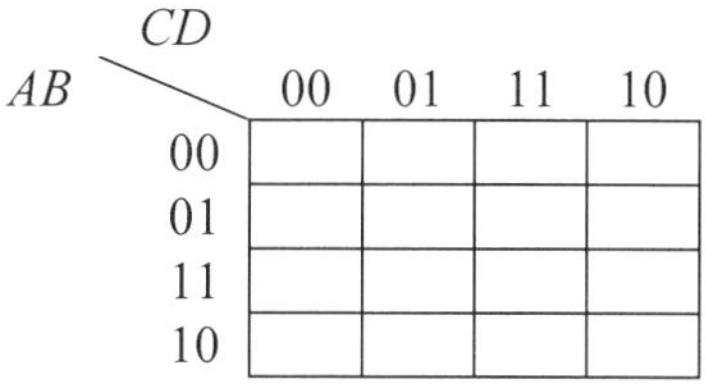

AB \ CD	00	01	11	10
00				
01				
11				
10				

Figure 7-4 Four-Input Karnaugh Map

Note that mapping the outputs from a larger truth table to a Karnaugh map is no different than it was for the two-by-two map except that there are more cells.

We are limited to four input variables when it comes to using Karnaugh maps on paper. Remember that the purpose of a Karnaugh map is to rearrange the truth table so that adjacent cells can be combined allowing for a term to drop out. In other words, the key to the effectiveness of a Karnaugh map is that each cell represents the output for a specific pattern of ones and zeros at the input, and that to move to an adjacent cell, one and only one of those inputs can change.

Take for instance the Karnaugh map in Figure 7-4. The cell in the third column of the second row represents the condition where A=0, B=1, C=1, and D=1. Moving to the cell immediately to the left will change only C; moving right will change D; moving up changes B; and moving down changes A. Therefore, there is an adjacent cell that represents a change in any of the four input variables.

If we were to add a fifth variable, not only would we need to double the number of cells in our map, we would also need to make sure that there were five directions to move adjacently out of every cell in the map. This is impossible to do and remain in two dimensions. A second layer of sixteen cells would have to be added on top of the four-input Karnaugh map to give us a fifth direction, i.e., perpendicular to the page. Although this can be done with a computer, we will not be addressing maps with more than four input variables here.

Example

Convert the three-input truth table below to its corresponding Karnaugh map.

A	B	C	X
0	0	0	0
0	0	1	1
0	1	0	0
0	1	1	1
1	0	0	1
1	0	1	0
1	1	0	1
1	1	1	1

Solution

The three-input Karnaugh map uses the two-by-four grid shown in Figure 7-3. It doesn't matter which row is used to begin the transfer. Typically, we begin with the top row.

A	B	C	X
0	0	0	0
0	0	1	1
0	1	0	0
0	1	1	1
1	0	0	1
1	0	1	0
1	1	0	1
1	1	1	1

```
         C
  AB      0   1
  00  →   0
  01
  11
  10
```

A few more of the transfers are shown in the map below.

A	B	C	X
0	0	0	0
0	0	1	1
0	1	0	0
0	1	1	1
1	0	0	1
1	0	1	0
1	1	0	1
1	1	1	1

```
         C
  AB      0   1
  00      0 → 1
  01    → 0
  11    → 1
  10    → 1
```

The final map is shown below.

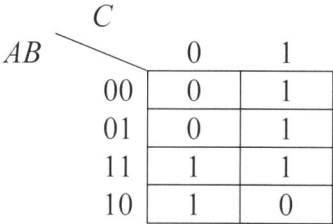

AB \ C	0	1
00	0	1
01	0	1
11	1	1
10	1	0

7.2 Using Karnaugh Maps

Each cell represents a boolean product just as a row in a truth table does. Figure 7-5 identifies the products for each cell containing a one from the previous example.

This shows that an SOP expression can be derived from a Karnaugh map just as it would be from a truth table.

$$X = (\overline{A} \cdot \overline{B} \cdot C) + (\overline{A} \cdot B \cdot C) + (A \cdot B \cdot \overline{C}) + (A \cdot B \cdot C) + (A \cdot \overline{B} \cdot \overline{C})$$

130 Computer Organization and Design Fundamentals

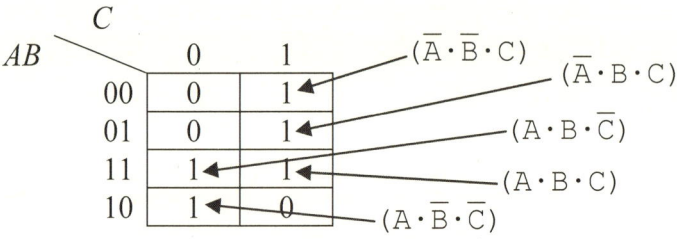

Figure 7-5 Identifying the Products in a Karnaugh Map

If this was all that Karnaugh maps could be used for, they wouldn't be of any use to us. Notice, however, that adjacent cells, either horizontally or vertically adjacent, differ by only one inversion. For example, the top right cell and the cell below it are identical except that B is inverted in the top cell and not inverted in the bottom cell. This implies that we can combine these two products into a single, simpler product depending only on A and C.

$$(\overline{A} \cdot \overline{B} \cdot C) + (\overline{A} \cdot B \cdot C) = \overline{A} \cdot C \cdot (B + \overline{B}) = \overline{A} \cdot C$$

The third row in the Karnaugh map in Figure 7-5 has another adjacent pair of products.

$$(A \cdot B \cdot \overline{C}) + (A \cdot B \cdot C) = A \cdot B \cdot (\overline{C} + C) = B \cdot C$$

Karnaugh maps can go even further though. If a pair of adjacent cells containing ones are adjacent to a second pair of adjacent cells containing ones, then all four cells can be represented with a single product with two variables dropping out. For example, the four adjacent cells in Figure 7-6 reduce to a single term with only one of the three original variables left.

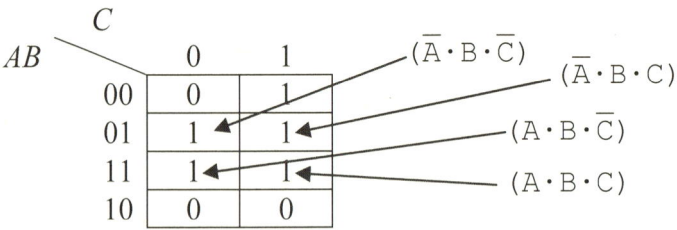

Figure 7-6 Karnaugh Map with Four Adjacent Cells Containing '1'

By applying the rules of boolean algebra, we can see how the products represented by these four cells reduce to a single product with only one variable.

$$X = \overline{A} \cdot B \cdot \overline{C} + \overline{A} \cdot B \cdot C + A \cdot B \cdot \overline{C} + A \cdot B \cdot C$$

$$X = \overline{A} \cdot B \cdot (\overline{C} + C) + A \cdot B \cdot (\overline{C} + C)$$

$$X = \overline{A} \cdot B + A \cdot B$$

$$X = B \cdot (\overline{A} + A)$$

$$X = B$$

So the key to effectively using Karnaugh maps is to find the largest group of adjacent cells containing ones. The larger the group, the fewer products and inputs will be needed to create the boolean expression that produces the truth table. In order for a group of cells containing ones to be considered adjacent, they must follow some rules.

- The grouping must be in the shape of a rectangle. There are no diagonal adjacencies allowed.

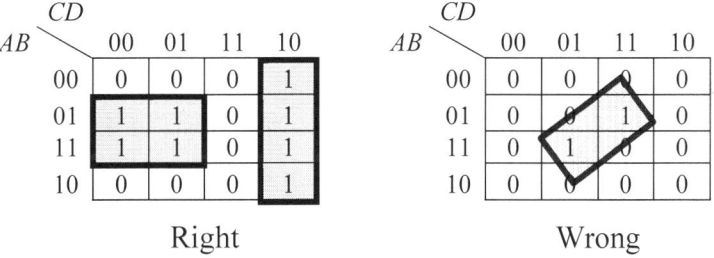

Right Wrong

- All cells in a rectangle must contain ones. No zeros are allowed.

AB \ CD	00	01	11	10
00	1	0	0	0
01	1	0	1	1
11	1	0	1	1
10	1	0	0	0

Right

AB \ CD	00	01	11	10
00	0	0	0	0
01	0	1	1	0
11	0	1	0	0
10	0	0	0	0

Wrong

- The number of cells in the grouping must equal a power of two, i.e., only groups of 1, 2, 4, 8, or 16 are allowed.

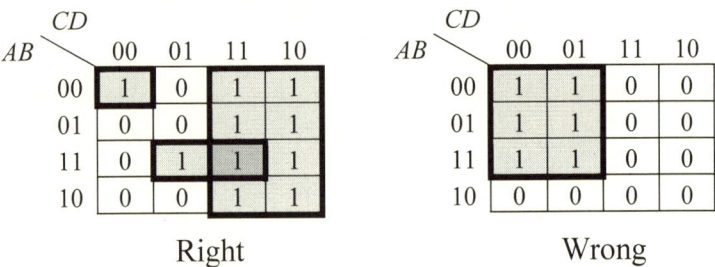

- Outside edges of Karnaugh maps are considered adjacent, so rectangles may wrap from left to right or from top to bottom.

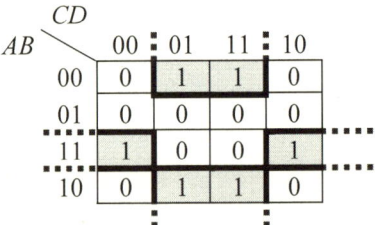

- Cells may be contained in more than one rectangle, but every rectangle must have at least one cell unique to it. (In wrong example, the horizontal rectangle is an unnecessary duplicate.)

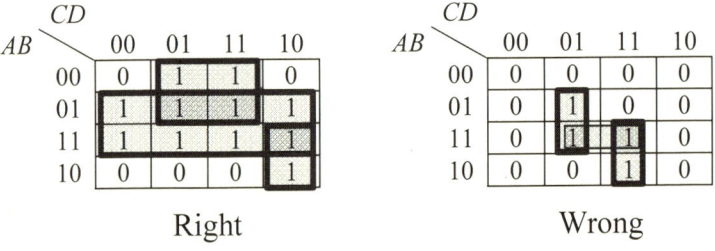

- Every rectangle must be as large as possible.

Chapter 7: Karnaugh Maps   133

- Every 1 must be covered by at least one rectangle.

CD AB	00	01	11	10
00	1	0	0	1
01	1	1	1	1
11	1	1	1	1
10	1	0	0	0

Right

CD AB	00	01	11	10
00	1	0	0	1
01	1	1	1	1
11	1	1	1	1
10	1	0	0	0

Wrong

The ultimate goal is to create the fewest number of valid rectangles while still covering every 1 in the Karnaugh map. Each rectangle represents a product, and the larger the rectangle, the fewer variables will be contained in that product.

For people new to Karnaugh maps, the easiest way to derive the product represented by a rectangle is to list the input values for all cells in the rectangle, and eliminate the ones that change. For example, the three-input Karnaugh map shown in Figure 7-7 has a four-cell rectangle with the following input values for each of its cells:

Top left cell: $A = 0$, $B = 1$, and $C = 0$
Top right cell: $A = 0$, $B = 1$, and $C = 1$
Bottom left cell: $A = 1$, $B = 1$, and $C = 0$
Bottom right cell: $A = 1$, $B = 1$, and $C = 1$

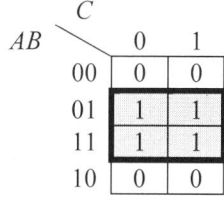

Figure 7-7 Sample Rectangle in a Three-Input Karnaugh Map

The inputs that are the same for *all* cells in the rectangle are the ones that will be used to represent the product. For this example, both A and C are 0 for some cells and 1 for others. That means that these inputs will drop out leaving only B which remains 1 for all four of the cells. Therefore, the product for this rectangle will equal 1 when B equals 1 giving us the same expression we got from simplifying the Figure 7-6 equation:

$$X = B$$

As for the benefits of simplification with Karnaugh maps, each time we are able to double the size of a rectangle, one input to the resulting product drops out. Rectangles containing only one cell will have all of the input variables represented in the final product. Two-cell rectangles will have one fewer input variables; four-cell rectangles will have two fewer input variables; eight-cell rectangles will have three fewer input variables; and so on.

Example

Determine the minimal SOP expression for the truth table below.

A	B	C	D	X
0	0	0	0	1
0	0	0	1	0
0	0	1	0	1
0	0	1	1	0
0	1	0	0	0
0	1	0	1	0
0	1	1	0	0
0	1	1	1	0
1	0	0	0	1
1	0	0	1	1
1	0	1	0	1
1	0	1	1	1
1	1	0	0	0
1	1	0	1	0
1	1	1	0	1
1	1	1	1	1

Solution

First, we need to convert the truth table to a Karnaugh map.

AB \ CD	00	01	11	10
00	1	0	0	1
01	0	0	0	0
11	0	0	1	1
10	1	1	1	1

Now that we have the Karnaugh map, it is time to create the rectangles. Two of them are easy to see: all four cells of the bottom row make one rectangle and the four cells that make up the lower right corner quadrant of the map make up a second rectangle.

Less obvious is the third rectangle that takes care of the two cells in the top row that contain ones. Remember that a rectangle can wrap from the left side of the map to the right side of the map. That means that these two cells are adjacent. What's less obvious is that this rectangle can wrap around from top to bottom too making it a four cell-rectangle.

```
                    CD              Rectangle 3
            AB     00  01  11  10
            00     1   0   0   1
Rectangle 1 01     0   0   0   0     Rectangle 2
            11     0   0   1   1
            10     1   1   1   1
```

It's okay to have the bottom right cell covered by three rectangles. The only requirement is that no rectangle can be fully covered by other rectangles and that no cell with a 1 be left uncovered.

Now let's figure out the products of each rectangle. Below is a list of the input values for rectangle 1, the one that makes up the bottom row of the map.

```
Rectangle 1:   A  B  C  D
               1  0  0  0
               1  0  0  1
               1  0  1  1
               1  0  1  0
```

A and B are the only inputs to remain constant for all four cells: A is always 1 and B is always 0. This means that for this rectangle, the product must output a one when A equals one and B equals zero, i.e., the *inverse* of B equals one. This gives us our first product.

Product for rectangle 1 = $A \cdot \overline{B}$

136 Computer Organization and Design Fundamentals

The product for rectangle 2 is found the same way. Below is a list of the values for A, B, C, and D for each cell of rectangle 2.

```
Rectangle 2:   A  B  C  D
               1  1  1  1
               1  1  1  0
               1  0  1  1
               1  0  1  0
```

In this rectangle, A and C are the only ones that remain constant across all of the cells. To make the corresponding product equal to one, they must both equal one.

Product for rectangle 2 = $A \cdot C$

Below is a list of the input values for each cell of rectangle 3.

```
Rectangle 3:   A  B  C  D
               0  0  0  0
               0  0  1  0
               1  0  0  0
               1  0  1  0
```

In rectangle 3, B and D are the only ones that remain constant across all of the cells. To make the corresponding product equal to one, they must both equal 0, i.e., their inverses must equal 1.

Product for rectangle 3 = $\overline{B} \cdot \overline{D}$

From these three products, we get our final SOP expression by OR'ing them together.

$$X = A \cdot \overline{B} + A \cdot C + \overline{B} \cdot \overline{D}$$

This is a significant simplification over what we would have gotten had we created a product for each row in the truth table. Since the four-input truth table had eight ones in it, the resulting SOP expression would have had eight products each with four input variables. This circuit would have taken eight four-input AND gates and one eight-input OR gate. The circuit from the expression derived from the

Karnaugh map, however, only requires three two-input AND gates and one three-input OR gate.

With practice, many Karnaugh map users can see the variables that will drop out of each rectangle without having to enumerate the input values for every cell. They usually do this by seeing where the rectangle spans variable changes for the rows and columns and drop out those variables. This skill is not necessary, however. Anyone can see which variables drop out by making a list of the bit patterns for each cell in the rectangle and identifying which input variables stay the same and which take on both one and zero as values.

7.3 "Don't Care" Conditions in a Karnaugh Map

Assume you've been invited to play some poker with some friends. The game is five card draw and jacks are wild. What does it mean that "jacks are wild"? It means that if you are dealt one or more jacks, then you can change them to whatever suit or rank you need in order to get the best possible hand of cards. Take for instance the following hand.

Three aces are pretty good, but since you can change the jack of diamonds to anything you want, you could make the hand better. Changing it to a two would give you a full house: three of a kind and a pair. Changing it to an ace, however, would give you an even better hand, one beatable by only a straight flush or five of a kind. (Note that five of a kind is only possible with wild cards.)

If a truth table contains a "don't care" element as its output for one of the rows, that "don't care" is transferred to corresponding cell of the Karnaugh map. The question is, do we include the "don't care" in a rectangle or not? Well, just like the poker hand, you do what best suits the situation.

For example, the four-input Karnaugh map shown in Figure 7-8 contains two "don't care" elements: one represented by the X in the far right cell of the second row and one in the lower left cell.

138 Computer Organization and Design Fundamentals

AB \ CD	00	01	11	10
00	1	0	0	0
01	1	0	0	X
11	1	0	1	1
10	X	0	0	0

Figure 7-8 Karnaugh Map with a "Don't Care" Elements

By changing the X in the lower left cell to a 1, we can make a larger rectangle, specifically one that covers the entire left column. If we didn't do this, we would need to use two smaller 2-cell rectangles to cover the ones in the left column.

If we changed the X in the second row to a one, however, it would force us to add another rectangle in order to cover it thereby making the final SOP expression more complex. Therefore, we will assume that that "don't care" represents a zero. Figure 7-9 shows the resulting rectangles.

AB \ CD	00	01	11	10
00	1	0	0	0
01	1	0	0	X
11	1	0	1	1
10	X	0	0	0

Figure 7-9 Karnaugh Map with a "Don't Care" Elements Assigned

The final circuit will have a one or a zero in that position depending on whether or not it was included in a rectangle. Later in this book, we will examine some cases where we will want to see if those values that were assigned to "don't cares" by being included or not included in a rectangle could cause a problem.

7.4 What's Next?

This chapter has shown how any truth table with up to four input variables can be quickly converted to its minimum SOP circuit expression. This means that if a designer can come up with a truth table, hardware can achieve it.

Chapter 7: Karnaugh Maps   139

Chapter 8 presents some common digital circuits by starting with their general concept, and then taking the reader all of the way through to the realization of the hardware. This is done so that the reader can get a feel for the more abstract parts of circuit design, specifically, taking the leap from a system level concept or specification to the boolean expression that will fulfill the requirements.

Problems

1. How many cells does a 3-input Karnaugh map have?

2. What is the largest number of input variables a Karnaugh map can handle and still remain two-dimensional?

3. In a 4-variable Karnaugh map, how many input variables (A, B, C, or D) does a product have if its rectangle of 1's contains 4 cells? Your answer should be 0, 1, 2, 3, or 4.

4. Identify the problems with each of the three rectangles in the Karnaugh map below.

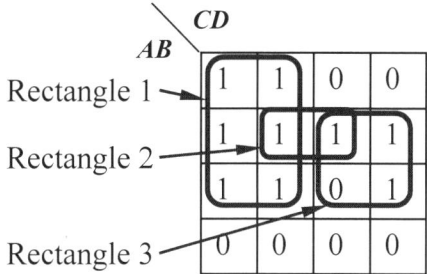

5. When a Karnaugh map has four rows or columns, they are numbered 00, 01, 11, 10 instead of 00, 01, 10, 11. Why?

6. Create Karnaugh maps for each of the truth tables below.

A	B	C	X		A	B	C	X		A	B	C	X
0	0	0	0		0	0	0	1		0	0	0	1
0	0	1	1		0	0	1	1		0	0	1	0
0	1	0	1		0	1	0	1		0	1	0	0
0	1	1	0		0	1	1	0		0	1	1	0
1	0	0	0		1	0	0	0		1	0	0	1
1	0	1	1		1	0	1	0		1	0	1	1
1	1	0	1		1	1	0	1		1	1	0	1
1	1	1	0		1	1	1	1		1	1	1	1

7. Derive the minimum SOP expressions for each of the Karnaugh maps below.

AB \ C	0	1
00	1	0
01	0	0
11	0	1
10	1	1

AB \ CD	00	01	11	10
00	1	0	0	1
01	1	0	0	1
11	1	0	1	1
10	1	0	0	1

AB \ C	0	1
00	0	1
01	1	1
11	1	1
10	0	1

AB \ CD	00	01	11	10
00	0	0	0	0
01	1	1	0	X
11	1	X	1	1
10	X	0	0	0

8. Create a Karnaugh map that shows there can be more than one arrangement for the rectangles of ones in a Karnaugh map.

CHAPTER EIGHT

Combinational Logic Applications

Thus far, our discussion has focused on the theoretical design issues of computer systems. We have not yet addressed any of the actual hardware you might find inside a computer. This chapter changes that.

The following sections present different applications used either as stand-alone circuits or integrated into the circuitry of a processor. Each section will begin with a definition of a problem to be addressed. From this, a truth table will be developed which will then be converted into the corresponding boolean expression and finally a logic diagram.

8.1 Adders

Most mathematical operations can be handled with addition. For example, subtraction can be performed by taking the two's complement of a binary value, and then adding it to the binary value from which it was to be subtracted. Two numbers can be multiplied using multiple additions. Counting either up or down (incrementing or decrementing) can be performed with additions of 1 or -1.

Chapter 3 showed that binary addition is performed just like decimal addition, the only difference being that decimal has 10 numerals while binary has 2. When adding two digits in binary, a result greater than one generates an "overflow", i.e., a one is added to the next position. This produces a sum of 0 with a carry of 1 to the next position.

```
                                              1
      0           0           1           1
    + 0         + 1         + 0         + 1
    ---         ---         ---         ---
      0           1           1          10
```

Figure 8-1 Four Possible Results of Adding Two Bits

A well-defined process such as this is easily realized with digital logic. Figure 8-2 shows the block diagram of a system that takes two binary inputs, A and B, and adds them together producing a bit for the sum and a bit indicating whether or not a carry occurred. This well-known circuit is commonly referred to as a *half-adder*.

142 Computer Organization and Design Fundamentals

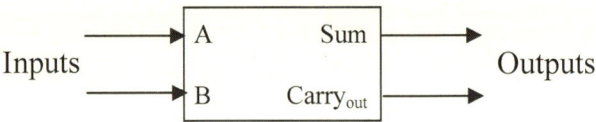

Figure 8-2 Block Diagram of a Half Adder

With two inputs, there are four possible patterns of ones and zeros.

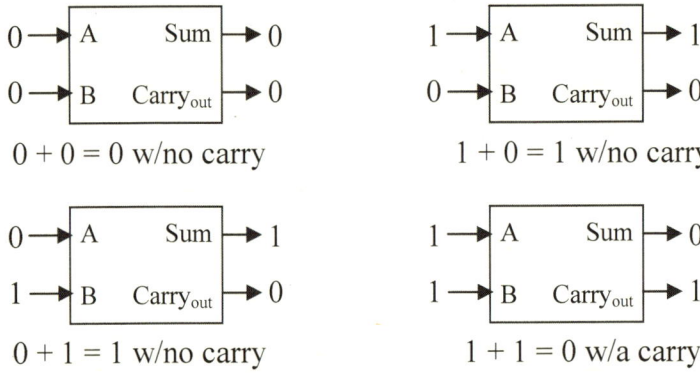

Figure 8-3 Four Possible States of a Half Adder

A truth table can be derived from Figure 8-3 from which the boolean expressions can be developed to realize this system.

A	B	Sum	$Carry_{out}$
0	0	0	0
0	1	1	0
1	0	1	0
1	1	0	1

The simplicity of a two-input truth table makes the use of a Karnaugh map unnecessary. Examining the Sum column shows that we should have an output of one when A=0 and B=1 and when A=1 and B=0. This gives us the following SOP expression:

$$Sum = \overline{A} \cdot B + A \cdot \overline{B}$$

Note that the output Sum is also equivalent to the 2-input XOR gate.

Chapter 8: Combinational Logic Applications   143

For Carry$_{out}$, the output equals 1 only when both A and B are equal to one. This matches the operation of the AND gate.

$$\text{Carry}_{out} = A \cdot B$$

Figure 8-4 presents the logic circuit for the half adder.

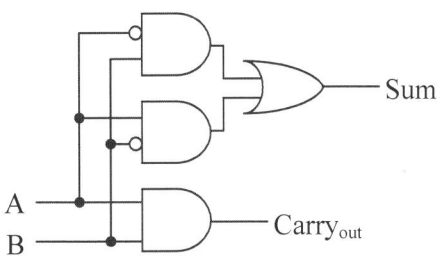

Figure 8-4   Logic Circuit for a Half Adder

The half-adder works fine if we're trying to add two bits together, a situation that typically occurs only in the rightmost column of a multi-bit addition. The remaining columns have the potential of adding a third bit, the carry from a previous column.

For example, assume we want to add two four bit numbers, A = 0110_2 and B = 1011_2. The addition would go something like that shown to the right.

```
  1 1
  0 1 1 0
+ 1 0 1 1
─────────
1 0 0 0 1
```

Adding the least significant bits of a multi-bit value uses the half-adder described above. Each input to the half-adder takes one of the least significant bits from each number. The outputs are the least significant digit of the sum and a possible carry to the next column.

What is needed for the remaining columns is an adder similar to the half-adder that can add two bits along with a carry from the previous column to produce a Sum and the Carry$_{out}$ to the next column. Figure 8-5 represents this operation where A_n is the bit in the nth position of A, B_n is the bit in the nth position of B, and S_n is the bit in the nth position in the resulting sum, S.

Notice that a Carry$_{out}$ from the addition of a pair of bits goes into the carry input of the adder for the next bit. We will call the input Carry$_{in}$. This implies that we need to create a circuit that can add three bits, A_n, B_n, and Carry$_{in}$ from the n-1 position. This adder has two outputs, the sum and the Carry$_{out}$ to the n+1 position. The resulting circuit is called a *full adder*. A block diagram of the full adder is shown in Figure 8-6.

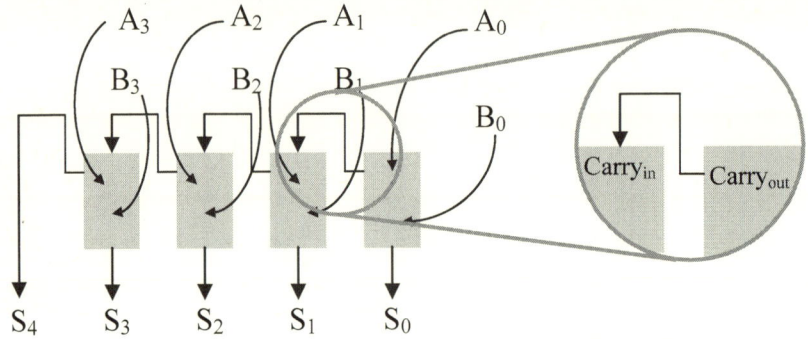

Figure 8-5 Block Diagram of a Multi-bit Adder

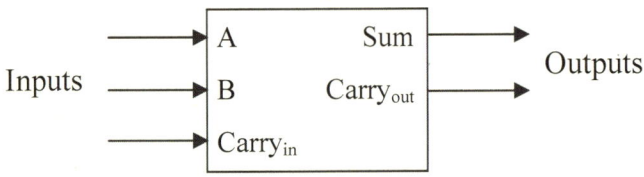

Figure 8-6 Block Diagram of a Full Adder

With three inputs there are $2^3 = 8$ possible patterns of ones and zeros that could be input to our full adder. Table 8-1 lists these combinations along with the results of their addition which range from 0 to 3_{10}.

Table 8-1 Addition Results Based on Inputs of a Full Adder

Inputs			Result	
A	B	Carry$_{in}$	Decimal	Binary
0	0	0	0_{10}	00_2
0	0	1	1_{10}	01_2
0	1	0	1_{10}	01_2
0	1	1	2_{10}	10_2
1	0	0	1_{10}	01_2
1	0	1	2_{10}	10_2
1	1	0	2_{10}	10_2
1	1	1	3_{10}	11_2

Chapter 8: Combinational Logic Applications   145

The two-digit binary result in the last column of this table can be broken into its components, the sum and a carry to the next bit position. This gives us two truth tables, one for the Sum and one for the $Carry_{out}$.

Table 8-2   Sum and $Carry_{out}$ Truth Tables for a Full Adder

A	B	$Carry_{in}$	Sum	A	B	$Carry_{in}$	$Carry_{out}$
0	0	0	0	0	0	0	0
0	0	1	1	0	0	1	0
0	1	0	1	0	1	0	0
0	1	1	0	0	1	1	1
1	0	0	1	1	0	0	0
1	0	1	0	1	0	1	1
1	1	0	0	1	1	0	1
1	1	1	1	1	1	1	1

With three inputs, a Karnaugh map can be use to create the logic expressions. One Karnaugh map will be needed for each output of the circuit. Figure 8-7 presents the Karnaugh maps for the Sum and the $Carry_{out}$ outputs of our full adder where C_{in} represents the $Carry_{in}$ input.

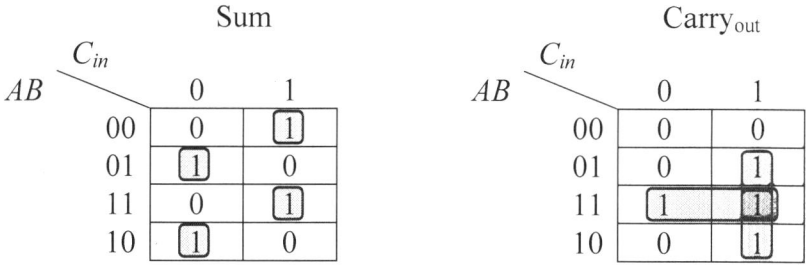

Figure 8-7   Sum and $Carry_{out}$ Karnaugh Maps for a Full Adder

The $Carry_{out}$ Karnaugh map has three rectangles, each containing two cells and all three overlapping on the cell defined by A=1, B=1, and C_{in}=1. By using the process presented in Chapter 7, we can derive the three products for the SOP expression defining $Carry_{out}$.

The Karnaugh map for the Sum is less promising. In fact, there is no way to make a more complex 3-input Karnaugh map than the one that

146 Computer Organization and Design Fundamentals

exists for the Sum output of the full adder. The addition or removal of a '1' in any cell of the map will result in a simpler expression. The four single-cell rectangles result in the four products of the SOP expression for the Sum output shown following the Carry$_{out}$ expression.

Rectangle 1:

A	B	C$_{in}$
0	1	1
1	1	1

$B \cdot C_{in}$

Rectangle 2:

A	B	C$_{in}$
1	1	0
1	1	1

$A \cdot B$

Rectangle 3:

A	B	C$_{in}$
1	1	1
1	0	1

$A \cdot C_{in}$

$$\text{Carry}_{out} = B \cdot C_{in} + A \cdot B + A \cdot C_{in}$$

$$\text{Sum} = \overline{A} \cdot \overline{B} \cdot C_{in} + \overline{A} \cdot B \cdot \overline{C_{in}} + A \cdot B \cdot C_{in} + A \cdot \overline{B} \cdot \overline{C_{in}}$$

Figure 8-8 presents the circuit for the full adder.

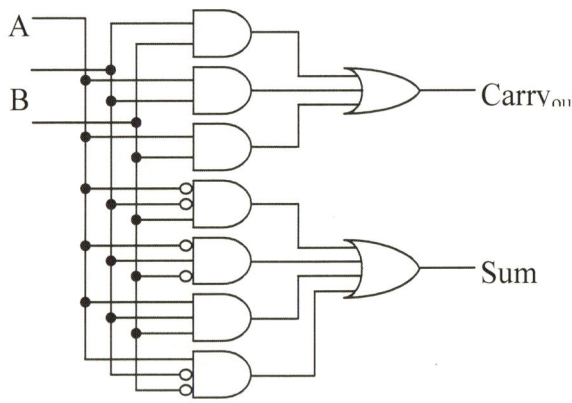

Figure 8-8 Logic Circuit for a Full Adder

Now we have the building blocks to create an adder of any size. For example, a 16-bit adder is made by using a half adder for the least

Chapter 8: Combinational Logic Applications 147

significant bit followed by fifteen full adders daisy-chained through their carries for the remaining fifteen bits.

This method of creating adders has a slight drawback, however. Just as with the addition of binary numbers on paper, the sum of the higher-order bits cannot be determined until the carry from the lower-order bits has been calculated and propagated through the higher stages. Modern adders use additional logic to predict whether the higher-order bits should expect a carry or not well before the sum of the lower-order bits is calculated. These adders are called *carry look ahead adders*.

8.2 Seven-Segment Displays

Most everyone has seen a seven-segment display. It is the most common way to display time on a clock radio, and it is one of the easiest ways to implement a numeric output for a digital circuit. The use of seven-segment displays is so extensive that special integrated circuits (ICs) have been developed to take a four-bit binary numeric input and create the output signals necessary to drive the display.

A seven-segment display consists of seven long, thin LEDs arranged in the pattern of an eight. Each segment is controlled individually so that any decimal digit can be displayed. Using a combination of both upper- and lower-case letters, A, B, C, D, E, and F can be displayed too allowing a seven-segment display to output all of the hexadecimal digits too.

Figure 8-9 shows a diagram of the typical seven-segment display with each segment lettered for identification.

Figure 8-9 7-Segment Display **Figure 8-10** Displaying a '1'

To make a digit appear, the user must know which segments to turn on and which to leave off. For example, to display a '1', we need to turn on segments b and c and leave the other segments off. This means that the binary circuits driving segments b and c would output 1 while the binary circuits driving segments a, d, e, f, and g would output 0. If the

148   Computer Organization and Design Fundamentals

binary inputs to the display are set to a=1, b=1, c=0, d=1, e=1, f=0, and g=1, a '2' would be displayed.

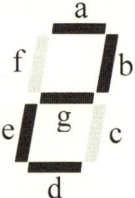

Figure 8-11   A Seven-Segment Display Displaying a Decimal '2'

The digital circuitry used to drive a seven-segment display consists of seven separate digital circuits, one for each LED. Each circuit takes as its input the binary nibble that is to be displayed. For example, if the binary nibble $0010_2 = 2_{10}$ is input to the digital circuitry driving the display, then the digital circuit for segment 'a' would output 1, the digital circuit for segment 'b' would output 1, the digital circuit for segment 'c' would output 0, and so on. Figure 8-12 shows a block diagram of the seven-segment display driver.

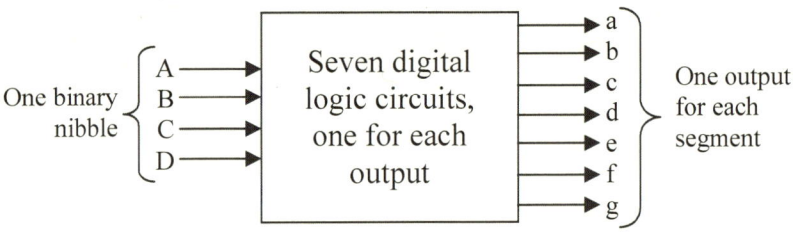

Figure 8-12   Block Diagram of a Seven-Segment Display Driver

To begin with, we need seven truth tables, one for the output of each circuit. The individual bits of the number to be displayed will be used for the inputs. Next, we need to know which segments are to be on and which are to be off for each digit. Figure 8-13 shows the bit patterns for each hexadecimal digit.

Using the information from Figure 8-13, we can build the seven truth tables. The truth table in Figure 8-14 combines all seven truth tables along with a column indicating which digit is displayed for the corresponding set of inputs. Note that the capital letters denote the input signals while the lower case letters identify the segments of the seven-segment display.

Chapter 8: Combinational Logic Applications 149

	Digit	Segments		Digit	Segments
0	0	a, b, c, d, e, f	1	1	b, c
2	2	a, b, d, e, g	3	3	a, b, c, d, g
4	4	b, c, f, g	5	5	a, c, d, f, g
6	6	a, c, d, e, f, g	7	7	a, b, c
8	8	a, b, c, d, e, f, g	9	9	a, b, c, d, f, g
A	A	a, b, c, e, f, g	b	B	c, d, e, f, g
C	C	a, d, e, f	d	D	b, c, d, e, g
E	E	a, d, e, f, g	F	F	a, e, f, g

Figure 8-13 Segment Patterns for all Hexadecimal Digits

Inputs				Hex Value	Segments					
A	B	C	D		a	b	c	d	e	f	g
0	0	0	0	0	1	1	1	1	1	1	0
0	0	0	1	1	0	1	1	0	0	0	0
0	0	1	0	2	1	1	0	1	1	0	1
0	0	1	1	3	1	1	1	1	0	0	1
0	1	0	0	4	0	1	1	0	0	1	1
0	1	0	1	5	1	0	1	1	0	1	1
0	1	1	0	6	1	0	1	1	1	1	1
0	1	1	1	7	1	1	1	0	0	0	0
1	0	0	0	8	1	1	1	1	1	1	1
1	0	0	1	9	1	1	1	1	0	1	1
1	0	1	0	A	1	1	1	0	1	1	1
1	0	1	1	B	0	0	1	1	1	1	1
1	1	0	0	C	1	0	0	1	1	1	0
1	1	0	1	D	0	1	1	1	1	0	1
1	1	1	0	E	1	0	0	1	1	1	1
1	1	1	1	F	1	0	0	0	1	1	1

Figure 8-14 Seven Segment Display Truth Table

150   Computer Organization and Design Fundamentals

The next step is to create a Karnaugh map for each of the seven segments in order to determine the minimum SOP expression and digital circuit to be used to drive each segment. Here we will only do one of the circuits, segment e. Figure 8-15 takes the column for segment e and maps it into a four-by-four Karnaugh map.

CD AB	00	01	11	10
00	1	0	0	1
01	0	0	0	1
11	1	1	1	1
10	1	0	1	1

Figure 8-15   Karnaugh Map for Segment 'e'

Next, we need to identify the optimum set of rectangles for the Karnaugh map. These rectangles are shown in Figure 8-16.

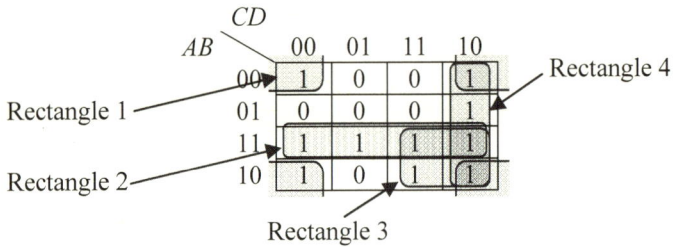

Figure 8-16   Karnaugh Map for Segment 'e' with Rectangles

From the rectangles, we can derive the SOP expression products.

Rectangle 1:	A	B	C	D		
	0	0	0	0	Product:	$\overline{B} \cdot \overline{D}$
	1	0	0	0		
	0	0	1	0		
	1	0	1	0		

Rectangle 2:	A	B	C	D		
	1	1	0	0		
	1	1	0	1	Product:	$A \cdot B$
	1	1	1	1		
	1	1	1	0		

Chapter 8: Combinational Logic Applications 151

Rectangle 3:   A B C D
               1 1 1 1
               1 1 1 0   Product: A·C
               1 0 1 1
               1 0 1 0

Rectangle 4:   A B C D
               0 0 1 0
               0 1 1 0   Product: C·$\overline{\text{D}}$
               1 1 1 0
               1 0 1 0

Our final SOP expression is then the OR of these four products.

Segment e = ($\overline{\text{B}}$·$\overline{\text{D}}$) + (A·B) + (A·C) + (C·$\overline{\text{D}}$)

Figure 8-17 presents the digital logic that would control segment e of the seven-segment display. The design of the display driver is not complete, however, as there are six more logic circuits to design.

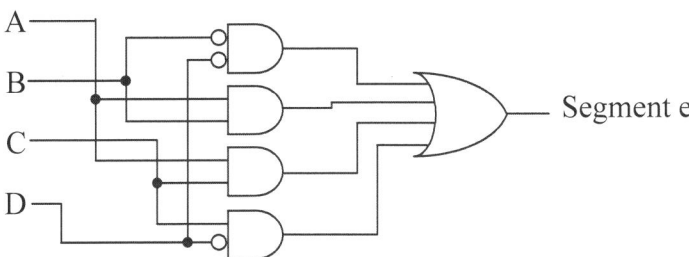

Figure 8-17   Logic Circuit for Segment e of 7-Segment Display

8.3 Active-Low Signals

Computer systems are composed of numerous subsystems, some of which may be idle, some of which may be operating independent of the processor, and some of which may be in direct contact with the processor. For systems that are in direct contact with the processor, only one may be enabled at any one time. For example, although a computer system may have multiple memory devices, when a piece of data is stored, it is sent to only one of the modules while the other modules must remain idle.

152   Computer Organization and Design Fundamentals

A scheme is needed to select or enable a specific device or to route data to an appropriate subsystem. This scheme is implemented with a separate binary line that is connected to each subsystem where one of the binary values enables the subsystem and the other binary value disables it, i.e., an on/off binary control.

Our discussion previous to this suggests that the "on" signal is equivalent to a logic 1, but for a number of reasons, the standard method of enabling a device is *not* to send a logic 1. Instead, due to the nature of electronics, it is standard practice to enable devices with a logic 0 and disable them with a logic 1. This is called *active-low* operation, i.e., the device is active when its enable signal is low or logic 0. The device is inactive when the enable is high or logic 1.

There is a special notation that identifies active-low signals. If you see a system's input or output labeled with a bar over it, then that signal is an active-low signal. Sometimes, the line that is drawn into or out of the system diagram will also pass through an inverter circle to identify the signal as active-low. For example, in the system shown in Figure 8-18, the input C and the output EN are both active-low.

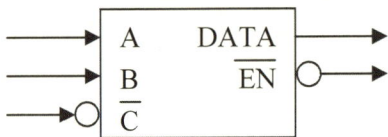

Figure 8-18   Labeling Conventions for Active-Low Signals

For the active-low circuits discussed in the remainder of this book, this notation will be used.

8.4 Decoders

One application where digital signals are used to enable a device is to identify the unique conditions to enable an operation. For example, the magnetron in a microwave is enabled *only* when the timer is running *and* the start button is pushed *and* the oven door is closed.

This method of enabling a device based on the condition of a number of inputs is common in digital circuits. One common application is in the processor's interface to memory. It is used to determine which memory device will contain a piece of data.

In the microwave example, the sentence used to describe the enabling of the magnetron joined each of the inputs with the word "and". Therefore, the enabling circuit for the magnetron should be realized with an AND gate as shown in Figure 8-19.

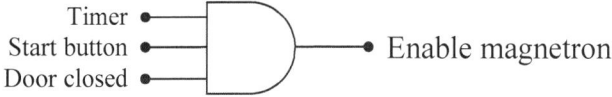

Figure 8-19 Sample Circuit for Enabling a Microwave

There are many other types of digital systems that enable a process based on a specific combination of ones and zeros from multiple inputs. For example, an automobile with a manual transmission enables the starter when the clutch is pressed *and* the ignition key is turned. A vending machine delivers a soda when enough money is inserted *and* a button is pushed *and* the machine is not out of the selected soda.

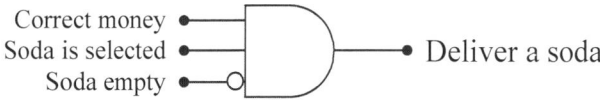

Figure 8-20 Sample Circuit for Delivering a Soda

An AND gate outputs a one only when all of its inputs equal one. If one or more inputs are inverted, the output of the AND gate is one if and only if all of the inputs without inverters equal one and all of the inputs with inverters equal zero.

The truth table for this type of circuit will have exactly one row with an output of one while all of the other rows output a zero. The row with the one can change depending on which inputs are inverted. For example, Figure 8-21 presents the truth table for the circuit that enables a device when A and B are true but C is false.

When SOP expressions were introduced in Chapter 6, we found that each row of a truth table with a '1' output corresponded to a unique product. Therefore, the circuit that is used to enable a device can be realized with a single AND gate. The conditions that activate that AND gate are governed by the pattern of inverters at its inputs. When we apply the tools of Chapter 6 to the truth table in Figure 8-21, we get the boolean expression $EN = A \cdot B \cdot \overline{C}$.

154 Computer Organization and Design Fundamentals

A	B	C	EN
0	0	0	0
0	0	1	0
0	1	0	0
0	1	1	0
1	0	0	0
1	0	1	0
1	1	0	1
1	1	1	0

Figure 8-21 Truth Table to Enable a Device for A=1, B=1, & C=0

Decoder circuits are a group of enable circuits that have an individual output that satisfies each row of the truth table. In other words, a decoder has a unique output for each combination of ones and zeros possible at its inputs.

For example, a 2-input decoder circuit with inputs A and B can have an output that is 1 only when A=0 and B=0, an output that is 1 only when A=0 and B=1, an output that is 1 only when A=1 and B=0, and an output that is 1 only when A=1 and B=1. The boolean expressions that satisfy this decoder circuit are:

$$EN_0 = \overline{A} \cdot \overline{B} \qquad EN_1 = \overline{A} \cdot B \qquad EN_2 = A \cdot \overline{B} \qquad EN_3 = A \cdot B$$

This two-input circuit is called a *1-of-4 decoder* due to the fact that exactly one of its four outputs will be enabled at any one time. A change at any of the inputs will change which output is enabled, but never change the fact that only one is enabled. As for the logic circuit, it has four AND gates, one satisfying each of the above boolean expressions. Figure 8-22 presents this digital circuit.

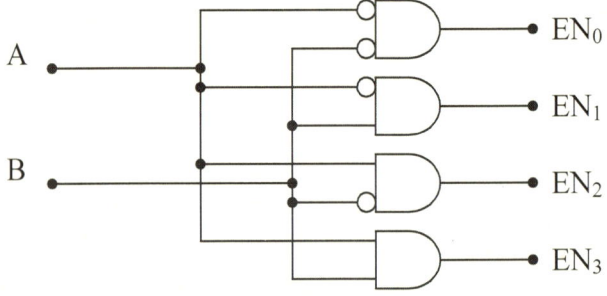

Figure 8-22 Digital Circuit for a 1-of-4 Decoder

As suggested in the previous section, it is common to implement enable signals as active-low due to the nature of electronics. To do this, the output of each AND gate must be inverted. This means that the active-low decoder circuit is implemented with NAND gates as shown in Figure 8-23. Notice the bar over the output names. This indicates the active-low nature of these signals.

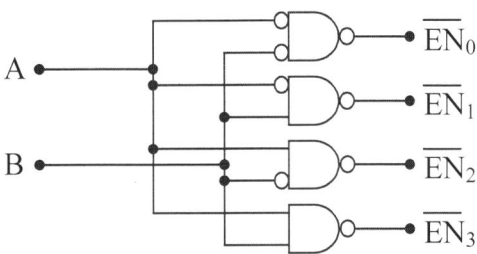

Figure 8-23 Digital Circuit for an Active-Low 1-of-4 Decoder

Decoder circuits can have any number of inputs. The number of outputs, however, is directly related to the number of inputs. If, for example, a decoder has four inputs signals, A, B, C, and D, then there are $2^4 = 16$ unique combinations of ones and zeros, each of which requires a NAND gate for its output. A decoder with four inputs is called a 1-of-16 decoder. Figure 8-24 presents the truth table for an active-low 1-of-8 decoder with three inputs.

A	B	C	EN_0	EN_1	EN_2	EN_3	EN_4	EN_5	EN_6	EN_7
0	0	0	0	1	1	1	1	1	1	1
0	0	1	1	0	1	1	1	1	1	1
0	1	0	1	1	0	1	1	1	1	1
0	1	1	1	1	1	0	1	1	1	1
1	0	0	1	1	1	1	0	1	1	1
1	0	1	1	1	1	1	1	0	1	1
1	1	0	1	1	1	1	1	1	0	1
1	1	1	1	1	1	1	1	1	1	0

Figure 8-24 Truth Table for an Active-Low 1-of-8 Decoder

8.5 Multiplexers

A multiplexer, sometimes referred to as a MUX, is a device that uses a set of control inputs to select which of several data inputs is to be connected to a single data output. With n binary "select lines," one of 2^n data inputs can be connected to the output. Figure 8-25 presents a block diagram of a multiplexer with three select lines, S_2, S_1, and S_0, and eight data lines, D_0 through D_7.

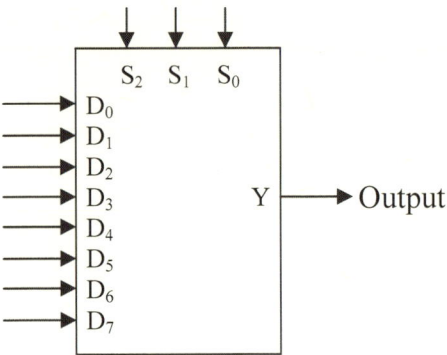

Figure 8-25   Block Diagram of an Eight Channel Multiplexer

A multiplexer acts like a television channel selector. All of the stations are broadcast constantly to the television's input, but only the channel that has been selected is displayed. As for the eight-channel multiplexer in Figure 8-25, its operation can be described with the truth table shown in Figure 8-26.

S_2	S_1	S_0	Y
0	0	0	D_0
0	0	1	D_1
0	1	0	D_2
0	1	1	D_3
1	0	0	D_4
1	0	1	D_5
1	1	0	D_6
1	1	1	D_7

Figure 8-26   Truth Table for an Eight Channel Multiplexer

For example, if the selector inputs are set to $S_2 = 0$, $S_1 = 1$, and $S_0 = 1$, then the data present at D_3 will be output to Y. If $D_3 = 0$, then Y will output a 0.

The number of data inputs depends on the number of selector inputs. For example, if there is only one selector line, S_0, then there can only be two data inputs D_0 and D_1. When S_0 equals zero, D_0 is routed to the

Chapter 8: Combinational Logic Applications   157

output. When S_0 equals one, D_1 is routed to the output. Two selector lines, S_1 and S_0, allow for four data inputs, D_0, D_1, D_2, and D_3.

Example

For the multiplexer shown below, sketch the output waveform Y for the inputs S_1 and S_0 shown in the graph next to it. Assume S_1 is the most significant bit.

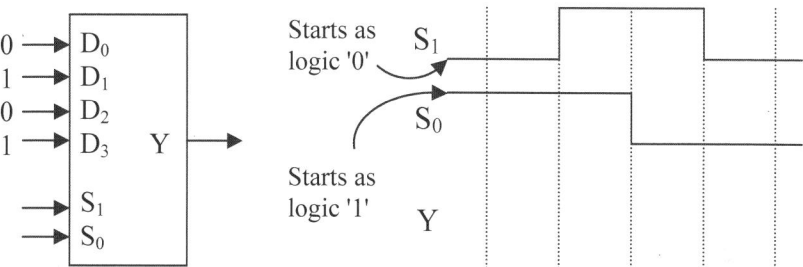

Solution

The decimal equivalent to the binary value input by the selector inputs indicates the subscript of the channel being connected to the output. For example, when S_1 equals one and S_0 equals zero, then their decimal equivalent is $10_2 = 2_{10}$. Therefore, D_2 is connected to the output. Since D_2 equals zero, then Y is outputting a zero.

The graph below shows the values of Y for each of the states of S_1 and S_0. The labels inserted above the waveform for Y indicate which channel is connected to Y at that time.

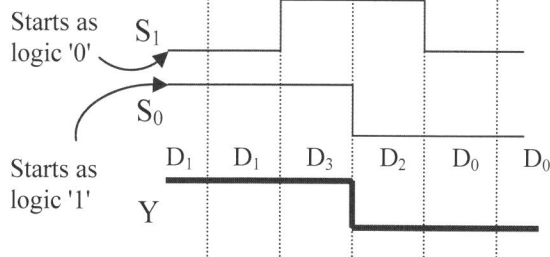

8.6 Demultiplexers

The previous section described how multiplexers select one channel from a group of input channels to be sent to a single output. Demultiplexers take a single input and select one channel out of a group of output channels to which it will route the input. It's like having multiple printers connected to a computer. A document can only be printed to one of the printers, so the computer selects one out of the group of printers to which it will send its output.

The design of a demultiplexer is much like the design of a decoder. The decoder selected one of many outputs to which it would send a zero. The difference is that the demultiplexer sends data to that output rather than a zero.

The circuit of a demultiplexer is based on the non-active-low decoder where each output is connected to an AND gate. An input is added to each of the AND gates that will contain the demultiplexer's data input. If the data input equals one, then the output of the AND gate that is selected by the selector inputs will be a one. If the data input equals zero, then the output of the selected AND gate will be zero. Meanwhile, all of the other AND gates output a zero, i.e., no data is passed to them. Figure 8-27 presents a demultiplexer circuit with two selector inputs.

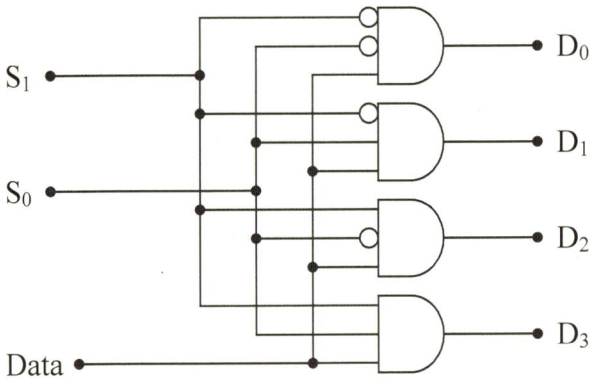

Figure 8-27 Logic Circuit for a 1-Line-to-4-Line Demultiplexer

In effect, the select lines, S_0, S_1, ... S_n, "turn on" a specific AND gate that passes the data through to the selected output. In Figure 8-27, if $S_1=0$ and $S_0=1$, then the D_1 output will match the input from the Data line and outputs D_0, D_2, and D_3 will be forced to have an output of zero. If $S_1=0$, $S_0=1$, and Data=0, then $D_1=0$. If $S_1=0$, $S_0=1$, and Data=1, then $D_1=1$. Figure 8-28 presents the truth table for the 1-line-to-4-line demultiplexer shown in Figure 8-27.

Chapter 8: Combinational Logic Applications 159

S_1	S_0	Data	D_0	D_1	D_2	D_3
0	0	0	0	0	0	0
0	0	1	1	0	0	0
0	1	0	0	0	0	0
0	1	1	0	1	0	0
1	0	0	0	0	0	0
1	0	1	0	0	1	0
1	1	0	0	0	0	0
1	1	1	0	0	0	1

Figure 8-28   Truth Table for a 1-Line-to-4-Line Demultiplexer

8.7 Integrated Circuits

It may appear that much of our discussion up to this point has been theoretical, but in reality, each of the circuits we've presented can easily be implemented given the right tools. Prototypes used to test or verify circuit designs can be made by wiring together small plastic chips that offer access to the internal components through thin metal pins. These chips, called integrated circuits (ICs), come in a wide variety of shapes, sizes, and pin configurations. Figure 8-29 presents a sample of some ICs.

Figure 8-29   Examples of Integrated Circuits

Connecting the metal pins of these chips with other metal pins from the same chip or additional chips is what allows us to create digital circuits.

As for what we are connecting to them, the metal pins of the ICs allow us access to the internal circuitry such as the inputs and outputs of logic gates. Detailed information is available for all ICs from the manufacturer allowing designers to understand the internal circuitry.

160   Computer Organization and Design Fundamentals

The documentation defining the purpose of each pin of the IC is usually referred to as the IC's "pin-out description." It provides information not only on the digital circuitry, but also any power requirements needed to operate the IC.

Figure 8-30 presents an example of the pin-out of a quad dual-input NAND gate chip, commonly referred to as a 7400.

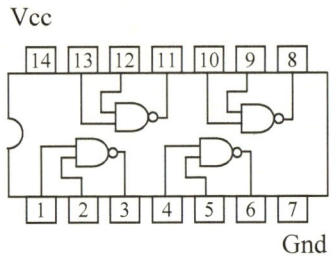

Figure 8-30   Pin-out of a Quad Dual-Input NAND Gate IC (7400)

Note that the pins are numbered. In order to properly use one of these ICs, you must be able to identify the pin numbers. To help you do this, the manufacturers identify the first pin, referred to as "pin 1", on every IC. The Figure 8-31 presents some of the ways this pin is identified.

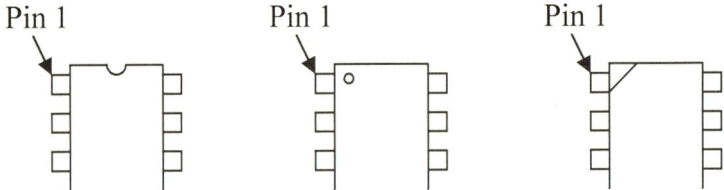

Figure 8-31   Sample Pin 1 Identifications

The pins are then numbered counter-clockwise around the chip. You can see this in the numbering of the pins in Figure 8-30.

Many circuits are then built and tested using prototype boards or protoboards. A protoboard is a long, thin plastic board with small holes in it that allow ICs and short wire leads to be plugged in. A generic protoboard is shown in Figure 8-32.

Chapter 8: Combinational Logic Applications   161

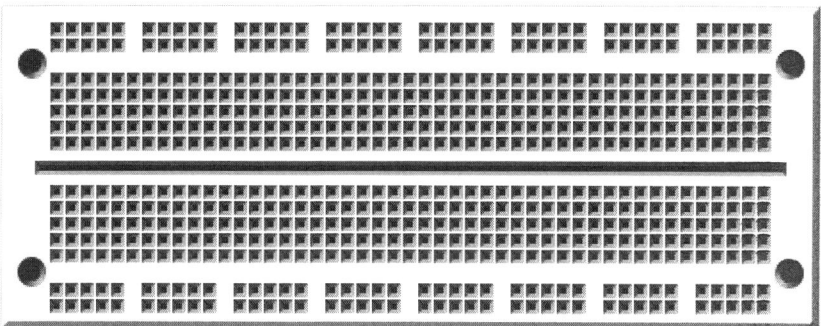

Figure 8-32   Generic Protoboard

Behind the sockets there is a pattern of metal connections that provides an electrical path between certain sockets on the protoboard. This allows us to interconnect and power ICs. Figure 8-33 below shows how the sockets are connected electrically.

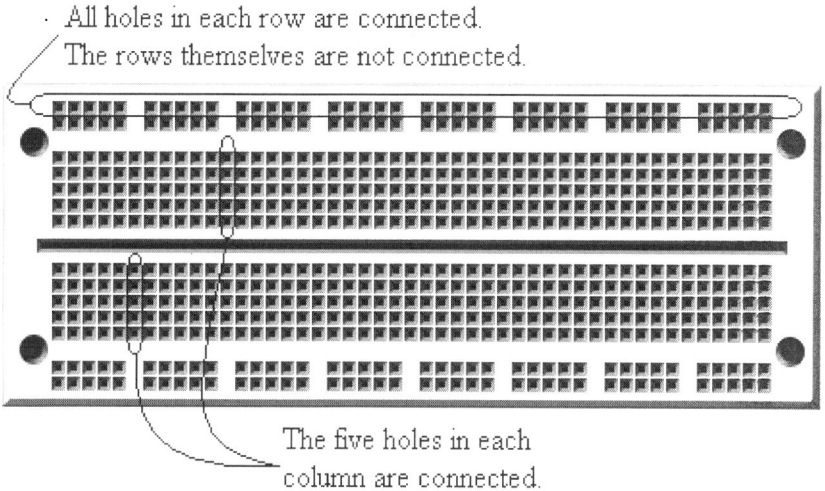

Figure 8-33   Generic Protoboard Internal Connections

The protoboard allows the user to insert an IC so that it straddles the gap running along the center of the board. Wires can then be used to connect the pins to other sockets on the protoboard. The rows on the top and bottom edges of the board in Figure 8-32 are used to connect

162   Computer Organization and Design Fundamentals

power (Vcc) and ground (GND) to the IC. Figure 8-34 shows a sample circuit with two chips wired together.

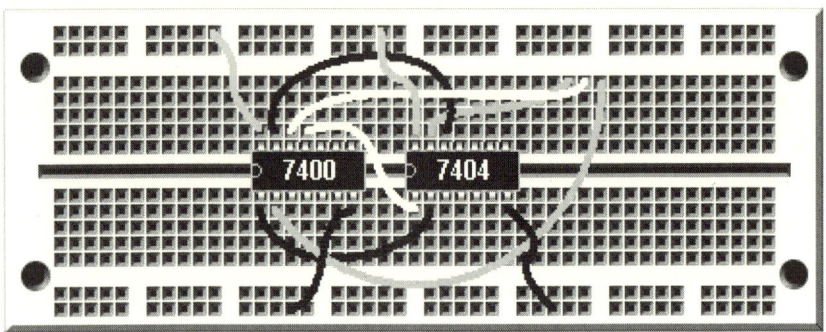

Figure 8-34   Sample Circuit Wired on a Protoboard

The next step is to add input and output that will allow us to communicate with our circuit. The simplest output from a digital circuit is an LED. Figure 8-35 presents the schematic symbol of an LED.

Figure 8-35   Schematic Symbol of a Light-Emitting Diode (LED)

An LED will turn on only when a small current passes through it from node A to node B. No light will appear if there is no current or if the current tries to flow in the opposite direction. By the way, if your LED doesn't work like you think it should, try to turn it around.

There are two things to note here. First, the current must be very small. In order to keep the current small enough to protect the LED, we need an electronic device called a resistor. This resistor is placed in series with the LED to limit the current. If you forget the resistor, you will hear a small pop and smell an awful burning odor when you power up your circuit. Figure 8-36 shows a typical LED circuit.

Chapter 8: Combinational Logic Applications 163

It is important to note that the LED will turn on only when the output from the IC equals zero. This is the best way to drive an LED. It keeps the ICs from having to supply too much current.

The simplest input to a digital circuit is a switch. It seems that the logical way to connect a switch to a digital circuit would be to connect it so that it toggles between a direct connection to a logic 1 and a direct connection to a logic 0. Switching back and forth between these connections should produce binary 1's and 0's, right?

Due to the electronics behind IC inputs, this is not the case. Instead, connections to positive voltages are made through resistors called ***pull-up resistors***. This protects the IC by limiting the current flowing into it while still providing a positive voltage that can be read as a logic one. Figure 8-37 presents a generic switch design for a single input to a digital circuit. It uses a pull-up resistor connected to 5 volts which represents the circuit's power source.

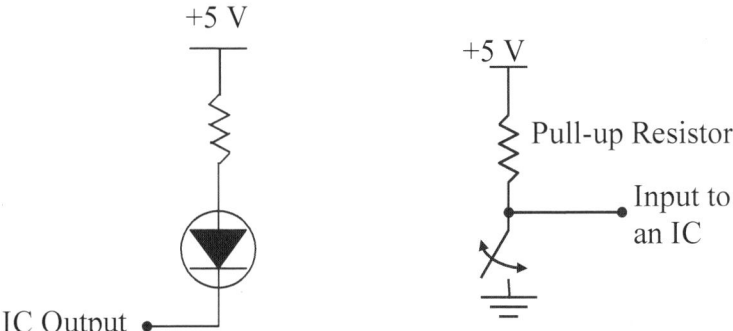

Figure 8-36 LED Circuit   **Figure 8-37** Switch Circuit

Any local electronics store should carry the protoboards, ICs, input switches, and output LEDs to create your prototype circuits. By using some simple circuits for switches and LEDs and the design principles outlined in this book, you can begin creating digital circuits of your own.

8.8 What's Next?

In this chapter, we have examined some of the lower-level hardware applications of digital logic. In the next chapter, we will present some applications that pertain more to the software and system levels of computer system design.

Problems

1. Design the digital logic for segments c, f, and g of the seven-segment display driver truth table in Figure 8-14.

2. Draw the decoding logic circuit with an active-low output for the inputs A = 1, B = 1, C = 0, and D = 1.

3. For the *active-low* output decoder shown to the right, fill in the values for the outputs D_0 through D_3. Assume S_1 is the most significant bit.

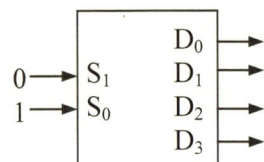

4. What is the binary value being output from Y in the multiplexer circuit shown to the right?

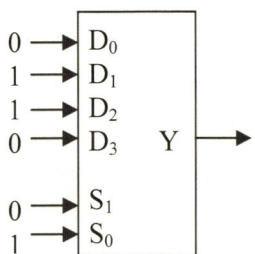

5. What is the purpose of the resistor in the digital circuit for the LED shown in Figure 8-36?

6. What is the purpose of the resistor in the digital circuit for the switch shown in Figure 8-37?

CHAPTER NINE

Binary Operation Applications

Our discussion so far has focused on logic design as it applies to hardware implementation. Frequently software design also requires the use of binary logic. This section presents some higher-level binary applications, ones that might be found in software. These applications are mostly for error checking and correction, but the techniques used should not be limited to these areas.

9.1 Bitwise Operations

Most software performs data manipulation using mathematical operations such as multiplication or addition. Some applications, however, may require the examination or manipulation of data at the bit level. For example, what might be the fastest way to determine whether an integer is odd or even?

The method most of us are usually taught to distinguish odd and even values is to divide the integer by two discarding any remainder then multiply the result by two and compare it with the original value. If the two values are equal, the original value was even because a division by two would not have created a remainder. Inequality, however, would indicate that the original value was odd. Below is an if-statement in the programming language C that would have performed this check.

```
if(((iVal/2)*2) == iVal)
    // This code is executed for even values
else
    // This code is executed for odd values
```

Let's see if we can't establish another method. As we discussed in Chapter 3, a division by two can be accomplished by shifting all of the bits of an integer one position to the right. A remainder occurs when a one is present in the rightmost bit, i.e., the least significant bit. A zero in this position would result in no remainder. Therefore, if the LSB is one, the integer is odd. If the LSB is zero, the integer is even. This is shown with the following examples.

$35_{10} = 00100011_2$ $124_{10} = 01111100_2$
$93_{10} = 01011101_2$ $30_{10} = 00011110_2$

This reduces our odd/even detection down to an examination of the LSB. The question is can we get the computer to examine only a single bit, and if we can, will it be faster than our previous example?

There is in fact a way to manipulate data at the bit level allowing us to isolate or change individual bits. It is based on a set of functions called *bitwise operations*, and the typical programming language provides operators to support them.

The term bitwise operation refers to the setting, clearing, or toggling of individual bits within a binary number. To do this, all processors are capable of executing logical operations (AND, OR, or XOR) on the individual pairs of bits within two binary numbers. The bits are paired up by matching their bit position, performing the logical operation, then placing the result in the same bit position of the destination value.

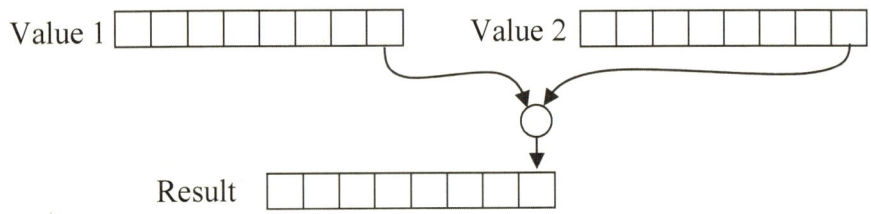

Figure 9-1   Graphic of a Bitwise Operation Performed on LSB

As an example, Figure 9-2 presents the bitwise AND of the binary values 01101011_2 and 11011010_2.

Value 1	0	1	1	0	1	0	1	1
Value 2	1	1	0	1	1	0	1	0
Resulting AND	0	1	0	0	1	0	1	0

Figure 9-2   Bitwise AND of 01101011_2 and 11011010_2

Remember that the output of an AND is one if and only if all of the inputs are one. In Figure 9-2, we see that ones only appear in the result in columns where both of the original values equal one. In a C program, the bitwise AND is identified with the operator '&'. The example in Figure 9-2 can then be represented in C with the following code.

Chapter 9: Binary Operation Applications 167

```
int iVal1 = 0b01101011;
int iVal2 = 0b11011010;
int result = iVal1 & iVal2;
```

Note that the prefix '0b' is a non-standard method of declaring a binary integer and is not supported by all C compilers. If your compiler does not support this type of declaration, use the hex prefix '0x' and declare iVal1 to be 0x6B and iVal2 to be 0xDA. As for the other bitwise operators in C, '|' (pipe) is the bitwise OR operator, '^' (caret) is the bitwise XOR operator, and '~' (tilde) is the bitwise NOT operator.

Typically, bitwise operations are intended to manipulate the bits of a single variable. In order to do this, we must know two things: what needs to be done to the bits and which bits to do it to.

As for the first item, there are three operations: clearing bits to zero, setting bits to one, and toggling bits from one to zero and from zero to one. Clearing bits is taken care of with the bitwise AND operation while setting bits is done with the bitwise OR. The bitwise XOR will toggle specific bits.

A bit mask is a binary value that is of the same length as the original value. It has a pattern of ones and zeros that defines which bits of the original value are to be changed and which bits are to be left alone.

The next three sections discuss each of the three types of bitwise operations: clearing bits, setting bits, and toggling bits.

9.1.1 Clearing/Masking Bits

Clearing individual bits, also known as bit masking, uses the bitwise AND to clear specific bits while leaving the other bits untouched. The mask that is used will have ones in the bit positions that are to be left alone while zeros are in the bit positions that need to be cleared.

This operation is most commonly used when we want to isolate a bit or a group of bits. It is the perfect operation for distinguishing odd and even numbers where we want to see how the LSB is set and ignore the remaining bits. The bitwise AND can be used to clear all of the bits except the LSB. The mask we want to use will have a one in the LSB and zeros in all of the other positions. In Figure 9-3, the results of three bitwise ANDs are given, two for odd numbers and one for an even number. By ANDing a binary mask of 00000001_2, the odd numbers have a non-zero result while the even number has a zero result.

This shows that by using a bitwise AND with a mask of 00000001_2, we can distinguish an odd integer from an even integer. Since bitwise

168 Computer Organization and Design Fundamentals

operations are one of the fastest operations that can be performed on a processor, it is the preferred method. In fact, if we use this bitwise AND to distinguish odd and even numbers on a typical processor, it can be twice as fast as doing the same process with a right shift followed by a left shift and over ten times faster than using a divide followed by a multiply.

35_{10} (odd)	0	0	1	0	0	0	1	1
Odd/Even Mask	0	0	0	0	0	0	0	1
Bitwise AND Result	0	0	0	0	0	0	0	1
93_{10} (odd)	0	1	0	1	1	1	0	1
Odd/Even Mask	0	0	0	0	0	0	0	1
Bitwise AND Result	0	0	0	0	0	0	0	1
30_{10} (even)	0	0	0	1	1	1	1	0
Odd/Even Mask	0	0	0	0	0	0	0	1
Bitwise AND Result	0	0	0	0	0	0	0	0

Figure 9-3 Three Sample Bitwise ANDs

Below is an if-statement in the programming language C that uses a bitwise AND to distinguish odd and even numbers.

```
if(!(iVal&0b00000001))
    // This code is executed for even values
else
    // This code is executed for odd values
```

The bitwise AND can also be used to clear specific bits. For example, assume we want to separate the nibbles of a byte into two different variables. The following process can be used to do this:

- Copy the original value to the variable meant to store the lower nibble, then clear all but the lower four bits
- Copy the original value to the variable meant to store the upper nibble, then shift the value four bits to the right. (See Section 3.7, "Multiplication and Division by Powers of Two," to see how to shift right using C.) Lastly, clear all but the lower four bits.

This process is demonstrated below using the byte 01101101_2.

Chapter 9: Binary Operation Applications   169

Isolating the lower nibble

```
Original value      0  1  1  0  1  1  0  1
Lower nibble mask   0  0  0  0  1  1  1  1
Resulting AND       0  0  0  0  1  1  0  1
```

Isolating the upper nibble

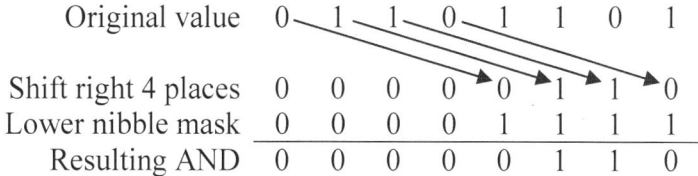

```
Shift right 4 places  0  0  0  0  0  1  1  0
Lower nibble mask     0  0  0  0  1  1  1  1
Resulting AND         0  0  0  0  0  1  1  0
```

The following C code will perform these operations.

```
lower_nibble = iVal & 0x0f;
upper_nibble = (iVal>>4) & 0x0f;
```

Example

Using bitwise operations, write a function in C that determines if an IPv4 address is a member of the subnet 192.168.12.0 with a subnet mask 255.255.252.0. Return a true if the IP address is a member and false otherwise.

Solution

An IPv4 address consists of four bytes or octets separated from one another with periods or "dots". When converted to binary, an IPv4 address becomes a 32 bit number.

The address is divided into two parts: a subnet id and a host id. All of the computers that are connected to the same subnet, e.g., a company or a school network, have the same subnet id. Each computer on a subnet, however, has a unique host id. The host id allows the computer to be uniquely identified among all of the computers on the subnet.

The subnet mask identifies the bits that represent the subnet id. When we convert the subnet mask in this example, 255.255.252.0, to binary, we get 11111111.11111111.11111100.00000000.

The bits that identify the subnet id of an IP address correspond to the positions with ones in the subnet mask. The positions with zeros in the subnet mask identify the host id. In this example, the first 22 bits of any IPv4 address that is a member of this subnet should be the same,

170 Computer Organization and Design Fundamentals

specifically they should equal the address 192.168.12.0 or in binary 11000000.10101000.00001100.00000000.

So how can we determine if an IPv4 address is a member of this subnet? If we could clear the bits of the host id, then the remaining bits should equal 192.168.12.0. This sounds like the bitwise AND. If we perform a bitwise AND on an IPv4 address of this subnet using the subnet mask 255.255.252.0, then the result must be 192.168.12.0 because the host id will be cleared. Let's do this by hand for one address inside the subnet, 192.168.15.23, and one address outside the subnet, 192.168.31.23. First, convert these two addresses to binary.

192.168.15.23 = 11000000.10101000.00001111.00010111
192.168.31.23 = 11000000.10101000.00011111.00010111

Now perform a bitwise AND with each of these addresses to come up with their respective subnets.

```
IP Address   11000000.10101000.00001111.00010111
Subnet mask  11111111.11111111.11111100.00000000
Bitwise AND  11000000.10101000.00001100.00000000


IP Address   11000000.10101000.00011111.00010111
Subnet mask  11111111.11111111.11111100.00000000
Bitwise AND  11000000.10101000.00011100.00000000
```

Notice that the result of the first bitwise AND produces the correct subnet address while the second bitwise AND does not. Therefore, the first address is a member of the subnet while the second is not.

The code to do this is shown below. It assumes that the type **int** is defined to be at least four bytes long. The left shift operator '<<' used in the initialization of **sbnt_ID** and **sbnt_mask** pushes each octet of the IP address or subnet mask to the correct position.

```
int subnetCheck(int IP_address)
{
   int sbnt_ID = (192<<24)+(168<<16)+(12<<8)+0;
   int sbnt_mask = (255<<24)+(255<<16)+(252<<8)+0;
   if((sbnt_mask & IP_address) == sbnt_ID)
     return 1;
   else return 0;
}
```

Chapter 9: Binary Operation Applications 171

9.1.2 Setting Bits

Individual bits within a binary value can be set to one using the bitwise logical OR. To do this, OR the original value with a binary mask that has ones in the positions to be set and zeros in the positions to be left alone. For example, the operation below sets bit positions 1, 3, and 5 of the binary value 10010110_2. Note that bit position 1 was already set. Therefore, this operation should have no affect on that bit.

Original value	1	0	0	1	0	1	1	0
Mask	0	0	1	0	1	0	1	0
Bitwise OR	1	0	1	1	1	1	1	0

In a C program, the bitwise OR is identified with the operator '|'.

Example

Assume that a control byte is used to control eight sets of lights in an auditorium. Each bit controls a set of lights as follows:

        bit 7 – House lighting   bit 3 – Emergency lighting
        bit 6 – Work lighting   bit 2 – Stage lighting
        bit 5 – Aisle lighting   bit 1 – Orchestra pit lighting
        bit 4 – Exit lighting   bit 0 – Curtain lighting

For example, if the house lighting, exit lighting, and stage lighting are all on, the value of the control byte should be 10010100_2. What mask would be used with the bitwise OR to turn on the aisle lighting and the emergency lighting?

Solution

The bitwise OR uses a mask where a one is in each position that needs to be turned on and zeros are placed in the positions meant to be left alone. To turn on the aisle lighting and emergency lighting, bits 5 and 3 must be turned on while the remaining bits are to be left alone. This gives us a mask of 00101000_2.

9.1.3 Toggling Bits

We can also toggle or switch the value of individual bits from 1 to 0 or vice versa. This is done using the bitwise XOR. Let's begin our discussion by examining the truth table for a two-input XOR.

172 Computer Organization and Design Fundamentals

Table 9-1 Truth Table for a Two-Input XOR Gate

A	B	X
0	0	0
0	1	1
1	0	1
1	1	0

If we cover up the bottom two rows of this truth table leaving only the rows where A=0 visible, we see that the value of B is passed along to X, i.e., if A=0, then X equals B. If we cover up the rows where A=0 leaving only the rows where A=1 visible, it looks like the inverse of B is passed to X, i.e., if A=1, then X equals the inverse of B. This discussion makes a two-input XOR gate look like a programmable inverter. If A is zero, B is passed through to the output untouched. If A is one, B is inverted at the output.

Therefore, if we perform a bitwise XOR, the bit positions in the mask with zeros will pass the original value through and bit positions in the mask with ones will invert the original value. The example below uses the mask 00101110_2 to toggle bits 1, 2, 3, and 5 of a binary value while leaving the others untouched.

```
Original value  1 0 0 1 0 1 1 0
         Mask   0 0 1 0 1 1 1 0
  Bitwise XOR   1 0 1 1 1 0 0 0
```

Example

Assume a byte is used to control the warning and indicator lights on an automotive dashboard. The following is a list of the bit positions and the dashboard lights they control.

bit 7 – Oil pressure light   bit 3 – Left turn indicator
bit 6 – Temperature light   bit 2 – Right turn indicator
bit 5 – Door ajar light   bit 1 – Low fuel light
bit 4 – Check engine light   bit 0 – High-beams light

Determine the mask to be used with a bitwise XOR that when used once a second will cause the left and right turn indicators to flash when the emergency flashers are on.

Chapter 9: Binary Operation Applications 173

Solution

The bitwise XOR uses a mask with ones is in the positions to be toggled and zeros in the positions to be left alone. To toggle bits 3 and 2 on and off, the mask should have ones only in those positions. Therefore, the mask to be used with the bitwise XOR is 00001100_2.

9.2 Comparing Bits with XOR

This brings us to our first method for detecting errors in data: comparing two serial binary streams to see if they are equal. Assume that one device is supposed to send a stream of bits to another device. An example of this might be a motion detector mounted in an upper corner of a room. The motion detector has either a zero output indicating the room is unoccupied or a one output indicating that something in the room is moving. The output from this motion detector may look like that shown in Figure 9-4.

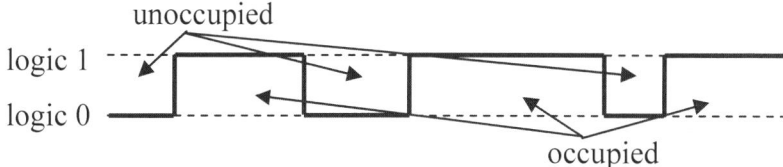

Figure 9-4 Possible Output from a Motion Detector

To verify the output of the motion detector, a second motion detector could be mounted in the room so that the two separate outputs could be compared to each other. If the outputs are the same, the signal can be trusted; if they are different, then one of the devices is in error. At this point in our discussion, we won't know which one.

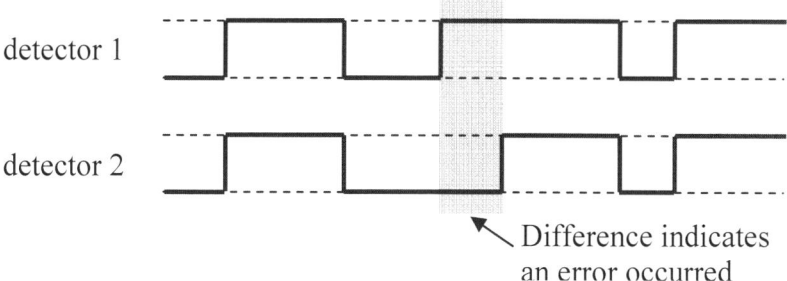

Figure 9-5 A Difference in Output Indicates an Error

A two-input XOR gate can be used here to indicate when an error has occurred. Remember that the output of a two-input XOR gate is a zero if both of the inputs are the same and a one if the inputs are different. This gives us a simple circuit to detect when two signals which should be identical are not.

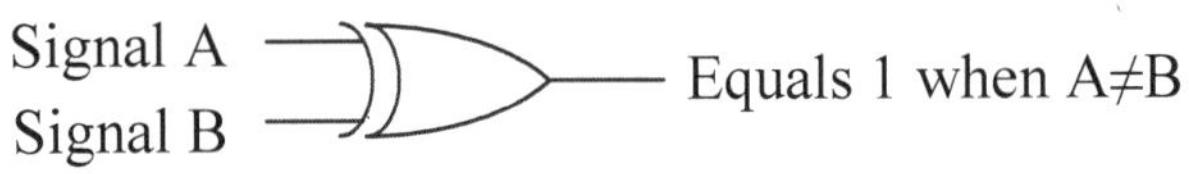

Signal A ⟶
Signal B ⟶ ⊕ ⟶ Equals 1 when A≠B

Figure 9-6 Simple Error Detection with an XOR Gate

This circuit will be used later in this chapter to support more complex error detection and correction circuits.

9.3 Parity

One of the most primitive forms of error detection is to add a single bit called a parity bit to each piece of data to indicate whether the data has an odd or even number of ones. It is considered a poor method of error detection as it sometimes doesn't detect multiple errors. When combined with other methods of error detection, however, it can improve their overall performance.

There are two primary types of parity: odd and even. Even parity means that the sum of the ones in the data element and the parity bit is an even number. With odd parity, the sum of ones in the data element and the parity bit is an odd number. When designing a digital system that uses parity, the designers decide in advance which type of parity they will be using.

Assume that a system uses even parity. If an error has occurred and one of the bits in either the data element or the parity bit has been inverted, then counting the number of ones results in an odd number. From the information available, the digital system cannot determine which bit was inverted or even if only one bit was inverted. It can only tell that an error has occurred.

One of the primary problems with parity is that if two bits are inverted, the parity bit appears to be correct, i.e., it indicates that the data is error free. Parity can only detect an odd number of bit errors.

Some systems use a parity bit with each piece of data in memory. If a parity error occurs, the computer will generate a non-maskable interrupt, a condition where the operating system immediately discontinues the execution of the questionable application.

Example

Assume the table below represents bytes stored in memory along with an associated parity bit. Which of the stored values are in error?

Data								Parity
1	0	0	1	0	1	1	0	0
0	0	1	1	1	0	1	0	1
1	0	1	1	0	1	0	1	1
0	1	0	1	1	0	0	1	0
1	1	0	0	0	1	0	1	1

Solution

To determine which data/parity combinations have an error, count the number of ones in each row. The rows with an odd sum have errors while the rows with an even sum are assumed to contain valid data.

Data								Parity	
1	0	0	1	0	1	1	0	0	4 ones – even → no error
0	0	1	1	1	0	1	0	1	5 ones – odd → Error!
1	0	1	1	0	1	0	1	1	6 ones – even → no error
0	1	0	1	1	0	0	1	0	4 ones – even → no error
1	1	0	0	0	1	0	1	1	5 ones – odd → Error!

9.4 Checksum

For digital systems that store or transfer multiple pieces of data in blocks, an additional data element is typically added to each block to provide error detection for the block. This method of error detection is common, especially for the transmission of data across networks.

One of the simplest implementations of this error detection scheme is the *checksum*. As a device transmits data, it takes the sum of all of the data elements it is transmitting to create an aggregate sum. This sum is called the *datasum*. The overflow carries generated by the additions are either discarded or added back into the datasum. The transmitting device then sends a form of this datasum appended to the end of the block. This new form of the datasum is called the *checksum*.

As the data elements are received, they are added a second time in order to recreate the datasum. Once all of the data elements have been received, the receiving device compares its calculated datasum with the checksum sent by the transmitting device. The data is considered error free if the receiving device's datasum compares favorably with the transmitted checksum. Figure 9-7 presents a sample data block and the datasums generated both by discarding the two carries and by adding the carries to the datasum.

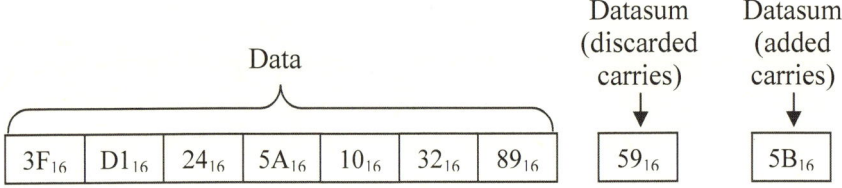

Figure 9-7 Sample Block of Data with Accompanying Datasums

Upon receiving this transmission, the datasum for this data block must be calculated. Begin by taking the sum of all the data elements.

$$3F_{16} + D1_{16} + 24_{16} + 5A_{16} + 10_{16} + 32_{16} + 89_{16} = 259_{16}$$

The final datasum is calculated by discarding any carries that went beyond the byte width defined by the data block (59_{16}) or by adding the carries to the final sum ($59_{16} + 2 = 5B_{16}$). This keeps the datasum the same width as the data. The method of calculating the datasum where the carries are added to the sum is called the ***one's complement sum***.

The checksum shown for the data block in Figure 9-7 is only one of a number of different possible checksums for this data. In this case, the checksum was set equal to the expected datasum. If any of the data elements or if the checksum was in error, the datasum would not equal the checksum. If this happens, the digital system would know that an error had occurred. In the case of a network data transmission, it would request the data to be resent.

The only difference between different implementations of the checksum method is how the datasum and checksum are compared in order to detect an error. As with parity, it is the decision of the designer as to which method is used. The type of checksum used must be agreed upon by both the transmitting and receiving devices ahead of time. The following is a short list of some of the different types of checksum implementations:

- A block of data is considered error free if the datasum is *equal* to the checksum. In this case, the checksum element is calculated by taking the sum of all of the data elements and discarding any carries, i.e., setting the checksum equal to the datasum.

Chapter 9: Binary Operation Applications 177

- A block of data is considered error free if the sum of the datasum and checksum results in a binary value with all ones. In this case, the checksum element is calculated by taking the 1's complement of the datasum. This method is called a *1's complement checksum*.
- A block of data is considered error free if the sum of the datasum and checksum results in a binary value with all zeros. In this case, the checksum element is calculated by taking the 2's complement of the datasum. This method is called a *2's complement checksum*.

As shown earlier, the basic checksum for the data block in Figure 9-7 is 59_{16} (01011001_2). The 1's complement checksum for the same data block is equal to the 1's complement of 59_{16}.

$$\text{1's complement of } 59_{16} = 10100110_2 = A6_{16}$$

The 2's complement checksum for the data block is equal to the 2's complement of 59_{16}.

$$\text{2s complement of } 59_{16} = 10100111_2 = A7_{16}$$

Example

Determine if the data block and accompanying checksum below are error free. The data block uses a 1's complement checksum.

Data						Checksum
06_{16}	00_{16}	$F7_{16}$	$7E_{16}$	01_{16}	52_{16}	31_{16}

Solution

First, calculate the datasum by adding all the data elements in the data block.

$$\begin{array}{cccccc} 06_{16} & 06_{16} & FD_{16} & 7B_{16} & 7C_{16} \\ +\,00_{16} & +\,F7_{16} & +\,7E_{16} & +\,01_{16} & +\,52_{16} \\ \hline 06_{16} & FD_{16} & 17B_{16} & 7C_{16} & CE_{16} \end{array}$$

This gives us a datasum of CE_{16}. If we add this to the checksum 31_{16} we get $CE_{16} + 31_{16} = FF_{16}$, which tells us the data block is error free.

There is a second way to check this data. Instead of adding the datasum to the checksum, you can use the datasum to recalculate the checksum and compare the result with the received checksum. Taking the 1's complement of CE_{16} gives us:

$$CE_{16} = 11001110_2$$
$$\text{1's complement of } CE_{16} = 00110001_2 = 31_{16}$$

Example

Write a C program to determine the basic checksum, 1's complement checksum, and 2's complement checksum for the data block 07_{16}, 01_{16}, 20_{16}, 74_{16}, 65_{16}, 64_{16}, $2E_{16}$.

Solution

Before we get started on this code, it is important to know how to take a 1's complement and a 2's complement in C. The 1's complement uses a bitwise not operator '~'. By placing a '~' in front of a variable or constant, the bitwise inverse or 1's complement is returned. Since most computers represent negative numbers with 2's complement notation, the 2's complement is calculated by placing a negative sign in front of the variable or constant.

The code below begins by calculating the datasum. It does this with a loop that adds each value from the array of data values to a variable labeled *datasum*. After each addition, any potential carry is stripped off using a bitwise AND with 0xff. This returns the byte value.

Once the datasum is calculated, the three possible checksum values can be calculated. The first one is equal to the datasum, the second is equal to the bitwise inverse of the datasum, and the third is equal to the 2's complement of the datasum.

```
int datasum=0;
int block[] = {0x07, 0x01, 0x20, 0x74,
               0x65, 0x64, 0x2E};

// This for-loop adds all of the data elements
for(int i=0; i < sizeof(block)/sizeof(int); i++)
     datasum += block[i];

// The following line discards potential carries
datasum &= 0xff;
// Compute each of the three types of checksums
int basic_checksum = datasum;
int ones_compl_checksum = 0xff&(~datasum);
int twos_compl_checksum = 0xff&(-datasum);
```

Chapter 9: Binary Operation Applications 179

If we execute this code with the appropriate output statements, we get the following three values for the checksums.

```
The basic checksum is 93
The 1's complement checksum is 6c
The 2's complement checksum is 6d
```

9.5 Cyclic Redundancy Check

The problem with using a checksum for error correction lies in its simplicity. If multiple errors occur in a data stream, it is possible that they may cancel each other out, e.g., a single bit error may subtract 4 from the checksum while a second error adds 4. If the width of the checksum character is 8 bits, then there are $2^8 = 256$ possible checksums for a data stream. This means that there is a 1 in 256 chance that multiple errors may not be detected. These odds could be reduced by increasing the size of the checksum to 16 or 32 bits thereby increasing the number of possible checksums to $2^{16} = 65,536$ or $2^{32} = 4,294,967,296$ respectively.

Assume Figure 9-8 represents a segment of an integer number line where the result of the checksum is identified. A minor error in one of the values may result in a small change in the checksum value. Since the erroneous checksum is not that far from the correct checksum, it is easy for a second error to put the erroneous checksum back to the correct value indicating that there hasn't been an error when there actually has been one.

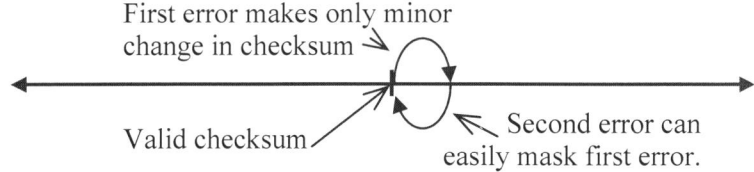

Figure 9-8 Small Changes in Data Canceling in Checksum

What we need is an error detection method that generates vastly different values for small errors in the data. The checksum algorithm doesn't do this which makes it possible for two bit changes to cancel each other in the sum.

A cyclic redundancy check (CRC) uses a basic binary algorithm where each bit of a data element modifies the checksum across its entire length regardless of the number of bits in the checksum. This means that an error at the bit level modifies the checksum so significantly that an equal and opposite bit change in another data element cannot cancel the effect of the first.

First, calculation of the CRC checksum is based on the remainder resulting from a division rather than the result of an addition. For example, the two numbers below vary only by one bit.

$$0111\ 1010\ 1101\ 1100_2 = 31{,}452_{10}$$
$$0111\ 1011\ 1101\ 1100_2 = 31{,}708_{10}$$

The checksums at the nibble level are:

$$0111 + 1010 + 1101 + 1100 = 1010_2 = 10_{10}$$
$$0111 + 1011 + 1101 + 1100 = 1011_2 = 11_{10}$$

These two values are very similar, and a bit change from another nibble could easily cancel it out.

If, on the other hand, we use the remainder from a division for our checksum, we get a wildly different result for the two values. For the sake of an example, let's divide both values by 9_{10}.

$$31{,}452 \div 9 = 3{,}494 \text{ with a remainder of } 6 = 0110_2$$
$$31{,}708 \div 9 = 3{,}523 \text{ with a remainder of } 1 = 0001_2$$

This is not a robust example due to the fact that 4 bits only have 16 possible bit patterns, but the result is clear. A single bit change in one of the data elements resulted in a single bit change in the addition result. The same change, however, resulted in three bits changing in the division remainder.

The problem is that division in binary is not a quick operation. For example, Figure 9-9 shows the long division in binary of $31{,}452_{10} = 0111101011011100_2$ by $9_{10} = 1001_2$. The result is a quotient of $110110100110_2 = 3{,}494_{10}$ with a remainder of $110_2 = 6_{10}$.

Remember that the goal is to create a checksum that can be used to check for errors, not to come up with a mathematically correct result. Keeping this in mind, the time it takes to perform a long division can be reduced by removing the need for "borrows". This would be the same as doing an addition while ignoring the carries. The truth table in Table 9-2 shows the single bit results for both addition and subtraction when carries and borrows are ignored.

Chapter 9: Binary Operation Applications 181

```
              110110100110
    1001 / 0111101011011100
          -1001
           1100
          -1001
           1110
          -1001
            1011
           -1001
             1010
            -1001
              1111
             -1001
              1100
             -1001
               110
```

Figure 9-9   Example of Long Division in Binary

Table 9-2   Addition and Subtraction Without Carries or Borrows

A	B	A+B	A − B
0	0	0	0
0	1	1	1 (no borrow)
1	0	1	1
1	1	0 (no carry)	0

The A + B and A − B columns of the truth table in Table 9-2 should look familiar; they are equivalent to the XOR operation. This means that a borrow-less subtraction is nothing more than a bitwise XOR. Below is an example of an addition and a subtraction where there is no borrowing. Note that an addition without carries produces the identical result as a subtraction without borrows.

```
   11011010        11011010
  +01101100       -01101100
   10110110        10110110
```

There is a problem when trying to apply this form of subtraction to long division: an XOR subtraction doesn't care whether one number is

182   Computer Organization and Design Fundamentals

larger than another. For example, 1111_2 could be subtracted from 0000_2 with no ill effect. In long division, you need to know how many digits to pull down from the dividend before subtracting the divisor.

To solve this, the assumption is made that one value can be considered "larger" than another if the bit position of its highest logic 1 is the same or greater than the bit position of the highest logic 1 in the second number. For example, the subtractions 10110 – 10011 and 0111 – 0011 are valid while 0110 – 1001 and 01011 – 10000 are not.

Figure 9-10 repeats the long division of Figure 9-9 using borrow-less subtractions. It is a coincidence that the resulting remainder is the same for the long division of Figure 9-9. This is not usually true.

```
                111010001010
        1001 ⌈ 0111101011011100
              -1001
               1100
              -1001
                1011
               -1001
                 1001
                -1001
                  01011
                  -1001
                    1010
                   -1001
                     110
```

Figure 9-10   Example of Long Division Using XOR Subtraction

Since addition and subtraction without carries or borrows are equivalent to a bitwise XOR, we should be able to reconstruct the original value from the quotient and the remainder using nothing but XORs. Table 9-3 shows the step-by-step process of this reconstruction. The leftmost column of the table is the bit-by-bit values of the binary quotient of the division of Figure 9-10.

Starting with a value of zero, 1001_2 is XORed with the result in the second column when the current bit of the quotient is a 1. The result is XORed with 0000_2 if the current bit of the quotient is a 0. The rightmost column is the result of this XOR. Before going to the next bit of the quotient, the result is shifted left one bit position. Once the end

Chapter 9: Binary Operation Applications   183

of the quotient is reached, the remainder is added. This process brings back the dividend using a multiplication of the quotient and divisor.

Table 9-3 Reconstructing the Dividend Using XORs

Quotient (Q)	Result from previous step shifted left one bit	XOR Value Q=0: 0000 Q=1: 1001	XOR result
1	0	1001	1001
1	10010	1001	11011
1	110110	1001	111111
0	1111110	0000	1111110
1	11111100	1001	11110101
0	111101010	0000	111101010
0	1111010100	0000	1111010100
0	11110101000	0000	11110101000
1	111101010000	1001	111101011001
0	1111010110010	0000	1111010110010
1	11110101100100	1001	11110101101101
0	111101011011010	0000	111101011011010
Add remainder to restore the dividend: 111101011011010 + 110 = **111101011011100**			

Example

Perform the long division of 110011011010101011_2 by 1011_2 in binary using the borrow-less subtraction, i.e., XOR function.

Solution

Using the standard "long-division" procedure with the XOR subtractions, we divide 1011_2 into 110011011010101011_2. Table 9-4 checks our result using the technique shown in Table 9-3. Since we were able to recreate the original value from the quotient and remainder, the division must have been successful.

Note that in Table 9-4 we are reconstructing the original value from the quotient in order to demonstrate the application of the XOR in this modified division and multiplication. This is not a part of the CRC implementation. In reality, as long as the sending and receiving devices use the same divisor, the only result of the division that is of concern is the remainder. As long as the sending and receiving devices obtain the same results, the transmission can be considered error free.

184 Computer Organization and Design Fundamentals

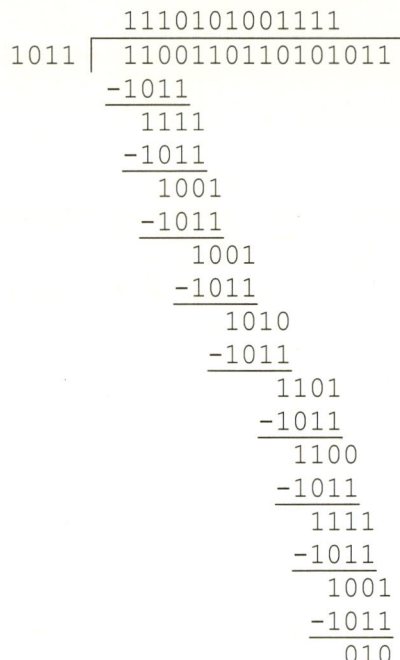

Table 9-4 Second Example of Reconstructing the Dividend

Quotient (Q)	Result from previous step shifted left one bit	XOR Value Q=0: 0000 Q=1: 1011	XOR result
1	0	1011	1011
1	10110	1011	11101
1	111010	1011	110001
0	1100010	0000	1100010
1	11000100	1011	11001111
0	110011110	0000	110011110
1	1100111100	1011	1100110111
0	11001101110	0000	11001101110
0	110011011100	0000	110011011100
1	1100110111000	1011	1100110110011
1	11001101100110	1011	11001101101101
1	110011011011010	1011	110011011010001
1	1100110110100010	1011	1100110110101001
Add remainder to restore the dividend: 1100110110101001 + 010 = **1100110110101011**			

Chapter 9: Binary Operation Applications 185

9.5.1 CRC Process

The primary difference between different CRC implementations is the selection of the divisor or polynomial as it is referred to in the industry. In the example used in this discussion, we used 1001_2, but this is by no means a standard value. Divisors of different bit patterns and different bit lengths perform differently. The typical divisor is 17 or 33 bits, but this is only because of the standard bit widths of 16 and 32 bits in today's processor architectures. A few divisors have been selected as performing better than others, but a discussion of why they perform better is beyond the scope of this text.

There is, however, a relationship between the remainder and the divisor that we do wish to discuss here. We made an assumption earlier in this section about how to decide whether one value is larger than another with regards to XOR subtraction. This made it so that in an XOR division, a subtraction from an intermediate value is possible only if the most significant one is in the same bit position as the most significant one of the divisor. This is true all the way up to the final subtraction which produces the remainder. These most significant ones cancel leaving a zero in the most significant bit position of each result including the remainder. Since the MSB is always a zero for the result of every subtraction in an XOR division, each intermediate result along with the final remainder must always be at least one bit shorter in length than the divisor.

There is another interesting fact about the XOR division that is a direct result of the borrow-less subtraction, and the standard method of CRC implementation has come to rely on this fact. Assume that we have selected an n-bit divisor. The typical CRC calculation begins by appending n-1 zeros to the end of the data (dividend). After we divide this new data stream by the divisor to compute the remainder, the remainder is added to the end of the new data stream effectively replacing the n-1 zeros with the value of the remainder.

Remember that XOR addition and subtraction are equivalent. Therefore, by adding the remainder to the end of the data stream, we have effectively subtracted the remainder from the dividend. This means that when we divide the data stream (which has the remainder added/subtracted) by the same divisor, **the new remainder should equal zero**. Therefore, if the receiving device generates a remainder of zero after dividing the entire data stream with the polynomial, the transmission was error-free. The following example illustrates this.

Example

Generate the CRC checksum to be transmitted with the data stream 1011011100101110_2 using the divisor 11011_2.

Solution

With a 5 bit divisor, append $5 - 1 = 4$ zeros to the end of the data.

New data stream = "1011011100101110" + "0000"
= "10110111001011100000"

Finish by computing the CRC checksum using XOR division.

```
                1100001010110010
        11011 | 10110111100101100000
                -11011
                 11011
                -11011
                   011100
                   -11011
                     11110
                    -11011
                      10111
                     -11011
                       11000
                      -11011
                        11000
                       -11011
                         0110
```

The data stream sent to the receiving device becomes the original data stream with the 4-bit remainder appended to it.

Transmitted data stream = "1011011100101110" + "0110"
= "10110111100101100110"

If the receiver divides the entire data stream by the same divisor used by the transmitting device, i.e., 11011_2, the remainder will be zero. This is shown in the following division. If this process is followed, the receiving device will calculate a zero remainder any time there is no error in the data stream.

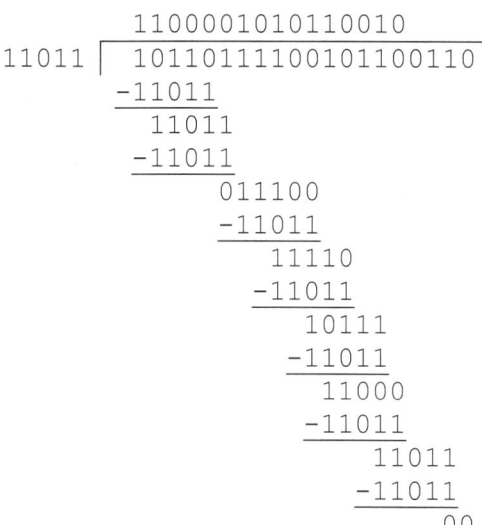

9.5.2 CRC Implementation

Up to now, the discussion has focused on the mathematics behind creating and using CRC checksums. As for the implementation of a CRC checksum, programmers use the following process:

- A single n-bit divisor is defined. Both the sending and receiving devices use the same n-bit divisor.
- The sending device adds n-1 zeros to the end of the data being sent, and then performs the XOR division in order to obtain the remainder. The quotient is thrown away.
- The sending device takes the original data (without the n–1 zeros) and appends the n–1 bit remainder to the end. This is the same as subtracting the remainder from the data with the appended zeros.
- The data and appended remainder is sent to the receiving device.
- The receiving device performs an XOR division on the received message and its appended n–1 bit remainder using the same divisor.
- If the result of the receiver's XOR division is zero, the message is considered error free. Otherwise, the message is corrupted.

A number of CRC divisors or polynomials have been defined for standard implementations. For example, the CRC-CCITT divisor is the 17-bit polynomial 11021_{16} while the divisor used in IEEE 802.3 Ethernet is the 33-bit polynomial $104C11DB7_{16}$.

188   Computer Organization and Design Fundamentals

As for implementing the XOR division, most data streams are far too large to be contained in a single processor register. Therefore, the data stream must be passed through a register that acts like a window revealing only the portion of the stream where the XOR subtraction is being performed. This is the second benefit of using the bitwise XOR. Without the XOR subtraction, the whole dividend would need to be contained in a register in order to support the borrow function.

Remember that the MSB of both the intermediate value and the divisor in an XOR subtraction are always 1. This means that the MSB of the subtraction is unnecessary as it always result in a zero. Therefore, for an n-bit divisor or polynomial, only an n-1 bit register is needed for the XOR operation.

The code presented in Figure 9-11 appends four zeros to the end of a 32-bit data stream (*data_stream*), then performs an XOR division on it with the 5-bit polynomial 10111_2 (*poly*). The division is done in a division register (*division_register*). This division register in theory should only be four bits wide, but since there is no four bit integer type in C, an 8-bit char is used. After every modification of the division register, a bitwise AND is performed on it with the binary mask 1111_2 in order to strip off any ones that might appear above bit 3. The binary mask is labeled *division_mask*.

Running this code with a 32-bit constant assigned to the variable *data_stream* will produce the four-bit CRC checksum 0010_2 for the polynomial 10111_2.

There are better ways to implement the CRC algorithm. This code is presented only to show how the division register might work.

9.6 Hamming Code

Errors can also occur in memory. One possibility is that a defect or a failure in the hardware could cause a memory cell to be un-writable. Random errors might also be caused by an electrical event such as static electricity or electromagnetic interference causing one or more bits to flip. Whatever the cause, we need to be able to determine if the data we are reading is valid.

One solution might be to store an additional bit with each data byte. This bit could act as a parity bit making it so that the total number of ones stored in each memory location along with the corresponding parity bit is always even. When it is time to read the data, the number of ones in the in the data and the parity bit are counted. If an odd result occurs, we know that there was an error.

Chapter 9: Binary Operation Applications   189

```
// This code generates a four-bit CRC from a 32 bit
// data stream by passing it through a four-bit
// division register where it is XORed with the last
// four bits of a five bit polynomial
__int32 data_stream = 0x48376dea;  // Data stream
#define poly 0x17                  // Polynomial=10111

// The XOR is performed in a char variable which will
// then be AND'ed with a 4-bit mask to clear the fifth
// bit. A mask allowing us to check for a fifth bit is
// also defined here.
char division_register = 0;
#define division_mask 0xf
#define division_MSB 0x10

// We will need to count how many times we've shifted
// the data stream so that we know when we are done.
// For a 32 bit stream, we need to shift 32+4 times.
int shift_count = 0;
#define shift_total (32+4)

__int32 temp_ds = data_stream;
while (shift_count < shift_total)
{
// The following code shifts bits into the division
// register from the data stream until a bit overflows
// past the length of the division register. Once this
// bit overflows, we know we have loaded a value from
// which the polynomial can be subtracted.
    while ((!(division_register & division_MSB))
        &&(shift_count < shift_total))
    {
        division_register <<= 1;
        if((temp_ds & 0x80000000) != 0)
            division_register+=1;
        temp_ds <<= 1;
        shift_count++;
    }
    division_register &= division_mask;
// If we have a value large enough to XOR with the
// polynomial, then we should do a bitwise XOR
    if(shift_count < shift_total)
        division_register ^= (poly & division_mask);
}
printf("The four-bit CRC for the 32 bit data stream
    0x%x using the polynomial 0x%x is 0x%x.\n",
    data_stream, poly, division_register);
```

Figure 9-11   Sample Code for Calculating CRC Checksums

190 Computer Organization and Design Fundamentals

As mentioned before, parity is not a very robust error checking method. If two errors occur, the parity still appears correct. In addition, it might be nice to detect *and* correct the error.

One way to do this is to use multiple parity bits, each bit responsible for the parity of a smaller, overlapping portion of the data. For example, we could use four parity bits to represent the parity of four different groupings of the four bits of a nibble. Table 9-5 shows how this might work for the four-bit value 1011_2. Each row of the table groups three of the four bits of the nibble along with a parity bit, P_n. The value shown for the parity bit makes the sum of all the ones in the grouping of three bits plus parity an even number.

Table 9-5 Data Groupings and Parity for the Nibble 1011_2

	Data Bits				Parity Bits			
	$D_3=1$	$D_2=0$	$D_1=1$	$D_0=1$	P_0	P_1	P_2	P_3
Group A	1	0	1		0			
Group B	1		1	1		1		
Group C	1	0		1			0	
Group D		0	1	1				0

In memory, the nibble would be stored with its parity bits in an eight-bit location as 10110100_2.

Now assume that the bit in the D_1 position which was originally a 1 is flipped to a 0 causing an error. The new value stored in memory would be 10010100_2. Table 9-6 duplicates the groupings of Table 9-5 with the new value for D_1. The table also identifies groups that incur a parity error with the data change.

Table 9-6 Data Groupings with a Data Bit in Error

	Data Bits				Parity Bits				Parity Result
	$D_3=1$	$D_2=0$	$D_1=0$	$D_0=1$	P_0	P_1	P_2	P_3	
Group A	1	0	0		0				Odd – Error
Group B	1		0	1		1			Odd – Error
Group C	1	0		1			0		Even – Okay
Group D		0	0	1				0	Odd – Error

Note that parity is now in error for groups A, C, and D. Since the D_1 position is the only bit that belongs to all three of these groups, then a

Chapter 9: Binary Operation Applications 191

processor checking for errors would not only know that an error had occurred, but also in which bit it had occurred. Since each bit can only take on one of two possible values, then we know that flipping the bit D_1 will return the nibble to its original data.

If an error occurs in a parity bit, i.e., if P_3 is flipped, then only one group will have an error. Therefore, when the processor checks the parity of the four groups, a single group with an error indicates that it is a parity bit that has been changed and the original data is still valid.

Table 9-7 Data Groupings with a Parity Bit in Error

	Data Bits				Parity Bits				Parity Result
	$D_3=1$	$D_2=0$	$D_1=1$	$D_0=1$	P_0	P_1	P_2	P_3	
Group A	1	0	1		0				Even – Okay
Group B	1		1	1		1			Even – Okay
Group C	1	0		1			0		Even – Okay
Group D		0	1	1				1	Odd – Error

It turns out that not all four data groupings are needed. If we only use groups A, B, and C, we still have the same level of error detection, but we do it with one less parity bit. Continuing our example without Group D, if our data is error-free or if a single bit error has occurred, one of the following eight situations is true.

Table 9-8 Identifying Errors in a Nibble with Three Parity Bits

Groups with bad parity	Bit in error
None	Error-free
A	P_0
B	P_1
C	P_2
A and B	D_1
A and C	D_2
B and C	D_0
A, B, and C	D_3

The use of multiple parity bits to "code" an error correction scheme for data bits is called the *Hamming Code*. It was developed by Richard Hamming during the late 1940's when he worked at Bell Laboratories.

192 Computer Organization and Design Fundamentals

The Hamming Code can be shown graphically using a Venn diagram. We begin by creating three overlapping circles, one circle for each group. Each of the parity bits P_n is placed in the portion of their corresponding circle that is not overlapped by any other circle. D_0 is placed in the portion of the diagram where circles B and C overlap, D_1 goes where circles A and B overlap, and D_2 goes where circles A and C overlap. Place D_3 in the portion of the diagram where all three circles overlap. Figure 9-12 presents just such an arrangement.

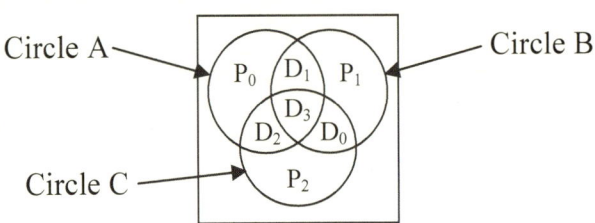

Figure 9-12 Venn Diagram Representation of Hamming Code

Figure 9-13a uses this arrangement to insert the nibble 1011_2 into a Venn diagram. Figures 9-13b, c, and d show three of the seven possible error conditions.

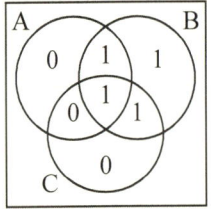 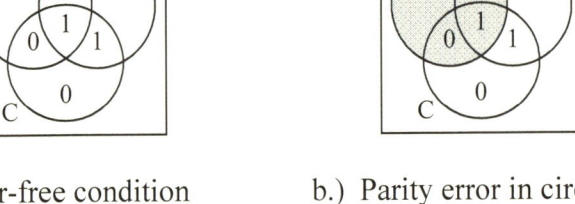

a.) Error-free condition   b.) Parity error in circle A

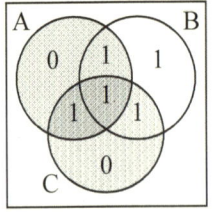 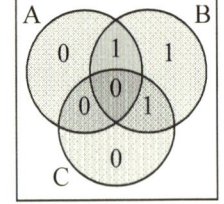

c.) Parity errors in A & C   d.) Parity errors in A, B, & C

Figure 9-13 Example Single-Bit Errors in Venn Diagram

Chapter 9: Binary Operation Applications   193

In 9-13b, a single error in circle A indicates only the parity bit P_0 is in error. In 9-13c, since both circles A and C have errors, then the bit change must have occurred in the region occupied only by A and C, i.e., where D_2 is located. Therefore, D_2 should be 0. Lastly, in 9-13d, an error in all three circles indicates that there has been a bit change in the region shared by all three circles, i.e., in bit D_3. Therefore, we know that bit D_3 is in error. Each of these errors can be corrected by inverting the value of the bit found in error.

Double errors, however, cannot be detected correctly with this method. In Figure 9-14b, both the parity bit P_1 and the data bit D_0 are in error. If we do a parity check on each of the three circles in this Venn diagram, we find erroneous parity only in circle C. This would indicate that only the parity bit P_2 is in error. This is a problem because it incorrectly assumes the data 1010_2 is correct.

This is a problem. Apparently, this error checking scheme can detect when a double-bit error occurs, but if we try to correct it, we end up with erroneous data. We need to expand our error detection scheme to be able to detect and correct single bit errors and distinguish them from double bit errors.

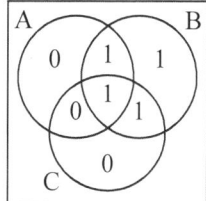
a.) Error-free condition

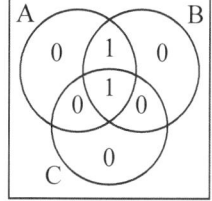
b.) Two-Bit Error Condition

Figure 9-14   Example of a Two-Bit Error

This can be done by adding one more bit that acts as a parity check for all seven data and parity bits. Figure 9-15 represents this new bit using the same example from Figure 9-14.

If a single-bit error occurs, then after we go through the process of correcting the error, this new parity bit will be correct. If, however, after we go through the process of correcting the error and the new parity bit is in error, then it can be assumed that a double-bit error has occurred and that correction is not possible. This is called ***Single-Error Correction/Doubled-Error Detection***.

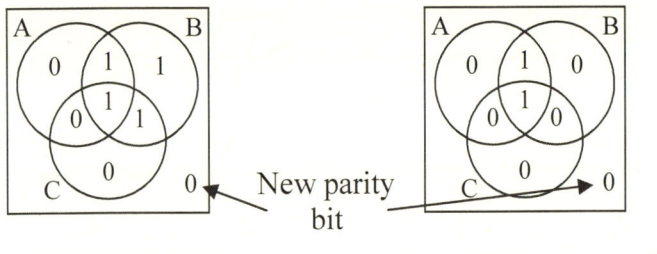

a.) Error-free condition   b.) Two-Bit Error Condition

Figure 9-15 Using Parity to Check for Double-Bit Errors

This error detection and correction scheme can be expanded to any number of bits. All we need to do is make sure there are enough parity bits to cover the error-free condition plus any possible single-bit error in the data or the parity. For example, in our four data bit and three parity bit example above, there can be one of seven single bit errors. Add the error-free condition and that makes eight possible conditions that must be represented with parity bits. Since there are three parity bits, then there are $2^3 = 8$ possible bit patterns represented using the parity bits, one for each of the outcomes.

For the general case, we see that p parity bits can uniquely identify $2^p - 1$ single-bit errors. Note that the one is subtracted from 2^p to account for the condition where there are no errors. If $2^p - 1$ is less than the number of data bits, n, plus the number of parity bits, p, then we don't have enough parity bits. This relationship is represented with equation 9-1.

$$p + n \leq 2^p - 1 \qquad (9.1)$$

Table 9-9 presents a short list of the number of parity bits that are required for a specific number of data bits. To detect double-bit errors, an additional bit is needed to check the parity of all of the $p + n$ bits.

Let's develop the error-checking scheme for 8 data bits. Remember from the four-bit example that there were three parity checks:

- P_0 was the parity bit for data bits for D_1, D_2, and D_3;
- P_1 was the parity bit for data bits for D_0, D_1, and D_3; and
- P_2 was the parity bit for data bits for D_0, D_2, and D_3.

Chapter 9: Binary Operation Applications 195

Table 9-9 Parity Bits Required for a Specific Number of Data Bits

Number of data bits (n)	Number of parity bits (p)	$p + n$	$2^p - 1$
4	3	7	7
8	4	12	15
16	5	21	31
32	6	38	63
64	7	71	127
128	8	136	255

In order to check for a bit error, the sum of ones for each of these groups is taken. If all three sums result in even values, then the data is error-free. The implementation of a parity check is done with the XOR function. Remember that the XOR function counts the number of ones at the input and outputs a 1 for an odd count and a 0 for an even count. This means that the three parity checks we use to verify our four data bits can be performed using the XOR function. Equations 9.2, 9.3, and 9.4 show how these three parity checks can be done. The XOR is represented here with the symbol $\oplus$.

Parity check for group A = $P_0 \oplus D_1 \oplus D_2 \oplus D_3$ (9.2)
Parity check for group B = $P_1 \oplus D_0 \oplus D_1 \oplus D_3$ (9.3)
Parity check for group C = $P_2 \oplus D_0 \oplus D_2 \oplus D_3$ (9.4)

The data bits of our four-bit example were $D_3 = 1$, $D_2 = 0$, $D_1 = 1$, and $D_0 = 1$ while the parity bits were $P_0 = 0$, $P_1 = 1$, and $P_2 = 0$. Substituting these into equations 9.2, 9.3, and 9.4 gives us:

Parity check for group A = $0 \oplus 1 \oplus 0 \oplus 1 = 0$
Parity check for group B = $1 \oplus 1 \oplus 1 \oplus 1 = 0$
Parity check for group C = $0 \oplus 1 \oplus 0 \oplus 1 = 0$

Assume that a single-bit error has occurred. If the single-bit error was a parity bit, then exactly one of the parity checks will be one while the others are zero. For example, if P_0 changed from a 0 to a 1, we would get the following parity checks.

196 Computer Organization and Design Fundamentals

Parity check for group A = 1 ⊕ 1 ⊕ 0 ⊕ 1 = 1
Parity check for group B = 1 ⊕ 1 ⊕ 1 ⊕ 1 = 0
Parity check for group C = 0 ⊕ 1 ⊕ 0 ⊕ 1 = 0

The single parity bit error reveals itself as a single parity check outputting a 1. If, however, a data bit changed, then we have more than one parity check resulting in a 1. Assume, for example, that D_1 changed from a 1 to a 0.

Parity check for group A = 0 ⊕ 0 ⊕ 0 ⊕ 1 = 1
Parity check for group B = 1 ⊕ 1 ⊕ 0 ⊕ 1 = 1
Parity check for group C = 0 ⊕ 1 ⊕ 0 ⊕ 1 = 0

Since D_1 is the only bit that belongs to both the parity check of groups A and B, then D_1 must have been the one to have changed.

Using this information, we can go to the eight data bit example. With four parity bits, we know that there will be four parity check equations, each of which will have a parity bit that is unique to it.

Parity check A = P_0 ⊕ (XOR of data bits of group A)
Parity check B = P_1 ⊕ (XOR of data bits of group B)
Parity check C = P_2 ⊕ (XOR of data bits of group C)
Parity check D = P_3 ⊕ (XOR of data bits of group D)

The next step is to figure out which data bits, D_0 through D_7, belong to which groups. Each data bit must have a unique membership pattern so that if the bit changes, its parity check will result in a unique pattern of parity check errors. Note that all of the data bits must belong to at least two groups to avoid an error with that bit looking like an error with the parity bit.

Table 9-10 shows one way to group the bits in the different parity check equations or groups. It is not the only way to group them.

By using the grouping presented in Table 9-10, we can complete our four parity check equations.

Parity check A = P_0 ⊕ D_0 ⊕ D_1 ⊕ D_3 ⊕ D_4 ⊕ D_6	(9.5)
Parity check B = P_1 ⊕ D_0 ⊕ D_2 ⊕ D_3 ⊕ D_5 ⊕ D_6	(9.6)
Parity check C = P_2 ⊕ D_1 ⊕ D_2 ⊕ D_3 ⊕ D_7	(9.7)
Parity check D = P_3 ⊕ D_4 ⊕ D_5 ⊕ D_6 ⊕ D_7	(9.8)

Chapter 9: Binary Operation Applications 197

Table 9-10 Membership of Data and Parity Bits in Parity Groups

	Parity check group			
	A	B	C	D
P_0	×			
P_1		×		
P_2			×	
P_3				×
D_0	×	×		
D_1	×		×	
D_2		×	×	
D_3	×	×	×	
D_4	×			×
D_5		×		×
D_6	×	×		×
D_7			×	×

When it comes time to store the data, we will need 12 bits, eight for the data and four for the parity bits. But how do we calculate the parity bits? Remember that the parity check must always equal zero. Therefore, the sum of the data bits of each parity group with the parity bit must be an even number. Therefore, if the sum of the data bits by themselves is an odd number, the parity bit must equal a 1, and if the sum of the data bits by themselves is an even number, the parity bit must equal a 0. This sounds just like the XOR function again. Therefore, we use equations 9.9, 9.10, 9.11, and 9.12 to calculate the parity bits before storing them.

$$P_0 = D_0 \oplus D_1 \oplus D_3 \oplus D_4 \oplus D_6 \quad (9.9)$$
$$P_1 = D_0 \oplus D_2 \oplus D_3 \oplus D_5 \oplus D_6 \quad (9.10)$$
$$P_2 = D_1 \oplus D_2 \oplus D_3 \oplus D_7 \quad (9.11)$$
$$P_3 = D_4 \oplus D_5 \oplus D_6 \oplus D_7 \quad (9.12)$$

Now let's test the system. Assume we need to store the data 10011100_2. This gives us the following values for our data bits:

$D_7 = 1 \quad D_6 = 0 \quad D_5 = 0 \quad D_4 = 1 \quad D_3 = 1 \quad D_2 = 1 \quad D_1 = 0 \quad D_0 = 0$

The first step is to calculate our parity bits. Using equations 9.9, 9.10, 9.11, and 9.12 we get the following values.

$$P_0 = 0 \oplus 0 \oplus 1 \oplus 1 \oplus 0 = 0$$
$$P_1 = 0 \oplus 1 \oplus 1 \oplus 0 \oplus 0 = 0$$
$$P_2 = 0 \oplus 1 \oplus 1 \oplus 1 = 1$$
$$P_3 = 1 \oplus 0 \oplus 0 \oplus 1 = 0$$

Once again, the XOR is really just a parity check. Therefore, if there is an odd number of ones, the result is 1 and if there is an even number of ones, the result is 0.

Now that the parity bits have been calculated, the data and parity bits can be stored together. This means that memory will contain the following value:

D_7	D_6	D_5	D_4	D_3	D_2	D_1	D_0	P_0	P_1	P_2	P_3
1	0	0	1	1	1	0	0	0	0	1	0

If our data is error free, then when we read it and substitute the values for the data and parity bits into our parity check equations, all four results should equal zero.

Parity check A = $0 \oplus 0 \oplus 0 \oplus 1 \oplus 1 \oplus 0 = 0$
Parity check B = $0 \oplus 0 \oplus 1 \oplus 1 \oplus 0 \oplus 0 = 0$
Parity check C = $1 \oplus 0 \oplus 1 \oplus 1 \oplus 1 = 0$
Parity check D = $0 \oplus 1 \oplus 0 \oplus 0 \oplus 1 = 0$

If, however, while the data was stored in memory, it incurs a single-bit error, e.g., bit D_6 flips from a 0 to a 1, then we should be able to detect it. If D_6 does flip, the value shown below is what will be read from memory, and until the processor checks the parity, we don't know that anything is wrong with it.

D_7	D_6	D_5	D_4	D_3	D_2	D_1	D_0	P_0	P_1	P_2	P_3
1	1	0	1	1	1	0	0	0	0	1	0

Start by substituting the values for the data and parity bits read from memory into our parity check equations. Computing the parity for all four groups shows that an error has occurred.

Parity check A = 0 ⊕ 0 ⊕ 0 ⊕ 1 ⊕ 1 ⊕ 1 = 1
Parity check B = 0 ⊕ 0 ⊕ 1 ⊕ 1 ⊕ 0 ⊕ 1 = 1
Parity check C = 1 ⊕ 0 ⊕ 1 ⊕ 1 ⊕ 1 = 0
Parity check D = 0 ⊕ 1 ⊕ 0 ⊕ 1 ⊕ 1 = 1

Since we see from Table 9-10 that the only bit that belongs to parity check groups A, B, and D is D_6, then we know that D_6 has flipped and we need to invert it to return to our original value.

The same problem appears here as it did in the nibble case if there are two bit errors. It is solved here the same way as it was for the nibble application. By adding a parity bit representing the parity of all twelve data and parity bits, then if one of the group parities is wrong but the overall parity is correct, we know that a double-bit error has occurred and correction is not possible.

9.7 What's Next?

In this chapter we've discussed how to correct errors that might occur in memory without having discussed the technologies used to store data. Chapter 10 begins our discussion of storing data by examining the memory cell, a logic element capable of storing a single bit of data.

Problems

1. Using an original value of 11000011_2 and a mask of 00001111_2, calculate the results of a bitwise AND, a bitwise OR, and a bitwise XOR for these values.

2. Assume that the indicators of an automotive dashboard are controlled by an 8-bit binary value named *dash_lights*. The table below describes the function of each bit. Assume that a '1' turns on the light corresponding to that bit position and a '0' turns it off.

   D_0 Low fuel D_4 Left turn signal
   D_1 Oil pressure D_5 Right turn signal
   D_2 High temperature D_6 Brake light
   D_3 Check engine D_7 Door open

   For each of the following situations, write the line of code that uses a bitwise operation to get the desired outcome.

a.) Turn on the low fuel, oil pressure, high temperature, check engine, and brake lights without affecting any other lights. This would be done when the ignition key is turned to start.
b.) Toggle both the right and left turn signals as if the flashers were on without affecting any other lights.
c.) Turn off the door open light when the door is closed.

3. True or False: A checksum changes if the data within the data block is sorted differently.

4. There are two ways of handling the carries that occur when generating the datasum for a checksum. One way is to simply discard all carries. What is the other way? (2 points)

5. Compute the basic checksum, the 1's complement checksum, and the 2's complement checksum for each of the following groups of 8-bit data elements using both the basic calculation of the datasum and the one's complement datasum. All data is in hexadecimal.

   a.) 34, 9A, FC, 28, 74, 45
   b.) 88, 65, 8A, FC, AC, 23, DC, 63
   c.) 00, 34, 54, 23, 5C, F8, F1, 3A, 34

6. Use the checksum to verify each of the following groups of 8-bit data elements. All of the data is represented in hexadecimal.

   a.) 54, 47, 82, CF, A9, 43   basic checksum = D8
   b.) 36, CD, 32, CA, CF, A8, 56, 88   basic checksum = 55
   c.) 43, A3, 1F, 8F, C5, 45, 43   basic checksum = E1

7. Identify the two reasons for using the XOR "borrow-less" subtraction in the long-division used to calculate the CRC.

8. What problem does the checksum error correction method have that is solved by using CRCs?

9. True or False: A CRC changes if the data within the data block is sorted differently.

10. True or False: By using the CRC process where the transmitting device appends the remainder to the end of the data stream, the remainder calculated by the receiving device should be zero.

11. How many possible CRC values (i.e., remainders) are possible with a 33-bit polynomial?

12. Assume each of the following streams of bits is received by a device and that each of the streams has appended to it a CRC checksum. Using the polynomial 10111, check to see which of the data streams are error free and which are not.

    a.) 1001011101011001001
    b.) 10110101001011010100100101
    c.) 110101101010101101110110111011

13. Compute the number of parity bits needed to provide single-bit error correction for 256 bits of data.

14. Using the error detection/correction equations 9.5 through 9.8, determine the single-bit error that would result from the following parity check values.

	Results of parity check			
	a.)	b.)	c.)	d.)
Parity check A	1	1	0	1
Parity check B	1	1	0	0
Parity check C	1	0	1	1
Parity check D	0	1	0	0

15. Using the programming language of your choice, implement the parity generating function of the single-bit error correction scheme for eight data bits discussed in this chapter. Use equations 9.9 through 9.12 to generate the parity bits. You may use the C prototype shown below as a starting point where the integer *data* represents the 8 data bits and the returned value will contain the four parity bits in the least significant four positions in the order P_0, P_1, P_2, and P_3.

    ```
    int generateParityBits (int data)
    ```

16. Using the programming language of your choice, implement the parity checking function of the single-bit error correction scheme for eight data bits discussed in this chapter. Use equations 9.5 through 9.8 to verify the data read from memory. You may use the C prototype shown below as a starting point where the integer *data* represents the 8 data bits and the integer *parity* represents the four parity bits in the least significant four positions in the order P_0, P_1, P_2, and P_3. The returned value is the data, unmodified if no error

was detected or corrected if a single-bit error was detected.

```
int generateCorrectedData (int data, parity);
```

17. Determine the set of parity check equations for eight data bits and four parity bits if we use the table to the right in place of the memberships defined by Table 9-10.

	Parity check group			
	A	B	C	D
P_0	×			
P_1		×		
P_2			×	
P_3				×
D_0	×	×		
D_1		×	×	
D_2	×		×	
D_3	×			×
D_4		×		×
D_5	×	×		×
D_6			×	×
D_7	×		×	×

18. Identify the error in the parity check equations below. Note that the expressions are supposed to represent a different grouping than those in equations 9.2, 9.3, and 9.4. There is still an error though with these new groupings.

Parity check for group A = $P_0 \oplus D_0 \oplus D_2 \oplus D_3$
Parity check for group B = $P_1 \oplus D_0 \oplus D_1$
Parity check for group C = $P_2 \oplus D_1 \oplus D_2$

CHAPTER TEN

Memory Cells

The previous chapters presented the concepts and tools behind processing binary data. This is only half of the battle though. For example, a logic circuit uses inputs to calculate an output, but where do these inputs come from? Some of them come from switches and other hardwired inputs, but many times a processor uses signals it has stored from previous operations. This might be as simple as adding a sequence of values one at a time to a running total: the running total must be stored somewhere so that it can be sent back to the inputs of the adder to be combined with the next value.

This chapter introduces us to memory by presenting the operation of a single memory cell, a device that is capable of storing a single bit.

10.1 New Truth Table Symbols

The truth tables that represent the operation of memory devices have to include a few new symbols in order to represent the functionality of the devices. For example, a memory cell is capable of storing a binary value, either a one or a zero. A new symbol, however, is needed to represent the stored value since its specific value is known only at the instant of operation.

10.1.1 Edges/Transitions

Many devices use as their input a change in a signal rather than a level of a signal. For example, when you press the "on" button to a computer, it isn't a binary one or zero from the switch that turns on the computer. If this was the case, as soon as you removed your finger, the machine would power off. Instead, the computer begins its power up sequence the instant your finger presses the button, i.e., the button transitions from an off state to an on state.

There are two truth table symbols that represent transitions from one logic value to another. The first represents a change in a binary signal from a zero to a one, i.e., a transition from a low to a high. This transition is called a *rising edge* and it is represented by the symbol ↑. The second symbol represents a transition from a one to a zero. This transition is called a *falling edge* and it is represented by the symbol ↓.

Figure 10-1 presents a binary signal with the points where transitions occur identified with these two new symbols.

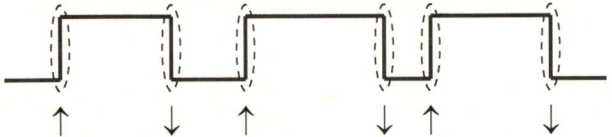

Figure 10-1 Symbols for Rising Edge and Falling Edge Transitions

10.1.2 Previously Stored Values

If a memory cell is powered, it contains a stored value. We don't know whether that value is a one or a zero, but there is something stored in that cell. If a logic circuit uses the stored value of that cell as an input, we need to have a way of labeling it so that it can be used within a boolean expression.

Just as A, B, C, and D are used to represent inputs and X is used to represent an output, a standard letter is used to represent stored values. That letter is Q. To indicate that we are referring to the last value of Q stored, we use Q_0.

10.1.3 Undefined Values

Some circuits have conditions that either are impossible to reach or should be avoided because they might produce unpredictable or even damaging results. In these cases, we wish to indicate that the signal is undefined. We do this with the letter U.

For example, consider the binary circuit that operates the light inside a microwave oven. The inputs to this circuit are a switch to monitor whether the door has been opened and a signal to indicate whether the magnetron is on or off. Note that the magnetron never turns on when the door is opened, so this circuit has an undefined condition.

Door	Magnetron	Light		D	M	L
Closed	Off	Off		0	0	0
Closed	On	On	$\Rightarrow$	0	1	1
Open	Off	On		1	0	1
Open	On	Shouldn't happen		1	1	U

Figure 10-2 Sample Truth Table Using Undefined Output

10.2 The S-R Latch

Computer memory is made from arrays of cells, each of which is capable of storing a single bit, a one or a zero. The goal is to send a logic one or a logic zero to a device, then after leaving it unattended for a period of time, come back and find the value still there. A simple wire alone cannot do this. A digital value placed on a wire will, after the value is removed, quickly loose the charge and vanish.

Early memory stored data in small doughnut shaped rings of iron. Wires that were woven through the centers of the iron rings were capable of magnetizing the rings in one of two directions. If each ring was allowed to represent a bit, then one direction of magnetization would represent a one while the other represented a zero. As long as nothing disturbed the magnetization, the value of the stored bit could be detected later using the same wires that stored the original value.

With the advent of digital circuitry, the magnetic material was replaced with gates. A circuit could be developed where the output could be routed back around to the circuit's inputs in order to maintain the stored value. This "ring" provided feedback which allowed the circuit's current data to drive the circuit's future data and thus maintain its condition. The circuit in Figure 10-3 is a simple example of this.

The output of the first inverter in the circuit of Figure 10-3 is fed into the input of a second inverter. Since the inverse of an inverse is the original value, the input to the first inverter is equal to the output of the second inverter. If we connect the output of the second inverter to the input of the first inverter, then the logic value will be maintained until power to the circuit is removed.

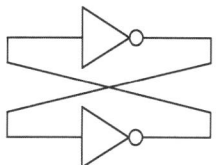

Figure 10-3 Primitive Feedback Circuit using Inverters

The problem with the circuit of Figure 10-3 is that there is no way to modify the value that is stored. We need to replace either one or both of the inverters with a device that has more than one input, but one that can also operate the same way as the inverter during periods when we want the data to be stable. It turns out that the NAND gate can do this.

Figure 10-4 presents the truth table for the NAND gate where one of the inputs is always connected to a one.

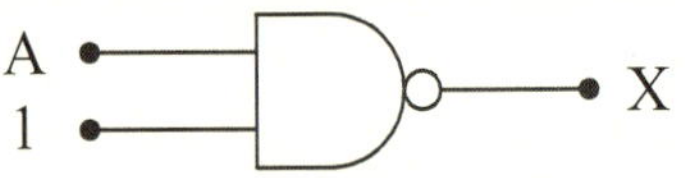

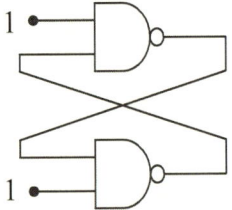

A	1	X
0	1	1
1	1	0

Figure 10-4   Operation of a NAND Gate with One Input Tied High

Notice that the output X is always the inverse of the input A. The NAND gate operates just like an inverter with a second input. Figure 10-5 replaces the inverters of Figure 10-3 with NAND gates.

Figure 10-5   Primitive Feedback Circuit Redrawn with NAND Gates

As long as the free inputs to the two NAND gates remain equal to one, the circuit will remain stable since it is acting as a pair of inverters connected together in series. It is also important to note that if the top inverter outputs a zero, the bottom inverter outputs a one. Likewise, if a one is output from the top inverter, then a zero is output from the bottom one. These two possible states are shown in Figure 10-6.

Figure 10-6   Only Two Possible States of Circuit in Figure 10-5

What happens if we change the free input of either NAND gate? Remember that if either input to a NAND gate is a zero, then the output is forced to be a 1 regardless of the other input. That means that if a

Chapter 10: Memory Cells   207

zero is placed on the free input of the top NAND gate, then the output of that NAND gate is forced to one. That one is routed back to the input of the lower NAND gate where the other input is one. A NAND gate with all of its inputs set to one has an output of zero. That zero is routed back to the input of the top NAND gate whose other input is a zero. A NAND gate with all of its inputs set to zero has an output of one. This means that the system has achieved a stable state.

If the free input of the top NAND gate returns to a one, the zero input to it from the lower NAND gate makes it so that there is no change to the one currently being output from it. In other words, returning the free input of the top NAND gate back to a one does not change the output of the circuit. These steps are represented graphically in the circuit diagrams of Figure 10-7.

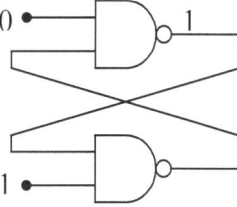

a.) A zero to the free input of the top NAND gate forces a one to its output

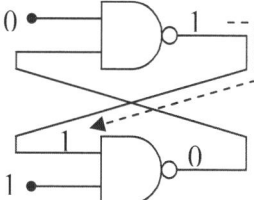

b.) That one passes to the bottom NAND which in turn outputs a zero

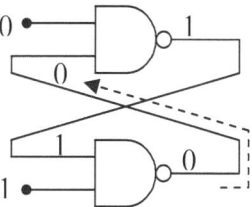

c.) A zero from the bottom NAND returns to the lower input of the top NAND

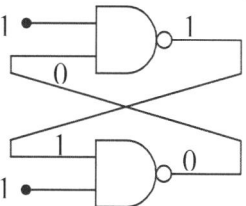

d.) The second zero at the top NAND holds its output even if the free input returns to 1

Figure 10-7 Operation of a Simple Memory Cell

This means that the circuit can be used to store a one in the top NAND gate and a zero in the bottom NAND gate by toggling the free input on the top NAND gate from a one to a zero and back to a one. Figure 10-8 shows what happens when we toggle the free input on the bottom NAND gate from a one to a zero and back to a one.

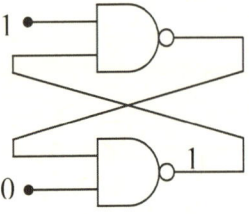

a.) A zero to the free input of the bottom NAND gate forces a one to its output

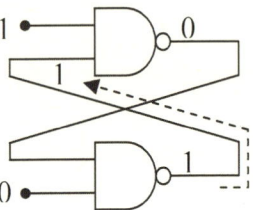

b.) That one passes to the top NAND which in turn outputs a zero

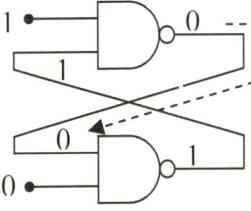

c.) A zero from the top NAND returns to the lower input of the bottom NAND

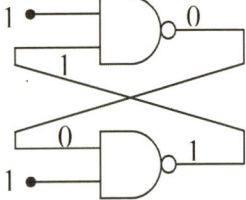

d.) The second zero at the bottom NAND holds its output even if the free input returns to 1

Figure 10-8 Operation of a Simple Memory Cell (continued)

This NAND gate circuit represents the basic circuit used to store a single bit using logic gates. Notice that in step d of both figures the circuit is stable with the opposing NAND gates outputting values that are inverses of each other. In addition, notice that the circuit's output is changed by placing a zero on the free input of one of the NAND gates.

Figure 10-9 presents the standard form of this circuit with the inputs labeled $\overline{S}$ and $\overline{R}$ and the outputs labeled Q and $\overline{Q}$. The bars placed over the inputs indicate that they are active low inputs while the bar over one of the outputs indicates that it is an inverted value of Q.

This circuit is referred to as the *S-R latch*. The output Q is *set* to a one if the $\overline{S}$ input goes low while $\overline{R}$ stays high. The output Q is *reset* to a zero if the $\overline{R}$ input goes low while $\overline{S}$ stays high. If both of these inputs are high, i.e., logic one, then the circuit maintains the current value of Q. The truth table for the S-R latch is shown in Figure 10-10.

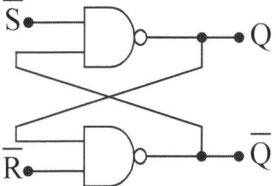

$\overline{S}$	$\overline{R}$	Q	$\overline{Q}$
0	0	U	U
0	1	1	0
1	0	0	1
1	1	Q_0	$\overline{Q_0}$

Figure 10-9 S-R Latch   **Figure 10-10** S-R Latch Truth Table

Notice that the row of the truth table where both inputs equal zero produces an undefined output. Actually, the output is defined: both Q and its inverse are equal to one. What makes this case undefined is that when both of the inputs return to one, the output of the system becomes unpredictable, and possibly unstable. It is for this reason that the top row of this truth table is considered illegal and is to be avoided for any implementation of the S-R latch circuit.

10.3 The D Latch

The S-R latch is presented here to show how latches store data. In general, every logic gate-based memory device has an S-R latch embedded in it. For the rest of this book, we will be treating latches as "black boxes" addressing only the inputs and how they affect Q.

The typical data storage latch is referred to as a data latch or a ***D latch***. There are slight variations between different implementations of the D latch, but in general, every D latch uses the same basic inputs and outputs. Figure 10-11 presents the block diagram of a fully implemented D-latch.

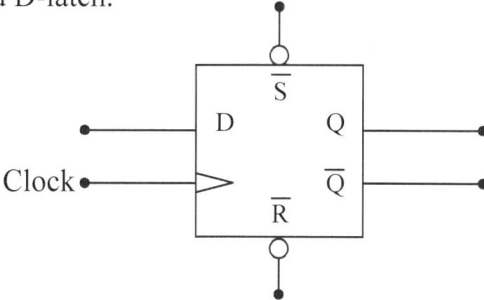

Figure 10-11 Block Diagram of the D Latch

The outputs Q and $\overline{Q}$ operate just as they did for the S-R latch outputting the stored data and its inverse. The active low inputs $\overline{S}$ and $\overline{R}$ also operate the same as they did for the S-R latch. If $\overline{S}$ goes low while $\overline{R}$ is held high, the output Q is set to a one. If $\overline{R}$ goes low while $\overline{S}$ is held high, the output Q is reset to zero. If both $\overline{S}$ and $\overline{R}$ are high, then Q maintains the data bit it was last storing. The output of the circuit is undefined for both $\overline{S}$ and $\overline{R}$ low.

The two new inputs, D and Clock, allow the circuit to specify the data being stored in Q. D, sometimes called the data input, is the binary value that we wish to store in Q. Clock tells the circuit when the data is to be stored.

This circuit acts much like a camera. Just because a camera is pointing at something does not mean that it is storing that image. The only way the image is going to be captured is if someone presses the button activating the shutter. Once the shutter is opened, the image is captured. The Clock input acts like the button on the camera. A specific transition or level of the binary value at the Clock input captures the binary value present at the D input and stores it to Q.

There is another characteristic of taking a picture with a camera that has an analogy with the storage of data in a D latch. Assume for a moment that we are talking about cameras that use film instead of digital media to store an image. If the camera's shutter is opened thus exposing the film to light for the entire time the user's finger was pressing the button, then every picture would be over exposed. The shutter should just open for an instant, typically, the instant that the user's finger is coming down on the button.

Alternatively, if the shutter was activated when the user's finger came up instead of down on the button, a number of good shots might be missed thus frustrating the user. It is important to define specifically when the image is captured with regards to the button.

Different implementations of the D latch use different definitions of when the data is captured with respect to Clock. Some operate like cameras do only capturing data when the Clock signal transitions, either rising edge or falling edge. These D latches are referred to as *edge-triggered latches*. The instant the D latch detects the appropriate transition, the binary value that is present at the input D is copied to Q. The data will remain at Q until the next appropriate transition. The truth tables in Figure 10-12 show how the inputs Clock and D of both the rising and falling edge-triggered latches affect the data stored at Q.

D	Clock	Q	$\overline{Q}$
X	0	Q_0	$\overline{Q_0}$
X	1	Q_0	$\overline{Q_0}$
X	↓	Q_0	$\overline{Q_0}$
0	↑	0	1
1	↑	1	0

a.) Rising Edge

D	Clock	Q	$\overline{Q}$
X	0	Q_0	$\overline{Q_0}$
X	1	Q_0	$\overline{Q_0}$
X	↑	Q_0	$\overline{Q_0}$
0	↓	0	1
1	↓	1	0

b.) Falling Edge

Figure 10-12 Edge-Triggered D Latch Truth Tables

Notice that the value on D does not affect the output if the Clock input is stable, nor does it have an effect during the clock transition other than the one for which it was defined. During these periods, the values stored at the latch's outputs remain set to the values stored there from a previous data capture.

D latches can also be designed to capture data during a specified level on the Clock signal rather than a transition. These are called *transparent latches*. They latch data much like an edge triggered latch, but while Clock is at the logic level previous to the transition, they pass all data directly from the D input to the Q output. For example, when a zero is input to the Clock input of a D latch designed to capture data when Clock equals zero, the latch appears to vanish, passing the signal D straight to Q. The last value present on D when the Clock switches from zero to one is stored on the output until Clock goes back to zero. Figure 10-13 presents this behavior using truth tables for both the active low and active high transparent D latches.

D	Clock	Q	$\overline{Q}$
X	1	Q_0	$\overline{Q_0}$
0	0	0	1
1	0	1	0

a.) Active Low

D	Clock	Q	$\overline{Q}$
X	0	Q_0	$\overline{Q_0}$
0	1	0	1
1	1	1	0

b.) Active High

Figure 10-13 Transparent D Latch Truth Tables

A transparent D latch acts like a door. If Clock is at the level that captures data to the output, i.e., the door is open, any signal changes on the D input pass through to the output. Once Clock goes to the opposite level, the last value in Q is maintained in Q.

The rest of this chapter presents some applications of latches including processor support circuitry, I/O circuits, and memory.

10.4 Divide-By-Two Circuit

In some cases, the frequency of a clock input on a circuit board is too fast for some of the computer's peripherals. An edge-triggered D latch can be used to divide a clock frequency in half. The circuit presented in Figure 10-14 does this.

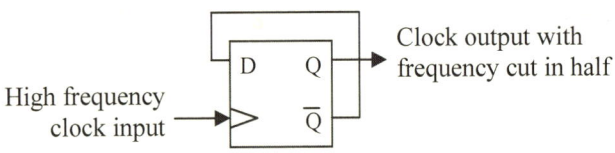

Figure 10-14   Divide-By-Two Circuit

Assume, for example, that we are using a rising edge-triggered latch for this circuit. By connecting the inverse of the Q output to the D input, the output Q is inverted or toggled every time the clock goes from a zero to a one. Since there is only one rising edge for a full cycle of a periodic signal, it takes two cycles to make the output Q go through a full cycle. This means that the frequency of the output Q is one half that of the input frequency at the clock input. Figure 10-15 presents a timing diagram of this behavior.

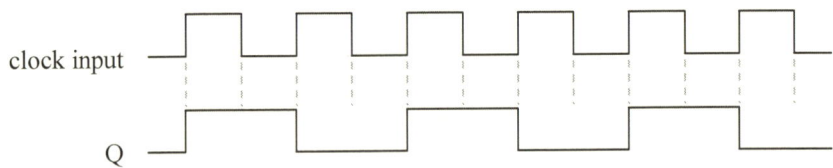

Figure 10-15   Clock and Output Timing in a Divide-By-Two Circuit

By cascading multiple divide-by-two circuits, we get divisions of the original frequency by 2, 4, 8, ... , 2^n as shown in Figure 10-16.

Chapter 10: Memory Cells   213

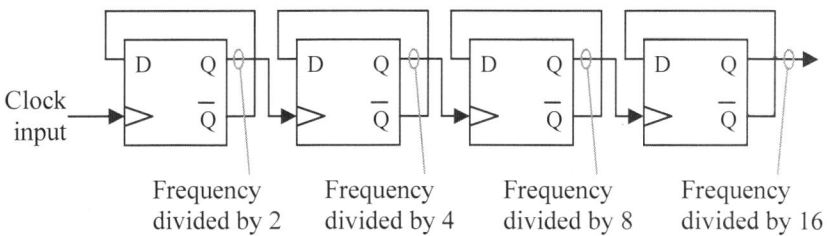

Figure 10-16   Cascading Four Divide-By-Two Circuits

10.5 Counter

By making a slight modification to the cascaded divide-by-two circuits of Figure 10-16, we can create a circuit with a new purpose. Figure 10-17 shows the modified circuit created by using the inverted outputs of the latches to drive the Clock inputs of the subsequent latches instead of using the Q outputs to drive them.

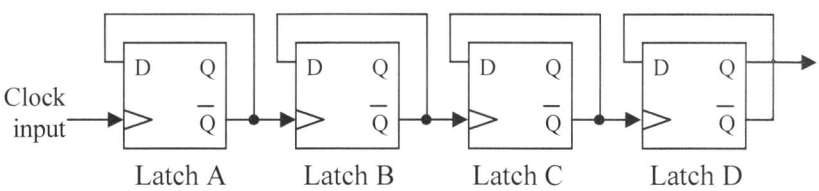

Figure 10-17   Counter Implemented with Divide-By-Two Circuits

If we draw the outputs of all four latches with respect to each other for this new circuit, we see that the resulting ones and zeros from their outputs have a familiar pattern to them, specifically, they are counting in binary.

If the leftmost latch is considered the LSB of a four-bit binary number and the rightmost latch is considered the MSB, then a cycle on the input clock of the leftmost latch will increment the binary number by one. This means that by connecting the inverted output of a divide-by-two circuit to the clock input of a subsequent divide-by-two circuit n times, we can create an n-bit binary counter that counts the pulses on an incoming frequency.

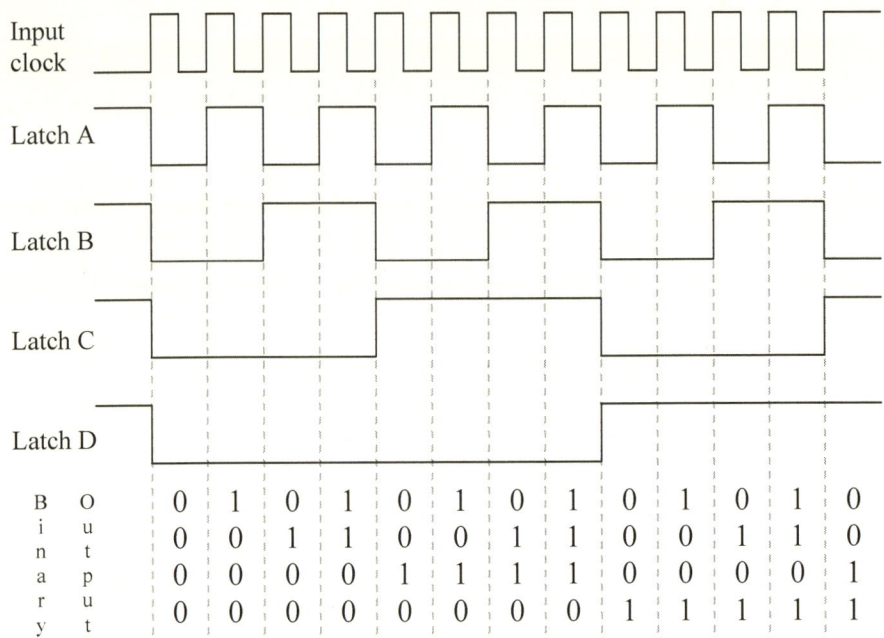

Figure 10-18 Output of Binary Counter Circuit

10.6 Parallel Data Output

Not all binary values stay inside the processor. Sometimes, external circuitry needs to have data sent to it. For example, before the advent of the USB port, computers used a 25-pin connector to transmit data. It was called the *parallel port*, and it was used to send and receive eight bits at a time to a device such as a printer or a storage device.

The processor needed to be able to place data on the eight data bits of this port, then latch it so that the data would remain stable while the processor performed another task. The device connected to the other end of the port could then access the data, and when it was done, alert the processor that it needed additional data. The processor would then latch another byte to the data lines for the external device.

The typical circuit used for the data lines of this port was the D latch. By placing an active-low transparent latch at each output bit, the processor could use the Clock to store data in each latch. This arrangement was so common that IC manufacturers made a single chip that contained all of the latches necessary for the circuit. Figure 10-19 presents that circuit.

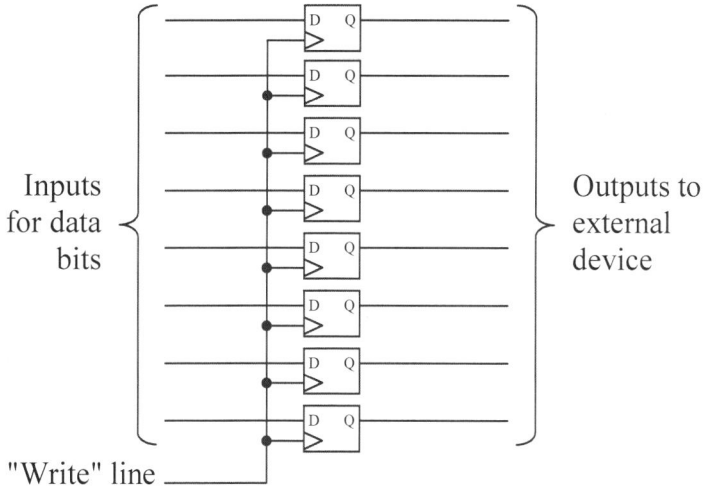

Figure 10-19 Output Port Data Latch Circuitry

By connecting all of the Clocks to a single "write" input, then the processor only needed to place the appropriate data on the data lines and toggle the write line. This would latch the data onto the Q lines of the eight latches where it would remain until the processor placed new data on the data lines and toggled the write line again.

Memory based on logic gates works the same way. To store data, the processor places the data it wants to store onto data lines, then pulses a write signal low then high. This stores the data into latches within the memory circuit.

10.7 What's Next?

The next chapter introduces state machines, the tools that are used to design them, and the circuits that are used to implement them. A state machine is any system that is designed to remember its condition. For example, for a traffic signal to turn yellow, it has to know that it was green. For an elevator to know that it should go down to get to the fifth floor must first know that it is currently on the eighth floor. State machines require memory, and therefore, many of the implementations of state machines use latches.

Problems

1. For the circuit shown to the right, what value does Q have?

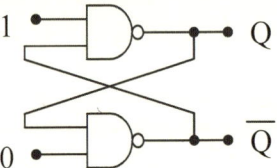

2. Describe why the S-R latch has an illegal condition.

3. Describe the purpose of each of the following truth table symbols.

   a.) ↓	b.) ↑	c.) U	d.) Q_0

4. What is the output Q of a D latch with $\overline{S}=0$, $\overline{R}=1$, $D=1$, and Clock = 0?

5. True or false: A D latch with only two inputs D and CLK has no illegal states.

6. Which of the following circuits is used to divide the frequency of the signal F in half?

   a.) 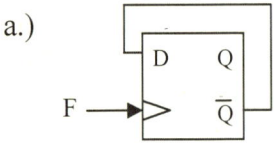   b.)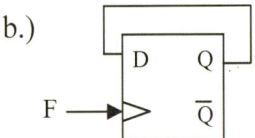

   c.) 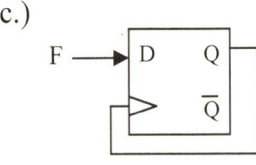   d.)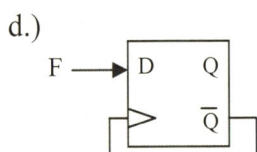

7. Show the D latch output waveform Q based on the inputs $\overline{R}$, D, and Clock indicated in the timing diagram shown to the right. Assume the latch captures on the rising edge.

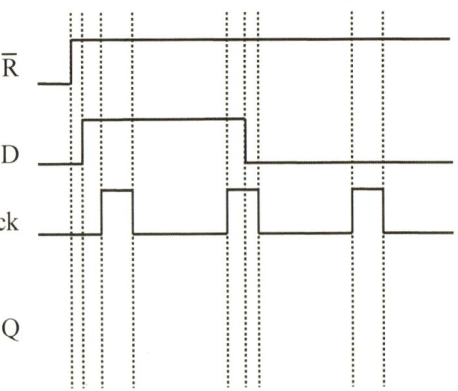

CHAPTER ELEVEN

State Machines

11.1 Introduction to State Machines

Now that Chapter 10 has introduced us to memory cells, we can begin designing circuits that rely on stored values. With a single latch, we can store a one or a zero. By combining latches, we can store larger binary numbers.

Our first design application using these latches will be *state machines*. A state machine is a digital circuit that relies not only on the circuit's inputs, but also the current state of the system to determine the proper output. For example, assume an elevator is stopped on the eighth floor and someone from the fourth floor presses the elevator call button. The elevator needs to decide whether to go up or down. As long as it remembers its current state, i.e., that it is on the eighth floor, it will know that it needs to go down to access the fourth floor.

To remember the current state of a system, memory will have to be added to our circuits. This memory will act as additional inputs to the circuitry used to create the outputs.

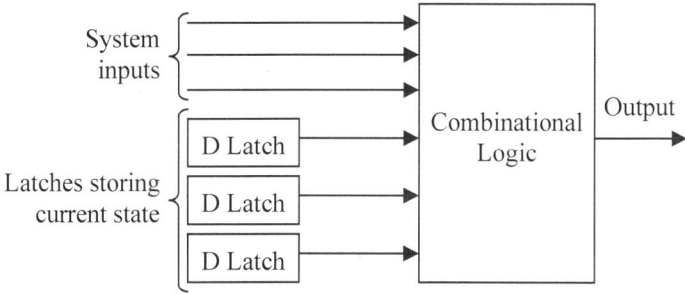

Figure 11-1 Adding Memory to a Digital Logic Circuit

11.1.1 States

So what is a state? A state defines the current condition of a system. It was suggested at the end of Chapter 10 that a traffic signal system is a state machine. The most basic traffic signal controls an intersection with two directions, North-South and East-West for example. There are

217

certain combinations of lights (on or off) that describe the intersection's condition. These are the system's states.

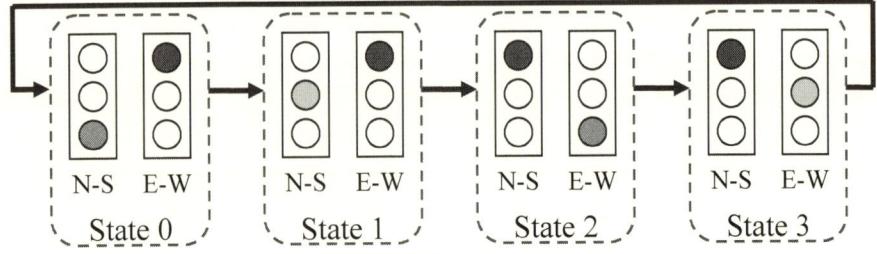

Figure 11-2   States of a Traffic Signal System

A state machine might also be as simple as a light bulb. The light bulb can have two states: on and off. The light switch moves the condition of the bulb from one state to another.

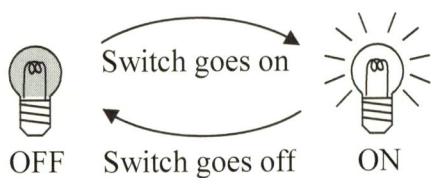

Figure 11-3   States of a Light Bulb

11.1.2 State Diagrams

We will begin our design of state machines by introducing the primary design tool: the ***state diagram***. A state diagram models a state machine by using circles to represent each of the possible states and arrows to represent all of the possible transitions between the states. For example, Figure 11-4 presents the state diagram for the light bulb state machine shown in Figure 11-3.

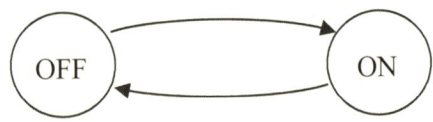

Figure 11-4   State Diagram for Light Bulb State Machine

This state diagram is incomplete. For example, what triggers a change from one state to the other? Even though the words ON and OFF mean something to you, they don't mean much to a computer. We need to include the boolean output associated with each of the states. Figure 11-5 presents the completed state diagram.

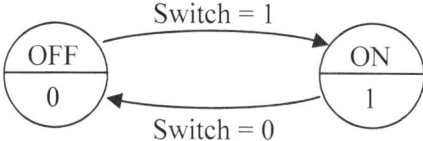

Figure 11-5 Complete State Diagram for Light Bulb State Machine

The upper half of each circle indicates the name of the state. The lower half indicates the binary output associated with that state. In the case of the light bulb state machine, a zero is output while we are in the OFF state and a one is output while we are in the ON state. The arrows along with the input value say that when we are in state OFF and the switch input goes to a 1, move to state ON. When we are in state ON and the switch input goes to a 0, move to state OFF.

Before creating a state diagram, we must define the parameters of the system. We begin with the inputs and outputs. The inputs are vital to the design of the state diagram as their values will be used to dictate state changes. As for the outputs, their values will be determined for each state as we create them.

It is also important to have an idea of what will define our states. For example, what happens to the states of our traffic signal system if we add a crosswalk signal? It turns out that the number of states we have will increase because there will be a difference between the state when the crosswalk indicator says "Walk" and when it flashes "Don't Walk" just before the traffic with the green light gets its yellow.

Here we will introduce an example to illustrate the use of state diagrams. Chapter 10 presented a simple counter circuit that incremented a binary value each time a pulse was detected. What if we wanted to have the option to decrement too? Let's design a state machine that stores a binary value and has as its input a control that determines whether we are incrementing that binary value or decrementing it when a pulse is received.

220   Computer Organization and Design Fundamentals

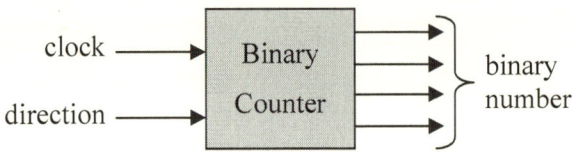

Figure 11-6   Block Diagram of an Up-Down Binary Counter

One of the inputs to this counter is a *clock*. Many state machines have a clock. It is used to drive the system from one state to the next. To do this, it is connected to the clock input of the latches. When a pulse is received, the next state is stored in the latches where it becomes the current state.

The other input to our system is *direction*. The *direction* signal is a binary input telling the system whether the stored value is to be incremented or decremented. Let's make a design decision now and say that when *direction* equals 0 we will be decrementing and when *direction* equals 1 we will be incrementing.

As for the states of our counter, the current state at any time can be represented with the binary number it is outputting. Therefore, the binary number is the state. For example, if the output from a three-bit counter is the binary number 110_2 and a pulse is detected on the *clock* input, the state of the system should change to state 101_2 if *direction* = 0 or state 111_2 if *direction* = 1.

We now have the characteristics of our counter specified well enough for us to begin creating the state diagram for a three-bit up-down counter. This counter has an output that is a three-bit number. Every time a clock pulse occurs, the counter will change state to either increment or decrement the output depending on the value of *direction*. For example, if *direction* equals one, then each clock pulse will increment the output through the sequence 000, 001, 010, 011, 100, 101, 110, 111, 000, 001, etc. If *direction* equals zero, then the output will decrement once for each clock pulse, i.e., 000, 111, 110, 101, 100, 011, 010, 001, 000, 111, 001, etc.

Figure 11-7 presents the state diagram for our system using the binary value to identify the states and the letter D to represent the input *direction*.

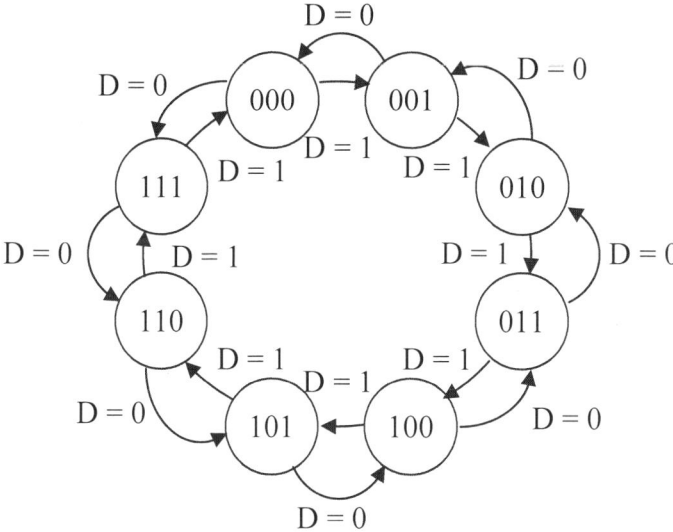

Figure 11-7 State Diagram for a 3-Bit Up-Down Binary Counter

In Figure 11-7, the arrows going clockwise around the inside of the diagram represent the progression through the states at each clock pulse when *direction* equals 1. Notice that each pulse from *clock* should take us to the next highest three-bit value. The arrows going counter-clockwise around the outside of the diagram represent the progression through the states at each clock pulse when *direction* equals zero.

There is an additional detail that must be represented with a state diagram. When a system first powers up, it should be initialized to a reset state. We need to indicate on the diagram which state is defined as the initial state. For example, the up-down counter may be initialized to the state 000_2 when it is first powered up. The state diagram represents this by drawing an arrow to the initial state with the word "reset" printed next to it. A portion of Figure 11-7 is reproduced in Figure 11-8 showing the reset condition.

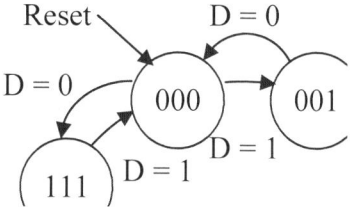

Figure 11-8 Sample of a Reset Indication in a State Diagram

11.1.3 Errors in State Diagrams

A state diagram must fully describe the operation of a state machine. It is for this reason that we need to watch for any missing or redundant information. Possible errors include the following situations.

- Any state other than an initial state that has no transitions going *into* it should be removed since it is impossible to reach that state.
- For a system with n inputs, there should be exactly 2^n transitions coming *out* of every state, one for each pattern of ones and zeros for the n inputs. Some transitions may come back to the current state, but every input must be accounted for. Missing transitions should be added while duplicates should be removed.

The following example shows how some of these errors might appear.

Example

Identify the errors in the following state diagram.

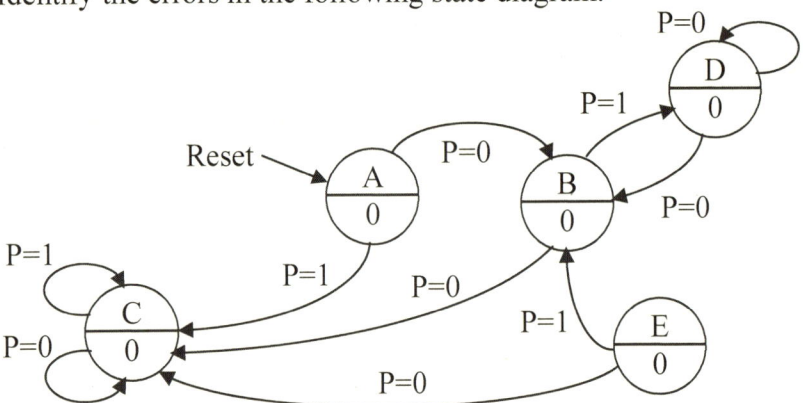

Solution

Error 1 – There is no way to get to state E. It should be removed. Although state A has no transitions to it, it is not a problem because it is the initial state.

Error 2 – The transition from state D for P=0 is defined twice while the transition for P=1 is never defined.

11.1.4 Basic Circuit Organization

From the state diagram, we can begin implementing the state machine. Figure 11-1 only revealed a portion of the organization of a state machine. Figure 11-9 presents a more accurate diagram of the state machine circuitry. The current state is contained in the latches while a block of logic is used to determine the next state from the current state and the external inputs. A second block of logic determines the system output from the current state.

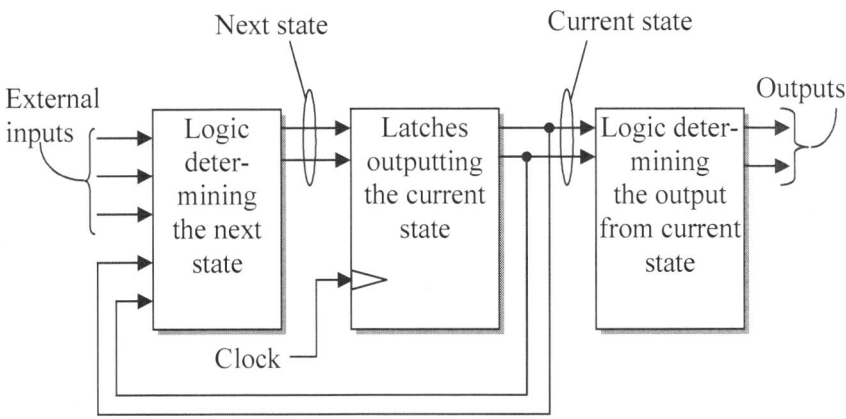

Figure 11-9 Block Diagram of a State Machine

There is a step-by-step process we will present here to design each block of logic. Although the three main pieces are connected, the design of the state machine involves three rather independent designs.

Let's begin with the latches, the center block of the block diagram of Figure 11-9. This component of the system consists only of one or more D latches, the combined outputs of which represent the current state of the state machine. The inputs to the latches represent what the next state would be if the clock were to pulse at that particular moment.

The number of latches in this portion of the circuit is based on the number of states the system can have. If, for example, a state diagram showed ten states for a system, then we would have to have enough latches so that their outputs, Q, could represent at least ten different patterns of ones and zeros. By numbering the ten states in binary, 0, 1, 10, 11, 100, 101, 110, 111, 1000, 1001, we see that we will need at least four latches, the number of digits it takes to represent the highest value, 1001.

The latches are labeled S_n where n represents the bit position of the number stored in that latch. For example, if a set of four latches stored the binary value 1101_2 indicating that the state machine was currently in state $1101_2 = 13_{10}$, then latch S_0 contains a 1, latch S_1 contains a 0, latch S_2 contains a 1, and latch S_3 contains a 1.

The D inputs serve to hold the binary value of the next state that the latches, and hence the state machine, will be set to. When a clock pulse occurs, the next state is stored in the latches making it the current state.

The leftmost block in the block diagram of Figure 11-9 represents the digital logic used to determine the next state of the system. It determines this from the inputs to the system and the current state of the system. We will use the state diagram to construct a truth table describing the operation of this block of logic.

The rightmost block in the block diagram of Figure 11-9 represents the digital logic used to determine the output of the system based on its current state. The state diagrams presented here have an output associated with each state. From this information, a truth table is developed which can be used to determine the output logic.

Example

The block diagram below represents a state machine. Answer the following questions based on the state machine's components and the digital values present on each of the connections.

- What is the maximum number of states this system could have?
- How many rows are in the truth table defining the output?
- How many rows are in the truth table defining the next state?
- What is the current state of this system?
- If the clock were to pulse right now, what would the next state be?

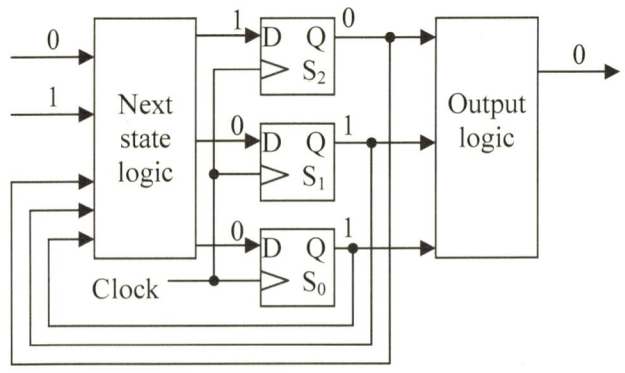

Solution

What is the maximum number of states this system could have? Since the system has 3 latches, then the numbers 000_2, 001_2, 010_2, 011_2, 100_2, 101_2, 110_2, and 111_2 can be stored. Therefore, this state machine can have up to **eight states**.

How many rows are in the truth table defining the output? Since the output is based on the current state which is represented by the latches, and since there are three latches, the logic circuit for the output has three inputs. With three inputs, there are $2^3 = 8$ possible patterns of ones and zeros into the circuit, and hence, **8 rows** in the truth table.

How many rows are in the truth table defining the next state? Since the next state of the state machine, i.e., the value on the input lines to the latches, depends on the current state fed back into the next state logic and the system inputs, then there are five inputs that determine the next state. Therefore, the inputs to the next state logic have $2^5 = 32$ possible patterns of ones and zeros. This means that the next state logic truth table has **32 rows**.

What is the current state of this system? The current state equals the binary value stored in the latches. Remembering that S_0 is the LSB while S_2 is the MSB, this means that the current state is $\mathbf{011_2 = 3_{10}}$.

If the clock were to pulse right now, what would the next state be? The next state is the binary value that is present at the D inputs to the latches. Once again, S_0 is the LSB and S_2 is the MSB. Therefore, the next state is $\mathbf{100_2 = 4_{10}}$.

11.2 State Machine Design Process

This section presents the state machine design process by taking an example through each of the design steps. The example we will be using is a push button circuit used to control a light bulb. When the button is pressed, the light bulb turns on. When the button is released, it stays on. Pushing the button a second time turns off the bulb, and the bulb stays off when the button is released.

First, let's define the system. It has a single input, i.e., the button. We will label this input 'B' and assume that when B = 0 the button is released and when B = 1 the button is pressed. The system has a single output, the light bulb. We will label this output 'L' and assume that L = 0 turns off the light and L = 1 turns on the light.

226 Computer Organization and Design Fundamentals

Now let's design the state diagram. We begin by assuming that the reset state has the light bulb off (L = 0) with the user's finger off of the button. Figure 11-10 presents this initial state labeled as state 0.

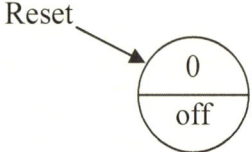

Figure 11-10 Initial State of the Push Button Light Control

The fact that we selected an initial state with the light bulb off might be clear, but it might not be clear why we added the condition that the user's finger is not touching the button. As we go through the design, we will see how the transitions between states depend on whether the button is currently pressed or released. This means that the condition of the button directly affects the state of the system.

So where do we go from this initial state? Well, when a clock pulse occurs, the decision of which state to go to from state 0 depends on the inputs to the system, namely whether the button is pressed (B=1) or released (B=0). Since the button has two possible conditions, then there will be two possible transitions out of state 0. Figure 11-11 shows how these transitions exit state 0 as arrows.

Each of these transitions must pass to a state, so the next step is to determine which state each transition goes to. To do this, we either need to create a new state or have the transition return to state 0.

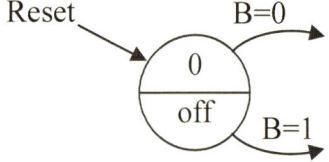

Figure 11-11 Transitions from State 0 of Push Button Circuit

If B=0, the button is not pressed and the light should stay off. We need to pass to a state that represents the condition that the light is off and the button is released. It just so happens that this is the same as the initial state, so the transition for B=0 should just return to state 0.

Chapter 11: State Machines   227

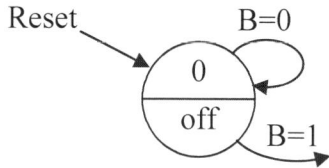

Figure 11-12   B=0 Transition from State 0 of Push Button Circuit

When the button is pressed, the light should come on. Therefore, the transition for B=1 should pass to a state where the light is on and the button is pressed. We don't have this state in our diagram, so we need to add it.

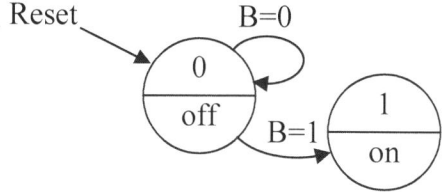

Figure 11-13   B=1 Transition from State 0 of Push Button Circuit

At this point, we have defined all of the transitions out of state 0. In the process, however, we created a new state. We now need to define all of the transitions for the input B for this new state.

If B=0 at the next clock pulse, then the button has been released. Going back to the original definition of the system, we see that if the button is pressed to turn on the light and then it is released, the light should stay on. Therefore, the transition out of state 1 for B=0 should go to a state where the light is on, but the button is released. We don't have this state, so we will need to make it. We will name it state 2.

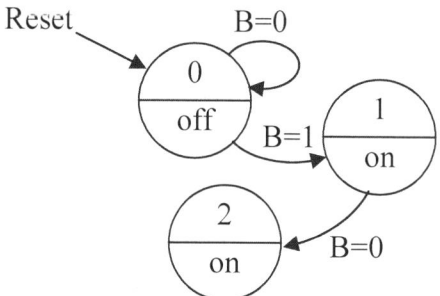

Figure 11-14   B=0 Transition from State 1 of Push Button Circuit

Going back to state 1, if the user's finger is still on the button (B=1) at the next clock pulse, then the light needs to remain on. We therefore need to go to a state where the button is pressed and the light is on. This is state 1, so the transition for B=1 needs to loop back into state 1.

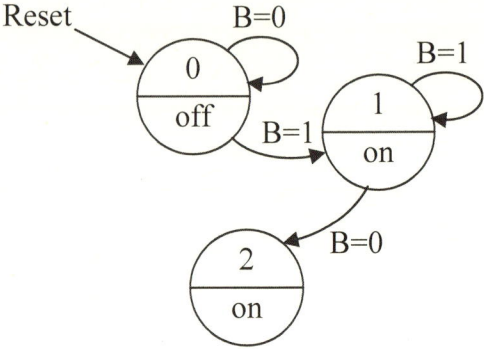

Figure 11-15 B=1 Transition from State 1 of Push Button Circuit

Now that all of the transitions from state 1 have been defined, we need to begin defining the transitions from state 2. If B=0, the button has not been pressed and the current state must be maintained. If the button is pressed, the light is supposed to turn off. Therefore, we need to pass to a state where the light is off and the button is pressed. This state doesn't exist, so we need to create state 3.

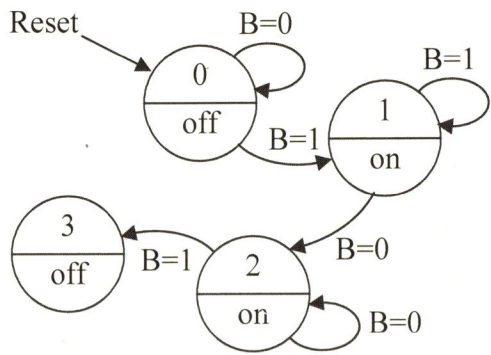

Figure 11-16 Transitions from State 2 of Push Button Circuit

As you can see, each time we create a new state, we need to add the transitions for both B=0 and B=1 to it. This will continue until the addition of all the transitions does not create any new states. The last

Chapter 11: State Machines   229

step added state 3 so we need to add the transitions for it. If B=0, then the button has been released, and we need to move to a state where the button is released and the light bulb is off. This is state 0. If B=1, then the button is still pressed and the bulb should remain off. This is state 3. Since we didn't create any new states, then the state diagram in Figure 11-17 should be the final state diagram for the system.

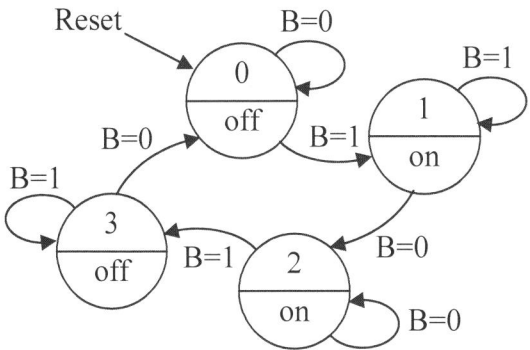

Figure 11-17 Final State Diagram for Push Button Circuit

At this point, there are a couple of items to note. First, as each state was created, it was assigned a number beginning with state 0 for the initial state. The order in which the states are numbered is not important right now. Advanced topics in state machine design examine how the numbering affects the performance of the circuit, but this chapter will not address this issue. It is a good idea not to skip values as doing this may add latches to your design.

The second item to note regards the operation of the state machine. The state diagram shows that to know which state we are going to be transitioning to, we need to know both the current state and the current values on the inputs.

The next step is a minor one, but it is necessary in order to determine the number of latches that will be used in the center block of Figure 11-9. Remember that the latches maintain the current state of the state machine. Each latch acts as a bit for the binary value of the state. For example, if the current state of the system is $2_{10} = 10_2$, then the state machine must have at least two latches, one to hold the '1' and one to hold the '0'. By examining the largest state number, we can determine the minimum number of bits it will take to store the current state. This is why we begin numbering out states at zero.

For our system, the largest state number is $3_{10} = 11_2$. Since 3 takes two bits to represent, then two latches will be needed to store any of the states the system could enter. Table 11-1 presents each of the states along with their numeric value in decimal and binary.

Table 11-1 List of States for Push Button Circuit

State	Numeric Value	
	Decimal	Binary
Bulb off; button released	0	00
Bulb on; button pressed	1	01
Bulb on; button released	2	10
Bulb off; button pressed	3	11

We will label the two bits used to represent these values S_1 and S_0 where S_1 represents the MSB and S_0 represents the LSB. This means, for example, that when $S_1 = 0$ and $S_0 = 1$, the bulb is on and the button is pressed. Each of these bits requires a latch. Using this information, we can begin building the hardware for our state machine.

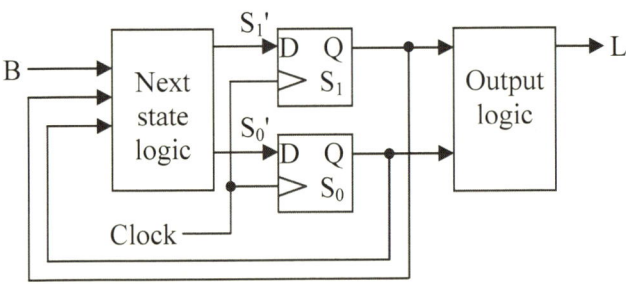

Figure 11-18 Block Diagram for Push Button Circuit

The next step is to develop the truth tables that will be used to create the two blocks of logic on either side of the latches in Figure 11-18. We begin with the "next state logic." The inputs to this logic will be the system input, B, and the current state, S_1 and S_0. The outputs represent the next state that will be loaded into the latches from their D inputs

Chapter 11: State Machines 231

when a clock pulse occurs. These are represented in Figure 11-18 by the signals S_1' and S_0'.

The ***next state truth table*** lists every possible combination of ones and zeros for the inputs which means that every possible state along with every possible system input will be listed. Each one of these rows represents an arrow or a transition on the state diagram. The output columns show the state that the system will be going to if a clock pulse occurs. For example, if the current state of our push button circuit is state 0 ($S_1 = 0$ and $S_0 = 0$) and the input B equals one, then we are going to state 1 ($S_1' = 0$ and $S_0' = 1$). If the current state is state 0 and the input B equals zero, then we are staying in state 0 ($S_1' = 0$ and $S_0' = 0$). Table 11-2 presents the truth table where each transition of the state diagram in Figure 11-17 has been translated to a row.

We also need to create a truth table for the output logic block of Figure 11-18. The output logic produces the correct output based on the current state. This means that the circuit will take as its inputs S_1 and S_0 and produce the system output, L. The truth table is created by looking at the output (the lower half of each circle representing a state), and placing it in the appropriate row of a truth table based on the values of S_1 and S_0. Table 11-3 presents the output truth table.

Table 11-2 Next State Truth Table for Push Button Circuit

S_1	S_0	B	S_1'	S_0'	
0	0	0	0	0	← State 0 stays in state 0 when B=0
0	0	1	0	1	← State 0 goes to state 1 when B=1
0	1	0	1	0	← State 1 goes to state 2 when B=0
0	1	1	0	1	← State 1 stays in state 1 when B=1
1	0	0	1	0	← State 2 stays in state 2 when B=0
1	0	1	1	1	← State 2 goes to state 3 when B=1
1	1	0	0	0	← State 3 goes to state 0 when B=0
1	1	1	1	1	← State 3 stays in state 3 when B=1

Table 11-3 Output Truth Table for Push Button Circuit

S_1	S_0	L	
0	0	0	← State 0: bulb is off
0	1	1	← State 1: bulb is on
1	0	1	← State 2: bulb is on
1	1	0	← State 3: bulb is off

Now that we have our system fully defined using truth tables, we can design the minimum SOP logic using Karnaugh maps. Figure 11-19 presents the Karnaugh maps for the outputs S_1', S_0', and L.

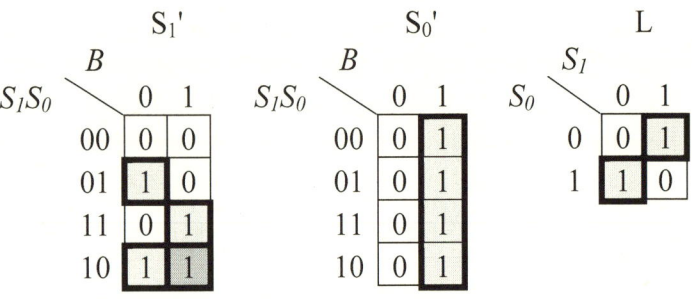

Figure 11-19 K-Maps for S_1', S_0', and L of Push Button Circuit

From these Karnaugh maps, we get the following boolean expressions:

$$S_1' = \overline{S_1} \cdot S_0 \cdot \overline{B} + S_1 \cdot B + S_1 \cdot \overline{S_0}$$

$$S_0' = B$$

$$L = \overline{S_1} \cdot S_0 + S_1 \cdot \overline{S_0} = S_1 \oplus S_0$$

These expressions give us the final implementation of our state machine. By converting the expressions to logic circuits and substituting them for the logic blocks in Figure 11-18, we get the circuit shown in Figure 11-20.

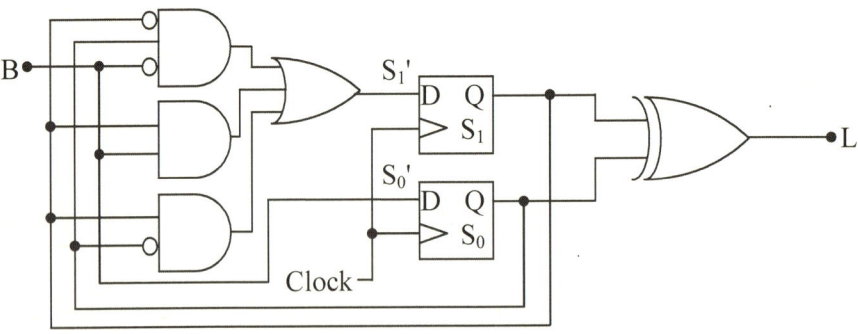

Figure 11-20 Finished Push Button Circuit

Chapter 11: State Machines 233

As was mentioned earlier, the numbering of the states directly affects the logic that results from a design. Let's use our design to see how this might happen. Assume we were to leave everything in the design of our circuit the same except for swapping the numbers for states 2 and 3. Table 11-4 shows the new binary values for our states.

Table 11-4 Revised List of States for Push Button Circuit

State	Numeric Value	
	Decimal	Binary
Bulb off; button released	0	00
Bulb on; button pressed	1	01
Bulb on; button released	3	11
Bulb off; button pressed	2	10

This modification affects all of the logic, but let's only look at how it affects the output logic that drives the signal L. In this case, the light is on in states 1 and 3, but off for states 0 and 2. Figure 11-21 presents the new output truth table and the resulting Karnaugh map.

S_1	S_0	L
0	0	0
0	1	1
1	0	0
1	1	1

S_0 \ S_1:

	0	1
0	0	**1**
1	0	**1**

Figure 11-21 Revised Truth Table and K Map for Push Button Circuit

This gives us a new boolean expression for L.

$$L = S_1$$

The final SOP expression for L with our previous numbering scheme used two AND gates and an OR gate. (This is the way an XOR gate is implemented.) Our new numbering scheme now consists only of a wire connecting the output of S_1 to the light bulb.

11.3 Another State Machine Design: Pattern Detection

A common application for state machines is to watch for a specific binary pattern within a serial data stream. The binary pattern may be used to indicate the start or end of a message or to alert the receiving device that a control sequence is about to come. Figure 11-22 presents a sample binary stream where the binary bit pattern "101" is identified.

1`101`00111`101`100`101`1`10`1`01`0000111`101`101`111001

Figure 11-22 Identifying the Bit Pattern "101" in a Bit Stream

If a clock can be produced that pulses once for each incoming bit, then we can develop a state machine that detects this pattern. The state machine will initially output a zero indicating no pattern match and will continue to output this zero until the full pattern is received. When the full pattern is detected, the state machine will output a 1 for one clock cycle.

The state machine used to detect the bit pattern "101" will have four states, each state representing the number of bits that we have received up to this point that match the pattern: 0, 1, 2, or 3. For example, a string of zeros would indicate that we haven't received any bits for our sequence. The state machine should remain in the state indicating no bits have been received.

If, however, a 1 is received, then it is possible we have received the first bit of the sequence "101". The state machine should move to the state indicating that we might have the first bit. If we receive another 1 while we are in this new state, then we know that the first 1 was not part of the pattern for which we are watching. The second 1, however, might indicate the beginning of the pattern, so we should remain in the state indicating that we might have received the first bit of the pattern. This thought process is repeated for each state.

The list below identifies each of the states along with the states they would transition to based on the input conditions.

- **State 0** – This is the initial state representing the condition that no bits of the sequence have been received. As long as zeros are received, we should remain in this state. Since the first bit of the sequence is a 1, whenever a 1 is received we should move to the state indicating that we *might* have received the first bit.

Chapter 11: State Machines   235

- **State 1** – This state is entered when we have received the first bit of the sequence. Receiving a 0, the second bit of the sequence, should move us to a state indicating that we've received "10". Receiving a 1 means that the last 1 was not part of the sequence, but this new 1 might be, so we should remain in State 1.
- **State 2** – We are in this state when we believe we *might* have the first two bits of the sequence, i.e., we got here after receiving "10". If we receive a 0, then the last three bits we received were "100". Since it is not possible to pull any part of the sequence out of this pattern, we should go back to state 0 indicating none of the sequence has been received. If, however, we receive a 1 while in this state, then the last three bits were "101" and we should go to the state indicating that the first three bits might have been received.
- **State 3** – This is the state we go to when we've received all three bits of the sequence, and therefore, it is the only state where a 1 will be output. If while in this state we receive a 0, then the last four bits we received were "1010". Notice that the last two bits of this sequence are "10" which are the first two bits of the pattern for which we are looking. Therefore, we should go to state 2 indicating that we've received two bits of the sequence. If we receive a 1, then the last four bits we received were "1011". This last 1 could be the first bit of a new pattern of "101", so we should go to state 1.

These states along with the appropriate transitions are presented in Figure 11-23 using the letter 'I' to represent the latest bit received from the input stream.

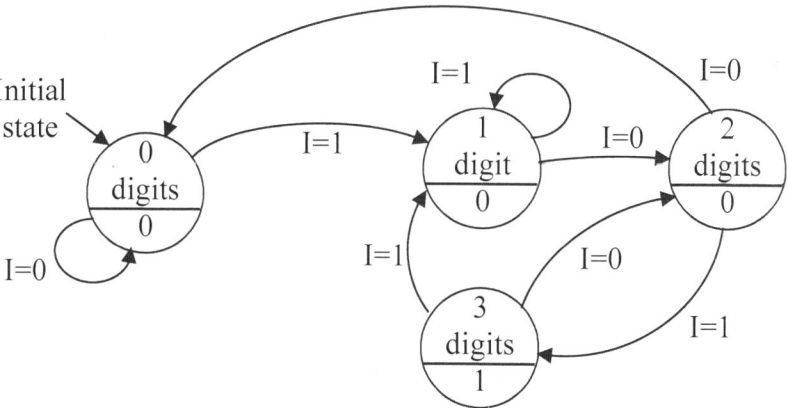

Figure 11-23   State Diagram for Identifying the Bit Pattern "101"

236 Computer Organization and Design Fundamentals

Next, we need to assign binary values to each of the states so that we know how many latches will be needed to store the current state and provide the inputs to the next state logic and the output logic. Table 11-5 presents the list of states along with their decimal and binary values.

From the state diagram and the numbering of the states, we can create the next state truth table and the output truth table. These are presented in Figure 11-24 with S_1 representing the MSB of the state, S_0 representing the LSB of the state, and P representing the output.

Table 11-5 List of States for Bit Pattern Detection Circuit

State	Numeric Value	
	Decimal	Binary
No bits of the pattern have been received	0	00
One bit of the pattern has been received	1	01
Two bits of the pattern have been received	2	10
Three bits of the pattern have been received	3	11

Next State					Output		
S_1	S_0	I	S_1'	S_0'	S_1	S_0	P
0	0	0	0	0	0	0	0
0	0	1	0	1	0	1	0
0	1	0	1	0	1	0	0
0	1	1	0	1	1	1	1
1	0	0	0	0			
1	0	1	1	1			
1	1	0	1	0			
1	1	1	0	1			

Figure 11-24 Next State and Output Truth Tables for Pattern Detect

Figure 11-25 shows the Karnaugh maps and resulting equations from the truth tables of Figure 11-24. Figure 11-26 presents the final circuit design.

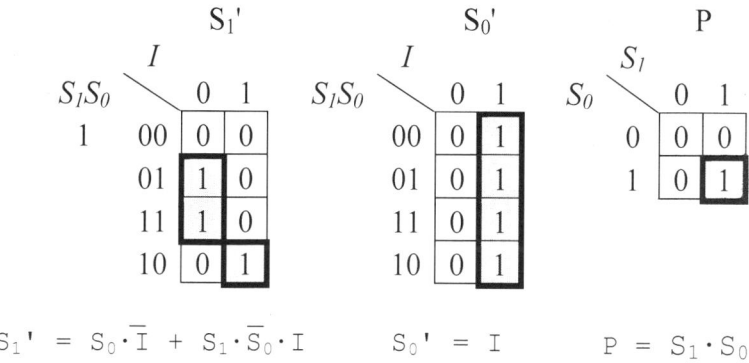

Figure 11-25 K-Maps for S_1', S_0', and P of Pattern Detect Circuit

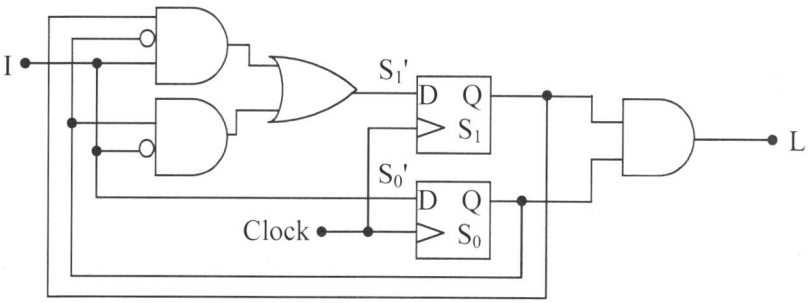

Figure 11-26 Final Circuit to Identify the Bit Pattern "101"

11.4 Mealy Versus Moore State Machines

The state machine design covered in the previous sections is referred to as a **Moore machine**. The distinguishing characteristic of a Moore machine is that its output is determined only by the current state.

The output of the second type of state machine, the **Mealy machine**, is based on both the current state of the machine *and* the system's input. Figure 11-27 shows how this is accomplished by including the system's inputs with the current state to drive the output logic.

To do this, the state diagram must be modified. The output values are removed from the states in the state diagram for a Mealy machine. The output values are then associated with each transition. Figure 11-28 shows how each transition is labeled using the format X/Y where X identifies the input driving the transition and Y is the resulting output.

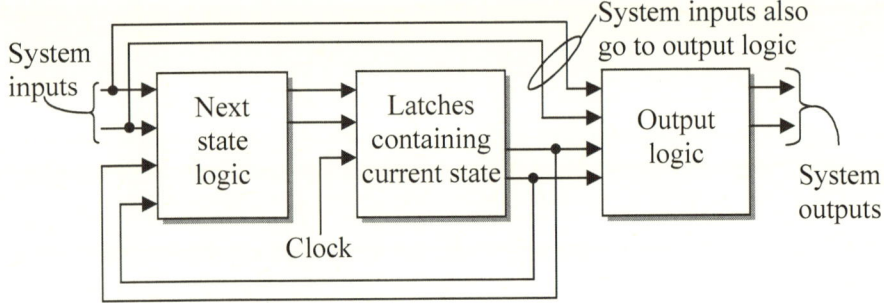

Figure 11-27 Basic Configuration of a Mealy Machine

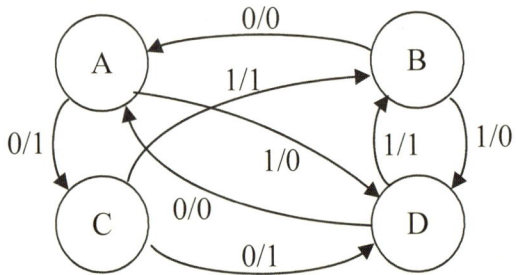

Figure 11-28 Sample State Diagram of a Mealy Machine

The next state truth table for the Mealy machine is the same as that for the Moore machine: the current state and the system input govern the next state. The Mealy machine's output truth table is different, however, since it now uses the system input as one of the truth table's inputs. Figure 11-29 presents the output truth table for the state diagram in Figure 11-28 where state A is $S_0 = 0$, $S_1 = 0$, B is $S_0 = 0$, $S_1 = 1$, C is $S_0 = 1$, $S_1 = 0$, and D is $S_0 = 1$, $S_1 = 1$.

11.5 What's Next?

Chapter 12 expands the application of latches to the arrays used in some forms of memory. It also presents the interface circuitry that the processor uses to communicate with memory. This may seem to be too detailed an examination of hardware for the typical computer science student, but the theories behind these designs are identical to those used to decode the subnet and host IDs of an IP network.

State	S_1	S_0	I	Y
A	0	0	0	1
A	0	0	1	0
B	0	1	0	0
B	0	1	1	0
C	1	0	0	1
C	1	0	1	1
D	1	1	0	0
D	1	1	1	1

Figure 11-29 Output Truth Table for Sample Mealy Machine

Problems

1. What is the maximum number of states a state machine with four latches can have?

2. How many latches will a state machine with 28 states require?

3. Apply the design process presented in Section 11.2 to design a two-bit up/down counter using the input *direction* such that when *direction* = 0, the system decrements (00 → 11 → 10 → 01 → 00) and when *direction* = 1, the system increments (00 → 01 → 10 → 11 → 00).

4. The three Boolean expressions below represent the next state bits, S_1' and S_0', and the output bit, X, based on the current state, S_1 and S_0, and the input I. Draw the logic circuit for the state machine including the latches and output circuitry. Label all signals.

$S_1' = \overline{S_1} \cdot S_0$ $\qquad$ $S_0' = S_1 \cdot S_0 \cdot I$ $\qquad$ $X = \overline{S_1} + S_0$

5. Create the next state truth table and the output truth table for the following state diagrams. Use the variable names S_1 and S_0 to represent the most significant and least significant bits respectively of the binary number identifying the state.

a.)

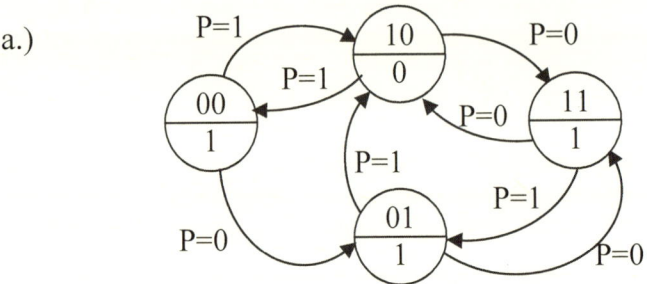

b.)

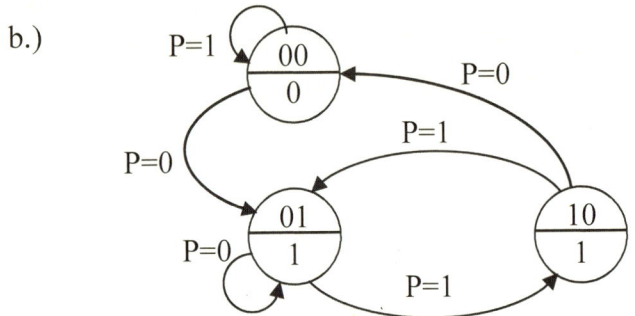

6. Identify the error in this state diagram. Be as specific as you can.

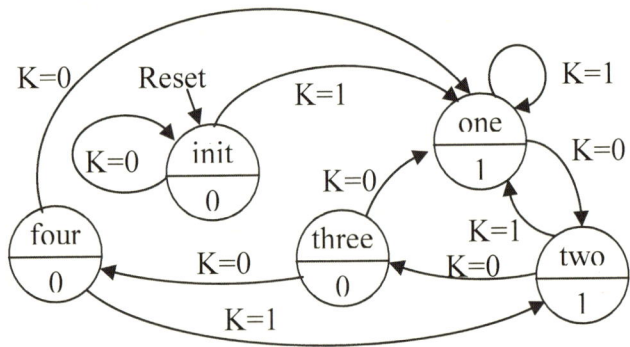

7. Design a state machine to detect the bit pattern "110" in a stream of bits.

8. How many latches would be needed in a state machine that detected the pattern "011110" in a stream of bits?

9. Create the logic diagram for the Mealy machine described in Figure 11-28.

CHAPTER TWELVE

Memory Organization

12.1 Early Memory

Every year new memory technologies are developed promising faster response and higher throughput. This makes it difficult to maintain a printed document discussing the latest advances in memory technologies. Although this chapter does present some basic memory technologies and how they are used to improve performance, the focus is on memory organization and interfacing with the processors.

One of the earliest types of computer memory was called *magnetic core memory*. It was made by weaving fine copper wires through tiny rings of magnetic material in an array. Figure 12-1 shows the basic arrangement of core memory.

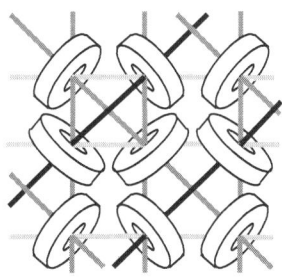

Figure 12-1 Diagram of a Section of Core Memory

Much like recording music to a magnetic tape, when electrical current was sent through the center of one of the magnetic rings, it polarized it with a magnetic charge. Each of these rings could have a charge that flowed clockwise or counter-clockwise. One direction was considered a binary 1 while the other was considered a binary 0.

The horizontal and vertical wires of the core memory were used to write data to a specific ring. By putting half the current necessary to polarize the magnetic material on one of the horizontal wires and the same level of current on one of the vertical wires, the ring where the two wires intersected had enough total current to modify the ring's polarity. The polarity of the remaining rings would be left unaltered.

The diagonal wires, called sense wires, were used to read data. They could detect when the polarity on one of the rings was changed. To read data, therefore, the bit in question would be written to with the horizontal and vertical wires. If the sense wire detected a change in polarity, the bit that had been stored there must have been opposite from the one just written. If no polarity change was detected, the bit written must have been equal to the one stored in that ring.

Magnetic core memory looks almost like fabric, the visible rings nestled among a lacework of glistening copper wires. It is for these reasons, however, that it is also impractical. Since the rings are enormous relative to the scale of electronics, a memory of 1024 bytes (referred to as a 1K x 8 or "1K by 8") had physical dimensions of approximately 8 inches by 8 inches. In addition, the fine copper wires were very fragile making manufacturing a difficult process. A typical 1K x 8 memory would cost thousands of dollars. Therefore, magnetic core memory disappeared from use with the advent of transistors and memory circuits such as the latch presented in Chapter 10.

12.2 Organization of Memory Device

Modern memory has the same basic configuration as magnetic core memory although the rings have been replaced with electronic memory cells such as the D-Latch. The cells are arranged so that each row represents a memory location where a binary value would be stored and the columns represent different bits of those memory locations. This is where the terminology "1K x 8" used in Section 12.1 comes from. Memory is like a matrix where the number of rows identifies the number of memory locations in the memory and the number of columns identifies the number of bits in each memory location.

To store to or retrieve data from a memory device, the processor must place a binary number called an address on special inputs to the memory device. This address identifies which row of the memory matrix or array the processor is interested in communicating with, and enables it.

Once a valid address is placed on the address lines, the memory cells from that row are connected to bi-directional connections on the memory device that allow *data* either to be stored to or read from the latches. These connections are called the data lines. Three additional lines, *chip select*, *read enable*, and *write enable*, are used to control the transaction.

Figure 12-2 presents the basic organization of a memory device.

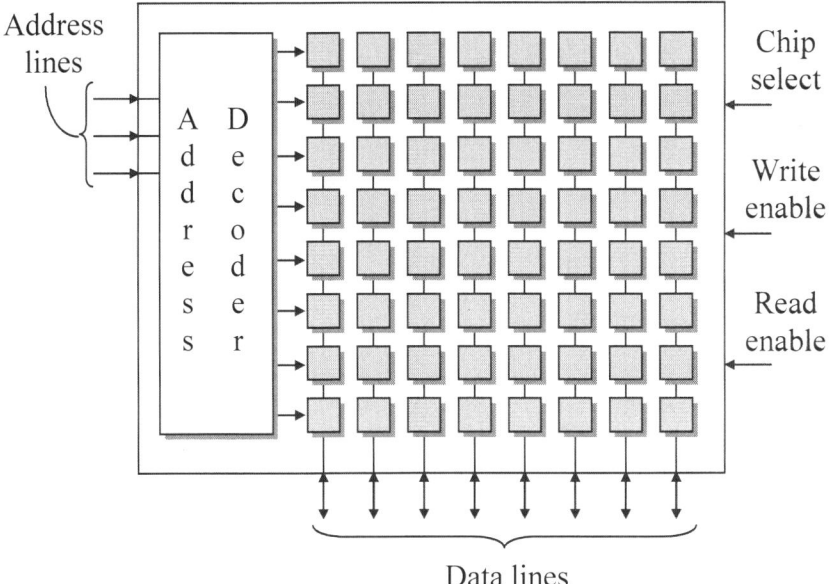

Figure 12-2 Basic Organization of a Memory Device

Remember from Chapter 8 that a decoder with n inputs has 2^n outputs, exactly one of which will be active for each unique pattern of ones and zeros at its input. For example, an active-low 2-input decoder will have four outputs. A different output will equal zero for each unique input pattern while all of the other inputs will be ones.

An **address decoder** selects exactly one row of the memory array to be active leaving the others inactive. When the microprocessor places a binary number onto the address lines, the address decoder selects a single row in the memory array to be written to or read from. For example, if $0111_2 = 3_{10}$ is placed on the address lines, the fourth row of the memory will be connected to the data lines. The first row is row 0.

The processor uses the inputs **read enable** and **write enable** to specify whether it is reading data from or writing data to the selected row of the memory array. These signals are active low. When read enable is zero, we are reading data from memory, and when write enable is zero, we are writing data to memory. These two signals should never be zero at the same time.

Sometimes, the read enable and write enable signals are combined into a single line called $R/\overline{W}$ (pronounced "read write-bar"). In this case, a one on $R/\overline{W}$ initiates a data read while a zero initiates a write.

If latches are used for the memory cells, then the data lines are connected to the D inputs of the memory location latches when data is written, and they are connected to the Q outputs when data is read.

The last input to the memory device shown in Figure 12-2 is the *chip select*. The chip select is an active low signal that enables and disables the memory device. If the chip select equals zero, the memory activates all of its input and output lines and uses them to transfer data. If the chip select equals one, the memory becomes idle, effectively disconnecting itself from all of its input and output lines. The reason for this is that the typical memory device shares the address and data lines of a processor with other devices.

Rarely does a processor communicate with only one memory device on its data lines. Problems occur when more than one device tries to communicate with the processor over shared lines at the same time. It would be like ten people in a room trying to talk at once; no one would be able to understand what was being said.

The processor uses digital logic to control these devices so that only one is talking or listening at a time. Through individual control of each of the chip select lines to the memory devices, the processor can enable only the memory device it wishes to communicate with. The processor places a zero on the chip select of the memory device it wants to communicate with and places ones on all of the other chip select inputs.

The next section discusses how these chip selects are designed so that no conflicts occur.

12.3 Interfacing Memory to a Processor

The previous section presented the input and output lines for a memory device. These lines are shared across all of the devices that communicate with the processor. If you look at the electrical traces across the surface of a motherboard, you should see collections of traces running together in parallel from the processor to then from one memory device to the next. These groups of wires are referred to as the *bus*, which is an extension of the internal structure of the processor. This section discusses how the memory devices share the bus.

12.3.1 Buses

In order to communicate with memory, a processor needs three types of connections: data, address, and control. The ***data lines*** are the electrical connections used to send data to or receive data from memory. There is an individual connection or wire for each bit of data. For example, if the memory of a particular system has 8 latches per memory location, i.e., 8 columns in the memory array, then it can store 8-bit data and has 8 individual wires with which to transfer data.

The *address lines* are controlled by the processor and are used to specify which memory location the processor wishes to communicate with. The address is an unsigned binary integer that identifies a unique location where data elements are to be stored or retrieved. Since this unique location could be in any one of the memory devices, the address lines are also used to specify which memory device is enabled.

The *control lines* consist of the signals that manage the transfer of data. At a minimum, they specify the timing and direction of the data transfer. The processor also controls this group of lines. Figure 12-3 presents the simplest connection of a single memory device to a processor with n data lines and m address lines.

Unfortunately, the configuration of Figure 12-3 only works with systems that have a single memory device. This is not very common. For example, a processor may interface with a BIOS stored in a non-volatile memory while its programs and data are stored in the volatile memory of a RAM stick. In addition, it may use the bus to communicate with devices such as the hard drive or video card. All of these devices share the data, address, and control lines of the bus. (BIOS stands for Basic Input/Output System and it is the low-level code used to start the processor when it is first powered up.)

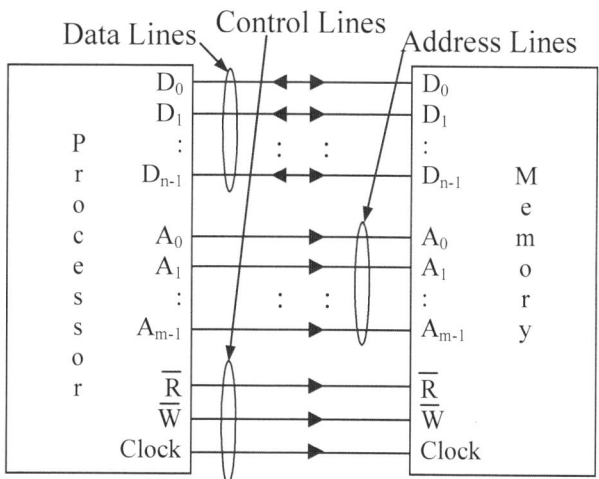

Figure 12-3 Basic Processor to Memory Device Interface

A method had to be developed to allow a processor to communicate to multiple memory devices across the same set of wires. If this wasn't done, the processor would need a separate set of data, address, and control lines for each device placing an enormous burden on circuit board designers for routing wires.

By using a bus, the processor can communicate with exactly one device at a time even though it is physically connected to many devices. If only one device on the bus is enabled at a time, the processor can perform a successful data transfer. If two devices tried to drive the data lines simultaneously, the result would be lost data in a condition called *bus contention*.

Figure 12-4 presents a situation where data is being read from memory device 1 while memory device 2 remains "disconnected" from the bus. Disconnected is in quotes because the physical connection is still present; it just doesn't have an electrical connection across which data can pass.

Notice that Figure 12-4 shows that the only lines disconnected from the bus are the data lines. This is because bus contention only occurs when multiple devices are trying to output to the same lines at the same time. Since only the microprocessor outputs to the address and control lines, they can remain connected.

In order for this scheme to work, an additional control signal must be sent to each of the memory devices telling them when to be connected to the bus and when to be disconnected. This control signal is called a *chip select*.

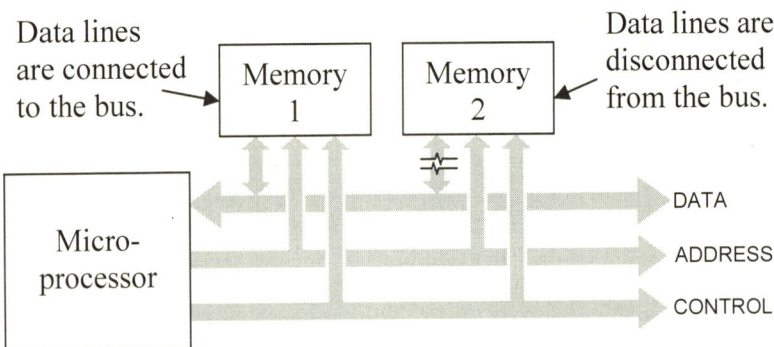

Figure 12-4 Two Memory Devices Sharing a Bus

A chip select is an active low signal connected to the enable input of the memory device. If the chip select is high, the memory device remains idle and its data lines are disconnected from the bus. When the processor wants to communicate with the memory device, it pulls that device's chip select low thereby enabling it and connecting it to the bus.

Each memory device has its own chip select, and at no time do two chip selects go low at the same time. For example, Table 12-1 shows the only possible values of the chip selects for a system with four memory devices.

Table 12-1 The Allowable Settings of Four Chip Selects

	CS_0	CS_1	CS_2	CS_3
Only memory device 0 connected	0	1	1	1
Only memory device 1 connected	1	0	1	1
Only memory device 2 connected	1	1	0	1
Only memory device 3 connected	1	1	1	0
All devices disconnected	1	1	1	1

The disconnection of the data lines is performed using *tristate outputs* for the data lines of the memory chips. A tristate output is digital output with a third state added to it. This output can be a logic 1, a logic 0, or a third state that acts as a high impedance or open circuit. It is like someone opened a switch and nothing is connected.

This third state is controlled by the chip select. When the active low chip select equals 1, data lines are set to high impedance, sometimes called the *Z state*. A chip select equal to 0 causes the data lines to be active and allow input or output.

In Figure 12-5a, three different outputs are trying to drive the same wire. This results in bus contention, and the resulting data is unreadable. Figure 12-5b shows two of the outputs breaking their connection with the wire allowing the first output to have control of the line. This is the goal when multiple devices are driving a single line. Figure 12-5c is the same as 12-5b except that the switches have been replaced with tristate outputs. With all but one of the outputs in a Z state, the top gate is free to drive the output without bus contention.

The following sections describe how memory systems are designed using chip selects to take advantage of tristate outputs.

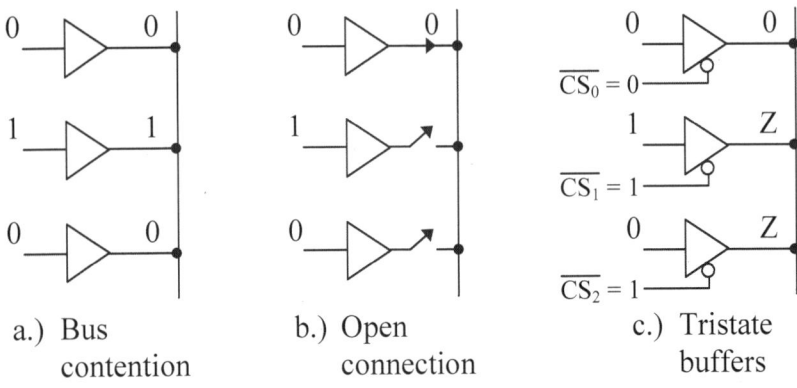

Figure 12-5 Three Buffers Trying to Drive the Same Output

12.3.2 Memory Maps

Think of memory as several filing cabinets where each folder can contain a single piece of data. The size of the stored data, i.e., the number of bits that can be stored in a single memory location, is fixed and is equal to the number of columns in the memory array. Each piece of data can be either code (part of a program) or data (variables or constants used in the program). Code and data are typically stored in the same memory, each piece of which is stored in a unique address or row of memory.

Some sections of memory are assigned to a predefined purpose which may place constraints on how they are arranged. For example, the BIOS from which the computer performs its initial startup sequence is located at a specific address range in non-volatile memory. Video memory may also be located at a specific address range.

System designers must have a method to describe the arrangement of memory in a system. Since multiple memory devices and different types of memory may be present in a single system, hardware designers need to be able to show what addresses correspond to which memory devices. Software designers also need to have a way to show how the memory is being used. For example, which parts of memory will be used for the operating system, which parts will be used to store a program, or which parts will be used to store the data for a program.

System designers describe the use of memory with a ***memory map***. A memory map represents a system's memory with a long, vertical column. It is meant to model the memory array where the rows correspond to the memory locations. Within the full range of addresses are smaller partitions where the individual resources are present. Figure 12-6 presents two examples of memory maps.

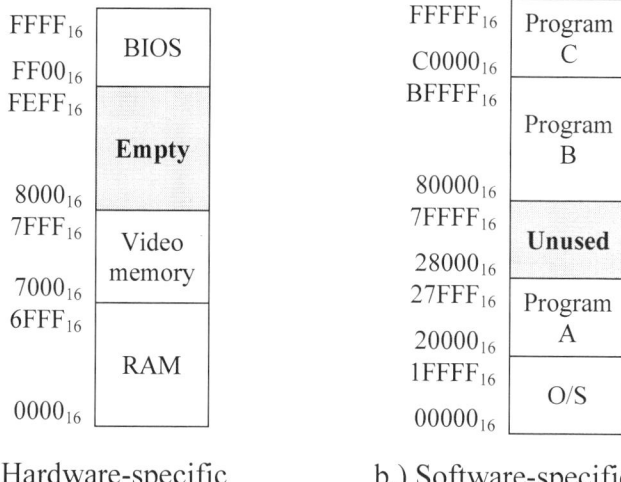

a.) Hardware-specific   b.) Software-specific

Figure 12-6 Sample Memory Maps

The numbers along the left side of the memory map represent the addresses corresponding to each memory resource. The memory map should represent the full address range of the processor. This full address range is referred to as the processor's *memory space*, and its size is represented by the number of memory locations in the full range, i.e., 2^m where m equals the number of address lines coming out of the processor. It is up to the designer whether the addresses go in ascending or descending order on the memory map.

As an example, let's calculate the memory space of the processor represented by the memory map in Figure 12-6b. The top address for this memory map is $FFFFF_{16} = 1111\ 1111\ 1111\ 1111\ 1111_2$. Since the processor accesses its highest address by setting all of its address lines to 1, we know that this particular processor has 20 address lines. Therefore, its memory space is $2^{20} = 1,048,576_{10} = 1$ Meg. This means that all of the memory resources for this processor must be able to fit into 1 Meg without overlapping.

In the next section, we will see how to compute the size of each partition of memory using the address lines. For now, however, we can determine the size of a partition in memory by subtracting the low address from the high address, then adding one to account for the fact that the low address itself is a memory location. For example, the range of the BIOS in Figure 12-6a starts at $FF00_{16} = 65,280_{10}$ and goes up to $FFFF_{16} = 65,535_{10}$. This means that the BIOS fits into $65,535 - 65,280 + 1 = 256$ memory locations.

It is vital to note that there is an exact method to selecting the upper and lower addresses for each of the ranges in the memory map. Take for example the memory range for Program A in Figure 12-6b. The lower address is 20000_{16} while the upper address is $27FFF_{16}$. If we convert these addresses to binary, we should see a relationship.

$$20000_{16} = 0010\ 0000\ 0000\ 0000\ 0000_2$$
$$27FFF_{16} = 0010\ 0111\ 1111\ 1111\ 1111_2$$

It is not a coincidence that the upper five bits of these two addresses are identical while the remaining bits go from all zeros in the low address to all ones in the high address. Converting the high and the low address of any one of the address ranges in Figure 12-6 should reveal the same characteristic.

The next section shows how these most significant address bits are used to define which memory device is being selected.

12.3.3 Address Decoding

Address decoding is a method for using an address to enable a unique memory device while leaving all other devices idle. The method described here works for many more applications than memory though. It is the same method that is used to identify which subnet a host computer is connected to based on its IP address.

All address decoding schemes have one thing in common: the bits of the full address are divided into two groups, one group that is used to identify the memory device and one group that identifies the memory location within the selected memory device. In order to determine how to divide the full address into these two groups of bits, we need to know how large the memory device is and how large the memory space is. Once we know the size of the memory device, then we know the number of bits that will be required from the full address to point to a memory location within the memory device.

Just as we calculated the size of the memory space of a processor, the size of the memory space of a device is calculated by raising 2 to a power equal to the number of address lines going to that device. For example, a memory device with 28 address lines going into it has 2^{28} = 256 Meg locations. This means that 28 address bits from the full address must be used to identify a memory location within that device. All of the remaining bits of the full address will be used to enable or disable the device. It is through these remaining address bits that we determine where the memory will be located within the memory map.

Table 12-2 presents a short list of memory sizes and the number of address lines required to access all of the locations within them. Remember that the memory size is simply equal to 2^m where m is the number of address lines going into the device.

Table 12-2 Sample Memory Sizes versus Required Address Lines

Memory size	Number of address lines	Memory size	Number of address lines
1 K	10	256 Meg	28
256 K	18	1 Gig	30
1 Meg	20	4 Gig	32
16 Meg	24	64 Gig	36

The division of the full address into two groups is done by dividing the full address into a group of most significant bits and least significant bits. The block diagram of an m-bit full address in Figure 12-7 shows how this is done. Each bit of the full address is represented with a_n where n is the bit position.

full address of m-bits

a_{m-1} a_{m-2} a_{m-3} ... a_k	a_{k-1} a_{k-2} ... a_2 a_1 a_0
$m-k$ bits defining when memory device is enabled	k bits wired directly to memory device

Figure 12-7 Full Address with Enable Bits and Device Address Bits

The bits used to enable the memory device are always the most significant bits while the bits used to access a memory location within the device are always the least significant bits.

Example

A processor with a 256 Meg address space is using the address $35E3C03_{16}$ to access a 16 Meg memory device.

- How many address lines are used to define when the 16 Meg memory space is enabled?
- What is the bit pattern of these enable bits that enables this particular 16 Meg memory device?
- What is the address within the 16 Meg memory device that this address is going to transfer data to or from?
- What is the lowest address in the memory map of the 16 Meg memory device?
- What is the highest address in the memory map of the 16 Meg memory device?

Solution

First, we need to determine where the division in the full address is so that we know which bits go to the enable circuitry and which are connected directly to the memory device's address lines. From Table 12-2, we see that to access 256 Meg, we need 28 address lines. Therefore, the processor must have 28 address lines coming out of it.

The memory device is only 16 Meg which means that it requires 24 address lines to uniquely identify all of its addresses.

a_{27} a_{26} a_{25} a_{24}	a_{23} a_{22} ... a_2 a_1 a_0
4 bits that enable memory device	24 bits going to address lines of memory device

Therefore, the *four most significant address lines* are used to enable the memory device.

By converting $35E3C03_{16}$ to binary, we should see the values of each of these bit positions for this memory location in this memory device.

$$35E3C03_{16} = 0011\ 0101\ 1110\ 0011\ 1100\ 0000\ 0011_2$$

The four most significant bits of this 28-bit address are 0011_2. This, therefore, is the bit pattern that will enable this particular 16 Meg memory device: $a_{27} = 0$, $a_{26} = 0$, $a_{25} = 1$, and $a_{24} = 1$. Any other pattern of bits for these four lines will disable this memory device and disallow any data transactions between it and the processor.

The 16 Meg memory device never sees the most significant four bits of this full address. The only address lines it ever sees are the 24 that are connected directly to its address lines: a_0 through a_{23}. Therefore, the address the memory device sees is:

$$0101\ 1110\ 0011\ 1100\ 0000\ 0011_2 = 5E3C03_{16}$$

As for the highest and lowest values of the full address for this memory device, we need to examine what the memory device interprets as its highest and lowest addresses. The lowest address occurs when all of the address lines *to the memory device* are set to 0. The highest address occurs when all of the address lines *to the memory device* are set to 1. Note that this does not include the four most significant bits of the full address which should stay the same in order for the memory device to be active. Therefore, from the standpoint of the memory map which uses the full address, the lowest address is the four enable bits set to 0011_2 followed by 24 zeros. The highest address is the four enable bits set to 0011_2 followed by 24 ones.

	4 bits that enable memory device				24 bits going to address lines of memory device					
	a_{27}	a_{26}	a_{25}	a_{24}	a_{23}	a_{22}	...	a_2	a_1	a_0
Highest address	0	0	1	1	1	1	...	1	1	1
Lowest address	0	0	1	1	0	0	...	0	0	0

Therefore, from the perspective of the memory map, the lowest and highest addresses of this memory device are:

Highest = $0011\ 1111\ 1111\ 1111\ 1111\ 1111\ 1111_2 = 3FFFFFF_{16}$
Lowest = $0011\ 0000\ 0000\ 0000\ 0000\ 0000\ 0000_2 = 3000000_{16}$

The following memory map shows how this 16 Meg memory is placed within the full range of the processor's memory space. The full address range of the processor's memory space is determined by the fact that there are 28 address lines from the processor. Twenty-eight ones is $FFFFFFF_{16}$ in hexadecimal and 28 zeros is 0000000_{16}.

254 Computer Organization and Design Fundamentals

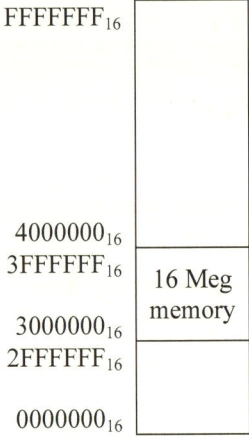

The method for resolving the subnet of an IP address is the same as enabling a specific memory device within a processor's memory space. When configuring a computer to run on a network that uses the Internet Protocol version 4 addressing scheme, it must be assigned a 32-bit address that uniquely identifies it among all of the other computers on that network. This 32-bit address serves a second purpose though: it identifies the sub-network or subnet that this computer is a member of within the entire network. A subnet within the entire IP network is equivalent to a memory device within the memory space of a processor.

$\leftarrow$ 32-bit IP address $\rightarrow$

Network address	Host or local address
Bits used to identify subnet	Bits used to identify host within subnet

Figure 12-8 IPv4 Address Divided into Subnet and Host IDs

According to IPv4 standard, there are four classes of addressing, Class A, Class B, Class C, and Class D. Each of these classes is defined by the number of bits that are assigned to identify the subnet and how many bits are left for the host ID. For example, a Class A subnet uses 8 bits to identify the subnet. This leaves 24 bits to identify the host within the subnet. Therefore, a Class A network can ideally contain a maximum of $2^{24} = 16,777,216$ hosts. The actual number of hosts is two less. Two addresses for every subnet are reserved: one for a broadcast address and one for the subnet itself.

A Class C network uses 24 bits to identify the subnet and 8 bits to identify the host within the subnet. Therefore, a Class C network can have at most $2^8 - 2 = 254$ machines on it, far fewer than a Class A. The drawback of a Class A network, however, is that if the entire network were assigned to Class A subnets, then there would ideally only be room for $2^8 = 256$ subnets. Whenever the number of bits used to identify the subnet is increased, the number of possible subnets is increased while the number of hosts within a subnet is decreased.

Example

The IPv4 address 202.54.151.45 belongs to a Class C network. What are the subnet and the host ids of this address?

Solution

First, IPv4 addresses are represented as four bytes represented in decimal notation. Therefore, let's convert the IP address above into its 32-bit binary equivalent.

$$202_{10} = 11001010_2$$
$$54_{10} = 00110110_2$$
$$151_{10} = 10010111_2$$
$$45_{10} = 00101101_2$$

This means that the binary address of 202.54.151.45 is:
11001010.00110110.10010111.00101101

Remember that the Class C network uses the first twenty-four bits for the subnet id. This gives us the following value for the subnet id.

Subnet $id_{202.54.151.45} = 110010100011011010010111_2$

Any IPv4 address with the first 24 bits equal to this identifies a host in this subnet.

The host id is taken from the remaining bits.

Host $id_{202.54.151.45} = 00101101_2$

12.3.4 Chip Select Hardware

What we need is a circuit that will enable a memory device whenever the full address is within the address range of the device and disable the memory device when the full address falls outside the address range of the device. This is where those most significant bits of the full address come into play.

Remember from our example where we examined the addressing of a 16 Meg memory device in the 256 Meg memory space of a processor that the four most significant bits needed to remain 0011_2. In other words, if the four bits a_{27}, a_{26}, a_{25}, and a_{24} equaled 0000_2, 0001_2, 0010_2, 0100_2, 0101_2, 0110_2, 0111_2, 1000_2, 1001_2, 1010_2, 1011_2, 1100_2, 1101_2, 1110_2, or 1111_2, the 16 Meg memory device would be disabled. Therefore, we want a circuit that is active when $a_{27} = 0$, $a_{26} = 0$, $a_{25} = 1$, and $a_{24} = 1$. This sounds like the product from an AND gate with a_{27} and a_{26} inverted. Chip select circuits are typically active low, however, so we need to invert the output. This gives us a NAND gate.

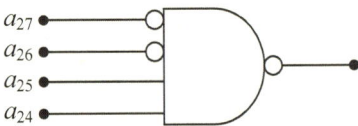

Figure 12-9 Sample Chip Select Circuit for a Memory Device

So the process of designing a chip select is as follows:

- Using the memory space of the processor and the size of the memory device, determine the number of bits of the full address that will be used for the chip select.
- Using the base address where the memory device is to be located, determine the values that the address lines used for the chip select are to have.
- Create a circuit with the address lines for the chip select going into the inputs of a NAND gate with the bits that are to be zero inverted.

Example

Using logic gates, design an active low chip select for a 1 Meg BIOS to be placed in the 1 Gig memory space of a processor. The BIOS needs to have a starting address of $1E00000_{16}$.

Solution

First of all, let's determine how many bits are required by the 1 Meg BIOS. We see from Table 12-2 that a 1 Meg memory device requires

20 bits for addressing. This means that the lower 20 address lines coming from the processor must be connected to the BIOS address lines. Since a 1 Gig memory space has 30 address lines (2^{30} = 1 Gig), then 30 – 20 = 10 address lines are left to determine the chip select.

Next, we figure out what the values of those ten lines are supposed to be. If we convert the starting address to binary, we get:

$$1E00000_{16} = 00\ 0001\ 1110\ 0000\ 0000\ 0000\ 0000\ 0000$$

Notice that enough leading zeros were added to make the address 30 bits long, the appropriate length in a 1 Gig memory space.

We need to assign each bit a label. We do this by labeling the least significant bit a_0, then incrementing the subscript for each subsequent position to the left. This gives us the following values for each address bit. (a_{18} through a_2 have been deleted in the interest of space.)

a_{29}	a_{28}	a_{27}	a_{26}	a_{25}	a_{24}	a_{23}	a_{22}	a_{21}	a_{20}	a_{19}	a_{18}	...	a_1	a_0
0	0	0	0	0	1	1	1	1	0	0	0	...	0	0

Bits a_{20} through a_{29} are used for the chip select.

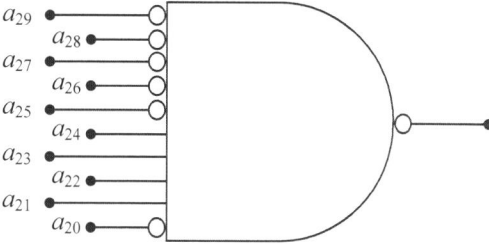

Example

What is the largest memory device that can be placed in a memory map with a starting address of $A40000_{16}$?

Solution

This may seem like a rather odd question, but it actually deals with an important aspect of creating chip selects. Notice that for every one of our starting addresses, the bits that go to the chip select circuitry can be ones or zeros. The bits that go to the address lines of the memory device, however, ***must all be zero.*** This is because the first address in any memory device is 0_{10}. The ending or highest address will have all ones going to the address lines of the memory device.

Let's begin by converting the address $A40000_{16}$ to binary.

$$A40000_{16} = 1010\ 0100\ 0000\ 0000\ 0000\ 0000_2$$

If we count the zeros starting with the least significant bit and moving left, we see that there are 18 zeros before we get to our first one. This means that the largest memory device we can place at this starting address has 18 address lines. Therefore, the largest memory device we can start at this address has $2^{18} = 256$ K memory locations.

Example

True or False: $B000_{16}$ to $CFFF_{16}$ is a valid range for a single memory device.

Solution

This is much like the previous example in that it requires an understanding of how the address lines going to the chip select circuitry and the memory device are required to behave. The previous example showed that the address lines going to the memory device must be all zero for the starting or low address and all ones for the ending or high address. The address lines going to the chip select, however, must all remain constant.

Let's begin by converting the low and the high addresses to binary.

	a_{15}	a_{14}	a_{13}	a_{12}	a_{11}	a_{10}	a_9	a_8	a_7	a_6	a_5	a_4	a_3	a_2	a_1	a_0
Low	1	0	1	1	0	0	0	0	0	0	0	0	0	0	0	0
High	1	1	0	0	1	1	1	1	1	1	1	1	1	1	1	1

Note that it is impossible to make a vertical division through both the high and the low addresses where all of the bits to the left are the same for both the high and the low addresses while every bit to the right goes from all zeros for the low address to all ones for the high address. Since we cannot do this, we cannot make a chip select for this memory device and the answer is *false*.

Example

What is the address range of the memory device that is enabled with the chip select shown?

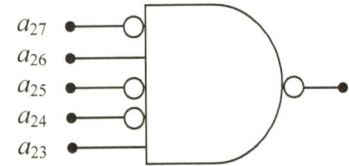

Solution

To begin with, the addressing can be determined from the subscripts of the address lines identified in the figure. The address lines coming out of the processor go from a_0 (always assumed to be the least significant bit of the address) to a_{27}. This means that the processor has 28 address lines and can access a memory space of 2^{28} = 256 Meg.

The chip select only goes low when all of the inputs to the NAND gate (after the inverters) equal 1. This means that $a_{27} = 0$, $a_{26} = 1$, $a_{25} = 0$, $a_{24} = 0$, and $a_{23} = 1$. We find the lowest address by setting all of the remaining bits, a_{22} through a_0, to zero and we find the highest address by setting all of the remaining bits to 1. This gives us the following binary addresses.

	a_{27}	a_{26}	a_{25}	a_{24}	a_{23}	a_{22}	a_{21}	...	a_1	a_0
High address	0	1	0	0	1	1	1	...	1	1
Low address	0	1	0	0	1	0	0	...	0	0

When we convert these values to hexadecimal, we get:

High address = 0100 1111 1111 1111 1111 1111 1111$_2$ = $4FFFFFF_{16}$
Low address = 0100 1000 0000 0000 0000 0000 0000$_2$ = 4800000_{16}

12.4 Memory Mapped Input/Output

Some devices do not contain a memory array, yet their interface to the processor uses data lines and control lines just like a memory device. For example, an analog-to-digital converter (ADC) reads an analog value and converts it to a digital number that the processor can use. The processor reads this digital value from ADC exactly the same way that it would read a value it had stored in a memory device.

The ADC may also require parameters to be sent to it from the processor. These parameters might include the method it uses for conversion, the time it waits between conversions, and which analog input channels are active. The processor sets these values by writing to the ADC in the same way it would store data to a memory device.

The practice of interfacing an input/output (I/O) device as if it was a memory device is called *memory mapping*. Just like the bus interface for a memory device, the memory mapped interface to a bus uses a chip select to tell the device when it's being accessed and data lines to pass data between the device and the processor. Some memory mapped I/O even use a limited number of address lines to identify internal registers. In addition, I/O devices use the write enable and read enable signals from the processor to determine whether data is being sent to the device or read from it. Some devices may only support writing (purely output) while others may only support reading (purely input).

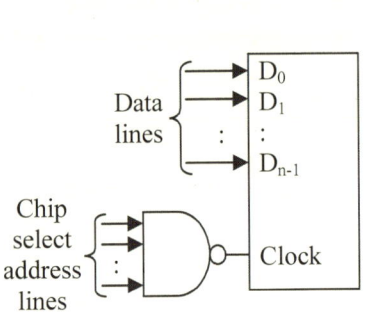
a.) Memory-mapped output device

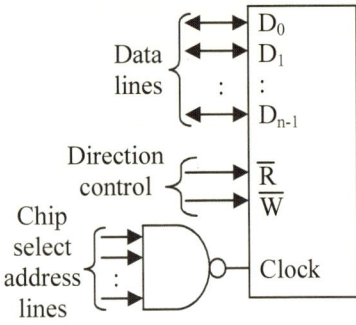
b.) Memory-mapped I/O device

Figure 12-10 Some Types of Memory Mapped I/O Configurations

12.5 Memory Terminology

There are many different purposes for memory in the operation of a computer. Some memory is meant to store data and programs only while the computer is turned on while other memory is meant to be permanent. Some memory contains application code while other memory is meant to store the low-level driver code to control devices such as an IDE interface or a video card. Some memory may have a larger capacity while other memory may be faster.

In order to understand what memory technologies to apply to which processor operation, we need to understand a little bit more about the technologies themselves. This section discusses some of the terminology used to describe memory.

12.5.1 Random Access Memory

The term **Random Access Memory** (RAM) is typically applied to memory that is easily read from and written to by the microprocessor. In actuality, this is a misuse of this term. For a memory to be random access means that any address can be accessed at any time. This is to differentiate it from storage devices such as tapes or hard drives where the data is accessed sequentially. We will discuss hard drive technologies in Chapter 13.

In general, RAM is the main memory of a computer. Its purpose is to store data and applications that are currently in use. The operating system controls the use of this memory dictating when items are to be loaded into RAM, where they are to be located in RAM, and when they need to be removed from RAM. RAM is meant to be very fast both for reading and writing data. RAM also tends to be volatile in that as soon as power is removed, all of the data is lost.

12.5.2 Read Only Memory

In every computer system, there must be a portion of memory that is stable and impervious to power loss. This kind of memory is called **Read Only Memory** or ROM. Once again, this term is a misnomer. If it was not possible to write to this type of memory, we could not store the code or data that is to be contained in it. It simply means that without special mechanisms in place, a processor cannot write to this type of memory. If through an error of some sort, the processor tries to write to this memory, an error will be generated.

The most common application of ROM is to store the computer's BIOS. Since the BIOS is the code that tells the processor how to access its resources upon powering up, it must be present even when the computer is powered down. Another application is the code for embedded systems. For example, it is important for the code in your car's computer to remain even if the battery is disconnected.

There are some types of ROM that the microprocessor can write to, but usually the time needed to write to them or the programming requirements needed to do so make it unwise to write to them regularly. Therefore, these memories are still considered read only.

In some cases, the processor cannot write to a ROM under any circumstances. For example, the code in your car's computer should never need to be modified. This ROM is programmed before it is installed. To put a new program in the car's computer, the old ROM is removed and discarded and a new ROM is installed in its place.

12.5.3 Static RAM versus Dynamic RAM

For as long as memory has existed, scientists and engineers have experimented with new technologies to make RAM faster and to cram more of it into a smaller space, two goals that are typically at odds.

Nowhere is this more obvious than in the two main classifications of RAM: Static RAM (SRAM) and Dynamic RAM (DRAM).

SRAM is made from an array of latches such as the D-latch we studied in Chapter 10. Each latch can maintain a single bit of data within a single memory address or location. For example, if a memory stores eight bits per memory address, then there are eight latches for a single address. If this same memory has an address space of 256 K, then there are $2^{18} \cdot 8 = 2^{21} = 2,097,152$ latches in the device.

Latches are not small devices as logic circuits go, but they are very fast. Therefore, in the pursuit of the performance goals of speed and size, SRAMs are better adapted to speed. In general, SRAMs:

- store data in transistor circuits similar to D-latches;
- are used for very fast applications such as RAM caches (discussed in Chapter 13);
- tend to be used in smaller memories which allows for very fast access due to the simpler decoding logic; and
- are volatile meaning that the data remains stored only as long as power is available.

There are circuits that connect SRAMs to a back up battery that allows the data to be stable even with a loss of power. These batteries, about the size of a watch battery, can maintain the data for long periods of time much as a battery in a watch can run for years. On the negative side, the extra battery and circuitry adds to the overall system cost and takes up physical space on the motherboard

A bit is stored in a DRAM using a device called a capacitor. A capacitor is made from a pair of conductive plates that are held parallel to each other and very close together, but not touching. If an electron is placed on one of the plates, its negative charge will force an electron on the other plate to leave. This works much like the north pole of a magnet pushing away the north pole of a second magnet.

If enough electrons are deposited on the one plate creating a strong negative charge, enough electrons will be moved away from the opposite plate creating a positive charge. Like a north pole attracting the south pole of a second magnet, the charges on these two plates will be attracted to each other and maintain their charge. This is considered a logic '1'. The absence of a charge is considered a logic '0'.

Since a capacitor can be made very small, DRAM technology is better adapted to high density memories, i.e., cramming a great deal of bits into a small space.

Capacitors do have a problem though. Every once in a while, one of the electrons will escape from the negatively charged plate and land on the positively charged plate. This exchange of an electron decreases the overall charge difference on the two plates. If this happens enough, the stored '1' will disappear. This movement of electrons from one plate to the other is referred to as *leakage current*.

The electrons stored on the plates of the capacitors are also lost when the processor reads the data. It requires energy to read data from the capacitors, energy that is stored by the position of the electrons. Therefore, each read removes some of the electrons.

In order to avoid having leakage current or processor reads corrupt the data stored on the DRAMs, i.e., turning the whole mess to zeros, additional logic called refresh circuitry is used that periodically reads the data in the DRAM then restores the ones with a full charge of electrons. This logic also recharges the capacitors each time the processor reads from a memory location. The refresh circuitry is included on the DRAM chip making the process of keeping the DRAM data valid transparent to the processor. Although it adds to the cost of the DRAM, the DRAM remains cheaper than SRAM.

The refresh process involves disabling memory circuitry, then reading each word of data and writing it back. This is performed by counting through the rows. The process does take time thus slowing down the apparent performance of the memory.

In general, DRAMs:

- have a much higher capacity due to the smaller size of the capacitor (The RAM sticks of your computer's main memory are DRAMs.);
- will "leak" charge due to the nature of capacitors eventually causing the data to disappear unless it is refreshed periodically;
- are much cheaper than SRAM; and
- are volatile meaning that the data is fixed and remains stored only as long as power is available.

12.5.4 Types of DRAM and Their Timing

The basic DRAM storage technology is unchanged since first RAM chips, but designers have used alternate techniques to improve the effective performance of the DRAM devices. For example, the number of pins that electrically connect the DRAM to the system can be quite large, one of the largest culprits being addressing. A 1 Gbyte memory, for example, requires 30 pins for addressing. If the number of pins could be reduced, the memory would have a smaller footprint on the circuit board and a more reliable connection.

The number of address lines can be cut in half by presenting the memory address to the DRAM in two stages. During the first stage, the first half of the address is presented on the address lines and stored or latched in the memory device. The second stage presents the last half of the address on the same pins. Once it receives both halves of the address, the DRAM can process the request.

	Time →		
	Cycle 1	Cycle 2	Cycle 3
Address lines:	1st half of addr.	2nd half of addr.	
Data lines:	No data	No data	Valid data

Figure 12-11   Basic Addressing Process for a DRAM

This allows the addressable space of the DRAM to be twice that which could be supported by the address pins. Unfortunately, it comes at the cost of the delay of the second addressing cycle. It will be shown later, however, that this can be turned into an advantage.

The presentation of the address in two stages is viewed as a logical reorganization of the memory into three-dimensions. The upper half of the address identifies a row. The lower half of the address identifies a column. The intersection of the row and column is where the data is stored, the multiple bits of the storage location is the third dimension. This concept of rows and columns is represented in Figure 12-12 for a memory with four data bits per addressable location.

To support the two-stage delivery of the address, two additional active-low control signals are needed. The first is called *row address select* or $\overline{RAS}$. This signal is used to strobe the row address into the DRAM's row address latch. The second, column address select or $\overline{CAS}$, strobes the column address into the DRAM's column address latch. This requires two additional input pins on the DRAM.

By using the two-stage addressing of a DRAM, the addition of a single address line will quadruple the memory size. This is because an additional address line doubles both the number of rows and the number of columns.

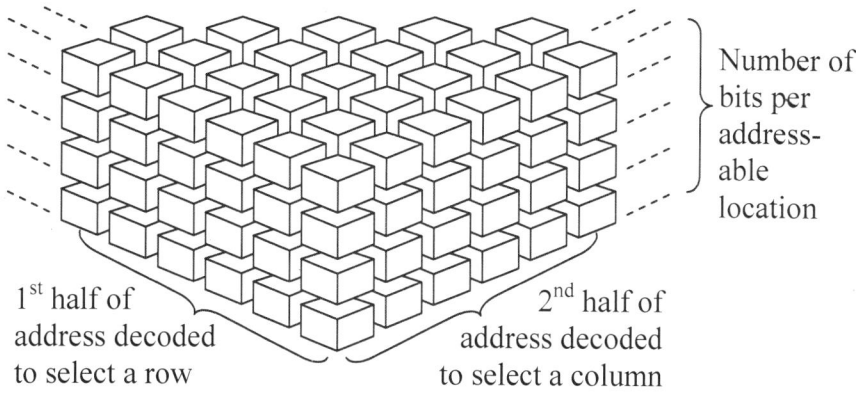

Figure 12-12 Organization of DRAM

Now let's get back to the issue of the delay added by a second address cycle. Most data transfers to and from main memory take the form of block moves where a series of instructions or data words are pulled from memory as a group. (For more information on memory blocks, see the section on caches in Chapter 13.)

If the processor needs a block from memory, the first half of the address should be the same for all the items of the block. Because of this, the memory access process begins with the row address then uses only the column address for subsequent retrievals. This is called Fast Page Mode (FPM), the data of a single row being referred to as a page. The $\overline{RAS}$ line is held low as long as the row address is valid. Figure 12-13 presents an example of FPM for a memory block of size four.

Address:	Row addr	Col. addr. 0		Col. addr. 1		Col. addr. 2		Col. addr. 3	
Data:	No data	No data	Data word 0	No data	Data word 1	No data	Data word 2	No data	Data word 3

Time →

Figure 12-13 Example of an FPM Transfer

FPM requires both the row and column addresses to be presented for the first cycle only. For subsequent addresses, only the column address is needed thereby saving one address cycle. Furthermore, since the decoding circuitry for the column address only uses half of the bits of the full address, the time it takes to decode each individual column address is shorter than it would have been for the full address.

The memory access time can be further shorted by having the processor present the column address for the next data element while the current data element is being returned on the data lines. This overlap of the DRAM returning a word of data while the processor is writing the column address for the next word is called Extended Data-Out (EDO). For data reads within the same page, EDO results in a savings of approximately 10 ns for each read. Figure 12-14 presents an example of EDO for a memory block of size four.

		Time →				
Address:	Row addr.	Column addr. 0	Column addr. 1	Column addr. 2	Column addr. 3	
Data:	No data	No data	Data word 0	Data word 1	Data word 2	Data word 3

Figure 12-14 Example of an EDO Transfer

If the processor needs to fetch a sequence of four data words from memory, Burst EDO (BEDO) can further speed up the process by using the initial column address, and then using a counter to step through the next three addresses. This means that the processor would only be required to send the row address and column address once, then simply clock in the four sequential data words.

12.5.5 Asynchronous versus Synchronous Memory Interfacing

In all logic circuits, there is a delay between the time that inputs are set and the outputs appear. The inputs of a memory include address lines and control lines while the data lines can be either inputs or outputs. When a processor sets the inputs of a memory device, it has to wait for the memory to respond. This is called **asynchronous** operation.

Asynchronous operation makes it difficult to design the timing of motherboards. The processor has to run slow enough to account for the slowest type and size of memory that is expected to be used. One memory may be ready with the data before the processor expects it while a different memory may take longer.

Some processors, however, are designed so that the memory follows a precise timing requirement governed by a clock that is added to the bus to keep everything attached in lock-step. This type of interface is referred to as *synchronous* and the memory that uses this type of interface is referred to as synchronous DRAM or SDRAM.

The main benefit derived from controlling the memory interface with a clock is that the memory's internal circuitry can be set up in what is referred to as a pipelined structure. Pipelining is discussed in Chapter 15, but at this point it is sufficient to say that pipelining allows a device to perform multiple operations at the same time. For example, an SDRAM might be able to simultaneously output data to the processor and receive the next requested address. Overlapping functions such as these allows the memory to appear faster.

One improvement to SDRAM allows two words of data to be written or read during a single clock cycle. This means that every time the processor accesses the memory it transfers two words, one on the rising edge of the clock and one on the falling edge. This type of memory is referred to as Double Data Rate SDRAM or DDR SDRAM. DDR2 and DDR3 double and quadruple the DDR rate by allowing four and eight data words respectively to be transferred during a single clock pulse. This is made possible by taking advantage of the fact that the when a DRAM row is accessed, simply counting through the columns retrieves consecutive bytes of data which can be buffered and send out the data lines as quickly as the processor can receive them.

12.6 What's Next?

This chapter has only examined a small part of the information storage solutions used in a computer system. In the next section, we will discuss the operation and purpose of all levels of data storage by examining the different characteristics of each. The major characteristics that will be examined are speed, size, and whether data is lost with a power loss. Each level has specific needs and therefore is implemented with different technologies.

Problems

1. What is the largest memory that can have a starting or lowest address of 160000_{16}?

2. What are the high and low addresses of the memory ranges defined by each of the chip selects shown below?

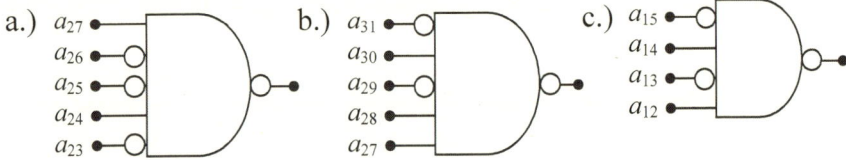

a.) $a_{27}, a_{26}, a_{25}, a_{24}, a_{23}$

b.) $a_{31}, a_{30}, a_{29}, a_{28}, a_{27}$

c.) $a_{15}, a_{14}, a_{13}, a_{12}$

3. What is the processor memory space for each chip select in problem 2?

4. What is the memory device size for each chip select in problem 2?

5. How many 16 K memories can be placed (without overlapping) in the memory space of a processor that has 24 address lines?

6. Using logic gates, design an active low chip select for the memory device described in each of the following situations.

   a.) A 256 K memory device starting at address 280000_{16} in a 4 Meg memory space

   b.) A memory device in the range 30000_{16} to $37FFF_{16}$ in a 1 Meg memory space.

7. How many latches are contained in a SRAM that has 20 address lines and 8 data lines?

8. True or false: DRAM is faster than SRAM.

9. True or false: DRAM is cheaper per bit than SRAM.

10. True or false: More DRAM can be packed into the same area (higher density) than SRAM.

11. Which is usually used for smaller memories, DRAM or SRAM?

12. When data is passed from a memory chip to the processor, what values do the bus signals $\overline{R}$ and $\overline{W}$ have?

13. What is the subnet and host id of the Class C IPv4 address 195.164.39.2?

14. Taking into account the addresses for the subnet and broadcast, how many hosts can be present on a Class C IPv4 subnet?

CHAPTER THIRTEEN

Memory Hierarchy

13.1 Characteristics of the Memory Hierarchy

We've discussed the organization and operation of RAM, but RAM is only one level of the group of components used to store information in a computer. The hard drive, for example, stores all of the data and code for the computer in a non-volatile format, and unless a file has been opened, this information can only be found on the hard drive.

Even though the hard drive stores all of the data necessary to operate the computer, other storage methods are needed. This is for a number of reasons, most notably the hard drive is slow and running programs from it would be impossible. When the processor needs data or applications, it first loads them into main memory (RAM).

Main memory and the hard drive are two levels of the computer's *memory hierarchy*. A memory hierarchy is an organization of storage devices that takes advantage of the characteristics of different storage technologies in order to improve the overall performance of a computer system. Figure 13-1 presents the components of the standard memory hierarchy of a computer. Each of these components and their function in the hierarchy is described in this chapter.

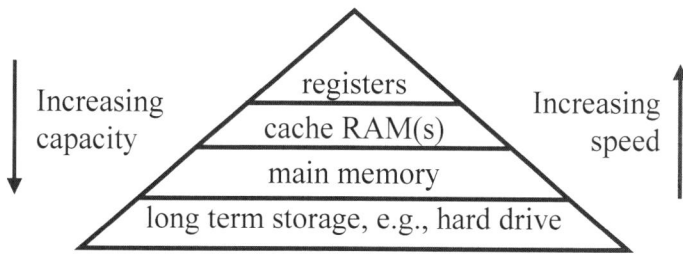

Figure 13-1   Block Diagram of a Standard Memory Hierarchy

13.2 Physical Characteristics of a Hard Drive

At the bottom of the hierarchy is long-term, high-capacity storage. This type of storage is slow making a poor choice for the processor to use for execution of programs and data access. It is, however, necessary to provide computer systems with high capacity, non-volatile storage.

269

Hard drives are the most cost-effective method of storing data. In the mid-1980's, a 30 Megabyte hard drive could be purchased for around $300 or about $10 per MB. In 2007, retailers advertised a 320 Gigabyte SATA Hard drive for around $80 or about $0.00025 per MB. In other words, the cost to store a byte of data is almost $1/40,000^{th}$ cheaper today than it was a little over two decades ago.

Hard drives store data in well-organized patterns of ones and zeros across a thin sheet of magnetic material. This magnetic material is spread either on one or both sides of a lightweight, rigid disk called a *substrate*. The substrate needs to be lightweight because it is meant to spin at very high speeds. The combination of magnetic material and substrate is called a *platter*.

The more rigid the substrate is, the better the reliability of the disk. This was especially true when the mechanisms that were used to read and write data from and to the disks were fixed making them prone to scraping across the substrate's surface if the substrate was not perfectly flat. The condition where the read-write mechanism comes in contact with the disk is called a "crash" which results in magnetic material being scraped away from the disk.

Substrates used to be made from aluminum. Unfortunately, extreme heat sometimes warped the aluminum disk. Now glass is used as a substrate. It improves on aluminum by adding:

- better surface uniformity which increases reliability;
- fewer surface defects which reduces read/write errors;
- better resistance to warping;
- better resistance to shock; and
- the ability to have the read/write mechanism ride closer to the surface allowing for better data density.

13.2.1 Hard Drive Read/Write Head

Data is recorded to the platter using a conductive coil called a head. Older drives and floppy drives use the same head for reading the data too. The head is shaped like a "C" with the gap between the ends positioned to face the magnetic material. A coil of wire is wrapped around the portion of the head that is furthest from the magnetic material. Figure 13-2 shows the configuration of this type of head.

In order to write data, an electrical current is passed through the wire creating a magnetic field within the gap of the head close to the disk.

This field magnetizes the material on the platter in a specific direction. Reversing the current would polarize the magnetic material in the opposite direction. By spinning the platter under the head, patterns of magnetic polarization can be stored in circular paths on the disk. By moving the head along the radius, nested circular paths can be created. The magnetized patterns on the platter represent the data.

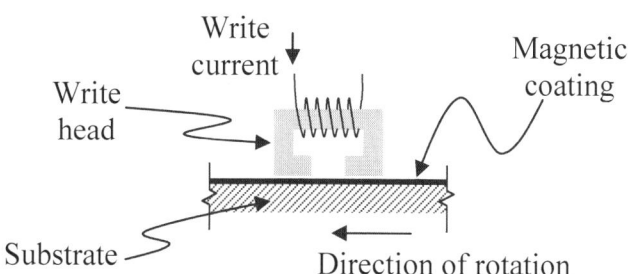

Figure 13-2 Configuration of a Hard Drive Write Head

It is possible to use the same head to read data back from the disk. If a magnetized material *moves* past a coil of wire, it produces a small current. This is the same principle that allows the alternator in your car to produce electricity. The direction of the current generated by the disk's motion changes if the direction of the magnetization changes. In this way, the same coil that is used to write the data can be used to read it. Just like the alternator in your car though, if the disk is not spinning, no current is generated that can be used to read the data.

Newer hard drives use two heads, one for reading and one for writing. The newer read heads are made of a material that changes its resistance depending on the magnetic field that is passing under it. These changes in resistance affect a current that the hard drive controller is passing through the read head during the read operation. In this way, the hard drive controller can detect changes in the magnetic polarization of the material directly under the read head.

There is another characteristic of the read/write head that is important to the physical operation of the hard drive. As was stated earlier, the area that is polarized by the head is equal to the gap in the write head. To polarize a smaller area thereby increasing the data density, the gap must be made smaller. To do this, the distance between the head and the platter must be reduced. Current technology allows heads to "fly" at less then three micro inches above the platter surface.

When the magnetic material is deposited on a flexible substrate such as a floppy diskette or a cassette tape, the flex in the material makes it possible for the head to come in contact with the substrate without experiencing reliability problems. This is not true for hard disks. Since the platters are rigid and because the platters spin at thousands of rotations per minute, any contact that the head makes with the platter will result in magnetic material being scraped off. In addition, the heat from the friction will eventually cause the head to fail.

These two issues indicate that the read/write head should come as close to the platters as possible without touching. Originally, this was done by making the platter as flat as possible while mounting the head to a rigid arm. The gap would hopefully stay constant. Any defects or warpage in the platter, however, would cause the head to crash onto the platter resulting in damaged data.

A third type of head, the **Winchester head** or "flying head" is designed to float on a cushion of air that keeps it a fixed distance from the spinning platter. This is done by shaping the head into an airfoil that takes advantage of the air current generated by the spinning platter. This means that the head can operate much closer to the surface of the platter and avoid crashing even if there are imperfections.

13.2.2 Data Encoding

It might seem natural to use the two directions of magnetic polarization to represent ones and zeros. This is not the case, however. One reason for this is that the controllers detect the *changes* in magnetic direction, not the direction of the field itself. Second, large blocks of data that are all ones or all zeros would be difficult to read because eventually the controller might lose track or synchronization of where one bit ended and the next began.

The typical method for storing data to a platter involves setting up a clock to define the bit positions, and watching how the magnetic field changes with respect to that clock. Each period of the clock defines a single bit time, e.g., if a single bit takes 10 nanoseconds to pass under the read-write head when the platter is spinning, then a clock with a period of 10 nanoseconds, i.e., a frequency of $(10\times 10^{-9})^{-1} = 100$ MHz is used to tell the controller when the next bit position is coming.

Originally, a magnetic field change at the beginning and middle of a bit time represented a logic one while a magnetic field change only at the beginning represented a logic zero. This method was referred to as **Frequency Modulation** (FM). Figure 13-3 uses an example to show the relationship between the bit-periods, the magnetic field changes, and the data stored using FM encoding.

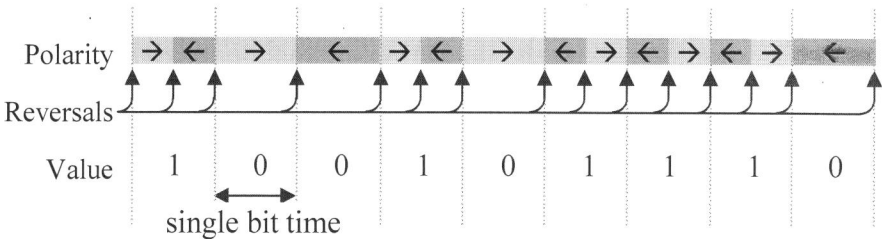

Figure 13-3 Sample FM Magnetic Encoding

To store a one using FM encoding, the polarization of the magnetic field must change twice within the space of a bit. This means that in order to store a single bit, FM encoding takes twice the width of the smallest magnetic field that can be written to the substrate. If the maximum number of polarity changes per bit could be reduced, more data could be stored to the same disk.

Modified Frequency Modulation (MFM) does this by changing the way in which the magnetic polarization represents a one or a zero. MFM defines a change in polarization in the middle of a bit time as a one and no change in the middle as a zero. If two or more zeros are placed next to each other, a change in polarization is made between each of the bit times. This is done to prevent a stream zeros from creating a long block of unidirectional polarization. Figure 13-4 uses an example to show the relationship between the bit-periods, the magnetic field changes, and the data stored using MFM encoding.

For MFM encoding, the longest period between polarity changes occurs for the bit sequence 1-0-1. In this case, the polarity changes are separated by two bit periods. The shortest period between polarity changes occurs when a one follows a one or a zero follows a zero. In these cases, the polarity changes are separated by a single bit period. This allows us to double the data density over FM encoding using the same magnetic surface and head configuration. The hard drive controller, however, must be able to handle the increased data rate.

Run Length Limited (RLL) encoding uses polarity changes to define sequences of bits rather than single bits. By equating different patterns of polarity changes to different sequences of ones and zeros, the density of bits stored to a platter can be further increased. There is a science behind generating these sequences and their corresponding polarity changes. It is based on satisfying the following requirements:

- to ensure enough polarity changes to maintain bit synchronization;
- to ensure enough bit sequences are defined so that any sequence of ones and zeros can be handled; and
- to allow for the highest number of bits to be represented with the fewest number of polarity changes.

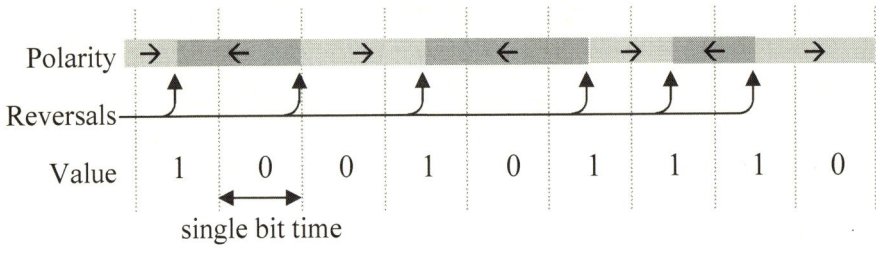

Figure 13-4 Sample MFM Magnetic Encoding

Figure 13-5 presents a sample set of RLL encoding polarity changes and the bit sequences that correspond to each of them. Any pattern of ones and zeros can be represented using this sample set of sequences.

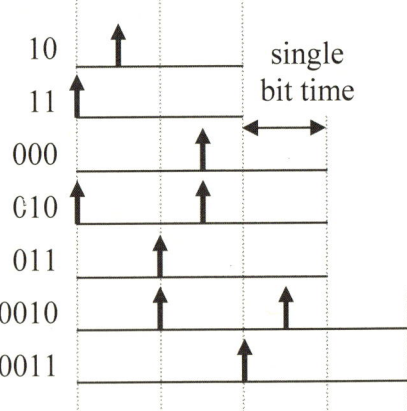

Figure 13-5 RLL Relation between Bit Patterns and Polarity Changes

Now the shortest period between polarity changes is one and a half bit periods producing a 50% increased density over MFM encoding. Figure 13-6 presents the same sample data with RLL encoding.

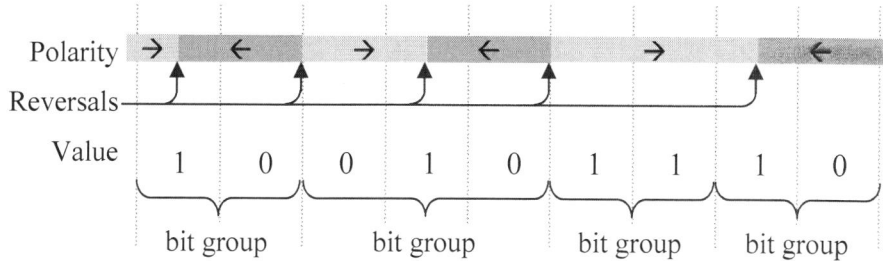

Figure 13-6 Sample RLL Magnetic Encoding

Improved encoding methods have been introduced since the development of RLL that use digital signal processing and other methods to realize better data densities. These methods include Partial Response, Maximum Likelihood (PRML) and Extended PRML (EPRML) encoding. A discussion of the details of these methods is beyond the scope of this text because it depends on a better understanding of sampling theory and electrical principles.

13.2.3 Hard Drive Access Time

There are a number of issues affecting the latency between a device requesting data and the hard drive responding with the data. Some of these issues depend on the current state of the system while others depend on the physical design of the drive and the amount of data being requested. There are four basic aspects to hard drive access time: queuing time, seek time, rotational latency, and transfer time.

After an initial request is made to a hard drive, the system must wait for the hard drive to become available. This is called queuing time. The hard drive may be busy serving another request or the bus or I/O channel that the hard drive uses may be busy serving another device that shares the link. In addition, the system's energy saving features may have powered down the drive meaning that an additional delay is incurred waiting for the drive to spin up.

The second aspect, seek time, is the amount of time it takes to get the read/write head from its current track to the desired track. Seek time is dependent on many things. First, it depends on the distance between the current and desired tracks. In addition, mechanical movement of any sort requires a ramping up before attaining maximum speed and a ramping down to avoid overshooting the desired target position. It is for these reasons that manufacturers publish a typical seek time.

Seek times have improved through the use of lighter components and better head positioning so that shorter seek distances are needed. As of this writing, the typical seek time for a hard drive is around 8 ms while higher performance drives might be as low as 4 ms. The heads used in CDROMs are heavier, and therefore, the seek time of a CDROM is longer than that of a hard drive. Older fixed head designs used multiple heads (one per track), each of which was stationary over its assigned track. In this case, the seek time was minimal, limited to the amount of time it took to electrically switch to the desired head.

Once the head has been positioned over the desired track, the drive must wait for the platters to rotate to the sector containing the requested data. This is called rotational latency. The worst case occurs when the start of the desired sector has just passed under the head when the drive begins looking for the data. This requires almost a full rotation of the platters before the drive can begin transferring the data. We can use the following calculation to determine the time required for a platter in a 7200 RPM drive to make a full rotation.

$$\frac{1 \text{ minute}}{7200 \text{ rotations}} \times \frac{60 \text{ seconds}}{1 \text{ minute}} = 8.3 \text{ ms per rotation}$$

If we make the assumption that on average the desired sector will be one half of a rotation away from the current position, then the average rotational latency should be half the time it takes for a full rotation. This means that for a 7200 RPM drive, the estimated rotational latency should be about 4.2 milliseconds.

Queuing time, seek time, and rotational latency are somewhat random in nature. Transfer time, however, is more predictable. Transfer time is the time it takes to send the requested data from the hard drive to the requesting device. Theoretically, the maximum transfer time equals the amount of time it takes for the data to pass beneath the head. If there are N sectors per track, then the amount of time it takes to retrieve a single sector can be calculated as shown below.

Theoretical transfer time for a sector = $(N \times \text{rotational speed})^{-1}$

Figure 13-7 presents a graphical representation of seek time, rotational latency, and transfer time.

As an example, let's calculate the amount of time it would take to read a 1 Mbyte file from a 7200 RPM drive with a typical 8 ms seek time that has 500 sectors per track each of which contains 512 bytes.

Begin by determining how many sectors the file requires. Dividing 1 Mbyte (1×10^6 bytes) by 512 bytes/sector shows that 1954 sectors will be required. There are two things to note about this number. First, $1 \times 10^6 \div 512$ actually equals 1953.125, but since files are stored on sector boundaries, the last sector must be partially empty. Second, authorities such as NIST, IEEE, and IEC have recommend Mbyte to represent 10^6 instead of 2^{20} as is used in the section on memory.

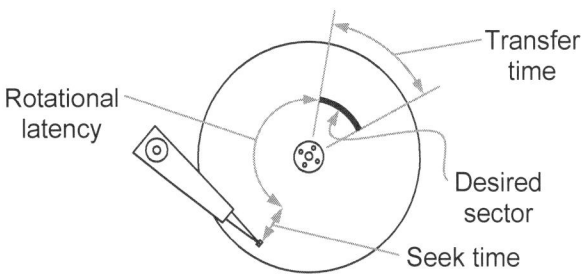

Figure 13-7 Components of Disk Access Time

Next, let's determine the transfer time for a single sector. If it takes 8.3 milliseconds for a complete revolution of the spindle, then during that time 500 sectors pass beneath the head. This means that a sector passes beneath the head every 8.3 ms/rotation ÷ 500 sectors/rotation = 16.7 microseconds/sector. This can also be calculated using the expression presented above.

Transfer time for a sector = $(500 \times 7200 \text{ RPM} \times 1/60 \text{ minutes/sec})^{-1}$
= 1/60000 seconds/sector
= 0.0000167 seconds/sector

Transferring 1954 sectors should take 1954 × 16.7 = 32.6 ms. By adding the average seek time and rotational latency, we can predict the total access time not counting queuing time.

Time to access 1 Mbyte file = 8 ms + 4.2 ms + 32.6 ms = 44.8 ms

There are a few of problems with this example. First, it will be discussed later how not all hard drives have a constant number of sectors per track. Therefore, the use of 500 sectors per track in the problem statement is not accurate. Second, this example assumes that the sectors of the file have been stored in consecutive locations. This is referred to as *sequential access*. Unfortunately sequential access is not always possible. File system fragmentation where the blocks of a file end up scattered across dissociated sectors of the hard disk hurts disk performance because each discontinuity in the order of the sectors forces the drive to incur an additional seek time and rotational latency.

Lastly, with 500 sectors per track, the almost 2000 sectors of this file will need to be stored on at least four tracks. Each time a drive is forced to switch tracks, an additional seek time and rotational latency will be incurred. In the case of our example, 12.2 ms must be added for each of the three additional tracks bringing the access time to 81.4 ms.

If the sectors of the file are stored randomly across the tracks of the platters, individual seek times and rotational latencies will be required for each sector. This is referred to as *random access*. In this case, each sector will take 8 ms + 4.2 ms + 0.017 ms = 12.217 ms to retrieve. Multiplying this by 1954 sectors means that retrieving the 1 Mbyte file in random access will take 23.872 seconds.

13.2.4 Self-Monitoring, Analysis & Reporting Technology System

A hard drive crash rarely comes without a warning. The user may be unaware of any changes in their hard drive's operation preceding a mechanical failure, but there are changes. For example, if a hard drive's platters are taking longer to get up to full speed, it may be that the bearings are going bad. A hard drive that has been experiencing higher than normal operating temperatures may also be about to fail.

Newer drives now support a feature referred to as **Self-Monitoring Analysis and Reporting Technology** (SMART). SMART enabled drives can provide an alert to the computer's BIOS warning of a parameter that is functioning outside of its normal range. This usually results in a message to the user to replace the drive before it fails.

SMART attribute values are stored in the hard drive as integers in the range from 1 to 253. Lower values indicate worse conditions. Depending on the parameter and the manufacturer, different failure thresholds are set for each of the parameters. The parameters measured vary from drive to drive with each drive typically monitoring about twenty. The following is a sample of some types of measurements:

- *Power On Hours*: This indicates the age of the drive.
- *Power Cycle Count*: This also might be an indication of age.

- **Spin Up Time**: A longer spin up time may indicate a problem with the assembly that spins the platters.
- **Temperature**: Higher temperatures also might indicate a problem with the assembly that spins the platters.
- **Head Flying Height**: A reduction in the flying height of a Winchester head may indicate it is about to crash into the platters.

There are still unpredictable failures such as the failure of an IC or a failure caused by a catastrophic event such as a power surge, but now the user can be forewarned of most mechanical failures.

13.3 Organization of Data on a Hard Drive

The width of a hard drive's read/write head is much smaller than that of the platter. This means that there are a number of non-overlapping positions for the read/write head along the platter's radius. By allowing the movable read/write head to be positioned at intervals along the radius of the disk, information can be recorded to any of a number of concentric circles on the magnetic material. Each one of these circles is called a *track*. A typical hard drive disk contains thousands of tracks per inch (TPI) on a single side of a platter, each track being the width of the read/write head. Figure 13-8 shows how these tracks correspond to the movement and size of the read/write head.

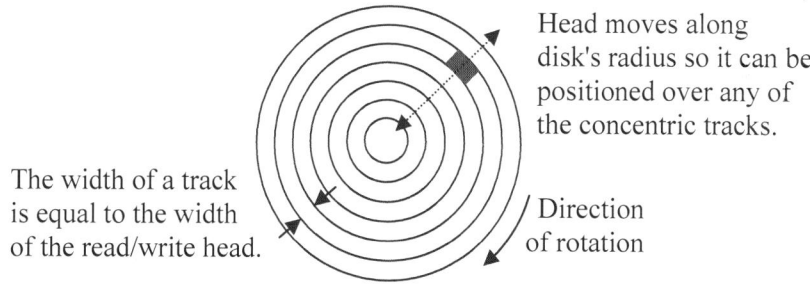

Figure 13-8 Relation between Read/Write Head and Tracks

A small gap called an *intertrack gap* is placed between the tracks to avoid interference from neighboring data. Reducing this gap allows for more data to be stored on a disk, but it also increases the risk of having data corrupted when data from an adjacent track bleeds over.

Each track is divided into sections of around 512 bytes apiece. These sections are called *sectors*. A platter may have sectors that are fixed in size for the whole platter or they may have variable amounts of data depending on their location on the platter relative to the center of rotation. There are typically hundreds of sectors per track.

In addition to the gaps left between the tracks, gaps are also left between the sectors. These gaps allow for a physical separation between the blocks of data and are typically used to help the hard drive controller when reading from or writing to the disk. These gaps are called *intersector gaps*. Figure 13-9 shows the relationship of these gaps to the tracks and sectors.

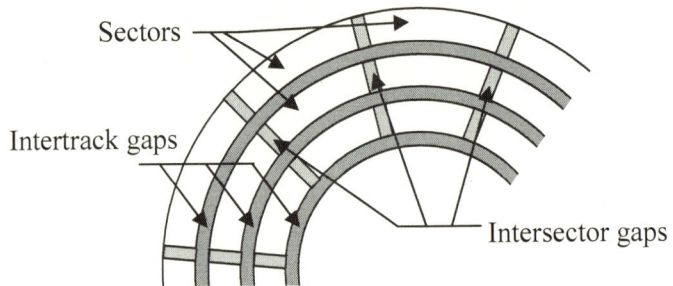

Figure 13-9 Organization of Hard Disk Platter

One way to increase the capacity of a hard drive is to increase the number of surfaces upon which the magnetic material is placed. The first way to do this is to place magnetic material on both sides of the platter. When this is done, a second read-write head must be placed on the opposite side of the platter to read the second magnetic surface. By using the same organization of sectors and tracks, this doubles the capacity of the hard drive.

A second method for increasing capacity is to mount multiple platters on a single spindle, the axis around which all of the platters rotate. Each additional magnetic surface adds to the capacity of the drive, and as with putting magnetic material on both sides of a single platter, all magnetic surfaces have the same organization of sectors and tracks, each sector lining up with the ones above it and below it. Every additional magnetic surface requires an additional read-write head.

All of the heads of a hard drive are locked together so that they are reading from the exact same location on each of their respective surfaces. Therefore, each track on each surface that is the same distance from the spindle can be treated as a unit because the hard drive controller is accessing them simultaneously. The set of all tracks, one from each surface, that are equidistant from the spindle are referred to as a *cylinder*. This virtual entity is depicted in Figure 13-10.

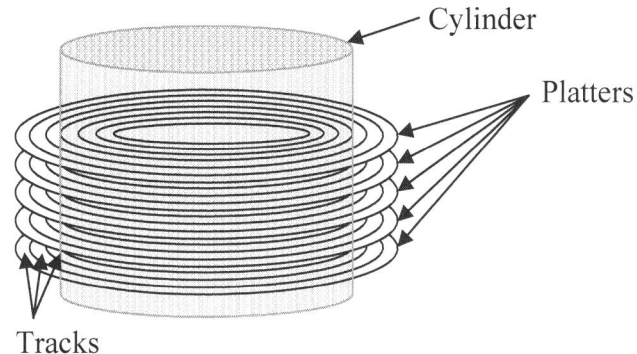

Figure 13-10 Illustration of a Hard Drive Cylinder

Using this information, we can develop a method for calculating the capacity of a hard drive. In general, the capacity of a hard drive equals the number of bytes per sector multiplied by the number of sectors per track multiplied by the number of cylinders multiplied by 2 if the platters have magnetic material on both sides and finally multiplied by the number of platters.

Figure 13-9 shows a platter that has the same number of sectors per track regardless of the radius of the track. From this figure, it can be seen that the physical size of a sector becomes smaller as its distance from the spindle is reduced. Since the number of bits per sector is constant, the size of a bit is also reduced.

Because the smallest allowable size for a bit is dictated by the size of the read-write head, the number of bits per track is limited by the number of bits that can fit on the smallest track, the one closest to the spindle. Because of this limitation, the outside tracks waste space when the bits become wider than is required by the head. Regardless of where the head is positioned, bits will pass under the head at a constant rate. This arrangement is called *constant angular velocity (CAV)*.

A better use of the space on the platter can be realized by letting the width of all bits be defined by the width of the read-write head regardless of the track position. This allows for more bits to be stored on the outer tracks. This tighter arrangement of bits can be seen in the comparison of CAV Figure 13-11a with the equal sized bits in Figure 13-11b.

282 Computer Organization and Design Fundamentals

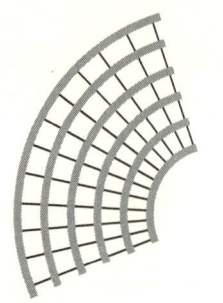   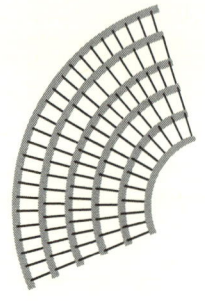

a.) Equal number of bits   b.) Equal sized bits

Figure 13-11   Equal Number of Bits per Track versus Equal Sized Bits

The problem with doing this is that as the read-write head moves to the outer tracks, the rate at which the bits pass under the head increases dramatically over that for the smallest track. This contrasts with the fixed number of bits per track which has the same data rate regardless of the position of the read-write head. This means that the hard drive with the equal sized bits requires a more complex controller.

Regardless of how the bits are arranged on the platters, the number of *bits per sector* must remain constant for all tracks. Since partial sectors are not allowed, additional bits cannot be added to tracks further from the spindle until a full sector's worth of bits can be added. This creates "zones" where groups of neighboring tracks have the same number of sectors, and therefore, the same number of bits. This method is called ***Zone Bit Recording (ZBR)***. Figure 13-12 compares CAV with ZBR.

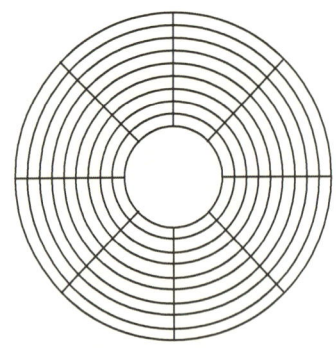   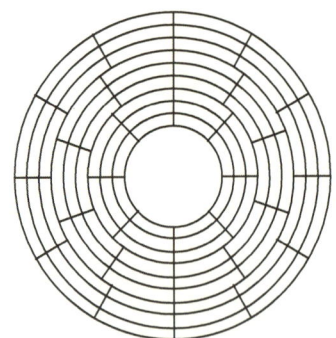

a.) Constant Angular Velocity   b.) Zone Bit Recording

Figure 13-12   Comparison of Sector Organizations

This brings us to the next layer of data organization on a hard drive: formatting. Formatting is the process of setting or clearing bits on the platters in an effort to organize and locate the files that will be stored on the hard drive. The methods used by hard drives to organize data can also be found on other rotational storage media such as floppy disks and Zip® disks.

Every hard drive utilizes two types of formatting: low-level and O/S-level. *Low-level formatting (LLF)* depends on the mechanics of the hard drive and its controller. It divides the platters into usable subsections by defining the tracks and sectors. In addition to defining the divisions, it also stores digital information allowing the controller to properly access the data. This additional information includes:

- Synchronization fields that provide timing and positional information to the controller;
- ID information to allow the controller to identify which track and sector its heads are currently positioned over; and
- Error correcting codes to detect and correct errors in the data.

LLF is driven by the mechanical operation of the hard drive and is independent of the operating system that uses it. At one time, an LLF could be performed with a computer's BIOS, but because of the complexity of modern hard drives, LLF is now performed at the factory only. The closest function currently available is a utility called a *zero fill*. This function erases all data on a hard drive by filling the sectors with zeroes.

O/S-level formatting is used to create a file system so that the operating system can find and load data from the hard drive. This includes information such as the folder structure, file attributes, and on which sectors the files are stored.

There is a level of logical hard drive organization between low-level formatting and O/S level formatting called *partitioning*. Partitioning uses a table contained on the hard drive that defines individual, non-overlapping "logical drives," i.e., drives that look like separate drives themselves, but in actuality are all contained on a single set of platters.

One of the original uses of partitioning was to divide a hard drive into smaller logical units when the hard drives that manufacturers produced became too large for a BIOS or operating system to handle. For example, to install a 2 Gigabyte hard drive on a system where the

BIOS was only capable of seeing 512 Megabyte drives, the hard drive has to be logically divided into at least four drives.

Another application of partitioning is if different O/S-level formatting is needed on a single hard drive. If, for example, a user wishes to load both Windows and Linux on the same hard drive, three logical drives would be needed, one with a Windows format, one with a Linux native format, and one with a Linux swap format.

At one time, performance benefits could be realized with effective partitioning, but this is no longer true with advances in hard drive design.

13.4 Cache RAM

Even with increases in hard drive performance, it will never be practical to execute programs or access data directly from these mechanical devices. They are far too slow. Therefore, when the processor needs to access information, it is first loaded from the hard drive into main memory where the higher performance RAM allows fast access to the data. When the processor is finished with the data, the information can either be discarded or used to update the hard drive.

Because of its expense, the capacity of a computer's main memory falls short of that of its hard drive. This should not matter though. Not all of the data on a hard drive needs to be accessed all of the time by the processor. Only the currently active data or applications need to be in RAM. Additional performance improvements can be realized by taking this concept to another level.

Remember from our discussion in Chapter 12 that there are two main classifications of RAM: static RAM (SRAM) and dynamic RAM (DRAM). SRAM is faster, but that speed comes at a price: it has a lower density and it is more expensive. Since main memory needs to be quite large and inexpensive, it is implemented with DRAM.

Could, however, the same relation that exists between main memory and a hard drive be realized between a small block of SRAM and a large main memory implemented in DRAM? Main memory improves the performance of the system by loading only the information that is currently in use from the hard drive. If a method could be developed where the code that is in immediate use could be stored in a small, fast SRAM while code that is not quite as active is left in the main memory, the system's performance could be improved again.

Due to the nature of programming, instructions that are executed within a short period of time tend to be clustered together. This is due primarily to the basic constructs of programming such as loops and subroutines that make it so that when one instruction is executed, the chances of it or its surrounding instructions being executed again in the near future are very good. Over a short period of time, a cluster of instructions may execute over and over again. This is referred to as the *principle of locality*. Data also behaves according to this principle due to the fact that related data is often defined in consecutive locations.

To take advantage of this principle, a small, fast SRAM is placed between the processor and main memory to hold the most recently used code and data under the assumption that they will most likely be used again soon. This small, fast SRAM is called a *RAM cache*.

Figure 13-13 Cache Placement between Main Memory and Processor

The reason the SRAM of the cache needs to be small is that larger address decoder circuits are slower than small address decoder circuits. The larger the memory is, the more complex the address decoder circuit. The more complex the address decoder circuit is, the longer it takes to select a memory location based on the address it received. Therefore, making a memory smaller makes it faster.

It is possible to take this concept a step further by placing an even smaller SRAM between the cache and the processor thereby creating two levels of cache. This new cache is typically contained inside of the processor. By placing the new cache inside the processor, the wires that connect the two become very short, and the interface circuitry becomes more closely integrated with that of the processor. Both of these conditions along with the smaller decoder circuit result in even faster data access. When two caches are present, the one inside the processor is referred to as a level 1 or *L1 cache* while the one between the L1 cache and memory is referred to as a level 2 or *L2 cache*.

Figure 13-14 L1 and L2 Cache Placement

The *split cache* is another cache system that requires two caches. In this case, a processor will use one cache to store code and a second cache to store data. Typically, this is to support an advanced type of processor architecture such as pipelining where the mechanisms that the processor uses to handle code are so distinct from those used for data that it does not make sense to put both types of information into the same cache.

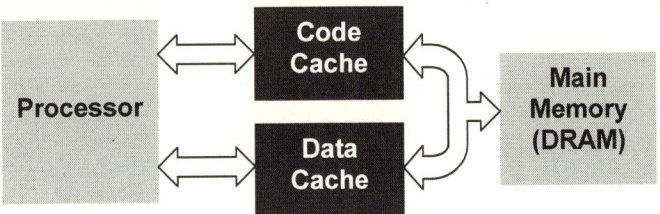

Figure 13-15 Split Cache Organization

13.4.1 Cache Organization

The success of caches is due primarily to the principle of locality. This suggests that when one data item is loaded into a cache, the items close to it in memory should be loaded too. For example, if a program enters a loop, most of the instructions that make up that loop will be executed multiple times. Therefore, when the first instruction of a loop is loaded into the cache, time will be saved if its neighboring instructions are loaded at the same time. That way the processor will not have to go back to main memory for subsequent instructions.

Because of this, caches are typically organized so that when one piece of data or code is loaded, the *block* of neighboring items is loaded too. Each block loaded into the cache is identified with a number called a *tag* that can be used to determine the original addresses of the data in main memory. This way, when the processor is looking for a piece of data or code (hereafter referred to as a word), it only needs to look at the tags to see if the word is contained in the cache.

The each block of words and its corresponding tag are combined in the cache to form a *line*. The lines are organized into a table much like that shown in Figure 13-16. It is important to note that when a word from within a block of words is needed from main memory, the whole block is moved into one of the lines of the cache along with the tag used to identify from where it came.

13.4.2 Dividing Memory into Blocks

Main memory stores all of its words in sequential addresses. The cache, however, has no sequential order. Therefore, it is the addressing scheme of main memory that is used to define the blocks of words and the method for locating them. The definition of blocks in main memory is logical only; it has no effect on how the words are stored.

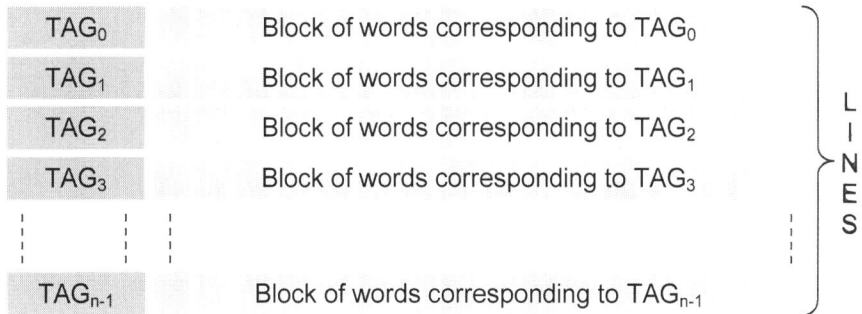

Figure 13-16 Organization of Cache into Lines

The full main memory address defines a specific memory location within memory. For example, a unique twenty-bit address such as $3E9D1_{16} = 0011\ 1110\ 1001\ 1101\ 0001_2$ points to exactly one memory location within a 1 Meg memory space.

If we "hide" the last bit of the address, i.e., that bit could be a one or a zero, than the resulting address could refer to one of two possible locations, $3E9D1_{16}$ ($0011\ 1110\ 1001\ 1101\ 0001_2$) or $3E9D0_{16}$ ($0011\ 1110\ 1001\ 1101\ 0000_2$). If we hide the last two bits, then the last two bits could be 00_2, 01_2, 10_2, or 11_2. Therefore, the address could be referring to one of the following four possible sequential locations:

$$3E9D0_{16} = 0011\ 1110\ 1001\ 1101\ 0000_2$$
$$3E9D1_{16} = 0011\ 1110\ 1001\ 1101\ 0001_2$$
$$3E9D2_{16} = 0011\ 1110\ 1001\ 1101\ 0010_2$$
$$3E9D3_{16} = 0011\ 1110\ 1001\ 1101\ 0011_2$$

This is how a block is defined. By removing a small group of bits at the end of an address, the resulting identifier points to a group of memory locations rather than a specific address. Every additional bit that is removed doubles the size of the group. This group of memory locations is what is referred to as a block.

The number of words in a block is defined by the number of bits removed from the end of the address to create the block identifier. For example, when one bit is removed, a block contains two memory locations. When two bits are removed, a block contains four memory locations. In the end, the size of a block, k, is defined by:

$$k = 2^w \qquad (13.1)$$

where w represents the number of bits "removed". Figure 13-17 shows an example of a 1 Meg memory space divided into four word blocks.

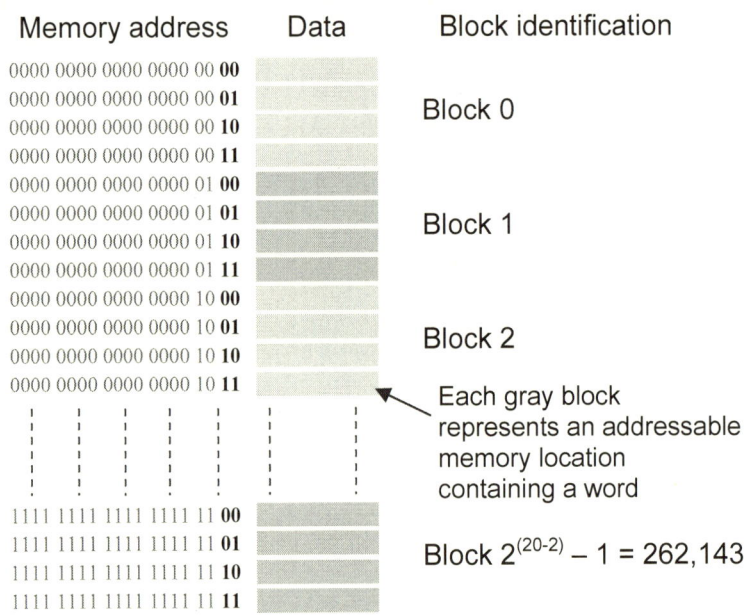

Figure 13-17 Division of Memory into Blocks

To organize memory into blocks, a memory address is divided into two logical sets of bits, one to represent the block number and one to identify the word's position or offset within the block. The memory address for the example in Figure 13-17 uses the most significant 18 bits to identify the block and the last two bits to identify a word's position within the block. Figure 13-18 presents this division using the address 10100101011010010110_2 ($A5696_{16}$).

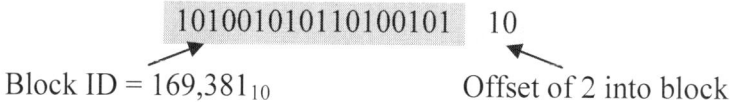

Block ID = $169{,}381_{10}$ Offset of 2 into block

Figure 13-18 Organization of Address Identifying Block and Offset

Example
How many blocks of 8 words are there in a 1 Gig memory space?

Solution
Eight words require three bits to uniquely identify their position within a block. Therefore, the last three bits of the address represent the word's offset into the block. Since a 1 Gig (2^{30}) address space uses 30 address lines, there are $30 - 3 = 27$ remaining bits in the address. These bits are used to identify the block. Below is a diagram of the logical organization of the address.

Memory address → a_{29} a_{28} a_{27} ... a_4 a_3 a_2 a_1 a_0

                         Bits identifying block   Bits identifying offset

13.4.3 Cache Operation

When the processor needs a word from memory, it first checks the cache. The circuits used to access the same word from main memory may be activated simultaneously so no time is lost in case the data is not available in the cache, a condition known as a **miss**. If the search of the cache is successful, then the processor will use the cache's word and disregard the results from main memory. This is referred to as a **hit**.

In the case of a miss, the entire block containing the requested word is loaded into a line of the cache, and the word is sent to the processor. Depending on the design of the cache/processor interface, the word is either loaded into the cache first and then delivered to the processor or it is loaded into the cache and sent to the processor at the same time. In the first case, the cache is in control of the memory interface and lies between memory and the processor. In the second case, the cache acts like an additional memory on the same bus with the main memory.

13.4.4 Cache Characteristics

The cache system used by a processor is defined by six traits:

- the size of the cache;
- the size of a block, which when combined with the size of the cache defines the number of lines;
- the number of caches (i.e., multiple levels or a split cache);
- the mapping function (the link between a block's address in memory and its location in the cache);
- the replacement algorithm (the method used to figure out which block to remove from the cache in order to free up a line); and
- the write policy (how the processor writes data to the cache so that main memory eventually gets updated).

As far as the size of a cache is concerned, designers need to perform a balancing act to determine the best size cache for a system. The larger a cache is, the more likely it is that the processor will find the word it needs in the cache. The problem is that as a cache gets larger, the address decoding circuits also get larger and therefore slower. In addition, more complicated logic is required to search a cache because of the seemingly random way that the blocks are stored in it. Larger caches are also more expensive.

There is also a relationship between size of a block and the performance of the cache. As the block size goes up, the possibility of getting a hit when looking for data could go up due to more words being available within a region of active code. For a fixed cache size, however, as the block size increases, the number of blocks that can be stored in a cache goes down thereby potentially reducing the number of hits. A typical size of a block is fairly low, between 4 and 8 words.

13.4.5 Cache Mapping Functions

There are three main methods used to map a line in the cache to an address in memory so that the processor can quickly find a word: direct mapping, full associative mapping, and set associative mapping. Let's begin with *direct mapping*.

Assume main memory is divided up into n blocks and the cache has room to contain exactly m blocks. Because of the nature of the cache, m is much smaller than n. If we divide m into n, we should get an integer which represents the number of times that the main memory could fill the cache with different blocks from its contents.

For example, if main memory is 128 Meg (2^{27}) and a block size is four words (2^2), then main memory contains $n = 2^{27-2} = 2^{25}$ blocks. If the cache for this system can hold 256 K (2^{18}) words, then $m = 2^{18-2} = 2^{16}$ blocks. Therefore, the main memory could fill the cache $n/m = 2^{25}/2^{16} = 2^{25-16} = 2^9 = 512$ times.

Another way of putting it is this: the memory is much larger than a cache, so each line in the cache is responsible for storing one of many blocks from main memory. In the case of our example above, each line of the cache is responsible for storing one of 512 different blocks from main memory at any one time.

Direct mapping is a method used to assign each memory block in main memory to a specific line in the cache. If a line is already filled with a memory block when a new block needs to be loaded, the old block is discarded from the cache. Figure 13-19 shows how multiple blocks from our example are mapped to each line in the cache.

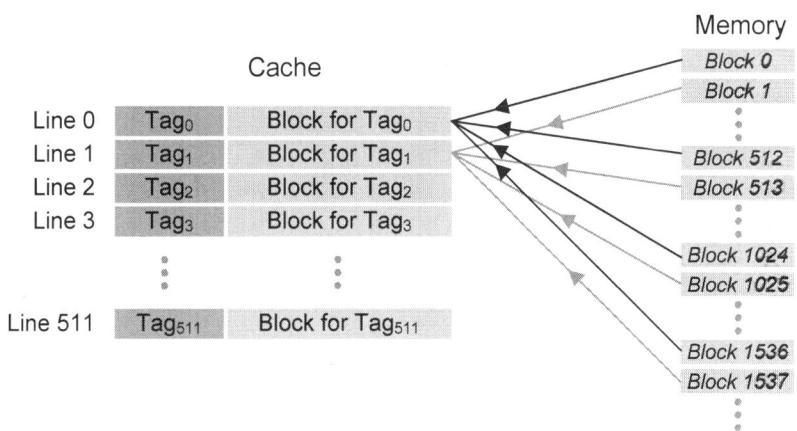

Figure 13-19 Direct Mapping of Main Memory to Cache

As with locating a word within a block, bits are taken from the main memory address to uniquely define the line in the cache where a block should be stored. For example, if a cache has $2^9 = 512$ lines, then a line would need 9 bits to be uniquely identified. Therefore, the nine bits of the address immediately to the left of the word identification bits would identify the line in the cache where the block is to be stored. The bits of the address not used for the word offset or the cache line would be used for the tag. Figure 13-20 presents this partitioning of the bits.

Once the block is stored in the line of the cache, the tag is copied to the tag location of the line. From the cache line number, the tag, and the word position within the block, the original address of the word can be reconstructed.

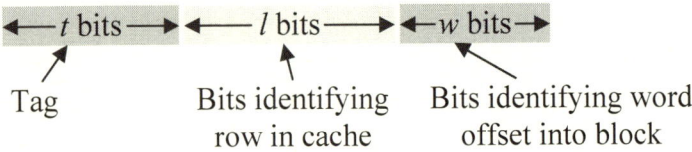

Figure 13-20 Direct Mapping Partitioning of Memory Address

In a nutshell, direct mapping breaks an address into three parts: t tag bits, l line bits, and w word bits. The word bits are the least significant bits identifying the specific word within a block of memory. The line bits are the next least significant identifying in which line of the cache the block will be stored. The remaining bits are stored with the block as the tag identifying where the block is located in main memory.

Example

Assume a cache system has been designed such that each block contains 4 words and the cache has 1024 lines, i.e., the cache can store up to 1024 blocks. What line of the cache is supposed to hold the block that contains the word from the twenty-bit address $3A456_{16}$? In addition, what is the tag number that will be stored with the block?

Solution

Start by dividing the address into its word id, line id, and tag bits. Since $4=2^2$, then the two least significant bits identify the word, i.e., $w = 2$. Since the cache has $1024=2^{10}$ lines, then the next 10 bits identify the line number where the data is supposed to be stored in the cache, i.e., $l = 10$. The remaining $t = 20 - w - l = 8$ bits are the tag bits. This partitions the address $3A456_{16} = 00111010010001010110_2$ as follows:

00111010	0100010101	10
tag bits	line id bits	word id bits

Therefore, the block from address $3A454_{16}$ to $3A457_{16}$ will be stored in line $0100010101_2 = 277_{10}$ of the cache with the tag 001110102_2.

Example

The first 10 lines of a 256 line cache are shown in the table below. Identify the address of the data that is shaded ($D8_{16}$). For this cache, a block contains 4 words. The tags are given in binary in the table.

Line #	Tag	word 00	word 01	word 10	word 11
0	110101	12	34	56	78
1	010101	54	32	6A	D3
2	000111	29	8C	ED	F3
3	001100	33	A2	2C	C8
4	110011	9A	BC	D8	F0
5	001101	33	44	55	66
6	010100	92	84	76	68
7	000100	FE	ED	00	ED
8	100000	00	11	22	33
9	101000	99	88	77	66

Solution

Start by finding the number of bits that represent each part of the address, i.e., the word id, the line id, and the tag. From the table, we can see that 2 bits represent the positions of each of the four words in a block and that 6 bits are used to represent the tag.

Since the cache has $256=2^8$ lines, then the line number in the cache is represented with 8 bits, and the address is partitioned as follows:

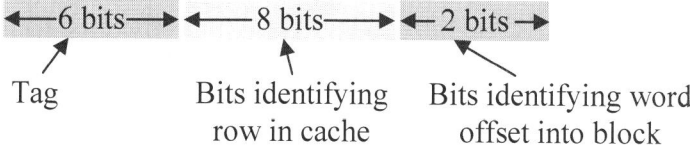

The shaded cell in the table has a tag number of 110011_2. The line number is 4, which in 8 bit binary is 00000100_2. Last of all, the word is in the third column which means that it is the 10_2 word within the block. (Remember to start counting from 00_2.) Putting the tag, line id, and word id bits together gives us:

294   Computer Organization and Design Fundamentals

110011	00000100	10
tag bits	line id bits	word id bits

Therefore, the address that the shaded cell containing $D8_{16}$ came from is 1100 1100 0001 0010$_2$ = $CC12_{16}$.

Example

Using the table from the previous example, determine if the data stored in main memory at address $101C_{16}$ is contained in this cache, and if it is, retrieve the data.

Solution

Converting $101C_{16}$ to binary gives us 0001 0000 0001 1100$_2$. By using the breakdown of bits for the tag, line id, and word id, the binary value can be divided into its components.

000100	00000111	00
tag bits	line id bits	word id bits

From this we see that the line in the cache where this data should be stored is 00000111$_2$ = 7_{10}. The tag currently stored in this line is 000100$_2$ which equals the tag from the above partitioned address. Therefore, the data from main memory address $101C_{16}$ is stored in this cache. If the stored tag did not match the tag pulled from the address, we would have known that the cache did not contain our address.

Lastly, we can find the data by looking at the offset 00$_2$ into the block at line 7. This gives us the value FE_{16}.

Example

Using the same table from the previous two examples, determine if the data from address 9827_{16} is in the cache.

Solution

Converting the hexadecimal address 9827_{16} to binary gives us 9827_{16} = 1001 1000 0010 0111$_2$. By using the breakdown of bits for the tag, line id, and word id, we can divide this value into its components.

100110	00001001	11
tag bits	line id bits	word id bits

From this we see that the tag is 100110_2, the line number is $00001001_2 = 9_{10}$, and the word offset into the block is 11_2. Looking at line number 9 we see that the tag stored there equals 101000_2. Since this does not equal 100110_2, the data from that address is not contained in this cache, and we will have to get it from the main memory.

Fully associative mapping does not use line numbers at all. It divides the main memory address into two parts: the word id and a tag. In order to see if a block is stored in memory, the tag is pulled from the memory address and a search is performed through all of the lines of the cache to see if the block is present.

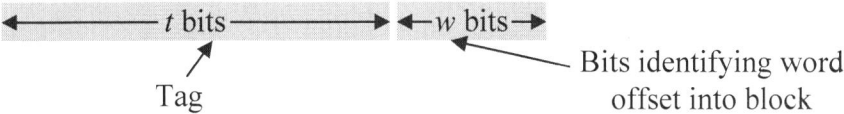

Figure 13-21 Fully Associative Partitioning of Memory Address

This method of searching for a block within a cache sounds like it might be a slow process, but it is not. Each line of the cache contains its own compare circuitry that is able to discern in an instant whether or not the block is contained at that line. With all of the lines performing this compare in parallel, the correct line is identified quickly.

This mapping algorithm is meant to solve a problem that occurs with direct mapping where two active blocks of memory map to the same line of the cache. When this happens, neither block of memory is allowed to stay in the cache long before it is replaced by the competing block. This results in a condition referred to as thrashing where a line in the cache goes back and forth between two or more blocks, usually replacing a block before the processor was through with it. Thrashing is avoided by allowing a block of memory to map to any line of the cache.

This benefit has a price, however. When a fully associative cache is full and the processor needs to load a new block from memory, a decision has to be made regarding which of the existing blocks is to be discarded. The selection method, known as a ***replacement algorithm***, should have a goal of replacing the block least likely to be needed by the processor in the near future.

There are numerous replacement algorithms, no one of which is significantly better then the others. In an effort to realize the fastest operation, each of these algorithms is implemented in hardware.

- **Least Recently Used (LRU)** – This method replaces the block that hasn't been read by the processor in the longest period of time.
- **First In First Out (FIFO)** – This method replaces the block that has been in cache the longest.
- **Least Frequently Used (LFU)** – This method replaces the block which has had fewest hits since being loaded into the cache.
- **Random** – This method randomly selects a block to be replaced. It has only slightly lower performance than LRU, FIFO, or LFU.

Example

The table below represents five lines from a cache that uses fully associative mapping with a block size of eight. Identify the address of the shaded data ($C9_{16}$).

Tag	\multicolumn{8}{c}{Word id bits (in binary)}							
	000	001	010	011	100	101	110	111
01101101100010_2	16	36	66	28	A1	3B	D6	78
01000110101101_2	54	C9	6A	63	54	32	00	D3
00010001110011_2	29	8C	ED	FD	29	54	12	F3
00011110011100_2	39	FA	B5	C1	33	9E	33	C8
10011001011011_2	23	4C	D2	40	6A	76	A3	F0

Solution

The tag for $C9_{16}$ is 01000110101101_2. When combining this with the word id of 001_2, the address in main memory from which $C9_{16}$ was retrieved is $01000110101101001_2 = 46A9_{16}$.

Example

Is the data from memory address $1E65_{16}$ contained in the table from the previous example?

Solution

For this cache, the last three bits identify the word and the rest of the bits act as the tag. Since $1E65_{16} = 0001111001100101_2$, then 101_2 is the word id and 0001111001100_2 is the tag. Scanning the rows shows that the fourth row contains this tag, and therefore the table contains the data in which we are interested. The word identified by 101_2 is $9E_{16}$.

The last mapping algorithm presented here is *set associative mapping*. Set associative mapping combines direct mapping with fully associative mapping by grouping together lines of a cache into sets. The sets are identified using a direct mapping scheme while the lines within each set are treated like a miniature fully associative cache where any block that is to be stored in the set can be stored to any line within the set. Figure 13-22 represents this arrangement with a sample cache that uses four lines to a set.

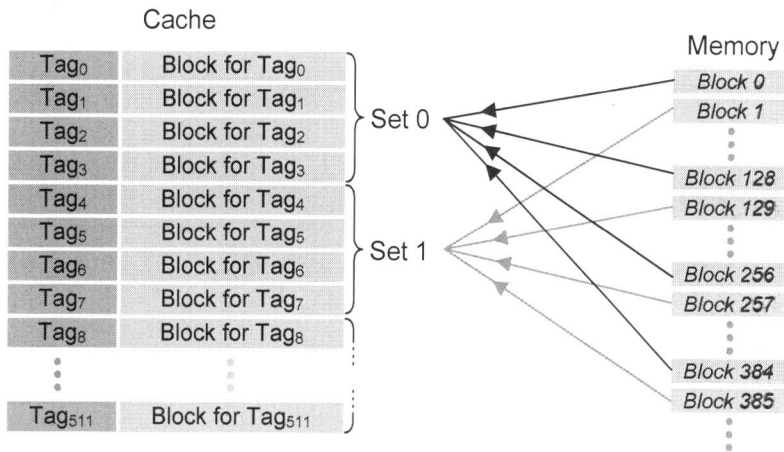

Figure 13-22 Set Associative Mapping of Main Memory to Cache

A set associative cache that has k lines per set is referred to as a k-way set associative cache. Since the mapping scheme uses the memory address just as direct mapping does, the number of lines contained in a set must be equal to an integer power of two, e.g., two, four, eight, sixteen, and so on.

Let's use an example to further explain set associative mapping. Assume that a system uses a cache with $2^9 = 512$ lines, a block of memory contains $2^3 = 8$ words, and the full memory space contains 2^{30} = 1 Gig words. In a direct mapping scheme, this would leave $30 - 9 - 3$

298 Computer Organization and Design Fundamentals

= 18 bits for the tag. Note that the direct mapping method is equivalent to the set associative method where the set size is equal to one line.

By going from direct mapping to set associative with a set size of two lines per set, the number of sets is equal to half the number of lines. In the case of the cache with 512 lines, that would give us 256 sets of two lines each which would require eight bits from the memory address to identify the set. This would leave 30 – 8 – 3 = 19 bits for the tag. By going to four lines per set, the number of sets is reduced to 128 sets requiring seven bits to identify the set and twenty bits for the tag.

Figure 13-23 shows how each time the number of lines per set in the example is doubled, the number of bits used to identify the set is reduced by one thereby increasing the number of tag bits by one.

Tag bits	Set ID bits	Word ID bits	
18 bits	9 bits	3 bits	Direct mapping (1 line/set)
19 bits	8 bits	3 bits	2-way set associative (2^1 lines/set)
20 bits	7 bits	3 bits	4-way set associative (2^2 lines/set)
21 bits	6 bits	3 bits	8-way set associative (2^3 lines/set)
⋮	⋮	⋮	
25 bits	2 bits	3 bits	128-way set associative (2^7 lines/set)
26 bits	1 bit	3 bits	256-way set associative (2^8 lines/set)
27 bits		3 bits	Fully associative (1 big set)

Figure 13-23 Effect of Cache Set Size on Address Partitioning

When a block from memory needs to be stored to a set already filled with other blocks, one of the replacement algorithms described for fully associative mapping is used. For a 2-way set associative cache, one of the easiest replacement algorithms to implement is the least recently used method. Each set contains a single bit identifying which of the two lines was used last. If the bit contains a zero, then the first line was used last and the second line is the one that should be replaced. If the bit contains a one, the first line should be replaced.

Example

Identify the set number where the block containing the address $29ABCDE8_{16}$ will be stored. In addition, identify the tag and the lower and upper addresses of the block. Assume the cache is a 4-way set associative cache with 4K lines, each block containing 16 words, with the main memory of size 1 Gig memory space.

Solution

First, we need to identify the partitioning of the bits in the memory address. A 1 Gig memory space requires 30 address lines. Four of those address lines will be used to identify one out of the 16 words within the block. Since the cache is a 4-way set associative cache, the number of sets equals 4K lines divided by four lines per set, i.e., $1K = 2^{10}$. Therefore, ten address lines will be needed to identify the set. The figure below represents the partitioning of the 30 bit address.

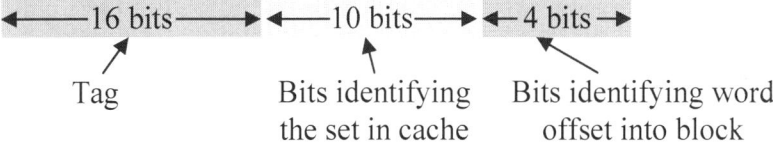

Tag   Bits identifying   Bits identifying word
                the set in cache   offset into block

Converting $29ABCDE8_{16}$ to a 30-bit binary value gives us $001010011010101111001101111010 00_2$. The first sixteen bits, $0010100110101011 11_2$, represent the tag. The next ten bits, $0011011110_2 = 222_{10}$, represent the set in which the block will be stored. The last four bits, $1000_2 = 8_{10}$, represent the word position within the block. The lowest address will be the one where word 0000_2 is stored and the highest address will be the one where the word 1111_2 is stored. Replacing the last four bits of $29ABCDE8_{16}$ with 0000_2 gives us a low address of $29ABCDE0_{16}$ while replacing them with 1111_2 gives us a high address of $29ABCDEF_{16}$

13.4.6 Cache Write Policy

The last characteristic of caches discussed here is the **cache write policy**, i.e., the method used to determine how memory is updated when the cache is written to by the processor. There are a number of issues surrounding this topic, most of which apply to multi-processor systems which are beyond the scope of this text. Basically, when the cache is written to, the corresponding location in memory becomes obsolete.

One method for resolving this is to have the cache update memory every time the processor writes to the cache. This is called a **write through policy**. The problem with this is that it creates a great deal of memory bus traffic, some of which might be unnecessary if the same memory location is being updated often. This policy also slows the write process since both memories are being updated at the same time.

A second method is to update main memory only when a line of the cache that has been modified to is about to be replaced with a new block from memory. This is called a ***write back policy***. This method runs into problems when more than one processor such as an I/O processor is sharing memory. Solutions include making shared memory non-cacheable, adding an additional processor to watch all of the caches and make appropriate updates when a write occurs, or giving all of the processors the ability to check other caches for updates.

13.5 Registers

At the top of the memory hierarchy is a set of memory cells called ***registers***. A register is a group of latches that have been combined in order to perform a special purpose. This group of latches may be used to store an integer, store an address pointing to memory, configure an I/O device, or indicate the status of a process. Whatever the purpose of the register is, all of the bits are treated as a unit.

Registers are contained inside the processor and are integrated with the circuitry used to perform the processor's internal operations. This integration places registers within millionths of a meter of the action resulting in very quick access times. In addition, the typical processor contains fewer than a hundred registers making decoding very simple and very fast. These two features combine to make registers by far the fastest memory unit in the memory hierarchy.

Because of the integral part they play in computer architecture, the details and applications of registers are presented in Chapter 15.

13.6 What's Next?

This chapter presented the system of memory components that serve the processor. This system will be revisited in Chapter 15 where a detailed examination of the organization of the components inside of the processor will be introduced.

Chapter 14 presents another important component supporting the processor: serial communications. Up to this point, our discussion of the processor has used the parallel bus to transfer data. The parallel bus has some drawbacks though. These include higher expense, lack of adaptability, and lower reliability. Chapter 14 presents the basic structure of a serial communications system followed by a presentation of two serial protocols.

Problems

1. Why is it important for hard drive substrates to be rigid?
2. Why is it important for hard drive substrates to be lightweight?
3. What is the advantage of a Winchester head, and how is it achieved?
4. Sketch the pattern of magnetic polarity found using the RLL encoding of Figure 13-5 for the bit pattern 0110100110100110101.
5. Calculate the amount of time it would take to read a 2 Mbyte file from a 15,000 RPM drive with a typical 4 ms seek time that has 500 sectors per track each of which contains 512 bytes. Assume the file is stored sequentially and take into account the delays incurred each time the drive must switch tracks.
6. Repeat the previous problem assuming the sectors of the file are scattered randomly across the tracks of the platters.
7. How many blocks of 16 words are there in a 256 Gig memory space? Draw the logical organization of the full address identifying the block ID portion and the word offset portion.
8. Identify the line number, tag, and word position for each of the 30-bit addresses shown below if they are stored in a cache using the direct mapping method.

   a.) Address: $23D94EA6_{16}$ Lines in cache: 4K   Block size: 2
   b.) Address: $1A54387F_{6}$ Lines in cache: 8K   Block size: 4
   c.) Address: $3FE9704A_{16}$ Lines in cache: 16K   Block size: 16
   d.) Address: $54381A5_{16}$ Lines in cache: 1K   Block size: 8

9. True or False: A block from main memory could possibly be stored in any line of a cache using fully associative mapping.
10. What problem is the fully or set-associative mapping methods for caches supposed to solve over the direct mapping method?
11. What is the easiest replacement algorithm to use with a 2-way set associative cache?

12. The table below represents five lines from a cache that uses fully associative mapping with a block size of eight. Identify the address of the shaded data ($3B_{16}$).

Tag	Word id bits (in binary)							
	000	001	010	011	100	101	110	111
100110110110001010_2	10	65	BA	0F	C4	19	6E	C3
001110000110101010_2	21	76	CB	80	D5	2A	7F	B5
101111000101110010_2	32	87	DC	91	E6	3B	F0	A6
011101100011010110_2	43	98	ED	A2	F7	4C	E1	97
001111001001110000_2	54	9A	FE	B3	08	5D	D2	88

13. Using the table from the previous problem, identify the data value represented by each of the following addresses.

    a.) 76359_{16} b.) $386AF_{16}$ c.) $BC5CC_{16}$

14. Identify the set number, tag, and word position for each of the 30-bit addresses stored in an 8K line set associative cache.

    a.) Address: $23D94EA6_{16}$ 2-way cache   Block size: 2
    b.) Address: $1A54387F_6$ 2-way cache   Block size: 4
    c.) Address: $3FE9704A_{16}$ 8-way cache   Block size: 16
    d.) Address: $54381A5_{16}$ 4-way cache   Block size: 8

15. Using the C declarations below of a simulated 256 line cache and a 64K memory, create two functions. The first function, **bool requestMemoryAddress(unsigned int address)**, takes as its parameter a 16-bit value and checks to see if it exists in the cache. If it does, simply return a value of TRUE. If it doesn't, load the appropriate line of the cache with the requested block from memory[] and return a FALSE. The second function, **unsigned int getPercentageOfHits(void)**, should return an integer from 0 to 100 representing the percentage of successful hits in the cache.

```
typedef struct {
    int tag;
    char block[4];
}cache_line;

cache_line cache[256];

char memory[65536];
```

CHAPTER FOURTEEN

Serial Protocol Basics

Whenever there is a need for information to be passed between two computer systems, a communication scheme must be developed to support it. This scheme must include clear definitions of the physical connection, e.g., the wires and voltage levels, the pattern of signals used to synchronize and define the data, methods of encryption and error checking, and so on. Entire books are written on the system of layers that define these communication schemes. This chapter focuses on a single aspect: the pattern of bits used to send data one bit at a time across a single wire.

14.1 OSI Seven-Layer Network Model

The Open Systems Interconnection (OSI) model of networks is a method for classifying the complex components of a communication scheme so that they are easier to describe and understand. There are seven layers to this model ranging from the physical implementation (the wires and such) to the more abstract layer of the applications where the details of the network are hidden. The following is a description of the seven layers:

- *Application Layer (layer 7)* – At this layer, one application must format the data so that a second application can properly interpret it. Examples include formatting data so that an e-mail agent or a web browser can properly display data to the user.
- *Presentation Layer (layer 6)* – This layer eliminates compatibility problems caused by serving different types of networks. It acts as a generic interface between the application and the details of the network.
- *Session Layer (layer 5)* – This layer starts, maintains, and stops the logical connection between two applications.
- *Transport Layer (layer 4)* – When a block of data is sent from one application to another, mechanisms are needed to provide error checking, the partitioning of large blocks of data into smaller packets, the reassembly of the data packets, and flow control. The transport layer is responsible for these functions.

- *Network Layer (layer 3)* – Once a packet from the transport layer is placed on the network, it needs to find its way from one physical host to another. This is the responsibility of the network layer. It provides routing, forwarding, sequencing, and logical addressing. Since the delivery of a packet may involve several types of networks, this layer must remain independent of the physical implementation of the network.
- *Datalink Layer (layer 2)* – The datalink layer handles the bit-level specifications used to deliver a message within a specific type of network. Examples of datalink protocols include the IEEE 802.3 protocol which defines how the bits are organized in an Ethernet frame and the Serial Line Internet Protocol (SLIP) which may be used on a dial-up network. While the network layer uses logical addresses to identify hosts, the datalink layer uses the physical addresses of the hardware.
- *Physical Layer (layer 1)* – This layer defines how the bits are transmitted. For example, logic ones and zeros may be identified by different voltage levels, the presence or absence of light, or the frequency of a radio signal. This hardware level description of the network is considered the physical layer.

Since most protocols are described with respect to the layer on which they function, it is important to have a basic understanding of the OSI layer definitions. This chapter discusses three different protocols, one from the datalink layer, one from the network layer, and one from the transport layer.

14.2 Serial versus Parallel Data Transmission

As discussed in Chapter 12, the processor communicates to devices on the motherboard across a group of parallel wires called the bus. A data element can be transferred in an instant by placing each individual bit on a different data line or wire. The data must be held on the lines for a moment so that the inputs of the receiving device stabilize enough for a successful read. This duration, however, is independent of the number of bits of the data element.

There are a few problems with this method of communication. First, wires cost money. At the level of the motherboard, this makes the ICs more expensive due to the greater number of pins and it makes the circuit board larger and more expensive due to the extra room needed for the extra wires. At the system level, i.e., for signals going outside of the computer, each additional data line requires an additional wire in the connecting cable. This results in:

- higher cost for the cable;
- higher cost for the connectors;
- physically larger connectors making miniaturization difficult; and
- decreased reliability of the system.

An increase in the number of connectors is the primary reason for the decrease in reliability of a parallel communication scheme. This is because most failures occur at the connectors. Reliability is also reduced because of a phenomenon known as *crosstalk*. All wires act like antennas capable of transmitting and receiving electronic signals. If two wires run close together for long distances, they have a tendency to blend their signals, each transmitting their own data and receiving their neighbor's transmitted data.

Another problem with parallel communication schemes that specify the purpose of each wire in the connection is a lack of flexibility. System characteristics such as the number of bits in a data element or the number of devices that can be attached to the bus cannot be modified in a system that uses parallel communication. If, for example, a system has twenty address lines and sixteen data lines, it is restricted to a memory space of 1 Meg and can only transmit unsigned integer values from 0 to 65,535.

The alternative to transmitting data over parallel wires is to send data serially, i.e., one bit at a time, across a single wire. This allows for smaller cables, smaller connectors, fewer pins on ICs, and a more flexible data format. It comes at the expense, however, of speed. If a single wire is used to transmit control, address, and data, then a period of time is used to specify a bit rather than an individual wire. For example, a parallel bus with twenty address lines and sixteen data lines could be converted to a serial connection that took 20 + 16 = 36 "bit periods" to send the same amount of data. Note that this calculation does not take into consideration the control information that would be needed.

The next section presents the basic format of a serial data transmission. It shows how control, addressing, and data information can be sent using a single bit stream.

14.3 Anatomy of a Frame or Packet

A computer system needs a number of pieces of information in order to transmit data from one device to another. This information includes:

- *Addressing information* – If more than one device is present on a network, then addressing information for both the sender and receiver is required.
- *Control information* – In order to maintain the serial connection, control signals are needed for things such as synchronization (timing), message type, data length, protocol control information such as sequence numbers, and error checking information.
- *Data* – While the purpose of some messages can be summed up with the message type, the majority of transmissions are used to send blocks of data.

Serial communication schemes use a single stream of data to send all of this information, each bit's purpose defined by its position with respect to the beginning of the stream. Since a bit's position in the stream of data defines its purpose, strict timing and signal definitions are needed. These definitions, called a *protocol*, describe a basic unit of communication between serial devices. At the datalink layer, this unit is called a *frame*. It is called a *packet* at higher levels.

In general, a datalink frame is divided into three parts: the *preamble*, the *packet*, and the *trailer*. The preamble is a recognizable bit pattern that is used to represent the start of a frame and provide timing and synchronization for the receiver's circuitry. The timing is necessary because of slight variances in the clock signals of different devices.

The packet of the frame is subsequently divided into two parts: the *header* and the data. The header may contain information such as:

- addressing for both the sender and receiver;
- packet numbering;
- message length; and
- message type.

The data may be either the raw data sent from one device to another or it may be an encapsulation of another packet. The datalink layer is not concerned with the pattern of bits within the data portion of the packet. This is to be interpreted at a higher layer in the network model.

The frame's only purpose is to get data successfully from one device to another within a network.

By embedding packets from upper layers of the OSI network model within packets or frames from lower layers, the implementations of the different layers can be swapped as needed. As long as a packet from the network layer gets from one logical address to another, it doesn't matter whether it was carried on a datalink layer implemented with Ethernet, dial-up, or carrier pigeon for that matter. The practice of embedding packets and frames is called a *protocol stack*.

There are a number of examples of a packet being encapsulated within the packet of another frame. Once again, this is the result of the implementation of the layers of the OSI network model. For example, a typical way to send a web page from a web server to a client is to begin by partitioning the file into smaller packets that are ordered, verified, and acknowledged using the *transmission control protocol* (TCP). These TCP packets are then encapsulated into network layer packets used to transport the message from one host to another. A common protocol for this is the *internet protocol* (IP). The network layer packets must then be encapsulated into packets used to transfer the data across a specific network such as Ethernet. This places the TCP/IP packets inside the packet of an Ethernet frame. Figure 14-1 shows how the TCP packet is embedded within the IP packet which is in turn embedded into the Ethernet frame.

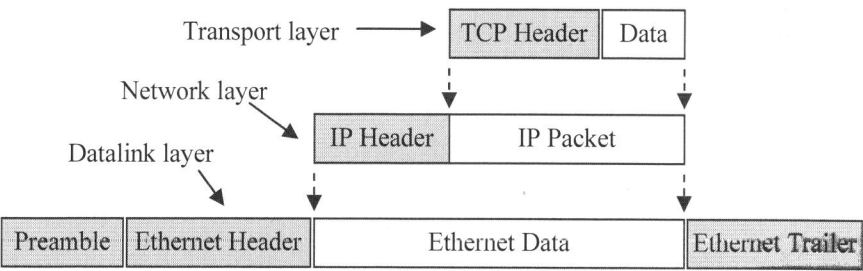

Figure 14-1 Sample Protocol Stack using TCP, IP, and Ethernet

The final part of the frame, the trailer, usually serves two purposes. The first is to provide error detection to verify that a frame has not been corrupted during transmission. Typically, this is a CRC using a predefined polynomial. (See Chapter 9) A second purpose of the trailer may be to include a special bit sequence defining the end of the frame.

14.4 Sample Protocol: IEEE 802.3 Ethernet

One commonly used datalink layer protocol is IEEE 802.3 Ethernet. This protocol is typically sent over a physical layer consisting of special grades of copper wire twisted in pairs to reduce crosstalk. A device on an Ethernet network can see all traffic placed on the network. Therefore, special mechanisms are needed in order to uniquely identify devices (hosts) and to handle messages that are lost when multiple devices attempt to send frames at the same time.

Theoretically, there is an upper limit of over 281 trillion devices on an Ethernet network. Of course this limit is not practical, but it is an indication of the level of addressing used by an Ethernet frame. A single Ethernet frame can transmit up to 1500 bytes, the integrity of which is verified using a 32-bit CRC checksum found in the frame's trailer.

Figure 14-2 presents the basic layout of an Ethernet frame. (Source: IEEE Computer Society. IEEE Std 802.3™-2002. Available on-line at http://standards.ieee.org/getieee802/download/802.3-2002.pdf)

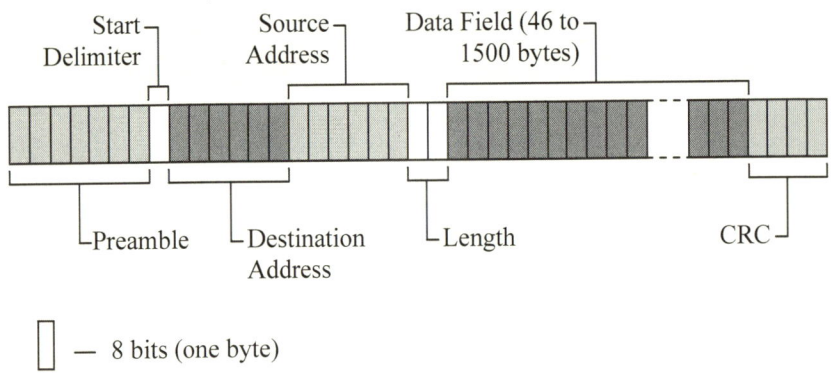

Figure 14-2 Layout of an IEEE 802.3 Ethernet Frame

The frame starts with the preamble, the start delimiter, the destination and source addresses, and the length. The preamble and start delimiter are used to tell the receiving devices when the message is going to start and to provide synchronization for the receive circuitry.

The preamble is 7 bytes (56 bits) of alternating ones and zeros starting with a one. This bit pattern creates a "square wave" which acts like a clock ensuring that all of the receiving devices are synchronized and will read the bits of the frame at the same point in each bit time.

The preamble is immediately followed by a single byte equal to 10101011_2 called the start delimiter. The first seven bits of the start delimiter continue the square wave pattern set up by the preamble. The last bit, which follows a one in the bit sequence, is also equal to a one. This pair of ones indicates to the receiving devices that the next portion of the frame, i.e., the destination address, will start at the next bit time.

The source and destination addresses come next in the frame. These are each 6 bytes long and they identify the hardware involved in the message transaction. It is important not to confuse these addresses with IP addresses which are assigned to a computer by a network administrator. The Ethernet addresses are hardwired into the physical hardware of the network interface card (NIC) and are unique to each device. They are referred to as a Medium Access Control (MAC) addresses and are loaded into the NIC by the manufacturer. They can not be modified. The first three bytes of the MAC address identify the manufacturer. If the destination address is all ones, then the message is meant to be a broadcast and all devices are to receive it.

The next field in the frame is the 2-byte length field. The value in this field represents the number of data bytes in the data field. With two bytes, it is possible to represent a value from 0 to 65,535. The definition of the IEEE 802.3 Ethernet, however, specifies that only values from 0 to 1500 are allowed in this field. Since $1500_{10} = 10111011100_2$, a value which uses only 11 bits, 5 bits are left over for other purposes. Ethernet uses these bits for special features.

The length field is followed by the data field which contains the transmitted data. Although the number of data bytes is identified by the two bytes in the length field, the definition of IEEE 802.3 Ethernet requires that the minimum length of the data field be 46 bytes. This ensures that the shortest Ethernet frame, not including the preamble and start delimiter, is 64 bytes long. If fewer than 46 bytes are being sent, additional bytes are used as padding to expand this field to 46 bytes. These filler bytes are added after the valid data bytes. The value in the length field represents only the valid data bytes, not the padding bytes.

The trailer of the Ethernet frame contains only an error detection checksum. This checksum is a 4-byte CRC. The polynomial for this CRC has bits 32, 26, 23, 22, 16, 12, 11, 10, 8, 7, 5, 4, 2, 1, and 0 set resulting in the 33-bit value $100000100110000010001110110110111_2$.

Remember from Chapter 9 that the polynomial for a CRC is one bit longer than the final CRC checksum.

Since any device can transmit data at any time, the Ethernet network must have a method for resolving when two devices attempt to send data at the same time. Simultaneous transmissions are called *collisions*, and each device, even the ones that are transmitting data, can detect when a collision occurs. It is assumed that no message survives a collision and both devices are required to retransmit.

In the event of a collision, an algorithm is executed at each of the devices that attempted to transmit data. The outcome of this algorithm is a pseudo-random number specifying how long the device is to wait before attempting to retransmit. The random numbers should be different making it so that one of the devices will begin transmitting before the other forcing the second device to wait until the end of the first device's transmission before sending its own message.

14.5 Sample Protocol: Internet Protocol

IP is a common protocol of the network layer. Remember that the network layer is used to identify logical addresses across a large network regardless of the datalink implementation. IPv4 does this by assigning a unique logical address to every host consisting of four 8-bit numbers. Using these addresses, IP is able to route blocks of data from one host to another.

The blocks of data, called datagrams, are sent either as single blocks or as partitioned fragments. Since error checking occurs at the datalink and transport layers, and since the transport layer provides mechanisms for reassembling packets, IP offers error checking only for its own header and has no mechanism for message-sequencing or flow-control.

In order to be sent across an IP network, an IP header is added to the beginning of a transport layer packet. This header contains information allowing an IP network to route the packet from one host to another. Figure 14-3 presents the basic layout of an IP packet header.

The first field of an IP header is four bits long, and it is used to identify the version of IP used to create the header. Immediately after these four bits is the four-bit length field. The value in this field, when multiplied by four, identifies the number of bytes in the header. This makes it possible to include variable length fields within the IP header.

Chapter 14: Serial Protocol Basics 311

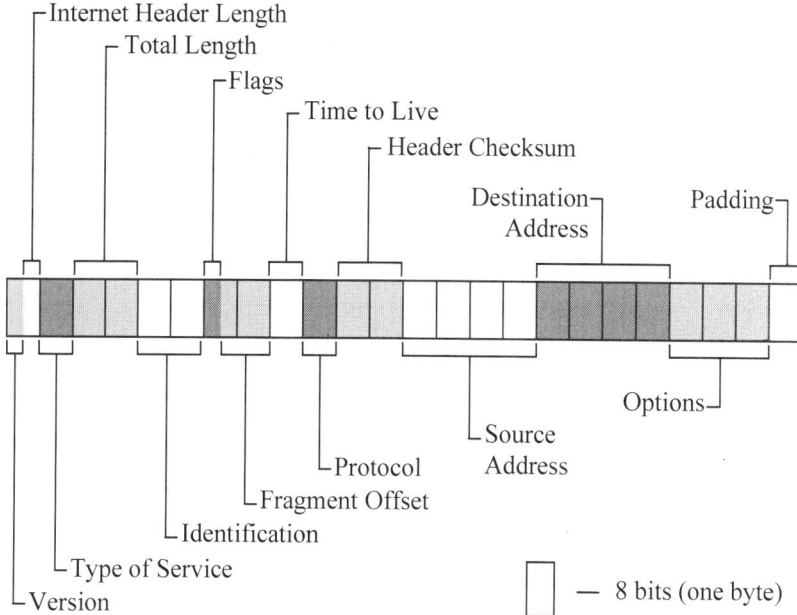

Figure 14-3 Layout of an IP Packet Header

The 8-bit field following the length field identifies the type of service. In large networks, there are usually many paths that a packet can take between two hosts. Each of these paths may have different degrees of speed, reliability, security, and so forth. The type of service field is used to specify the type of link across which a message is to be sent.

The next two bytes define the total length of the message. It is calculated by adding the number of bytes in the IP header to the number of bytes contained in the packet that follows it. This value does not count any bytes from the frame in which the IP packet may be contained.

Sixteen bits would suggest that an Ethernet packet can be up to 65,535 bytes in length. Note, however, that many networks will not allow packets of this size. For example, for an IP packet to be contained within an Ethernet frame, the packet can be at most 1500 bytes long.

The two bytes following the total length field are referred to as the identification field. They are used by the destination host in order to group the fragments contained in multiple IP packets so that they can be reassembled into a single datagram.

The next byte is divided into two parts. The first three bits represent the flag field while the last five bits are coupled with the following byte to create the fragment offset field. The first bit of the flag field is reserved. The second bit indicates whether the datagram may be partitioned into fragments. The last bit is used to identify the current packet as the last fragment.

When a datagram has been partitioned into fragments, a mechanism must be in place to reorder the fragments. This is due to the nature of large networks in which different paths of varying duration can be taken by different packets. This makes it impossible for the receiving device to determine the order in which the packets were sent merely by relying on the order in which they were received.

The fragment offset field contains thirteen bits which are used to identify the starting position of a fragment within the full datagram. Because the partitioning of datagrams must occur on 64-bit boundaries, the value in the fragment offset field is multiplied by eight to determine the fragment's offset in bytes. An offset of zero identifies the fragment as the first fragment within the datagram.

It is possible for a packet to become lost or undeliverable within a large network. Therefore, each packet is sent with a field identifying how long the packet is allowed to remain on the network. This field is referred to as the time to live field. Every time the packet encounters a module on the network, the value in the time to live field is decremented. If the value in this field is decremented to zero before reaching its destination, the packet is discarded.

The next eight bits of the IP header identify the protocol of the packet contained in the data field.

In order to verify the integrity of the IP header, a sixteen bit header checksum is calculated and inserted as the next field. IP uses the one's complement of the one's complement datasum discussed in Chapter 9. Remember that a checksum was identified as being less reliable than a CRC. The one's complement checksum, however, has proven adequate for use with IP headers.

Since the checksum is part of the IP header, this field must be filled with zeros during the checksum calculation to avoid a recursive condition. In addition, since the time to live field changes as the packet is routed across the network, the header checksum will need to be recalculated as it traverses the network.

As was mentioned earlier, IP uses logical addresses to identify both the sending and receiving devices. The next two fields of the IP header contain these addresses. The first four byte field represents the source address while the next four bytes represent the destination address field.

Some IP packets may have special requirements such as security restrictions and routing needs. These requirements are listed next in the IP header in a field referred to as the options field. Depending on the needs of a specific packet, a number of options can be represented. Therefore, this field is variable in length.

Finally, the length of an IP header must be a multiple of 32 bits. To ensure this, a padding field filled with zeros is added to the end of the IP header. Any data contained in the packet immediately follows the padding.

14.6 Sample Protocol: Transmission Control Protocol

A network layer packet such as IP may in turn contain a packet from the transport layer. A common protocol used to define a transport layer packet is the transmission control protocol (TCP). The mechanisms provided by TCP allow large blocks of data to be partitioned, delivered, reassembled, and checked for errors.

TCP uses no host addressing. Instead, TCP uses a set of logical (as opposed to physical) connections called *ports* to uniquely identify target and source applications. For example, a TCP port number may identify the data it carries as being part of a web page. Since a TCP packet contains no addressing, it depends on the network layer packet containing it to guarantee it reaches its destination.

Port numbers are identified with 16 bits and therefore can take on values from 0 to 65535. The first 1,024 ports (0 through 1023) are reserved for well-established types of applications such as http (port 80) and version 3 of the post office protocol (POP3) (port 110). Ports 1024 through 49151 are called registered ports, and like the first 1,024 ports, the purpose of these ports is well defined. Unlike the first 1,024 ports, the registered ports typically represent a specific application. For example, port 1433 is reserved for Microsoft SQL Server applications while port 3689 is reserved for Apple iTunes music sharing. The remaining ports, from 49152 through 65535, are dynamically allocated to applications requiring ports not defined by 0 to 49151.

One of the benefits of TCP is its ability to break large blocks of data into smaller packets. This makes it so that one message does not tie up the network for a long period of time. In addition, when an error occurs, only a small portion of the data must be resent rather than the whole data block.

To do this, each byte of the entire data block has a unique integer offset representing the byte's position with respect to the start of the block. This offset is used in each packet for things such as identifying the position of the current packet's data within the completed data block (sequence number) or telling the sending device the position of the data the receiver next expects to receive (acknowledgement number).

Like IP, TCP uses a header inserted before a block of data in order to contain all of the information needed to manage the packet. The layout of this header is presented in Figure 14-4.

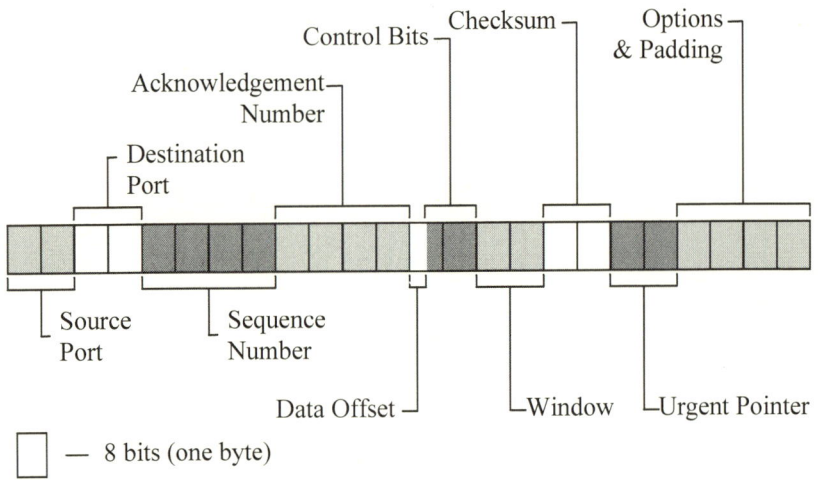

Figure 14-4 Layout of a TCP Packet Header

The first two of the ten fields of the TCP packet header identify the service that sent the message (source port) and the service that is to receive it (destination port) respectively.

The next field is a 32 bit sequence number. The sequence number identifies position of each packet within a block of data using its offset with respect to the beginning of the block. The receiver uses sequence numbers to order the received packets. If packets are received out of order, the sequence number indicates how many bytes to reserve for the missing packet(s). Both the sender and the receiver keep track of the sequence numbers in order to maintain the integrity of the data block.

The next field, the acknowledgement number, is also a 32 bit field. The receiver acknowledges a received message by placing the next expected sequence number in this field.

The next field, the data offset field, is used to identify where the TCP header ends and the data of the packet begins. The value contained in these four bits must be multiplied by four (two left shifts) to calculate the true data offset. This means that a TCP header must have a length equal to an integer multiple of 32 bits (four bytes).

The twelve bits following the data offset field are the control bits of the TCP header. The first six bits are reserved. The last six flag bits are used either to request service such as a connection reset or to identify characteristics of the packet. Figure 14-5 identifies the position and purpose of the flags in the control bits.

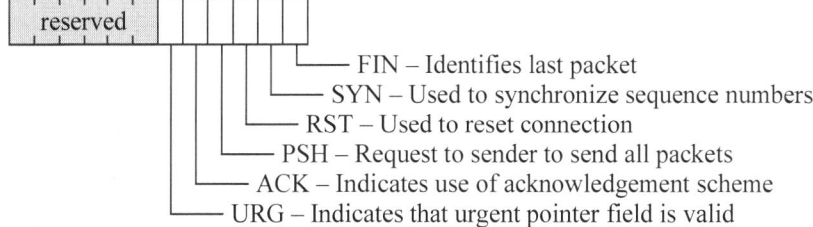

Figure 14-5 Position and Purpose of TCP Control Flags

The next field, the window field, is used by the device requesting data to indicate how much data it or its network has the capacity to receive. A number of things affect the value in this field including the amount of available buffer space the receiver has or the available network bandwidth.

A sixteen bit checksum field is next. Like IP, it contains the one's complement of the one's complement datasum. The difference is that the sum is computed across three groups of bytes:

- the TCP header without the checksum field;
- the data or payload field (if this is an odd number of bytes, pad with a byte of zeros at the end); and
- a pseudo header created using information from the IP header.

316   Computer Organization and Design Fundamentals

The pseudo header consists of the source and destination IP addresses, the protocol field of the IP header, and a count of the number of bytes in both the TCP header and the TCP data or payload field. Figure 14-6 presents the arrangement of the fields in the pseudo header.

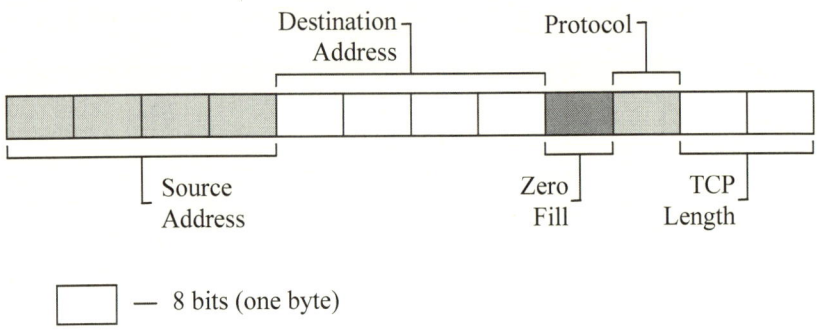

Figure 14-6 Layout of a TCP Pseudo Header

One of the flags in the control block is the urgent flag (URG). By setting this flag to a 1, the sending device is indicating that the data block contains urgent data. When this happens, the sixteen bit field following the checksum is used to identify where that data is contained within the data block. This field is referred to as the urgent pointer field. The value contained in this field is added to the sequence number to identify the position of the urgent data within the packet.

As with the IP protocol, some packets have special requirements. These requirements are identified in a variable length list of options. These options occur in the header immediately after the urgent pointer field. The options identify packet requirements such maximum receive segment size.

Because the option field is variable in length, an additional field referred to as the padding field must be added to ensure the length of the header is a multiple of four bytes. (Remember that the data offset field identifies the length of the header using integer multiples of 32 bits.) The padding field appends zeros to the header after the options field to do this.

14.7 Dissecting a Frame

Remember that the purpose of a protocol is to allow a device receiving a serial data stream to correctly interpret its contents. Figure 14-7 represents one such data stream where a TCP header and data segment is contained within an IP packet which in turn is contained within an Ethernet frame. This section uses the data in this figure to identify the components and data of the frame and its packets.

```
offset                        data
0000:    00 04 76 48 35 AD 00 B0 D0 C1 6B 31 08 53 45 00
0010:    00 53 6D F4 40 00 80 06 CC 3C C5 A8 1A 8C C5 A8
0020:    1A 97 17 0C 0D BE DE B1 57 C5 79 59 3E D4 50 18
0030:    42 18 B6 3E 00 00 00 B4 00 30 00 22 00 0E 00 00
0040:    00 05 1A 99 D6 04 DA DE 00 07 FC FF 20 DD 00 00
0050:    08 00 DA DE 09 04 02 FC FF 0E 00 00 FC FF 01 00
0060:    0D
```

Figure 14-7 Simulated Raw Data Capture of an Ethernet Frame

Note that the captured data does not include the preamble, start delimiter, or CRC of the Ethernet frame. In general, this information is used by the network interface card for synchronization of the electronics and error checking, but is not made available to the user. Therefore, the frame shown above starts with the destination and source MAC addresses of the Ethernet frame and ends with its data field.

From Figure 14-2, we see that the first six bytes after the start delimiter represent the destination address. Therefore, the MAC address of the destination card is 00:04:76:48:35:AD. Remember that the first three bytes represents the manufacturer. The three bytes 00:04:76 represents 3Com® Corporation.

The next six bytes represent the source address, i.e., the device sending the frame. In this case, the MAC address of the source is 00:B0:D0:C1:6B:31. 00:B0:D0 identifies the card as a NIC from Dell® Computer Corporation.

The next two bytes, 08:53, identifies the both the frame type and the length of the frame. Converting this value to a sixteen-bit binary value gives us $0853_{16} = 0000100001010011_2$. The most significant 5 bits represent the type, and in this case (00001_2) it is an IP version 4 type. The least significant 11 bits represent the length of the data in the frame. In this case, $000010100011_2 = 83_{10}$ indicating the data field of the Ethernet frame contains 83 bytes.

Immediately after the length field of the Ethernet frame is the start of the IP header. By using Figure 14-3 as a reference, the details of the IP packet can also be revealed.

The first four bits identifies the IP version being used. In this case, the first four bits of the byte 45_{16} equal 4, i.e., IP version 4. The next four bits in this byte equal 5. Multiplying this value by four gives us the length of the IP header: 20 bytes.

Next comes one byte identifying the type of service, i.e., the special requirements of this packet. Zeros in this field indicate that this packet has no special needs.

The next two bytes identify the total length of the IP packet, i.e., the number of bytes in the IP header plus the number of bytes of data. A 53_{16} indicates that header and data together total 83 bytes. Subsequent fields are:

- Identification field = $6DF4_{16} = 28148_{10}$
- Flags = first three bits of $40_{16} = 010_2$ (Do not fragment flag is set)
- Fragment offset = last thirteen bits of $4000_{16} = 0000000000000_2$
- Time to live = $80_{16} = 128_{10}$
- Protocol contained in data field = 06_{16} (TCP)
- Header checksum = $CC3C_{16}$
- Source address = C5.A8.1A.8C = 197.168.26.140
- Destination address = C5.A8.1A.97 = 197.168.26.151

To verify the checksum, divide the IP header into words (byte pairs), and add the words together. Doing this for our message give us:

```
  4500
  0053
  6DF4
  4000
  8006
  CC3C
  C5A8
  1A8C
  C5A8
 +1A97
  ────
  3FFFC
```

Remember that IP uses the one's complement datasum which means that the carries must be added to the datasum. This gives us a datasum of $FFFC_{16} + 3 = FFFF_{16}$ which indicates that the checksum is correct.

Immediately after the IP header is the TCP packet. Using Figure 14-4, the components of the TCP header can be identified too.

First two bytes represent the source port. In the sample data, the source port's value is $170C_{16} = 5900_{10}$. This represents a port for a virtual computing network (VNC). Next two bytes represent the destination port, which in the sample data is $0DBE_{16} = 3518_{10}$. This represents the Artifact Message Server port.

The next four bytes, $DEB157C5_{16}$, identifies the sequence number. The four-byte acknowledgement number comes next, $79593ED4_{16}$.

The first four bits of the byte following the acknowledgement number is the data offset. This is $0101_2 = 5$. Multiplying this value by four gives us the length of the TCP header, i.e., twenty bytes.

The last four bits of the same byte joined with the eight bits of the next byte represent the twelve control bits. In binary, this value is 000000011000_2. From Figure 14-5, we see that the first six bits of these twelve are reserved. After that, they come in order URG, ACK, PSH, RST, SYN, and FIN. From our data we see that the ACK and PSH flags are set.

Following the control bits is the two byte value representing the window size. This is $4218_{16} = 16920_{10}$ in our sample data.

The next two bytes represent a sixteen bit checksum of $B63E_{16}$. To verify the checksum, the one's complement datasum must be calculated from the TCP header (minus the checksum field), the data field (everything after the TCP header not including any Ethernet trailer), and the pseudo header. Note that since the data field contains 43 bytes which is an odd number, an additional byte of zeros must be added to the end to allow for the computation of a sixteen-bit checksum.

To generate the pseudo header, combine the IP source address ($C5A81A8C_{16}$), the IP destination address ($C5A81A97_{16}$), a byte of zeros concatenated with the protocol from the IP header (0006_{16}), and the length of the TCP header and the payload or data field combined (20 bytes for the header plus 43 bytes of data equals $63_{10} = 003F_{16}$).

Adding the pseudo header, the TCP header, and the data field for the sample data results in the following:

320   Computer Organization and Design Fundamentals

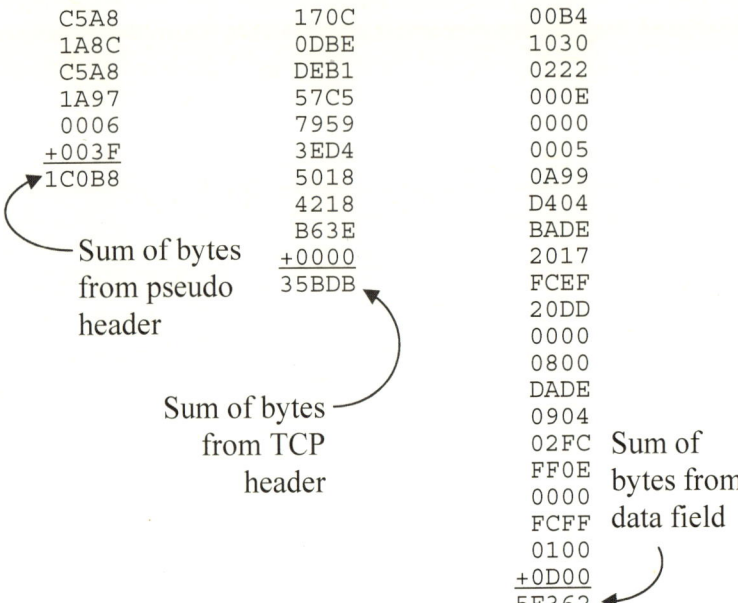

Adding these three sums together produces the result $1C0B8_{16}$ + $35BDB_{16}$ + $5E362_{16}$ = $AFFF5_{16}$. By adding the carries to the lower sixteen bits, the checksum result is $FFF5_{16}$ + A_{16} = $FFFF_{16}$. Therefore, the checksum is correct.

Following the checksum is the sixteen bit urgent pointer. The sample data has this field set to 0000_{16}. This makes sense since the URG flag was not set which causes the receiver to ignore this field.

The last field of the TCP header is the option and padding field. By using the length of the header calculated earlier, we can see that the option and padding field (which serve to fill the rest of the header) must have been left out. The header is 20 bytes without them.

14.8 Additional Resources

This chapter has provided an overview of serial protocols using examples from Ethernet, IP, and TCP. An entire book could be written on the details of any one of these protocols. This section presents a few additional references that might be helpful to gain further information on these topics.

One of the basic references for Internet protocols can be found in a list of documents referred to as *requests for comments* (RFCs). This list of RFCs is maintained by the Internet Engineering Task Force. The two RFCs used for this chapter are RFC 791 (the standard for IP) and RFC 793 (the standard for TCP). These can be found on the web at the following locations:

- Internet Protocol - DARPA Internet Program Protocol Specification (RFC 791) – http://www.faqs.org/rfcs/rfc791.html
- Transmission Control Protocol - DARPA Internet Program Protocol Specification (RFC 793) – http://www.faqs.org/rfcs/rfc793.html

The Institute of Electrical and Electronics Engineers (IEEE) maintains the standard for the Ethernet protocol. It too can be found on the web at:

- IEEE Std 802.3™-2002 – http://standards.ieee.org/getieee802/download/802.3-2002.pdf.

In the discussion of the Ethernet frame, it was shown how the first three bytes of the MAC address identify the manufacturer. A list of these manufacturer codes, called the Organization Unique Identifiers (OUI), is also maintained by the Institute of Electrical and Electronics Engineers (IEEE). It can be found at:

- IEEE OUI and Company_id Assignments – http://standards.ieee.org/regauth/oui/oui.txt

It also might be of help to be able to identify the ports identified in a TCP packet. A list of registered port numbers is maintained by the Internet Corporation for Assigned Names and Numbers (ICANN). There are a number of resources on the web that allow users to search for a specific port using the number found in the TCP header. Once such service is the Internet Ports Database which can be found at:

- The Internet Ports Database – http://www.portsdb.org/

Last of all, there are a number of programs that allow a user to capture and examine data captured by a NIC. These programs are called protocol analyzers or sniffers. Once such program, Packetyzer, is available for the Windows® operating systems under the GNU license agreement. It is available on the web from Network Chemistry at:

- Network Chemistry: Packetyzer Network Packet Analyzer – http://www.packetyzer.com

14.9 What's Next?

This chapter has shown how each bit position of a serial frame has a defined purpose allowing information to be transmitted from one device to another as long as the frame is well-defined. Although serial communication is favored as a long-distance computer system interface due to its reliability, flexibility, and cost effectiveness, there is a drawback. All of the information pertaining to the delivery of the message including addressing and control must be contained within a single stream of bits. This reduces the performance of the network.

Chapter 15 brings us back to the hardware of the computer through an introduction to the architecture of a processor. This takes us from the detailed view of logic gates to the system level view of the computer and its major components. The study of computer architecture will allow us to better understand how the components work together and how they can be used to improve the computer's performance.

Problems

1. List the two primary causes for reduced reliability in a parallel communication scheme.

2. In the IEEE 802.3 Ethernet frame format, what is the purpose of the 7 byte preamble of alternating ones and zeros sent at the beginning of the frame?

3. What is the binary value of the start delimiter of the IEEE 802.3 Ethernet frame?

4. True or false: The two-byte length field of the IEEE 802.3 Ethernet frame contains the length of the entire message including preamble and start delimiter.

5. What are the minimum and maximum values that can be contained in the length field of an IEEE 802.3 Ethernet frame?

6. What are the minimum and maximum lengths of the data field of an IEEE 802.3 Ethernet frame?

Chapter 14: Serial Protocol Basics **323**

7. True or false: If the amount of data being sent using an IEEE 802.3 Ethernet frame is less than the minimum data field length, the data is padded to 46 bytes and the length field is set to 46.

8. True or false: All devices can see all of the messages that pass across their Ethernet network, even the ones not meant for them.

9. True or false: If two Ethernet devices try to transmit at the same time and a collision occurs, this means that only one message got through and one device will have to retransmit.

10. List all of the components of the packet that are summed together to create the IP checksum?

11. List all of the components of the packet that are summed together to create the TCP checksum?

12. Describe the addressing used in an Ethernet frame.

13. Describe the addressing used in an IP packet.

14. Describe the addressing used in a TCP packet.

15. Using the data shown below, identify each of the components of the Ethernet frame and the IP and TCP packets it contains. Be sure to verify the IP and TCP checksums. (Note that the Ethernet preamble and trailer are not shown.)

```
offset                     data
0000:    00 B0 D0 FE DF 9F 00 07 B3 18 F0 00 08 00 45 60
0010:    00 B4 00 7B 40 00 2F 06 0C 86 81 2A 3A 8C 97 8D
0020:    EA 9F 1F 40 0A 49 2F 1B 57 77 91 28 81 88 50 18
0030:    40 00 E2 14 00 00 CA B1 00 00 00 86 01 00 00 A2
0040:    4C CB 2D 36 0D 13 7A 00 00 00 00 00 00 00 08 00
0050:    00 00 0F 00 00 00 2F 00 00 00 0B 02 07 66 4F 02
0060:    00 04 00 00 00 00 00 04 00 00 00 00 19 24 54 4F
0070:    50 49 43 2F 77 69 6D 2F 74 65 6E 6E 69 73 2F 73
0080:    63 6F 72 65 2F 54 07 66 4F 02 00 00 2B 74 00 00
0090:    00 00 00 00 00 00 00 00 00 00 00 26 1F 8B 08 00
00A0:    00 00 00 00 00 03 33 35 30 36 AD 71 AE 71 AA 71
00B0:    76 AC 71 72 AC 31 AC 31 06 00 11 83 33 5B 12 00
00C0:    00 00
```

CHAPTER FIFTEEN

Introduction to Processor Architecture

15.1 Organization versus Architecture

Up to this point, the discussion has focused on the components from which computers are built, i.e., computer organization. In contrast, computer architecture is the science of integrating those components to achieve a level of functionality and performance. It is as if computer organization examines the lumber, bricks, nails, and other building material while computer architecture looks at the design of the house.

We've already discussed a number of the components of computer architecture. For example, when we discussed memory in Chapter 12, we introduced the interface that the processor uses to communicate with the memory and other peripherals of the system. Chapter 13 showed how internal registers and the cache RAM improve the processor's performance.

This chapter puts these components together and introduces a few new ones to complete the architecture of a general purpose processor. A few advanced architecture topics are also examined to see how the general architecture can modified to deliver improved performance.

15.2 Components

Before going into detail on how the processor operates, we need to discuss some of its sub-assemblies. The following sections discuss some of the general components upon which the processor is built.

15.2.1 Bus

As shown in Chapter 12, a bus is a bundle of wires grouped together to serve a single purpose. The main application of the bus is to transfer data from one device to another. The processor's interface to the bus includes connections used to pass data, connections to represent the address with which the processor interested, and control lines to manage and synchronize the transaction. These lines are "daisy-chained" from one device to the next.

The concept of a bus is repeated here because the memory bus is not the only bus used by the processor. There are internal buses that the processor uses to move data, instructions, configuration, and status between its subsystems. They typically use the same number of data lines found in the memory bus, but the addressing is usually simpler. This is because there are only a handful of devices between which the data is passed.

In this chapter we will introduce new control lines that go beyond the read control, write control, and timing signals discussed in Chapter 12. These new lines are needed by the processor in order to service external devices and include interrupt and device status lines.

15.2.2 Registers

As stated when they were introduced in Chapter 13, a register stores a binary value using a group of latches. For example, if the processor wishes to add two integers, it may place one of the integers in a register labeled A and the second in a register labeled B. The contents of the latches can then be added by connecting their Q outputs to the addition circuitry described in Chapter 8. The output of the addition circuitry is then directed to another register in order to store the result. Typically, this third register is one of the original two registers, e.g., A = A + B.

Although variables and pointers used in a program are all stored in memory, they are moved to registers during periods in which they are the focus of operation. This is so that they can be manipulated quickly. Once the processor shifts its focus, it stores the values it doesn't need any longer back in memory.

The individual bit positions of the register are identified by the power of two that the position represents as an integer. In other words, the least significant bit is bit 0, the next position to the left is bit 1, the next is bit 2, and so on.

For the purpose of our discussion, registers may be used for one of four types of operations.

- *Data registers* – These registers hold the values on which to perform arithmetic or logical functions.
- *Address registers* – Sometimes, the processor may need to store an address rather than a value. A common use of an address register is to hold a pointer to an array or string. Another application is to hold the address of the next instruction to execute.
- *Instruction registers* – Remember that instructions are actually numeric values stored in memory. Each number represents a different command to be executed by the processor. Some registers

are meant specifically to hold instructions so that they can be interpreted to see what operation is to be performed.
- ***Flag registers*** – The processor can also use individual bits grouped together to represent the status of an operation or of the processor itself. The next section describes the use of flags in greater detail.

15.2.3 Flags

Picture the instrumentation on the dash board of a car. Beside the speedometer, tachometer, fuel gauge, and such are a number of lights unofficially referred to as "idiot lights". Each of these lights has a unique purpose. One comes on when the fuel is low; another indicates when the high beams are on; a third warns the driver of low coolant. There are many more lights, and depending on the type of car you drive, some lights may even replace a gauge such as oil pressure.

How is this analogous to the processor's operation? There are a number of indicators that reveal the processor's status much like the car's idiot lights. Most of these indicators represent the results of the last operation. For example, the addition of two numbers might produce a negative sign, an erroneous overflow, a carry, or a value of zero. Well, that would be four idiot lights: sign, overflow, carry, and zero.

These indicators, otherwise known as flags, are each represented with a single bit. Going back to our example, if the result of an addition is negative, the sign flag would equal 1. If the result was not a negative number, (zero or greater than zero) the sign flag would equal 0.

For the sake of organization, these flags are grouped together into a single register called the ***flags register*** or the ***processor status register***. Since the values contained in its bits are typically based on the outcome of an arithmetic or logical operation, the flags register is connected to the mathematical unit of the processor.

One of the primary uses of the flags is to remember the results of the previous operation. It is the processor's short term memory. This function is necessary for ***conditional branching***, a function that allows the processor to decide whether or not to execute a section of code based on the results of a condition statement such as "if".

The piece of code shown in Figure 15-1 calls different functions based on the relative values of *var1* and *var2*, i.e., the flow of the program changes depending on whether *var1* equals *var2*, *var1* is greater than *var2*, or *var1* is less than *var2*. So how does the processor determine whether one variable is less than or greater than another?

```
if(var1 == var2)
    equalFunction();
else if(var1 > var2)
    greaterThanFunction();
else
    lessThanFunction();
```

Figure 15-1 Sample Code Using Conditional Statements

The processor does this using a "virtual subtract." This is a subtraction that occurs in the mathematical unit of the processor where it affects the flags, but the result is discarded.

Referring back to our example, the results of a subtraction of *var2* from *var1* is used to select one of three paths through the code.

- ***var1* is equal to *var2*** – When one value is subtracted from an equal value, the result is zero. Therefore, if the zero flag is set after the subtraction, the function *equalFunction()* should be executed.
- ***var1* is greater than *var2*** – If *var1* is larger, then no borrow is needed in the subtraction which results in a non-zero value. (A borrow will set the carry flag.) Therefore, after a subtraction, if the carry flag and the zero flag are both cleared, *var1* was greater than *var2* and the function *greaterThanFunction()* is called.
- ***var1* is less than *var2*** – If *var1* is smaller, then a borrow is needed setting the carry flag. Therefore, after a subtraction, if the carry flag is set, *var1* was less than *var2* and *lessThanFunction()* is called.

Later in this chapter, there is a more detailed examination of this process including a list of the many other program flow control options that are available, each of which tests the flags to determine which code to jump to after one of these virtual subtracts.

15.2.4 Buffers

Rarely does a processor operate in isolation. Typically there are multiple processors supporting the operation of the main processor. These include video processors, the keyboard and mouse interface processor, and the processors providing data from hard drives and CDROMs. There are also processors to control communication interfaces such as USB, Firewire, and Ethernet networks. These processors all operate independently, and therefore one may finish an operation before a second processor is ready to receive the results.

If one processor is faster than another or if one processor is tied up with a process prohibiting if it from receiving data from a second process, then there needs to be a mechanism in place so that data is not lost. This mechanism takes the form of a block of memory that can hold data until it is ready to be picked up. This block of memory is called a buffer. Figure 15-2 presents the basic block diagram of a system that incorporates a buffer.

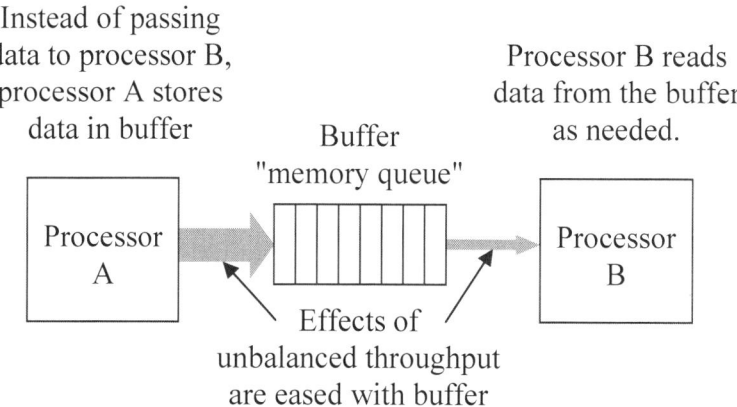

Figure 15-2 Block Diagram of a System Incorporating a Buffer

The concept of buffers is presented here because the internal structure of a processor often relies on buffers to store data while waiting for an external device to become available.

15.2.5 The Stack

During the course of normal operation, there will be a number of times when the processor needs to use a temporary memory, a place where it can store a number for a while until it is ready to use it again. For example, every processor has a finite number of registers. If an application needs more registers than are available, the register values that are not needed immediately can be stored in this temporary memory. When a processor needs to jump to a subroutine or function, it needs to remember the instruction it jumped from so that it can pick back up where it left off when the subroutine is completed. The return address is stored in this temporary memory.

The *stack* is a block of memory locations reserved to function as temporary memory. It operates much like the stack of plates at the start of a restaurant buffet line. When a plate is put on top of an existing stack of plates, the plate that was on top is now hidden, one position lower in the stack. It is not accessible until the top plate is removed.

The processor's stack works in the same way. When a processor puts a piece of data, a plate, on the top of the stack, the data below it is hidden and cannot be removed until the data above it is removed. This type of buffer is referred to as a "last-in-first-out" or LIFO buffer.

There are two main operations that the processor can perform on the stack: it can either store the value of a register to the top of the stack or remove the top piece of data from the stack and place it in a register. Storing data to the stack is referred to as "pushing" while removing the top piece of data is called "pulling" or "popping".

The LIFO nature of the stack makes it so that applications must remove data items in the opposite order from which they were placed on the stack. For example, assume that a processor needs to store values from registers A, B, and C onto the stack. If it pushes register A first, B second, and C last, then to restore the registers it must pull in order C, then B, then A.

Example

Assume registers A, B, and C of a processor contain 25, 83, and 74 respectively. If the processor pushes them onto the stack in the order A, then B, then C then pulls them off the stack in the order B, then A, then C, what values do the registers contain afterwards?

Solution

First, let's see what the stack looks like after the values from registers A, B, and C have been pushed. The data from register A is pushed first placing it at the bottom of the stack of three data items. B is pushed next followed by C which sits at the top of the stack. In the stack, there is no reference identifying which register each piece of data came from.

Chapter 15: Introduction to Processor Architecture 331

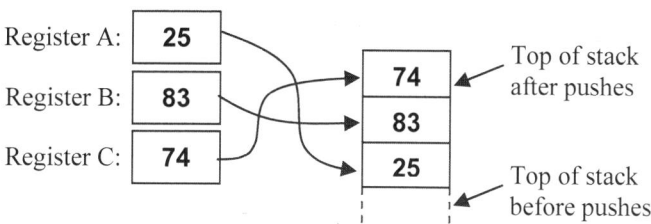

When the values are pulled from the stack, B is pulled first and it receives the value from the top of the stack, i.e., 74. Next, A is pulled. Since the 74 was removed and placed in B, A gets the next piece of data, 83. Last, 25 is placed in register C.

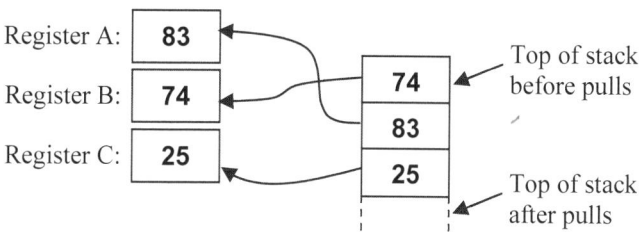

15.2.6 I/O Ports

Input/output ports or I/O ports refer to any connections that exist between the processor and its external devices. A USB printer or scanner, for example, is connected to the computer system through an I/O port. The computer can issue commands and send data to be printed through this port or receive the device's status or scanned images.

As described in the section on memory mapping in Chapter 12, some I/O devices are connected directly to the memory bus and act just like memory devices. Sending data to the port is done by storing data to a memory address and retrieving data from the port is done by reading from a memory address.

In some cases, however, the processor has special hardware just for I/O ports. This is done in one of two ways: either the device interface hardware is built into the processor or the processor has a second bus designed to communicate with the I/O devices. In Chapter 16 we will see that the Intel 80x86 family of processors uses the later method.

If the device is incorporated into the processor, then communication with the port is done by reading and writing to registers. This is sometimes the case for simple serial and parallel interfaces such as a printer port or keyboard and mouse interface.

15.3 Processor Level

Figure 15-3 presents the generic block diagram of a processor system. It represents the interface between the processor, memory, and I/O devices through the bus that we discussed in the section on memory interfacing in Chapter 12.

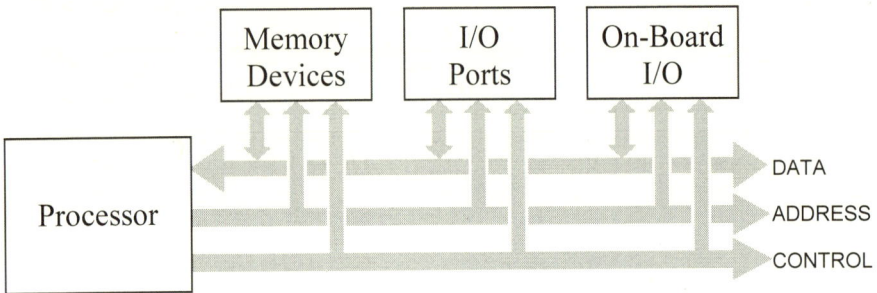

Figure 15-3   Generic Block Diagram of a Processor System

The internals of a processor are a microcosm of the processor system shown in Figure 15-3. Figure 15-4 shows a central processing unit (CPU) acting as the brains of the processor connected to memory and I/O devices through an internal bus within a single chip.

The internal bus is much simpler than the bus the processor uses to connect its external devices. There are a number of reasons for this. First, there are fewer devices to interface with, so the addressing scheme does not need to be that complex. Second, the external bus needs to be able to adapt to many different configurations using components from many different manufacturers. The internal bus will never change for that particular model of processor. Third, the CPU accesses the internal components in a well-defined, synchronized manner allowing for more precise timing logic.

The following is a description of the components of the processor shown in Figure 15-4.

- *Central processing unit (CPU)* – This is the brain of the processor. The execution of all instructions occurs inside the CPU along with the computation required to determine addressing.
- *Internal memory* – A small, but extremely quick memory. It is used for any internal computations that need to be done fast without the added overhead of writing to external memory. It is also used

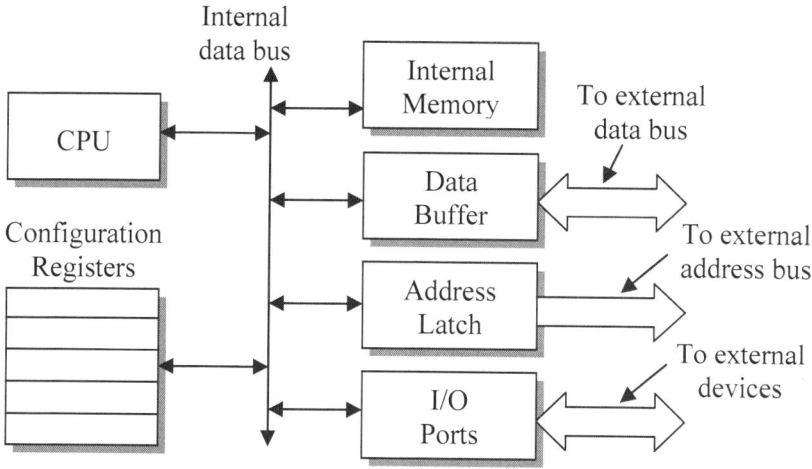

Figure 15-4 Generic Block Diagram of Processor Internals

for storage by processes that are transparent to the applications, but necessary for the operation of the processor.
- *Data buffer* – This buffer is a bidirectional device that holds outgoing data until the memory bus is ready for it or incoming data until the CPU is ready for it. This circuitry also provides signal conditioning ensuring the output signals are strong enough and the fragile internal components of the CPU are protected.
- *Address latch* – This group of latches maintains the address that the processor wishes to exchange data with on the memory bus. It also provides signal conditioning and circuit protection for the CPU.
- *I/O ports* – These ports represent the device interfaces that have been incorporated into the processor's hardware.
- *Configuration registers* – A number of features of the processor are configurable. These registers contain the flags that represent the current configuration of the processor. These registers might also contain addressing information such as which portions of memory are protected and which are not.

15.4 CPU Level

If we look at the organization inside the CPU, we see that it in turn is a microcosm of the processor block diagram of Figure 15-4. Figure 15-5 presents the organization inside a typical CPU.

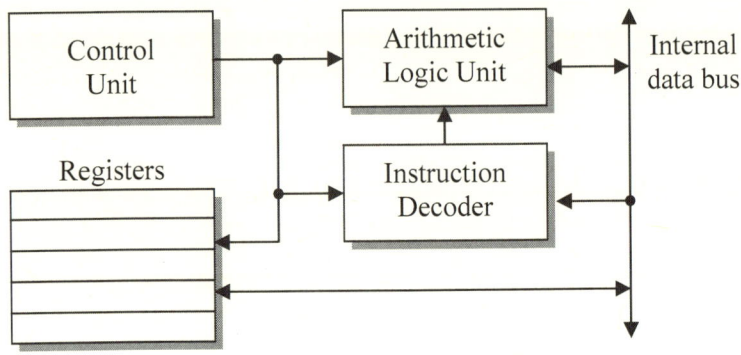

Figure 15-5 Generic Block Diagram of a Typical CPU

- *Control unit* – Ask anyone who has worked in a large business what middle management does and they might say something like, "Not a darn thing." Ask them what expertise middle management has and you are likely to get a similar answer. This of course is not true. Middle management has a very important task: they know what needs to be done, who best can do it, and when it needs to be done. This is the purpose of the control unit. It knows the big picture of what needs to be done, it knows which of the CPU's components can do it, and it controls the timing to do it.
- *Arithmetic logic unit (ALU)* – The ALU is a collection of logic circuits designed to perform arithmetic (addition, subtraction, multiplication, and division) and logical operations (not, and, or, and exclusive-or). It's basically the calculator of the CPU. When an arithmetic or logical operation is required, the values and command are sent to the ALU for processing.
- *Instruction decoder* – All instructions are stored as binary values. The instruction decoder receives the instruction from memory, interprets the value to see what instruction is to be performed, and tells the ALU and the registers which circuits to energize in order to perform the function.
- *Registers* – The registers are used to store the data, addresses, and flags that are in use by the CPU.

15.5 Simple Example of CPU Operation

Each component of the CPU has a well-defined allocation of duties. In addition, the interaction between the components is based on a lock-step communication scheme that places data where it is needed when it is needed. The power of the modern processor is the combination of its ability to execute digital commands quickly and the compiler's ability to take a complex program written in a high-level language and convert it to an efficient sequence of digital commands to be used by the CPU.

Let's examine a short piece of code to see how the CPU might execute it. The following for-loop is presented to show how a compiler might transform it to a sequence of processor commands.

```
int sum = 0, max = 0;
for (int i=0; i<100; i ++)
{
    sum += array[i];
    if (max < array[i]) max = array[i];
}
```

The first thing a compiler might do to create executable code for the processor is to determine how it is going to use its internal registers. It needs to decide which pieces of data require frequent and fast operations and which pieces can be kept in the slower main memory.

First, the index i is accessed repeatedly throughout the block of code, so the compiler would assign one of the data registers inside the CPU to contain i. Depending on the size of the registers provided by the CPU, it would only need to be an 8-bit register.

Second only to i in the frequency of their use are the values *sum* and *max*. They too would be assigned to registers assuming that enough registers existed in the CPU to support three variables. Since *sum* and *max* are defined as integers, they would need to be assigned to registers equivalent to the size of an integer as defined for this CPU. In the Pentium processor, this would be a 32-bit register.

The data contained in *array* would not be loaded into a register, at least not all at once. First of all, each element of *array* is accessed only once, and it isn't even modified during that access. Second, and more important, only a few special application processors have enough registers to hold 100 data elements.

There is one element of *array* that will be stored in a register, and that is the pointer or address that identifies where *array* is stored in memory. Each time the code needs to access an element of *array*, it multiplies the index i by the size of an integer, then adds it to the base address of *array*. This provides a pointer to the specific element of *array* in which the CPU is interested.

The sequence shown below is one possible way that a compiler might convert the sample for-loop into CPU commands.

Step 1: Clear registers assigned for i, sum, and max
Step 2: Initialize an address register to point to start of $array$
Step 3: Use address generated by adding i multiplied by the size of an integer to the starting address of $array$ to retrieve $array[i]$ from memory
Step 4: Add retrieved value to register assigned to sum
Step 5: Compare retrieved value to register assigned to max
Step 6: If the value in the register assigned to max was less than retrieved value, jump to Step 8
Step 7: Copy retrieved value to register assigned to max
Step 8: Increment register assigned to i
Step 9: Compare register assigned to i to 100
Step 10: If register assigned to i is less than 100, jump to Step 3
Step 11: Store values in registers assigned to sum and max to the appropriate memory locations for later use. Since i is visible only within this loop, it does not need to be stored.

There are two things to notice about these steps. First, the steps are very minimal. The instruction set that a CPU uses for its operation is made from short, simple commands. The typical instruction for a CPU involves either a single transaction of data (movement from a register to a register, from memory to a register, or from a register to memory), or a simple operation such as the addition of two registers.

The second thing to notice is that this simple sequence uses a two-step process to handle program flow control. In section 15.2.3, it was shown how a "virtual subtraction" is performed to compare two values. This operation sets or clears the zero flag, the sign flag, the carry flag, and the overflow flag depending on the relationship of the magnitude of the two values. For our example, this virtual subtraction occurs in Step 5 where max is compared to the next value retrieved from $array$ and in Step 9 where i is compared to the constant 100.

Every compare is followed immediately by a **conditional jump** that checks the flags to see if the flow of the program needs to be shifted to a new address or if it can just continue to the next address in the sequence. There are many more options for conditional jumps than were presented in the processor flags section. For example, a conditional "jump if greater than" might work differently when using 2's complement values rather than unsigned integer values.

Table 15-1 presents some of the many options that can be used for conditional jumps after a compare. High-level language compilers use these conditional jumps to transform if-statements, for-loops, while-loops, and switch-case blocks into code useable by the processor. Even though programmers are told to avoid using any type of "jump" commands in their code, compiled CPU instructions are full of them.

Table 15-1 Conditional Jumps to be Placed After a Compare

Jump to new address if...	Flag conditions
equal	zero flag = 1
not equal	zero flag = 0
greater than or equal (unsigned)	carry flag = 0
greater than (unsigned)	carry flag = 0 & zero flag = 0
less than or equal (unsigned)	carry flag = 1 or zero flag = 1
less than (unsigned)	carry flag = 1
greater than or equal (signed)	sign flag = overflow flag
greater than (signed)	sign flag = overflow flag & zero flag = 0
less than or equal (signed)	sign flag != overflow flag or zero flag = 1
less than (signed)	sign flag != overflow flag

The application of conditional jumps is not limited only to use with a compare command. Any operation that affects the flags can be used to change the flow of the code using conditional jumps. For example, a section of code may need to be executed if the result of a multiplication is negative while another section is to be executed if the result is positive. Table 15-2 presents some of the options that can be used for conditional jumps after an arithmetic instruction that affects the flags.

Notice that the flag settings for a conditional jump checking for equality and the conditional jump checking for a zero are the same in both Table 15-1 and Table 15-2. The processor treats these instructions the same. In fact, the processor thinks they are exactly the same command and they are represented in memory using the same code.

The only reason there are two different commands is to assist the programmer by creating syntax that makes more sense linguistically.

Table 15-2 Conditional Jumps to be Placed After an Operation

Jump to new address if…	Flag conditions
result is zero	zero flag = 1
result is not zero	zero flag = 0
result is positive	sign flag = 0
result is negative	sign flag = 1
operation generated a carry	carry flag = 1
operation generated no carry	carry flag = 0

15.6 Assembly and Machine Language

Processor designers create a basic set of instructions for every processor they design. As we have already discussed, these instructions are very simplistic, mere baby steps as compared with high-level languages such as C, C++, or BASIC. In order for the instruction decoder to decipher what an instruction represents, the instruction itself must be a number. These numbers are referred to as *machine code*. Machine code is the instruction set that the processor uses.

Humans, however, understand words, so each machine code is given a lexical equivalent. These instructions in text form are called *assembly language*. There is a one-to-one correlation between assembly language instructions and the machine code.

These definitions do not do a good job of showing how processors execute code. For that, let's design the instruction set for a mock processor and use those instructions to create some short programs.

To begin with, assume our mock processor has two registers, A and B. Next, let's assume that the processor is an 8-bit machine, i.e., both A and B are 8-bit registers and can hold unsigned values from 0 to 255 or signed values from −128 to 128. Lastly, let's assume that the processor has 16 address lines. This will give us a memory space of 2^{16} = 64K.

Now let's begin creating the instruction set by brainstorming a list of possible operations we could perform on these two registers and some of the conditional branches that we might need. Of course if you do this exercise on your own, you will come up with a completely different list of operations. Below is the instruction set we will use for our example.

Chapter 15: Introduction to Processor Architecture   339

- Move data from A to memory
- Move data from memory to A
- Load A with a constant
- Move data from B to memory
- Move data from memory to B
- Load B with a constant
- Exchange values contained in A and B
- Add A and B and put result in A
- Take the 2's complement of A (make A negative)
- Take the 2's complement of B (make B negative)
- Compare A and B
- Compare A to a constant
- Compare B to a constant
- Jump if equal
- Jump if first value is greater than second value (signed)
- Jump if first value is less than second value (signed)
- Unconditional jump (jump always)

This is a good start except that processors understand binary values, not English. By numbering the instructions, the instruction decoder can identify the requested operation by matching it with the corresponding integer (machine code). Table 15-3 presents one possible numbering.

Unfortunately, human beings are not very adept at programming with numbers. Words are far more natural for us, so each machine code instruction is given a text abbreviation to describe its operation. The resulting collection of words is called *assembly language*. The one-to-one correspondence between machine code and assembly language is used by a program called an assembler to create the machine code that will be executed by the CPU. Table 15-4 presents a suggested assembly language for the instruction set of our imaginary processor.

We need to define one last item for our instruction set before we can begin programming. Some of the processor's instructions require additional information in order to be executed. This might be a constant to be loaded into a register, an address pointing to a memory location, or some other attribute that the CPU needs in order to properly execute the instruction. These additional pieces of data are called *operands*. Table 15-5 takes the list of instructions for our processor and shows the size and type of operand that would be needed with each.

Table 15-3 Numbered Instructions for Imaginary Processor

Machine code	Instruction
01	Move data from A to memory
02	Move data from memory to A
03	Load A with a constant
04	Move data from B to memory
05	Move data from memory to B
06	Load B with a constant
07	Exchange values contained in A and B
08	Add A and B and put result in A
09	Take the 2's complement of A (negative)
0A	Take the 2's complement of B (negative)
0B	Compare A to B
0C	Compare A to a constant
0D	Compare B to a constant
0E	Jump if equal
0F	Jump if first value is greater than second value
10	Jump if first value is less than second value
11	Jump unconditionally (jump always)

Table 15-4 Assembly Language for Imaginary Processor

Machine code	Assembly language	Instruction
01	STORA	Move data from A to memory
02	LOADA	Move data from memory to A
03	CNSTA	Load A with a constant
04	STORB	Move data from B to memory
05	LOADB	Move data from memory to B
06	CNSTB	Load B with a constant
07	EXCAB	Exchange values in A and B
08	ADDAB	Add A and B and put result in A
09	NEGA	Take the 2's complement of A
0A	NEGB	Take the 2's complement of B
0B	CMPAB	Compare A to B
0C	CMPAC	Compare A to a constant
0D	CMPBC	Compare B to a constant
0E	JEQU	Jump if equal
0F	JGT	Jump if first value is greater
10	JLT	Jump if second value is greater
11	JMP	Jump always

Table 15-5 Operand Requirements for Imaginary Processor

Instruction	Operands required
Move data from A to memory (STORA)	16-bit memory address
Move data from memory to A (LOADA)	16-bit memory address
Load A with a constant (CNSTA)	8-bit constant
Move data from B to memory (STORB)	16-bit memory address
Move data from memory to B (LOADB)	16-bit memory address
Load B with a constant (CNSTB)	8-bit constant
Exchange values in A & B (EXCAB)	None
Add A and B and put result in A (ADDAB)	None
Take the 2's complement of A (NEGA)	None
Take the 2's complement of B (NEGB)	None
Compare A to B (CMPAB)	None
Compare A to a constant (CMPAC)	8-bit constant
Compare B to a constant (CMPBC)	8-bit constant
Jump if equal (JEQU)	16-bit destination address
Jump if 1st val. Is greater than 2nd val. (JGT)	16-bit destination address
Jump if 1st val. Is less than 2nd val. (JLT)	16-bit destination address
Jump always (JMP)	16-bit destination address

Now that we have a set of instructions, let's create a simple program. This first program adds two variables together and puts the result into a third variable. In a high-level language, this is a single line of code.

RESULT = VAR1 + VAR2

To do this in assembly language, however, takes a few more steps. First, our instruction set does not support the addition of variables in memory. Therefore, the data will need to be copied from memory into registers where the addition can be performed. Second, since the result of the addition will be in a register, we will need to store the data back to memory in order to free up the register. The code below is the assembly language equivalent of RESULT = VAR1 + VAR2.

```
LOADA     VAR1
LOADB     VAR2
ADDAB
STORA     RESULT
```

The next step is to have an assembler convert this assembly language code to machine language so the processor can execute it.

There is another thing that must be done before a processor can execute code: the variable names must be converted into addresses. For the purpose of our example, assume that VAR1 is stored at address $5E00_{16}$, VAR2 is stored at $5E01_{16}$, and RESULT is stored at $5E02_{16}$. By using Table 15-4 to convert the assembly language to machine code and by substituting the addresses shown above, the assembly language program becomes the following sequence of numbers. (All of the values are shown in hexadecimal.)

```
02    5E00
05    5E01
08
01    5E02
```

This is what the processor reads and executes. In memory, it appears as a sequence of binary values, but to the instruction decoder, each byte becomes executable code and data. The following sequence of values is how the data would appear in memory.

```
02 5E 00 05 5E 01 08 01 5E 02
```

Now that it has been shown how assembly language is converted into machine code, let's go the other way and see how the CPU might interpret a sequence of numbers stored as code in memory. Table 15-6 presents a sample of some code stored in memory starting at address 1000_{16}. Each location stores a byte which is the size of a single machine code instruction, an 8-bit constant, or one half of a 16-bit address. All of the values are shown in hexadecimal.

Table 15-6 A Simple Program Stored at Memory Address 1000_{16}

Address	Data	Address	Data	Address	Data
1000_{16}	02_{16}	1005_{16}	$0F_{16}$	$100A_{16}$	05_{16}
1001_{16}	12_{16}	1006_{16}	10_{16}	$100B_{16}$	08_{16}
1002_{16}	$3E_{16}$	1007_{16}	09_{16}	$100C_{16}$	01_{16}
1003_{16}	$0C_{16}$	1008_{16}	09_{16}	$100D_{16}$	12_{16}
1004_{16}	FF_{16}	1009_{16}	06_{16}	$100E_{16}$	$3E_{16}$

Assuming that the instruction decoder is told to begin executing code starting at address 1000_{16} and by using the machine code to assembly language translations found in Table 15-4, this string of values can be decoded into executable instructions. Starting at address 1000_{16}, we see that the first instruction is 02_{16}. Table 15-4 equates 02_{16} to the LOADA instruction while Table 15-5 shows that LOADA uses a 16-bit address. Therefore, the next two bytes in memory (addresses 1001_{16} and 1002_{16}) contain the address from which register A will be loaded. This gives us the first instruction: LOADA 123E.

The next instruction comes after the operands of the LOADA instruction. This puts us at address 1003_{16}. Address 1003_{16} contains $0C_{16}$ which we see from Table 15-4 represents CMPAC, i.e., compare A with a constant. Table 15-5 shows that CMPAC uses a single 8-bit constant as its operand. Since 1004_{16} contains FF_{16}, the 2's complement representation of -1, the next instruction is CMPAC -1.

The CMPAC -1 instruction is followed by the machine code $0F_{16}$ at address 1005_{16}. $0F_{16}$ represents the assembly language JGT, "Jump if first value is greater than second value." When this instruction is executed, it will jump if the value loaded into accumulator A is greater than -1, i.e., if it is a positive number or zero. The next two bytes represent the address that will be jumped to, 1009_{16}.

By continuing this process for the remainder of the code, the assembly language program that is represented by this machine code is revealed. Figure 15-6 presents the final code with the leftmost column presenting the address where the instruction begins and the rightmost column representing an in-line comment field.

1000_{16}	LOADA	$123E_{16}$	;Put data from address $123E_{16}$ in A
1003_{16}	CMPAC	-1	;Compare A to -1
1005_{16}	JGT	1009_{16}	;If A>-1, jump to address 1009_{16}
1008_{16}	NEGA		;A = $-$A
1009_{16}	CNSTB	5	;Put a constant 5 in B
$100B_{16}$	ADDAB		;A = A + B
$100C_{16}$	STORA	$123E_{16}$	;Store A at address $123E_{16}$

Figure 15-6 Decoded Assembly Language from Table 15-6

Notice that if A is positive or zero, the compare and subsequent JGT at addresses 1003_{16} and 1005_{16} respectively will force the processor to skip over the instruction at 1008_{16} and execute the CNSTB 5 at address 1009_{16}. In a high-level language, the code above might look like the following two instructions where the address of VAR is $123E_{16}$.

```
if (VAR > -1) VAR = -VAR;
VAR = VAR + 5;
```

It is important to note that not only does machine language require variable names to be replaced with references to memory addresses, but jumps must also use addresses. Second, note that a comment field has been added to the code in Figure 15-6. All assembly languages have a provision commenting. Usually it is of the in-line variety where a character, in this case a semi-colon (;), is used to comment out all of the subsequent characters until the end of the line is reached.

Every processor has an assembly language associated with it. Since the processors have different architectures, functions, and capabilities, the languages are usually quite different. There are, however, similarities. For example, there are three general categories of instructions for all processors: data transfer, data manipulation, and program control Data transfer instructions are used to pass data between different parts of the processor and memory. These include:

- Register-to-register transfers
- Register-to-memory or port transfers
- Memory or port-to-register transfers
- Memory or port-to-memory or port transfers

Data manipulation instructions make use of the ALU to operate on values contained in the registers or in memory. These include:

- Math operations such as add, subtract, multiply, and divide
- Logic operations such as and, or, xor, and not
- Bit manipulation such as shifting

Within the CPU is a register that contains an address pointing to the next instruction to be executed. There are a number of different names given to this register such as ***program counter*** or ***instruction pointer***. Every time an instruction is executed, this pointer is modified so that it points to the next instruction to be executed. Program control instructions are used to assign new values to this register so that control can jump to a new position in the program. Some of the program control instructions use the CPU's flags to determine whether a jump in the code will be performed or not. These are the conditional jumps described earlier. The following is a short list of some of the major program control instructions:

- Jump to a new address of the code
- Jump to a subroutine or function
- Return from a subroutine or function
- Conditional jumps

There are a number of reasons to program in assembly language just as there are a number of reasons to avoid it. The tiny, almost primitive processor dependent assembly language instructions cause many problems for programmers. The result is code that is:

- complicated to learn and use;
- hard to debug;
- more time consuming to write;
- unable to be directly transferred to a different processor; and
- harder to decipher if the programmer is unfamiliar with it.

The main benefits of programming in assembly language are due to the fact that the programmer is working much closer to the electronics of the processor. This makes it so that the details of the processor are not hidden by the operating system or compiler. Programming in assembly language gives the programmer:

- full access to all processor resources;
- the ability to make much faster code; and
- the ability to make far more compact code.

15.7 Big-Endian/Little-Endian

In the previous section, some of the operands were 16-bits in length and had to be broken into 8-bit values in order to be stored in memory. It is not much of a problem to store numbers larger than the width of the data bus in memory. By partitioning the value to be stored into chunks that are the size of the data bus, the processor simply uses sequential memory locations to store large values. For example, if a processor with an 8-bit data bus needs to store the 32-bit value $3A2B48CA_{16}$, it uses four memory locations: one to store $3A_{16}$, one for $2B_{16}$, one for 48_{16}, and one for CA_{16}. When it retrieves the data, it reads all four values and reconstructs the data in one of its registers. The processor designer must ensure that the order in which the smaller chunks are stored remains consistent for both reading and writing, or the value will become corrupted. This should not be a problem.

It can become a problem, however, when data is being transferred between processors that use different orders. Big-endian and little-endian are terms used to identify the order in which the smaller words or bytes are stored. Big-endian means that the first byte or word stored is the most significant byte or word. Little-endian means that the first byte or word stored is the least significant byte or word. The method selected does not affect the starting address, nor does it affect the ordering of items in a data structure.

15.8 Pipelined Architectures

Microprocessor designers, in an attempt to squeeze every last bit of performance from their designs, try to make sure that every circuit of the CPU is doing something productive at all times. Circuitry is added that tries to predict what each CPU component should be doing as soon as it finishes its current task. Even if the prediction was wrong, nothing is lost; the result is simply ignored. If, however, the outcome was useful, then time has been saved and code executed faster.

The most common application of this practice applies to the execution of instructions. It is based on the fact that there are steps to the execution of an instruction, each of which uses entirely different components of the CPU.

Let's begin our discussion by assuming that the execution of a machine code instruction can be broken into three stages:

- *Fetch* – get the next instruction to execute from its location in memory
- *Decode* – determine which circuits to energize in order to execute the fetched instruction
- *Execute* – use the ALU and the processor to memory interface to execute the instruction

By comparing the definitions of the different components of the CPU shown in Figure 15-5 with the needs of these three different stages or cycles, it can be seen that three different circuits are used for these three tasks.

- The internal data bus and the instruction pointer perform the fetch.
- The instruction decoder performs the decode cycle.
- The ALU and CPU registers are responsible for the execute cycle.

Once the logic that controls the internal data bus is done fetching the current instruction, what's to keep it from fetching the next instruction? It may have to guess what the next instruction is, but if it guesses right, then a new instruction will be available to the instruction decoder immediately after it finishes decoding the previous one.

Once the instruction decoder has finished telling the ALU what to do to execute the current instruction, what's to keep it from decoding the next instruction while it's waiting for the ALU to finish? If the internal data bus logic guessed right about what the next instruction is, then the ALU won't have to wait for a fetch and subsequent decode in order to execute the next instruction.

This process of creating a queue of fetched, decoded, and executed instructions is called *pipelining*, and it is a common method for improving the performance of a processor.

Figure 15-7 shows the time-line sequence of the execution of five instructions on a non-pipelined processor. Notice how a full fetch-decode-execute cycle must be performed on instruction 1 before instruction 2 can be fetched. This sequential execution of instructions allows for a very simple CPU hardware, but it leaves each portion of the CPU idle for 2 out of every 3 cycles. During the fetch cycle, the instruction decoder and ALU are idle; during the decode cycle, the bus interface and the ALU are idle; and during the execute cycle, the bus interface and the instruction decoder are idle.

Figure 15-8 on the other hand shows the time-line sequence for the execution of five instructions using a pipelined processor. Once the bus interface has fetched instruction 1 and passed it to the instruction decoder for decoding, it can begin its fetch of instruction 2. Notice that the first cycle in the figure only has the fetch operation. The second cycle has both the fetch and the decode cycle happening at the same time. By the third cycle, all three operations are happening in parallel.

348   Computer Organization and Design Fundamentals

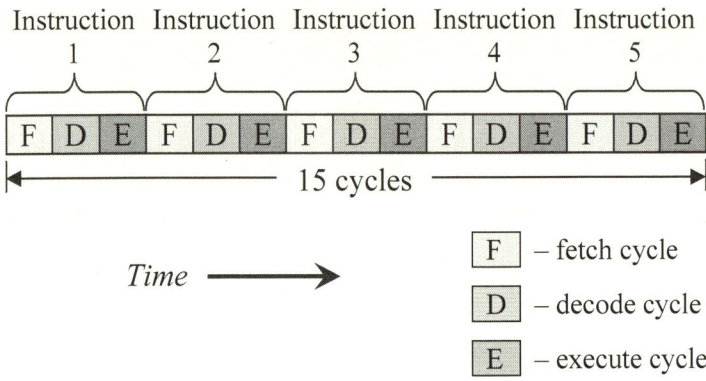

Figure 15-7   Non-Pipelined Execution of Five Instructions

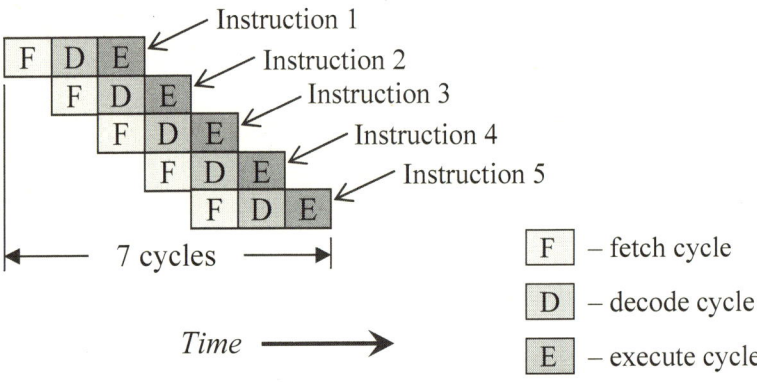

Figure 15-8   Pipelined Execution of Five Instructions

Without pipelining, five instructions take 15 cycles to execute. In a pipelined architecture, those same five instructions take only 7 cycles to execute, a savings of over 50%.

In general, the number of cycles it takes for a non-pipelined architecture using three cycles to execute an instruction is equal to three times the number of instructions.

Num. of cycles (non-pipelined) = 3 × number of instructions   (15.1)

For the pipelined architecture, it takes two cycles to "fill the pipe" so that all three CPU components are fully occupied. Once this occurs, then an instruction is executed once every cycle. Therefore, the formula used to determine the number of cycles used by a pipelined processor to execute a specific number of instructions is:

Num. of cycles (pipelined) = 2 + number of instructions (15.2)

As the number of instructions grows, the number of cycles required of a pipelined architecture approaches 1/3 that of the non-pipelined.

Example

Compare the number of cycles required to execute 50 instructions between a non-pipelined processor and a pipelined processor.

Solution

Using equations 15.1 and 15.2, we can determine the number of cycles necessary for both the non-pipelined and the pipelined CPUs.

number of cycles (non-pipelined) = 3 * 50 = 150 cycles

number of cycles (pipelined) = 2 + 50 = 52 cycles

By taking the difference, we see that the pipelined architecture will execute 50 instructions in 98 fewer cycles.

There is one more point that needs to be addressed when discussing pipelined architectures. In order for the bus interface logic to retrieve the next instruction, it needs to know where to find it. For most instructions, it is only a matter of knowing how many memory locations to move forward from the current position.

For example, assume that the bus interface logic for our mock processor has retrieved the machine code 03. It doesn't need to know that this instruction is CNSTA, "Load A with a constant," it only needs to know how many memory locations the instruction uses. From Table 15-5 we see that CNSTA uses an 8-bit operand. Therefore, including the instruction itself, this particular instruction uses 2 bytes in memory. This means that the bus interface logic needs to increment 2 positions in order to point to the next instruction.

The address of the next instruction can be found even for the unconditional jump instruction, JMP. In this case, the bus interface logic needs to load the instruction pointer with the two bytes following the JMP = 11_{16} machine code to point to the next instruction to fetch.

There is one group of instructions for which there is no method to reliably predict where to find the next instruction in memory: conditional jumps. For our mock processor, this group of instructions includes "Jump if equal" (JEQU), "Jump if first value is greater than second value" (JGT), and "Jump if first value is less than second value" (JLT). Each of these instructions has two possible outcomes: either control is passed to the next instruction or the processor jumps to a new address. The decision, however, cannot be made until after the instruction is executed, the last cycle of the sequence. This is because the flags from the previous instruction must be evaluated before the processor knows which address to load into the instruction pointer.

There are a number of methods used to predict what the next instruction will be, but if this prediction fails, the pipeline must be flushed of all instructions fetched after the conditional jump. The bus interface logic then starts with a new fetch from the address determined by the execution of the conditional jump. Each time the pipeline is flushed, two cycles are added to the execution time of the code.

15.9 Passing Data To and From Peripherals

Although the vast majority of data transactions within a computer occur between the processor and its memory, sometimes the processor must communicate with external devices. This means that the processor must be able to transfer data to and from devices such as a hard drive or a flash RAM, receive data from inputs such as the keyboard and mouse, and send data to outputs such as the video system.

Every year brings technology that allows for higher and higher densities of digital circuitry. This makes it so that every new processor design contains greater functionality. One of these improvements is to incorporate greater levels of interface circuitry into the processor. This might include a built-in keyboard/mouse interface or a communication interface. When this is done, exchanging data with the interface is performed by reading from or writing to a set of special registers contained within the processor.

Sometimes though, the processor will still need a special interface to an external device. In these cases, the external device can be connected through the same bus that the processor uses to communicate with the memory.

15.9.1 Memory-Mapped I/O

Recall the process that the processor uses to read and write from memory. It begins by placing the address of the memory location it wishes to exchange data with on its address lines. If it is writing data, it places the data to store in memory on the data lines and pulls the write line low while leaving the read line high. If it is reading data, it pulls the read line low while leaving the write line high, then retrieves the data from the data lines.

Sending data to and receiving data from an external input/output (I/O) device can be done using the same process. The major difference is that a memory device will have a great deal more memory locations than an I/O device. Where a memory device may require an address space on the order of Megabytes, an I/O device may require only a few addresses. These addresses may be used for configuring the device, reading its status, receiving captured data, or sending data.

The chip select design discussion in Chapter 12 showed that the address lines are divided into two groups, one that specifies the chip select bit pattern and one that is used to determine the address within the memory device. The number of bits used for the address within the memory device is determined by the size of the device itself. For example, a 256 Meg device uses 28 address lines (2^{28} = 256 Meg).

Assume that an interface needs to be designed for an I/O device that has two registers that are written to, one for writing a configuration and one for writing data, and two registers that are read from, one for reading the device's status and one for reading data. This means that the device requires only two addresses. This can be handled with a single address line, A_0. Table 15-7 presents the signal settings for communicating with such a device.

Table 15-7 Signal Values for Sample I/O Device

A_0	R	W	Function
0	0	1	Reading from device's status register
1	0	1	Reading from device's data register
0	1	0	Writing to device's configuration register
1	1	0	Writing to device's data register
X	1	1	No data transaction

By using the remaining address lines for the chip select, this I/O device can be inserted into the memory map of the processor using the processor's memory bus. This method of interfacing an I/O device to a processor is called ***memory mapping***. Figure 15-9 shows a basic memory mapped device circuit that uses four addresses.

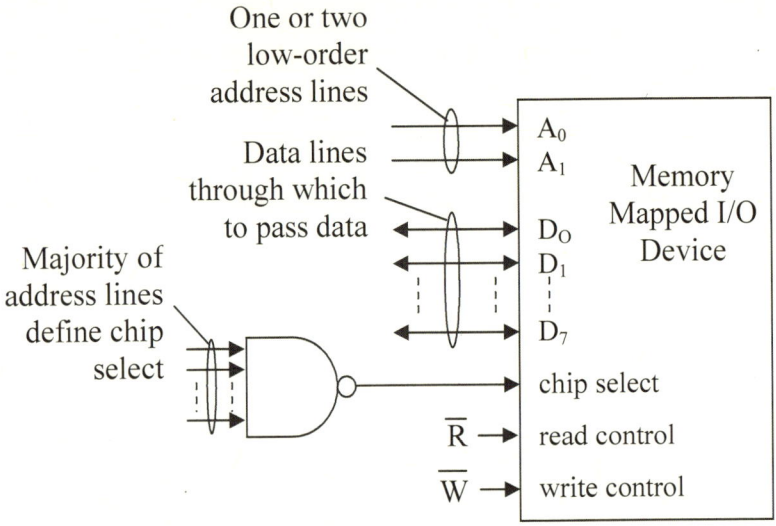

Figure 15-9 Sample Memory Mapped Device Circuit

Some processors add a second read control line and a second write control line specifically for I/O devices. These new lines operate independently of the read and write control lines set up for memory. This does two things for the system. First, it allows the I/O devices to be added to the main processor bus without stealing memory addresses from the memory devices. Second, it makes it so that the I/O devices are not subject to the memory handling scheme of the operating system.

Typically, there is a different set of assembly language instructions that goes along with these new control lines. This is done to distinguish a read or write with a memory device from a read or write with an I/O device. Table 15-8 summarizes how the processor uses the different read and write control lines to distinguish between an I/O device transaction and a memory transaction.

Table 15-8 Control Signal Levels for I/O and Memory Transactions

R_{memory}	W_{memory}	$R_{I/O\ device}$	$W_{I/O\ device}$	Operation
0	1	1	1	Reading from memory
1	0	1	1	Writing to memory
1	1	0	1	Reading from I/O device
1	1	1	0	Writing to I/O device
1	1	1	1	Bus is idle

The methods used to physically connect the processor with an I/O device are only half of the story. The next thing to understand is how the operating system or the software application accesses the device while maintaining responsibility for its other duties.

15.9.2 Polling

The method used by the operating system and its software applications to communicate with I/O devices directly affects the performance of the processor. This is due to the asynchronous nature of I/O. In other words, the I/O device is never ready exactly when the processor needs it to be. For example, the processor cannot predict when a user might press a key, a network connection is not as fast as the processor that's trying to send data down it, and the mechanical nature of a hard drive means that the processor will have to wait for the data it requested. If an I/O interface is not designed properly, the processor will be stalled as it waits for access to the I/O device.

There are four basic methods used for communicating with an I/O device: polling, interrupts, direct memory access, and I/O channels. The first of these, ***polling***, is by far the lowest performer, but it is presented here due to its simplicity.

When an I/O device needs attention from the processor, it usually indicates this by changing a flag in one of its status registers. For example, a network interface may have a bit in one of its status registers that is set to a one when its receive buffer is full. If the processor does not attend to this situation immediately, new incoming data may overwrite the buffer causing the old data to be lost.

In the polling method, the processor continually reads the status registers of the I/O device to see if it needs attention. There are two problems with this method. First, data might be missed if the register is not read often enough. Second, by forcing the processor to continuously monitor the I/O inputs, considerable processing time is eaten up without having much to show for it. The majority of the reads are not going to show any change in the input values.

15.9.3 Interrupts

The problems caused by using the polling method of communication with an I/O device can be solved if a mechanism is added to the system whereby each I/O device could "call" the processor when it needed attention. This way the processor could tend to its more pressing duties and communicate with the I/O device only when it is asked to. If each call was handled with enough priority, the chance of losing data would be greatly reduced.

This system of calling the processor is called ***interrupt driven I/O***. Each device is given a software or hardware interface that allows it to request the processor's attention. This request might be to tell the processor that new data is available to be read, that the device is ready to receive data, or that a process has completed. The call to the processor requesting service is called an ***interrupt***.

It is as if someone was reading a book when the telephone rings. The reader, concerned about keeping her place in the book, places a book mark to indicate where she left off. She then answers the phone and carries on a conversation while the book "waits" for her attention to return. While chatting on the phone, the person notices the dog standing at the door waiting to be let out. She tells the person on the other end of the line, "Hold that thought, I'll be right back." After she lets out the dog, she returns to the phone call, picks up where she left off. When she finishes talking on the phone, she hangs up and returns to her reading exactly where she left off.

The processor handles devices that need service in a similar way. When the processor receives a device interrupt, it needs to remember exactly what it was doing when it was interrupted. This includes the current condition of its registers, the address of the line of code it was about to execute, and the settings of all of its flags. It does this by storing its registers and instruction pointer to the stack using pushes.

Once its current status is stored, the processor executes a function to handle the device's request. This function is called an ***interrupt service routine (ISR)***. There could be a single ISR for a group of devices or a different ISR for each device. By using interrupts and ISRs, the processor is able to concentrate on running applications while it is the responsibility of the devices themselves to monitor their condition.

It is important to note that unlike subroutines, ISRs are not called with function calls from the application or operating system code. The processor maintains a list of the ISRs that correspond to each device. When a device interrupts the processor, the processor halts the execution of the main code, looks up the address of the appropriate ISR, and jumps to it. Once the ISR is complete, the processor restores its previous condition by pulling the register values and instruction pointer from the stack so as to pick up the main code where it left off. Figure 15-10 presents a basic diagram of this operation.

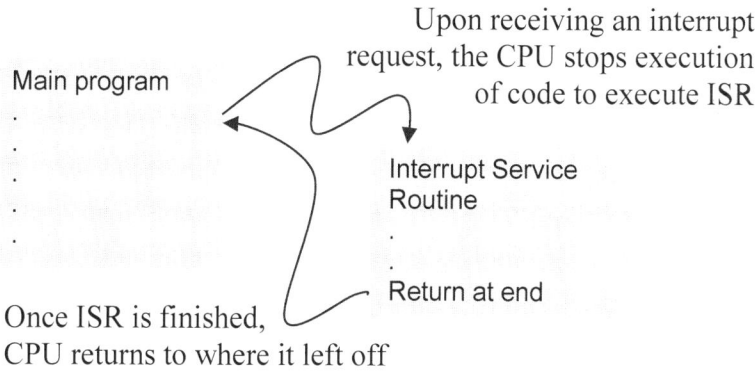

Figure 15-10 Basic Operation of an ISR

Although interrupts greatly improve the performance of a system by requiring the processor's attention only when it is needed, there is still a large burden placed on the processor if the device requires the transfer of a large block of data.

15.9.4 Direct Memory Access

Assume that a communication device receives a large block of data that needs to be placed into memory. It interrupts the processor which in turn initiates the execution of an ISR. The function of the ISR is to make the processor read the data one piece at a time from the device, then store it to memory. This repetitive read-write process takes processing time away from the applications. In addition, each piece of data goes through a two step process, a read from the device then a store to memory, in order to complete a transfer.

It would be far more efficient for the data to be transferred directly from the I/O device to memory. A process such as this would not need to involve the processor at all. If the processor could remain off of the bus long enough for the device to perform the transfer, the processor would only need to be told when the transfer was completed. It could even continue to perform functions that did not require bus access.

This type of data transfer is called *direct memory access (DMA)*, and although it still requires an interrupt, it is far more efficient since the processor does not need to perform the data transfer. The typical system uses a device called a DMA controller that is used to take over the bus when the device needs to make a transfer to or from memory. The controller either waits for a time when the processor does not need the bus or it sends the processor a signal asking it to suspend its bus access for one cycle while the I/O device makes a transfer.

A DMA transaction involves a three step process. In the first step, the processor sets up the transfer by telling the DMA controller the direction of the transfer (read or write), which I/O device is to perform the transfer, the address of the memory location where the data will be stored to or read from, and the amount of data to be transferred.

Once the processor has set up the transfer, it relinquishes control to the DMA controller. As the I/O device receives or requires data, it communicates directly with memory under the supervision of the DMA controller. The last step comes when the transfer is complete. At this point, the DMA controller interrupts the processor to tell it that the transfer is complete.

15.9.5 I/O Channels and Processors

As I/O devices become more sophisticated, more and more of the processing responsibility can be taken off of the processor and placed on the I/O device itself. Some I/O devices can access and execute application software directly from main memory without any processor intervention. These are *I/O channels*. Other I/O devices, *I/O processors*, are computer systems in their own right taking the functionality of the processor and distributing it to the end devices.

15.10 What's Next?

At this point, the reader should have enough of a background in computer architecture to begin examining a specific processor. In Chapter 16, we will study the Intel 80x86 processor architecture from the point of view of the hardware. Following that, Chapter 17 presents a basic introduction to the Intel 80x86 assembly language.

Problems

1. List the types of registers utilized by the processor and describe their operation.

2. Determine the settings of the zero flag, the carry flag, the overflow flag, and the sign flag for each of the following 8-bit operations.

    ```
      10110110        01011011        10011001
    + 01001010      + 01110010      - 00001000
    ```

3. If registers A, B, and C contain the values 12, 65, and 87 respectively, and they are pushed to the stack in the order A, then B, then C, what values do A, B, and C have if they then are pulled from the stack in the order C, then A, then B?

4. List and describe the purpose of each of the components of the processor.

5. List and describe the purpose of each of the components of the CPU.

6. Using Tables 15-4 and 15-5, convert the following assembly language to machine code.

    ```
               LOADA    1000₁₆
               LOADB    1001₁₆
               CMPAB
               JGT      AGREATER
               EXCAB
    AGREATER:  STORA    1002₁₆
    ```

7. What is the purpose of an instruction pointer?

8. List the four drawbacks presented in the text to programming in assembly language.

9. List the three benefits presented in the text to programming with assembly language.

10. Using Tables 15-4 and 15-5, convert the following machine code to assembly language starting at address 2000_{16}.

Address	Data
2000_{16}	02
2001_{16}	13
2002_{16}	4E
2003_{16}	05
2004_{16}	13
2005_{16}	4F
2006_{16}	08
2007_{16}	05
2008_{16}	13
2009_{16}	50
$200A_{16}$	0A
$200B_{16}$	08
$200C_{16}$	01
$200D_{16}$	13
$200E_{16}$	51

11. What type of instruction might force the processor to flush the pipeline?

12. List the two benefits of using separate read/write control lines for I/O devices instead of using memory mapped I/O.

13. What two problems does the polling method to monitor the I/O devices have that are solved by interrupt-driven I/O?

14. What problem does non-DMA interrupt-driven I/O have that is solved by DMA?

15. How would the 32-bit value $1A2B3C4D_{16}$ be stored in an 8-bit memory with a processor that used big-endian? Little-endian?

CHAPTER SIXTEEN

Intel 80x86 Base Architecture

16.1 Why Study the 80x86?

Any introduction to processor architecture should be followed by an investigation of the architecture of a specific processor. The choice then becomes which processor to examine. There are so many. Some approaches use a virtual processor, i.e., one that exists only on paper or as a simulator. This method simplifies the learning process by concealing the complexities and idiosyncrasies of a real processor.

At the other extreme, we could examine a modern processor such as the Intel® Pentium® 4 Processor Extreme Edition with its Hyper-Threading Technology™, Hyper-Pipelined Technology™, enhanced branch prediction, three levels of 8-way cache including a split L1 cache, and multiple ALUs. Or we could look at the Apple® PowerPC® G5 with its 64-bit architecture, two double-precision floating point units, and twelve functional units. If you are a student who has just been introduced to processor architecture, this can be like trying to swallow an elephant. Too many new concepts must be explained before even a minimal understanding of the processor can be had.

A third method is to examine the simplest processor from a family of existing processors. This particular processor should provide the closest match to the processor architecture discussed in Chapter 15 while providing a link to the most modern processor of the family. It eliminates the need for a discussion of advanced computer architecture concepts while giving the student a real processor that they can program.

The processor we present here is the original 16-bit Intel processor, the 80186, the root of the Intel processor family that is commonly referred to as the 80x86 family. The 'x' in 80x86 represents the generation of the processor, 1, 2, 3, and so on. Table 16-1 presents a summary of the bus characteristics of some of the 80x86 processors.

The 80186 has 16 data lines allowing it to perform operations on unsigned integers from 0 to $2^{16} - 1 = 65,535$ and signed integers from $-32,768$ to 32767. It has 20 address lines providing access to a memory space of $2^{20} = 1$ Meg.

Table 16-1 Summary of Intel 80x86 Bus Characteristics

Processor	Data bus width	Address bus width	Size of address space
80186	16	20	2^{20} = 1 Meg
80286	16	24	2^{24} = 16 Meg
80386SX	16	24	2^{24} = 16 Meg
80386DX	32	32	2^{32} = 4 Gig
80486	32	32	2^{32} = 4 Gig
80586 "Pentium"	64	32	2^{32} = 4 Gig

16.2 Execution Unit

The 80x86 processor is divided into two main components: the execution unit and the bus interface unit. The *execution unit* (EU) is the 80x86's CPU as discussed in Chapter 15. It is controlled by the EU control system which serves a dual purpose: it acts as the control unit and also as a portion of the instruction decoder. The EU also contains the ALU, the processor flags, and the general purpose and address registers. Figure 16-1 presents a block diagram of the EU.

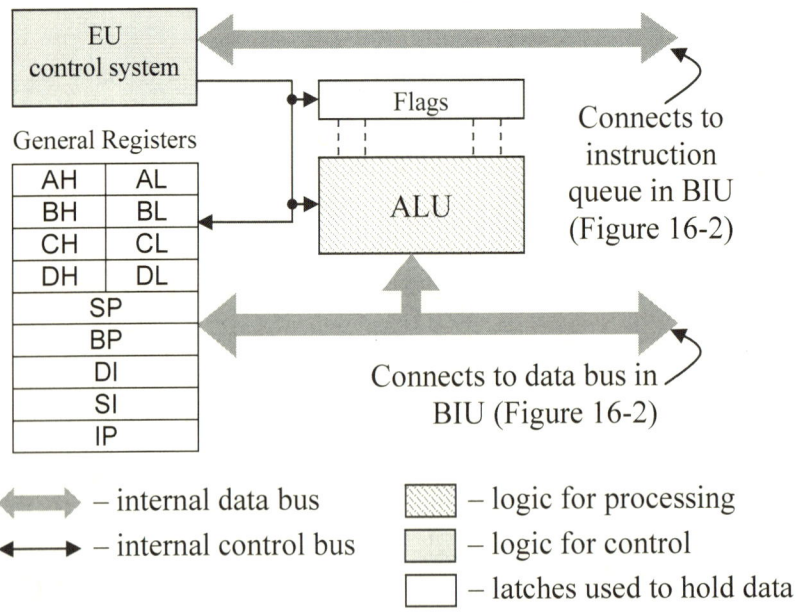

Figure 16-1 Block Diagram of 80x86 Execution Unit (EU)

16.2.1 General Purpose Registers

The registers of the 80x86 are grouped into two categories: general purpose and address. The general purpose registers are for manipulating or transferring data; the address registers contain memory addresses and are used to point to the locations in memory where data will be retrieved or stored.

Figure 16-1 shows that there are eight general purpose registers: AH, AL, BH, BL, CH, CL, DH, and DL. Each of these registers is eight bits. Earlier we said that the 80186 is a 16-bit processor. How can this be since we only have 8-bit registers?

The 80186 processor creates a 16-bit register by combining two 8-bit registers. AH and AL, for example, can function as a pair. This larger register is referred to as AX. The 8-bit registers are combined by linking them together so that the 8 bits of AH are the 8 most significant bits of AX and AL are the 8 least significant bits of AX. For example, if AH contains $10110000_2 = B0_{16}$ and AL contains $01011111_2 = 5F_{16}$, then the virtual register AX contains $1011000001011111_2 = B05F_{16}$.

Example

If CX contains the binary value 0110110101101011_2, what value does CH have?

Solution

Since the register CH provides the most significant 8 bits of CX, then the upper eight bits of CX is CH, i.e., CH contains 01101101_2.

Each of the general purpose registers is named according to their default purpose. For the most part, these purposes are not set in stone. The programmer still has some flexibility in how the registers are used. The following discussion presents their suggested use.

AX is called the ***accumulator register***, and it is used mostly for arithmetic, logic, and the general transfer of data. Many of the assembly language instructions for higher level mathematical operations such as multiply and divide don't even let the programmer specify a register other than AX to be used.

BX is called the ***base register***, and it is used as a base address or pointer to things like data arrays. We will find out later that there are a number of other registers that are used as pointers, but those are special purpose pointers. BX tends to be more of a general purpose pointer.

CX is called the *counter register*. When a programmer uses a for-loop, the index for that loop is usually stored in CX. Intel designed a number of special purpose instructions that use CX in order to get better performance out of loops.

DX is called the *data register*. This register is used with AX for special arithmetic functions allowing for things such as storing the upper half of a 32-bit result of a 16-bit multiply or holding the remainder after an integer division.

16.2.2 Address Registers

Below the general purpose registers in Figure 16-1 are the address registers: SP, BP, DI, SI, and IP. These are 16-bit registers meant to contain addresses with which to point to locations in memory. At this point, do not worry about how a 16-bit register can reference something in a memory space that uses a 20-bit address bus. The process involves using the segment registers of the BIU. We will address the mechanics behind the use of the segment registers later in this chapter.

These address registers are classified into two groups: the pointer registers, SP, BP, and IP, and the index registers, DI and SI. Although they all operate in the same manner, i.e., pointing to addresses in memory, each address register has a specific purpose.

SP is the *stack pointer* and it points to the address of the last piece of data stored to the stack. To store something to the stack, the stack pointer is decremented by the size of the value to be stored, i.e., SP is decremented by 2 for a word or 4 for a double word. The value is then stored at the new address pointed to by the stack pointer. To retrieve a value from the stack, the value is read from the address pointed to by the stack pointer, then the stack pointer is incremented accordingly.

BP is the *base pointer* and its primary use is to point to the parameters that are passed to a function during a function call. For example, if the function myfunc(var1, var2) is called, the values for var1 and var2 are placed in the temporary memory of the stack. BP contains the address in the stack where the list of variables begins.

IP is the *instruction pointer*. As we discussed in Chapter 15, the CPU goes step-by-step through memory loading, interpreting, and then executing machine code. It uses the memory address contained in IP as a marker pointing to where to retrieve the next instruction. Each time it retrieves an instruction, it increments IP so that it points to the next instruction to retrieve. In some cases, the instruction decoder needs to increment IP multiple times to account for data or operands that might follow an element of machine code.

SI, the *source index*, and *DI*, the *destination index*, also contain addresses that point to memory. They are used for string operations where strings may be copied, searched, or otherwise manipulated. SI points to memory locations from which characters are to be retrieved while DI points to memory locations where characters will be stored.

16.2.3 Flags

The flags of the 80x86 processor are contained in a 16-bit register. Not all 16 bits are used, and it isn't important to remember the exact bit positions of each of the flags inside the register. The important thing is to understand the purpose of each of the flags.

Remember from Chapter 15 that the flags indicate the current status of the processor. Of these, the majority report the results of the last executed instruction to affect the flags. (Not all instructions affect all the flags.) These flags are then used by a set of instructions that test their state and alter the flow of the software based on the result.

The flags of the 80x86 processor are divided into two categories: control flags and status flags. The control flags are modified by the software to change how the processor operates. There are three of them: trap, direction, and interrupt.

The *trap flag (TF)* is used for debugging purposes and allows code to be executed one instruction at a time. This allows the programmer to step through code address-by-address so that the results of each instruction can be inspected for proper operation.

The *direction flag (DF)* is associated with string operations. In particular, DF dictates whether a string is to be examined by incrementing through the characters or decrementing. This flag is used by the 80x86 instructions that automate string operations.

Chapter 15 introduced us to the concept of interrupts by showing how devices that need the processor's attention can send a signal interrupting the processor's operation in order to avoid missing critical data. The *interrupt flag (IF)* is used to enable or disable this function. When this flag contains a one, any interrupt that occurs is serviced by the processor. When this flag contains a zero, the maskable interrupts are ignored by the processor, their requests for service remaining in a queue waiting for the flag to return to a one.

364　Computer Organization and Design Fundamentals

The IF flag is cleared and set by software using two different assembly language commands: **STI** for setting and **CLI** for clearing. Some interrupts known as non-maskable interrupts cannot be disabled. Either their purpose is considered to be a priority over all other processor functions or the software itself calls the interrupt.

The remaining flags are the status flags. These are set or cleared based on the result of the last executed instruction. There are six of them: overflow, sign, zero, auxiliary carry, parity, and carry. The following describes the operation of each of these bits.

- *Overflow flag (OF)* – indicates when an overflow has occurred in a mathematical operation.
- *Sign flag (SF)* – follows the sign bit of a mathematical or logical result, i.e., it is cleared to 0 when the result is positive and set to 1 when the result is negative.
- *Zero flag (ZF)* – is set to 1 when the result of a mathematical or logical function is zero. The flag is cleared to 0 otherwise.
- *Auxiliary carry flag (AF)* – equals the carry from the bit 3 column of an addition into the bit 4 column. If you recall the section on BCD addition from Chapter 3, a carry out of a nibble is one indication that error correction must be taken. This flag represents the carry out of the least significant nibble.
- *Parity flag (PF)* – is set to 1 if the result contains an even number of ones and cleared to 0 otherwise.
- *Carry flag (CF)* – represents the carry out of the most significant bit position. Some shift operations also use the carry to hold the bit that was last shifted out of a register.

Example

How would the status flags be set after the processor performed the 8-bit addition of 10110101_2 and 10010110_2?

Solution

This problem assumes that the addition affects all of the flags. This is not true for all assembly language instructions, i.e., a logical OR does not affect AF.

Let's begin by adding the two numbers to see what the result is.

```
                    ⎛1⎞  1 1   1
      carry out    ⎝ ⎠  1 0 1 1 0 1 0 1
                      + 1 0 0 1 0 1 1 0
                        0 1 0 0 1 0 1 1
```

Now go through each of the flags to see how it is affected.

OF=1 – There was an overflow, i.e., adding two negative numbers resulted in a positive number.
SF=0 – The result is positive.
ZF=0 – The result does not equal zero.
AF=0 – No carry occurred from the fourth column (bit 3) to the fifth column (bit 4).
PF=1 – The result contains four ones which is an even number.
CF=1 – There was a carry.

16.2.4 Internal Buses

There are two internal buses in the EU that are used to pass information between the components. The first is used to exchange data and addressing information between the registers and the ALU. This same bus is also used to transfer data to and from memory by way of the bus interface unit. Each assembly language instruction that uses operands must move those operands from their source to a destination. These transfers occur along the data bus.

The second bus has one purpose: to transfer instructions that have been obtained by the bus interface unit to the instruction decoder contained in the EU control system.

The next section discusses how the bus interface unit performs data transactions with the memory space.

16.3 Bus Interface Unit

The *bus interface unit* (BIU) controls the transfer of information between the processor and the external devices such as memory, I/O ports, and storage devices. Basically, it acts as the bridge between the EU and the external bus. A portion of the instruction decoder as defined in Chapter 15 is located in the BIU. The instruction queue acts as a buffer allowing instructions to be queued up as they wait for their turn in the EU. Figure 16-2 presents the block diagram of the BIU.

366   Computer Organization and Design Fundamentals

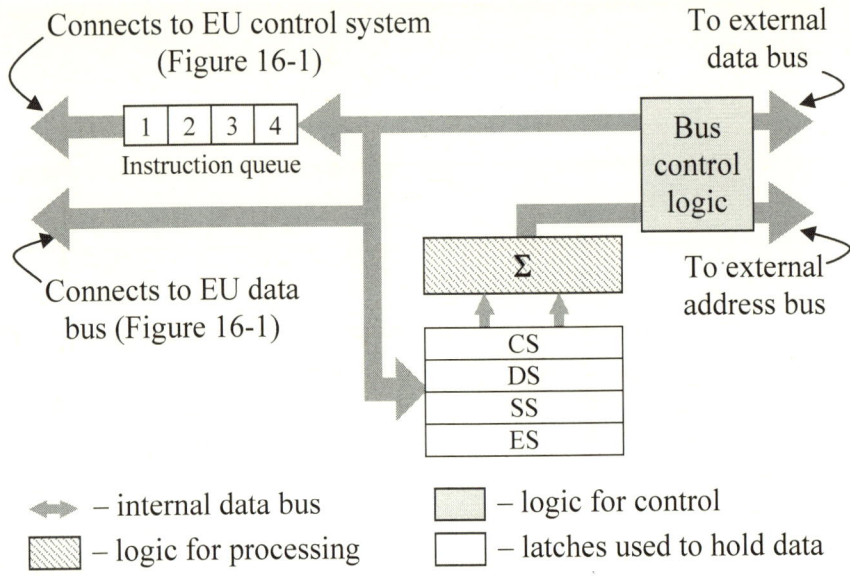

Figure 16-2   Block Diagram of 80x86 Bus Interface Unit (BIU)

The main purpose of the BIU is to take the 16-bit pointers of the EU and modify them so that they can point to data in the 20-bit address space. This is done using the four registers CS, DS, SS, and ES. These are the segment registers.

16.3.1 Segment Addressing

In the center of the BIU block diagram is a set of segment registers labeled CS, DS, SS, and ES. These four 16-bit registers are used in conjunction with the pointer and index registers to store and retrieve items from the memory space.

So how does the processor combine a 16-bit address register with a 16-bit segment register to create a 20-bit address? Well, it is all done in the address summing block located directly above the segment registers in the block diagram of the BIU in Figure 16-2. Every time the processor goes out to its memory space to read or write data, this 20-bit address must be calculated based on different combinations of address and segment registers.

Chapter 16: Intel 80x86 Base Architecture 367

Next time your Intel-based operating system throws up an execution error, look to see if it gives you the address where the error occurred. If it does, you should see some hexadecimal numbers in a format similar to the one shown below:

$$3241{:}A34E$$

This number is a special representation of the segment register (the number to the left of the colon) and the pointer or index register (the number to the right of the colon). Remember that a 4-digit hexadecimal number represents a 16-bit binary number. It is the combination of these two 16-bit registers that creates the 20-bit address.

The process works like this. First take the value in the segment register and shift if left four places. This has the effect of adding a zero to the right side of the hexadecimal number or four zeros to the right side of the binary number. In our example above, the segment is 3241_{16} = $0011\ 0010\ 0100\ 0001_2$. Adding a zero nibble to the right side of the segment gives us 32410_{16} = $0011\ 0010\ 0100\ 0001\ 0000_2$.

The pointer or index register is then added to this 20-bit segment address. Continuing our example gives us:

```
  0011 0010 0100 0001 0000          32410₁₆
+           1010 0011 0100 1110  or + A34E₁₆
  0011 1100 0111 0101 1110          3C75E₁₆
```

For the rest of this book, we will use the following terminology to represent these three values.

- The 20-bit value created by shifting the value in a segment register four places to the left will be referred to as the ***segment address***. It points to the lowest address to which a segment:pointer combination can point. This address may also be referred to as the ***base address*** of the segment.
- The 16-bit value stored in a pointer or index register will be referred to as the ***offset address***. It represents an offset from the segment address to the address in memory that the processor needs to communicate with.
- The resulting 20-bit value that comes out of the address summing block points to a specific address in the processor's memory space.

This address will be referred to as the *physical address*, and it is the address that is placed on the address lines of the memory bus.

If we look at the function of the segment and pointer registers from the perspective of the memory space, the segment register adjusted with four binary zeros filled in from the right points to an address somewhere in the full memory space. Because the least significant four bits are always zero, this value can only point to memory in 16-byte increments. The 16-bit offset address from the pointer register is then added to the segment address pointing to an address within the 2^{16} = 65,535 (64K) locations above where the segment register is pointing. This is the physical address. Figure 16-3 shows how the segment and pointer addresses relate to each other when pointing to a specific address within the memory space.

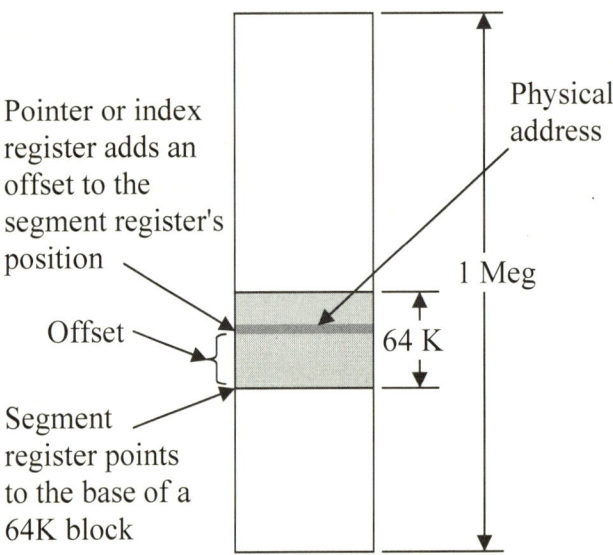

Figure 16-3 Segment/Pointer Relation in the 80x86 Memory Map

There is a second purpose for this segment:pointer addressing method beyond allowing the 80x86 processor to control 20 address lines using 16-bit registers. This second reason is actually of greater importance as it allows for greater functionality of the operating system.

By assigning the responsibility of maintaining the segment registers to the operating system while allowing the application to control the address and pointer registers, applications can be placed anywhere in memory without affecting their operation. When the operating system loads an application to be executed, it selects a 64 K block of memory called a *segment* and uses the lowest address of that block as the base address for that particular application. During execution, the application modifies only the pointer registers keeping its scope within the 64K block of its segment.

As long as the application modifies only the address registers, then the program remains in the 64 K segment it was assigned to. By using this process, the operating system is free to place an application wherever it wants to in memory. It also allows the operating system to maintain several concurrent applications in memory by keeping track of which application is assigned to which segment.

Although the programmer may force a segment register to be used for a different purpose, each segment register has an assigned purpose. The following describes the uses of the four segment registers, CS, DS, SS, and ES.

- *Code Segment (CS)* – This register contains the base address of the segment assigned to contain the code of an application. It is paired with the Instruction Pointer (IP) to point to the next instruction to load into the instruction decoder for execution.
- *Data Segment (DS)* – This register contains the base address of the segment assigned to contain the data used by an application. It is typically associated with the SI register.
- *Stack Segment (SS)* – This register contains the base address of the stack segment. Remember that there are two pointer registers that use the stack. The first is the stack pointer, and the combination of SS and SP points to the last value stored in this temporary memory. The other register is the base pointer which is used to point to the block of data elements passed to a function.
- *Extra Segment (ES)* – Like DS, this register points to the data segment assigned to an application. Where DS is associated with the SI register, ES is associated with the DI register.

Example

If CS contains $A487_{16}$ and IP contains 1436_{16}, then what is the physical address of the next instruction in memory to be executed?

Solution

The physical address is found by shifting $A487_{16}$ left four bits and adding 1436_{16} to the result.

```
  A4870₁₆              1010 0100 1000 0111 0000
+  1436₁₆      or   +       0001 0100 0011 0110
  A5CA6₁₆              1010 0101 1100 1010 0110
```

Therefore, the physical address pointed to by A487:1436 is $A5CA6_{16}$.

16.3.2 Instruction Queue

As discussed in Chapter 15, there are times during the execution of an instruction when different portions of the processor are idle. In the case of the 80x86 processor for example, while the BIU is retrieving the next instruction to be executed from memory, the EU control system and the ALU are standing by waiting for the instruction.

The 80186 divides the process of executing an instruction into three cycles: fetch, decode, and execute. These cycles are described below:

- *Fetch* – Retrieve the next instruction to execute from its location in memory. This is taken care of by the BIU.
- *Decode* – Determine which circuits to energize in order to execute the fetched instruction. This function is performed by the instruction decoding circuitry in the EU control system.
- *Execute* – Perform the operation dictated by the instruction using the ALU, registers, and data transfer mechanisms.

The purpose of the instruction queue of the BIU is to maintain a sequence of fetched instructions for the EU to execute. In some cases, branches or returns from functions can disrupt the sequence of instructions and require a change in the anticipated order of execution. An advanced instruction queue can handle this by loading both paths of execution allowing the EU to determine which one it will need after executing the previous instructions.

16.4 Memory versus I/O Ports

In order to communicate with external hardware devices without taking up space in the 1 Meg memory space of the 80x86 processor, two additional control lines are added to the bus that effectively turn it into two buses, one for data and one for I/O. This second bus uses the same address and data lines that are used by the memory bus. The difference is that the I/O devices use different read and write control lines.

To read data from memory, the 80x86 processor uses the active-low signal MRDC. When MRDC is low, the addressed memory device on the bus knows to pass the appropriate data back to the processor.

To write data to memory, the 80x86 processor uses the active-low signal MWTC. When MWTC is low, the addressed memory device on the bus knows that the processor will be sending data to it. Once the memory device receives this data, it knows to store it in the appropriate memory location.

If both MRDC and MWTC are high, then the memory devices remain inactive. By adding a second pair of read and write control lines, the processor can communicate with a new set of devices on the same set of address and data lines. These new devices are called *I/O ports*, and they connect the processor to the external environment. By placing an address on the address lines, an I/O port is selected in the same way that a memory chip is selected using chip select circuitry.

The read control for the I/O ports is called IORC, and it too is an active low signal. When IORC equals zero, the selected I/O port places data on the data lines for the processor to read. This data might be the value of a key press, the digital value of an analog input, the status of a printer, or anything else that the processor needs to input from the external devices.

The write control for the I/O ports is called IOWC. This active low signal goes low when the processor wants to send data to an external device. This data might be the characters of a document to be printed, a command to the video system, or any other value that the processor needs to send to the external devices.

Table 16-2 summarizes the settings of these four read and write control signals based on their functions.

Table 16-2 Summary of the 80x86 Read and Write Control Signals

Function	MRDC	MWTC	IORC	IOWC
Reading from memory	0	1	1	1
Writing to memory	1	0	1	1
Reading from an I/O device	1	1	0	1
Writing to an I/O device	1	1	1	0

Even though they use the same address and data lines, there are slight differences between the use of memory and the use of I/O ports. First, regardless of the generation of the 80x86 processor, only the lowest 16 address lines are used for I/O ports. This means that even if the memory space of an 80x86 processor goes to 4 Gig, the I/O port address space will always be $2^{16} = 65,536 = 64K$. This is not a problem as the demand on the number of external devices that a processor needs to communicate with has not grown nearly at the rate of demand on memory space.

The second difference between the memory space and the I/O port address space is the requirement placed on the programmer. Although we have not yet discussed the 80x86 assembly language instruction set, the assembly language commands for transferring data between the registers and memory are of the form MOV. This command cannot be used for input or output to the I/O ports because it uses MRDC and MWTC for bus commands. To send data to the I/O ports, the assembly language commands OUT and OUTS are used while the commands for reading data from the I/O ports are IN and INS.

16.5 What's Next?

Now that you have a general idea of the architecture of the 80x86, we can begin programming with it. In Chapter 17, we will present some of the instructions from the 80x86 assembly language along with the format of the typical assembly language program. In addition, the syntax used to differentiate between registers, memory, and constants in 80x86 assembly language code will be presented. This information will then be used to take you though some sample programs.

Problems

Answer problems 1 though 7 using the following settings of the 80x86 processor registers.

$AX = 1234_{16}$ $BP = 1212_{16}$ $CS = A101_{16}$
$BX = 8721_{16}$ $SP = 3434_{16}$ $DS = B101_{16}$
$CX = 5678_{16}$ $DI = 5656_{16}$ $SS = C101_{16}$
$DX = 8765_{16}$ $IP = 7878_{16}$ $ES = D101_{16}$

1. What is the value in the register AL?

2. What is the value in the register CH?

3. What is the physical address pointed to by ES:DI?

4. What is the physical address of the next instruction to be executed in memory?

5. What is the physical address of the last data item to be stored in the stack?

6. Assuming a function has been called and the appropriate address and segment registers have been set, what is the physical address of the location of the function parameters in the stack?

7. What would the settings of the flags OF, SF, ZF, AF, PF, and CF be after the addition of BH to AL?

8. True or false: Every 80x86 assembly language instruction modifies the flags.

9. What is the purpose of the internal bus that connects the instruction queue in the BIU with the EU control system?

10. List the two benefits of segmented addressing.

11. What are the values of MRDC, MWTC, IORC, and IOWC when the processor is storing data to memory?

12. What are the values of MRDC, MWTC, IORC, and IOWC when the processor is reading data from a device on the I/O port bus?

13. What 80x86 assembly language commands are used to write data to a memory device on the I/O port bus?

14. On an 80486 processor with its 32 address lines, what is the maximum number of I/O ports it can address?

CHAPTER SEVENTEEN

Intel 80x86 Assembly Language

In Chapter 15, we developed a generic assembly language and its associated machine code. This language was presented to create a few simple programs and present how the CPU executed code. In this chapter, the assembly language of the Intel 80x86 processor family is introduced along with the typical syntax for writing 80x86 assembly language programs. This information is then used to write a sample program for the 80x86 processor.

This chapter is meant to serve as an introduction to programming the Intel 80x86 using assembly language. For more detailed instruction, refer to one of the resources listed at the end of this chapter.

17.1 Assemblers versus Compilers

For a high-level programming language such as C, there is a two-step process to produce an application from source code. To begin with, a program called a *compiler* takes the source code and converts it into machine language instructions. This is a complex task that requires a detailed understanding of the architecture of the processor. The compiler outputs the resulting sequence of machine code instructions to a file called an *object file*. The second step takes one or more object files and combines them by merging addressing information and generating necessary support code to make the final unit operate as an application. The program that does this is called a *linker*.

In order for the linker to operate properly, the object files must follow certain rules for format and addressing to clearly show how one object file interrelates with the others.

A similar two-step process is used to convert assembly language source code into an application. It begins with a program called an *assembler*. The assembler takes an assembly language program, and using a one-to-one conversion process, converts each line of assembly language to a single machine code instruction. Because of this one-to-one relation between assembly language instructions and machine code instructions, the assembly language programmer must have a clear understanding of how the processor will execute the machine code. In other words, the programmer must take the place of the compiler by converting abstract processes to the step-by-step processor instructions.

As with the compiler, the output of the assembler is an object file. The format and addressing information of the assembler's object file should mimic that of the compiler making it possible for the same linker to be used to generate the final application. This means that as long as the assembly language programmer follows certain rules when identifying shared addressing, the object file from an assembler should be capable of being linked to the object files of a high-level language compiler.

The format of an assembly language program depends on the assembler being used. There are, however, some general formatting patterns that are typically followed. This section presents some of those standards.

Like most programming languages, assembly language source code must follow a well-defined syntax and structure. Unlike most programming languages, the lines of assembly language are not structurally interrelated. In a language such as C, for example, components such as functions, if-statements, loops, and switch/case blocks utilize syntax to indicate the beginning and end of a block of code that is to be treated as a unit. Blocks of code may be contained within larger blocks of code producing a hierarchy of execution. In assembly language, there is no syntax to define blocks of code; formatting only applies to a single line of code. It is the execution of the code itself that is used to logically define blocks within the program.

17.2 Components of a Line of Assembly Language

As shown in Figure 17-1, a line of assembly language code has four fields: a label, an opcode, a set of operands, and comments. Each of these fields must be separated by horizontal white space, i.e., spaces or tabs. No carriage returns are allowed as they identify the beginning of a new line of code. Depending on the function of a particular line, one or more of the fields may be omitted.

The first field of a line is an optional *label field.* A label is used to identify a specific line of code or the memory location of a piece of data so that it may be referenced by other lines of assembly language. The assembler will translate the label into an address for use in the object file. As far as the programmer is concerned, however, the label may be used any time an address reference is needed to that particular line. It is not necessary to label all lines of assembly language code, only the ones that are referred to by other lines of code.

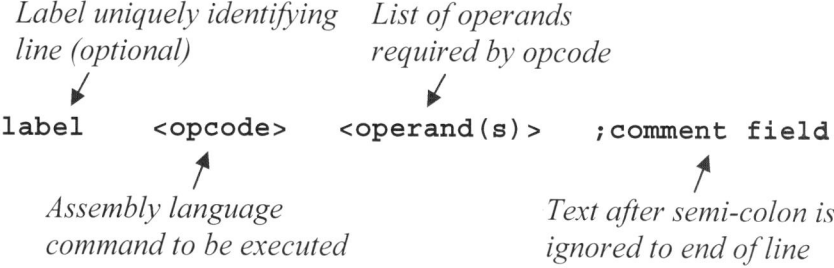

Figure 17-1 Format of a Line of Assembly Language Code

A label is a text string much like a variable name in a high-level language. There are some rules to be obeyed when defining a label.

- Labels must begin in the first column with an alphabetic character. Subsequent characters may be numeric.
- It must not be a reserved string, i.e., it cannot be an assembly language instruction nor can it be a command to the assembler.
- Although a label may be referenced by other lines of assembly language, it cannot be reused to identify a second line of code within the same file.
- In some cases, a special format for a label may be required if the label's function goes beyond identification of a line within a file. A special format may be needed, for example, if a high-level programming language will be referencing one of the assembly language program's functions.

The next field is the *instruction* or *opcode field*. The instruction field contains the assembly language command that the processor is supposed to execute for this line of code. An instruction must be either an assembly language instruction (an opcode) or an instruction to the assembler (an assembler directive).

The third field is the *operand field*. The operand field contains the data or operands that the assembly language instruction needs for its execution. This includes items such as memory addresses, constants, or register names. Depending on the instruction, there may be zero, one, two, or three operands, the syntax and organization of which also depends on the instruction.

The last field in a line of assembly language is the *comment field*. As was mentioned earlier, assembly language has no structure in the syntax to represent blocks of code. Although the specific operation of a line of assembly language should be clear to a programmer, its purpose within the program usually is not. It is therefore imperative to comment assembly language programs. In addition to the standard use of comments, comments in assembly language can be used to:

- show where functions or blocks of code begin and end;
- explain the order or selection of commands (e.g., where a shift left has replaced a multiplication by a power of two); or
- identify obscure values (e.g., that address 0378_{16} represents the data registers of the parallel port).

A comment is identified with a preceding semi-colon, ';'. All text from the semi-colon to the end of the line is ignored. This is much like the double-slash, "//", used in C++ or the quote used in Visual Basic to comment out the remaining text of a line. A comment may be alone in a line or it may follow the last necessary field of a line of code.

17.3 Assembly Language Directives

There are exceptions in an assembly language program to the opcode/operand lines described in the previous section. One of the primary exceptions is the *assembler directive*. Assembler directives are instructions to the assembler or the linker indicating how the program should be created. Although they have the same format as an assembly language instruction, they do not translate to object code. This section will only address a few of the available directives. Please refer to one of the resources listed at the end of this chapter for more information on the assembler directives used with the Intel 80x86.

17.3.1 SEGMENT Directive

One of the most important directives with respect to the final addressing and organization of the application is **SEGMENT**. This directive is used to define the characteristics and or contents of a segment. (See Chapter 16 for a description of segments and their use with the 80x86 processor.)

There are three main segments: the code segment, the data segment, and the stack segment. To define these segments, the assembly language file is divided into areas using the SEGMENT directive. The beginning of the segment is defined with the keyword SEGMENT while its end is defined using the keyword ENDS. Figure 17-2 presents the format and parameters used to define a segment.

```
label    SEGMENT     alignment    combine    'class'
           .            .
           .            .
           .            .
label    ENDS
```

Figure 17-2 Format and Parameters Used to Define a Segment

The *label* uniquely identifies the segment. The SEGMENT directive label must match the corresponding ENDS directive label.

The *alignment* attribute indicates the "multiple" of the starting address for the segment. For a number of reasons, either the processor or the operating system may require that a segment begin on an address that is divisible by a certain power of two. The align attribute is used to tell the assembler what multiple of a power of two is required. The following is a list of the available settings for alignment.

- BYTE – There is no restriction on the starting address.
- WORD – The starting address must be even, i.e., the binary address must end in a zero.
- DWORD – The starting address must be divisible by four, i.e., the binary address must end in two zeros.
- PARA – The starting address must be divisible by 16, i.e., the binary address must end in four zeros.
- PAGE – The starting address must be divisible by 256, i.e., the binary address must end in eight zeros.

The *combine* attribute is used to tell the linker if segments can be combined with other segments. The following is a list of a few of the available settings for the combine attribute.

- NONE – The segment is to be located independently of the other segments and is logically considered separate.
- PUBLIC or COMMON – The segment may be combined with other segments of the same name and class.
- STACK – Works like PUBLIC for stack segments.

The *class* attribute helps the assembler classify the information contained in the segment. This is important in order to organize the data, code, and other information that the linker will be partitioning into segments when it comes time to create the final application. Typical values are 'Data', 'Code', or 'Stack'. Note that the apostrophes are to be included as part of the attribute value.

17.3.2 .MODEL, .STACK, .DATA, and .CODE Directives

Instead of going to the trouble of defining the segments with the SEGMENT directive, a programmer may select a memory model. By defining the memory model for the program, a basic set of segment definitions is assumed. The directive **.MODEL** can do this. Figure 17-3 presents the format of the .MODEL directive.

```
.MODEL    memory_model
```

Figure 17-3 Format of the .MODEL Directive

Table 17-1 presents the different types of memory models that can be used with the directive. The memory models LARGE and HUGE are the same except that HUGE may contain single variables that use more than 64K of memory.

There are three more directives that can be used to simplify the definition of the segments. They are **.STACK**, **.DATA**, and **.CODE**. When the assembler encounters one of these directives, it assumes that it is the beginning of a new segment, the type being defined by the specific directive used (stack, data, or code). It includes everything that follows the directive in the same segment until a different segment directive is encountered.

The .STACK directive takes an integer as its operand allowing the programmer to define the size of the segment reserved for the stack.

Chapter 17: Intel 80x86 Assembly Language 381

The .CODE segment takes a label as its operand indicating the segment's name.

Table 17-1 Memory Models Available for use with .MODEL

Memory Model	Segment Definitions
TINY	Code, data, and, stack in one 64K segment
SMALL	One code segment less than or equal to 64K One data segment less than or equal to 64K
MEDIUM	Multiple code segments of any size One data segment less than or equal to 64K
COMPACT	One code segment less than or equal to 64K Multiple data segments of any size
LARGE	Multiple code segments of any size Multiple data segments of any size
HUGE	Multiple code segments of any size Multiple data segments of any size
FLAT	One 4 Gig memory space

17.3.3 PROC Directive

The next directive, **PROC**, is used to define the beginning of a block of code within a code segment. It is paired with the directive **ENDP** which defines the end of the block. The code defined between PROC and ENDP should be treated like a procedure or a function of a high-level language. This means that jumping from one block of code to another is done by calling it like a procedure.

```
label     PROC    NEAR or FAR
  .         .
  .         .
  .         .
label     ENDP
```

Figure 17-4 Format and Parameters Used to Define a Procedure

As with the SEGMENT directive, the labels for the PROC directive and the ENDP directive must match. The attribute for PROC is either

NEAR or FAR. A procedure that has been defined as NEAR uses only an offset within the segment for addressing. Procedures defined as FAR need both the segment and offset for addressing.

17.3.4 END Directive

Another directive, **END**, is used to tell the assembler when it has reached the end of *all* of the code. Unlike the directive pairs SEGMENT and ENDS and PROC and ENDP, there is no corresponding directive to indicate the beginning of the code.

17.3.5 Data Definition Directives

The previous directives are used to tell the assembler how to organize the code and data. The next class of directives is used to define entities that the assembler will convert directly to components to be used by the code. They do not represent code; rather they are used to define data or constants on which the application will operate.

Many of these directives use integers as their operands. As an aid to programmers, the assembler allows these integers to be defined in binary, decimal, or hexadecimal. Without some indication as to their base, however, some values could be interpreted as hex, decimal, or binary (e.g., 100). Hexadecimal values have an 'H' appended to the end of the number, binary values have a 'B' appended to the end, and decimal values are left without any suffix.

Note also that the first digit of any number must be a numeric digit. Any value beginning with a letter will be interpreted by the assembler as a label instead of a number. This means that when using hexadecimal values, a leading zero must be placed in front of any number that begins with A, B, C, D, E, or F.

The first of the defining directives is actually a set of directives used for reserving and initializing memory. These directives are used to reserve memory space to hold elements of data that will be used by the application. These memory spaces may either be initialized or left undefined, but their size will always be specified.

The primary form of these directives is **Dx** where a character is substituted for the 'x' to indicate the incremental size of memory that is being reserved. For example, a single byte can be reserved using the directive DB. Figure 17-5 presents some of the define directives and their format.

```
label    DB    expression    ;define a byte
label    DW    expression    ;define a word (2 bytes)
label    DD    expression    ;define a double word
label    DQ    expression    ;define a quad word
```

Figure 17-5 Format and Parameters of Some Define Directives

The label, which is to follow the formatting guidelines of the label field defined earlier, is not required. When it is used, the assembler assigns it the address corresponding to the next element of memory being reserved. The programmer may then use it throughout their code to refer back to that address.

The expression after the directive is required. The expression is used to tell the assembler how much memory is to be reserved and if it is to be initialized. There are four primary formats for the expression.

- Constants – The expression can be a list of one or more constants. These constants will be converted to binary and stored in the order that they were defined.
- String – The expression can be a string. The assembler will divide the string into its characters and store each character in the incremental space required by the selected define directive, i.e., DB reserves memory a byte at a time, DW reserves memory a word at a time, DD reserves memory a double word at a time, and DQ reserves memory a quad word at a time.
- Undefined – A question mark (?) can be used to tell the assembler that the memory is to be reserved, but left undefined.
- Duplicated elements – The keyword DUP may be used to replicate the same value in order to fill a block of memory.

Figure 17-6 presents some examples of the define directives where the comment field is used to describe what will be stored in the reserved memory.

17.3.6 EQU Directive

The next directive, **EQU**, is in the same class as the define directives. It is like the #define directive used in C, and like #define, it is used to define strings or constants to be used during assembly. The format of the EQU directive is shown in Figure 17-7.

```
VAR01   DB   23H          ;Reserve byte/initialized to
                          ;hexadecimal 23
VAR01   DB   10010110B    ;Reserve byte/initialized to
                          ;binary 10010110
VAR02   DB   ?            ;Reserve byte/undefined
STR01   DB   'hello'      ;Store 'h', 'e', 'l', 'l',
                          ;and 'o' in 5 sequential bytes
ARR01   DB   3, 2, 6      ;Store the numbers 3, 2, and 6
                          ;in 3 sequential bytes
ARR02   DB   4 DUP(?)     ;Reserve 4 bytes/undefined
ARR03   DW   4 DUP(0)     ;Reserve 4 words (8 bytes) and
                          ;initialize to 0
```

Figure 17-6   Example Uses of Define Directives

```
         label    EQU    expression
```

Figure 17-7   Format and Parameters of the EQU Directive

Both the label and the expression are required fields with the EQU directive. The label, which also is to follow the formatting guidelines of the label field, is made equivalent to the expression. This means that whenever the assembler comes across the label later in the file, the expression is substituted for it. Figure 17-8 presents two sections of code that are equivalent because of the use of the EQU directive.

```
ARRAY    DB    12 DUP(?)
```

a.) Reserving 12 bytes of memory without EQU directive

```
COUNT    EQU   12
ARRAY    DB    COUNT DUP(?)
```

b.) Reserving 12 bytes of memory using EQU directive

Figure 17-8   Sample Code with and without the EQU Directive

Note that EQU only assigns an expression to a name at the time of assembly. No data segment storage area is allocated with this directive.

17.4 80x86 Opcodes

Assembly language instructions can be categorized into four groups: data transfer, data manipulation, program control, and special operations. The next four sections introduce some of the Intel 80x86 instructions by describing their function.

17.4.1 Data Transfer

There is one Intel 80x86 opcode that is used to move data: **MOV**. As shown in Figure 17-9, the MOV opcode takes two operands, *dest* and *src*. MOV copies the value specified by the *src* operand to the memory or register specified by *dest*.

```
MOV     dest, src
```

Figure 17-9 Format and Parameters of the MOV Opcode

Both *dest* and *src* may refer to registers or memory locations. The operand *src* may also specify a constant. These operands may be of either byte or word length, but regardless of what they are specifying, the sizes of *src* and *dest* must match for a single MOV opcode. The assembler will generate an error if they do not.

Section 16.4 showed how the Intel 80x86 uses separate control lines for transferring data to and from its I/O ports. To do this, it uses a pair of special data transfer opcodes: **IN** and **OUT**. The opcode IN reads data from an I/O port address placing the result in either AL or AX depending on whether a byte or a word is being read. The OUT opcode writes data from AL or AX to an I/O port address. Figure 17-10 shows the format of these two instructions using the operand *accum* to identify either AL or AX and *port* to identify the I/O port address of the device.

```
IN      accum, port
OUT     port, accum
```

Figure 17-10 Format and Parameters of the IN and OUT Opcodes

None of the data transfer opcodes modifies the processor's flags.

17.4.2 Data Manipulation

Intel designed the 80x86 family of processors with plenty of instructions to manipulate data. Most of these instructions have two operands, *dest* and *src*, and just like the MOV instruction, they read from *src* and store in *dest*. The difference is that the *src* and *dest* values are combined somehow before being stored in *dest*. Another difference is that the data manipulation opcodes typically affect the flags.

Take for example the **ADD** opcode shown in Figure 17-11. It reads the data identified by *src*, adds it to the data identified by *dest*, then replaces the original contents of *dest* with the result.

```
ADD     dest, src
```

Figure 17-11 Format and Parameters of the ADD Opcode

The ADD opcode modifies the processor's flags including the carry flag (CF), the overflow flag (OF), the sign flag (SF), and the zero flag (ZF). This means that any of the Intel 80x86 conditional jumps can be used after an ADD opcode for program flow control.

Many of the other data manipulation opcodes operate the same way. These include logic operations such as **AND**, **OR**, and **XOR** and mathematical operations such as **SUB** (subtraction) and **ADC** (add with carry). **MUL** (multiplication) and **DIV** (division) are different in that they each use a single operand, but since two pieces of data are needed to perform these operations, the AX or AL registers are implied.

Some operations by nature only require a single piece of data. For example, **NEG** takes the 2's-complement of a value and stores it back in the same location. The same is true for **NOT** (bit-wise inverse), **DEC** (decrement), and **INC** (increment). These commands all use a single operand identified as *dest*.

```
NEG     dest        ;Take 2's complement of dest
NOT     dest        ;Invert each of the bits of dest
DEC     dest        ;Subtract 1 from dest
INC     dest        ;Add 1 to dest
```

Figure 17-12 Format and Parameters of NEG, NOT, DEC, and INC

As with most processors, the Intel 80x86 processor has a group of opcodes that are used to shift data. There are two ways to classify shift instructions: left versus right and arithmetic versus logical. The area where these classifications are of greatest concern is with a right shift.

Remember from Chapter 3 that left and right shifts are equivalent to multiplication and division by powers of two. When using a right shift to perform a division, the most significant bit must be replicated or the sign of a two's complement value might change from negative to positive. Therefore, if it is important to maintain the sign of a right-shifted value, an arithmetic shift right (**SAR**) should be used, not a logical shift right (**SHR**). Since a left shift doesn't have this constraint, an arithmetic shift left (**SAL**) and logical shift left (**SHL**) perform the same operation and are even identified with the same machine code.

All four of the shift commands use two operands. The first operand, *dest*, contains the data to be shifted. It is also the location where the result will be stored. The second operand, *count*, indicates the number of bit positions the piece of data will be shifted.

```
SAR     dest, count    ;Arithmetic shift right
SHR     dest, count    ;Logical shift right
SAL     dest, count    ;Arithmetic shift left
SHL     dest, count    ;Logical shift left
```

Figure 17-13 Format and Parameters of SAR, SHR, SAL, and SHL

17.4.3 Program Control

As with the generic processor described in Chapter 15, the 80x86 uses both unconditional and conditional jumps to alter the sequence of instruction execution. When the processor encounters an unconditional jump or "jump always" instruction (**JMP**), it loads the instruction pointer with the address that serves as the JMP's operand. This makes it so that the next instruction to be executed is at the newly loaded address. Figure 17-14 presents an example of the JMP instruction.

```
        JMP    LBL01        ;Always jump to LAB01
          :      :
LBL01:                      ;Destination for jump
```

Figure 17-14 Example of a JMP Instruction

The 80x86 has a full set of conditional jumps to provide program control based on the results of execution. Each conditional jump examines the flags before determining whether to load the jump opcode's operand into the instruction pointer or simply move to the next sequential instruction. Table 17-2 presents a summary of most of the 80x86 conditional jumps along with the flag settings that force a jump. (Note that "!=" means "is not equal to")

Table 17-2 Summary of 80x86 Conditional Jumps

Mnemonic	Meaning	Jump Condition
JA	Jump if Above	CF=0 and ZF=0
JAE	Jump if Above or Equal	CF=0
JB	Jump if Below	CF=1
JBE	Jump if Below or Equal	CF=1 or ZF=1
JC	Jump if Carry	CF=1
JE	Jump if Equal	ZF=1
JG	Jump if Greater (signed)	ZF=0 and SF=OF
JGE	Jump if Greater or Equal (signed)	SF=OF
JL	Jump if Less (signed)	SF != OF
JLE	Jump if Less or Equal (signed)	ZF=1 or SF != OF
JNA	Jump if Not Above	CF=1 or ZF=1
JNAE	Jump if Not Above or Equal	CF=1
JNB	Jump if Not Below	CF=0
JNBE	Jump if Not Below or Equal	CF=0 and ZF=0
JNC	Jump if Not Carry	CF=0
JNE	Jump if Not Equal	ZF=0
JNG	Jump if Not Greater (signed)	ZF=1 or SF != OF
JNGE	Jump if Not Greater or Equal (signed)	SF != OF
JNL	Jump if Not Less (signed)	SF=OF
JNLE	Jump if Not Less or Equal (signed)	ZF=0 and SF=OF
JNO	Jump if No Overflow	OF=0
JNS	Jump if Not Signed (signed)	SF=0
JNZ	Jump if Not Zero	ZF=0
JO	Jump if Overflow	OF=1
JPE	Jump if Even Parity	PF=1
JPO	Jump if Odd Parity	PF=0
JS	Jump if Signed (signed)	SF=1
JZ	Jump if Zero	ZF=1

Typically, these conditional jumps come immediately after a compare. In the Intel 80x86 instruction set, the compare function is **CMP**. It uses two operands, setting the flags by subtracting the second operand from the first. Note that the result is not stored.

The 80x86 provides an additional instruction over that of the generic processor discussed in Chapter 15. The **LOOP** instruction was added to support the operation of a for- or a while-loop. It takes as its only operand the address of the first instruction of the loop.

Before entering the loop, the CX register is loaded with a count of the number of times the loop is to be executed. Each time the LOOP opcode is executed, CX is decremented. As long as CX has not yet been decremented to zero, the instruction pointer is set back to the first instruction of the loop, i.e., the address given as the operand of the LOOP instruction. When CX has been decremented to zero, the LOOP instruction does not return to the beginning of the loop; instead, it goes to the instruction after LOOP. Figure 17-15 presents an example where the LOOP instruction executes a loop 25 times.

```
          MOV   CX,25      ;Load CX with the integer 25
LBL02:                     ;Beginning of loop
            :     :
          LOOP  LBL02      ;Decrement CX and jump to
                           ; LBL02 as long as CX!=0
```

Figure 17-15 Example of a LOOP Instruction

There is one last set of instructions used to control the flow of the program, and although they were not mentioned in Chapter 15, they are common to all processors. These instructions are used to call and return from a procedure or function.

The **CALL** opcode is used to call a procedure. It uses the stack to store the address of the instruction immediately after the CALL opcode. This address is referred to as the *return address*. This is the address that the processor will jump back to after the procedure is complete.

The CALL instruction takes as its operand the address of the procedure that it is calling. After the return address is stored to the stack, the address of the procedure is loaded into the instruction pointer.

To return from a procedure, the instruction **RET** is executed. The only function of the RET instruction is to pull the return address from the stack and load it into the instruction pointer. This brings control back to the original sequence. Figure 17-16 presents an example of the organization of a procedure call using the CALL and RET instructions.

```
        CALL PROC01   ;Procedure call to PROC01
        xxx           ;Instruction that is returned
                      ; to after procedure is called
            :
PROC01:               ;Beginning of procedure
            :
        RET           ;Return to instruction after
                      ; CALL
```

Figure 17-16 Sample Organization of a Procedure Call

17.4.4 Special Operations

The special operations category is for opcodes that do not fit into any of the first three categories, but are necessary to fully utilize the processor's resources. They provide functionality ranging from controlling the processor flags to supporting the 80x86 interrupt system.

To begin with, there are seven instructions that allow the user to manually alter the flags. These are presented in Table 17-3.

Table 17-3 80x86 Instructions for Modifying Flags

Mnemonic	Meaning
CLC	Clear Carry Flag
CLD	Clear Direction Flag
CLI	Clear Interrupt Flag (disables maskable interrupts)
CMC	Complement Carry Flag
STC	Set Carry Flag
STD	Set Direction Flag
STI	Set Interrupt Flag (enables maskable interrupts)

The next two special instructions are **PUSH** and **PULL**. These instructions operate just as they are described in chapters 15 and 16. The Intel 80x86 processor's stack is referred to as a post-increment/pre-decrement stack. This means that the address in the stack pointer is decremented before data is stored to the stack and incremented after data is retrieved from the stack.

There are also some special instructions that are used to support the operation of the Intel 80x86 interrupts. **IRET**, for example, is the instruction used to return from an interrupt service routine. It is used in the same manner as the RET instruction in a procedure. IRET, however, is required for interrupts because an interrupt on the 80x86 pushes not only the return address onto the stack, but also the code segment and processor flags. IRET is needed to pull these two additional elements off of the stack before returning to the code being executed before the interrupt.

Another special instruction is the software interrupt, **INT**. It is a non-maskable interrupt that calls an interrupt routine just like any hardware interrupt. In a standard PC BIOS, this interrupt has a full array of functions ranging from keyboard input and video output to file storage and retrieval.

The last instruction presented here may not make sense to the novice assembly language programmer. The **NOP** instruction has no operation and it does not affect any flags. Typically, it is used to delete a machine code by replacing it and its operands with this non-executing opcode. In addition, a sequence of NOPs can be inserted to allow a programmer to write over them later with new machine code. This is only necessary under special circumstances.

17.5 Addressing Modes

The previous section described the 80x86 opcodes and their operands. This section shows the format that the programmer needs to use to properly identify the operands. Specifically, the assembler needs to know whether the programmer is referring to a register, a constant, or a memory address. Special syntax is used to do just that.

17.5.1 Register Addressing

To identify a register as an operand, simply use the name of the register for either *src* or *dest*. For the 80x86 architecture described in Chapter 16, these registers include both the 8- and 16-bit general purpose registers (AX, BX, CX, DX, AL, AH, BL, BH, CL, CH, DL, and DH), the address registers (SP, BP, DI, SI, and IP), and the segment registers (CS, DS, SS, and ES). Figure 17-17 presents some examples of instructions using register addressing.

```
MOV   AL,BL         ;Copy the contents of BL to AL
CMP   BX,CX         ;Compare the contents of CX to
                    ; the contents of BX
INC   DX            ;Increment the contents of DX
```

Figure 17-17   Examples of Register Addressing

17.5.2 Immediate Addressing

The use of a constant as an operand is referred to as immediate addressing. In this case, a constant is used instead of a stored value such as that retrieved from a register or memory. As with the directives used to define constants in memory, hex, decimal, and binary values must be identified by appending an 'H' to the end of a hexadecimal number, appending a 'B' to the end of a binary number, and leaving the decimal values without any suffix.

Because of the nature of constants, they can only be used as the *src* operand. They reserve no space in the data segment, and therefore cannot have data stored to them. Figure 17-18 presents some examples of instructions using immediate addressing.

```
MOV   AX,67D1H      ;Place the hex value 67D1 in AX
CMP   BL,01101011B  ;Compare the contents of BL to
                    ; the binary value 01101011
ADD   CX,9          ;Add decimal 9 to CX
```

Figure 17-18   Examples of Immediate Addressing

17.5.3 Pointer Addressing

It might be misleading not to distinguish between the six different forms used to identify an address as an operand. This chapter, however, is only an introduction to assembly language. At this point it is sufficient to say that an operand is identified as an address by surrounding it with brackets []. For example, to make a reference to hexadecimal address 1000, the operand would be identified as [1000H].

Although the data segment identified by DS is the default segment when using an address as an operand, the segment may still be specified within this notation. By using a colon to separate the segment from the offset, any segment may be used. For example, to ensure that

Chapter 17: Intel 80x86 Assembly Language   393

the address 1000 was coming from the data segment, the operand would be identified as [DS:1000H].

The processor can also use the contents of a register as a pointer to an address. In this case, the register name is enclosed in brackets to identify it as a pointer. For example, if the contents of BX are being used as an address pointing to memory, the operand should be entered as [BX] or [DS:BX].

A constant offset can be added to the pointer if necessary by adding a constant within the brackets. For example, if the address of interest is 4 memory locations past the address pointed to by the contents of BX, the operand should be entered as [BX+4] or [DS:BX+4].

While this is not a comprehensive list of the methods for using a memory address as an operand, it should be a sufficient introduction. Figure 17-19 presents some examples of using addresses for operands.

```
MOV   AX,[6000H]    ;Load AX w/data from address 6000H
MOV   AX,[BX]       ;Load AX w/data pointed to by the
                    ; address contained in BX
MOV   AX,[BX+4]     ;Load AX w/data 4 memory locations
                    ; past address pointed to by BX
```

Figure 17-19 Examples of an Address being used as an Operand

17.6 Sample 80x86 Assembly Language Programs

Now we need to tie the concepts of assembly language presented in Chapter 15 to the specifics of the 80x86 assembly language. The best way to do this is to create a simple program. We begin with the general framework used to support the program. Figure 17-20 presents the basic skeleton code of an 80x86 assembly language program.

```
        .MODEL  SMALL
        .STACK  100H
        .DATA
        .CODE
MAIN    PROC    FAR

MAIN    ENDP
        END     MAIN
```

Figure 17-20 Skeleton Code for a Simple Assembly Program

394   Computer Organization and Design Fundamentals

Let's examine this code line-by-line.

- The first line contains the string ".MODEL SMALL". We see from Table 17-1 that this tells the compiler to use one code segment less than or equal to 64K and one data segment less than or equal to 64K. The program we are writing here is quite small and will easily fit in this memory model.
- The next line, ".STACK 100H", tells the instructor to reserve 256 bytes (hexadecimal 100) for the stack.
- The next line, ".DATA", denotes the beginning of the data segment. All of the data for the application will be defined between the .DATA and .CODE directives.
- The next line, ".CODE", denotes the beginning of the code segment. All of the code will be defined after this directive.
- "MAIN PROC FAR" identifies a block of code named main that will use both the segment and offset for addressing.
- "MAIN ENDP" identifies the end of the block of code named MAIN.
- "END MAIN" tells the assembler when it has reached the end of all of the code.

The next step is to insert the data definitions and code that go after the .DATA and .CODE directives respectively.

The first piece of code we need to write will handle some operating system house keeping. First, we need to start the program by retrieving the address that the operating system has assigned to the data segment. This value needs to be copied to the DS register. We do this with the two lines of code presented in Figure 17-21. These lines need to be placed immediately after the MAIN PROC FAR line.

```
MOV   AX,@DATA    ;Get assigned data segment
                  ; address from O/S
MOV   DS,AX       ;Copy it to the DS register
```

Figure 17-21 Code to Assign Data Segment Address to DS Register

When the program ends, we need to transfer control back to the operating system. This is done using a software interrupt. At this point it is not necessary to understand this process other than to say that when the O/S receives this interrupt, it knows that the application is finished and can be removed from memory. Placing the lines from Figure 17-22 immediately before the line MAIN ENDP in the code will do this.

```
MOV   AX,4C00H    ;Load code indicating normal
                  ; program termination
INT   21H         ;Call interrupt to end program
```

Figure 17-22   Code to Inform O/S that Program is Terminated

At this point, our skeleton code should look like that shown in Figure 17-23.

```
        .MODEL  SMALL
        .STACK  100H
        .DATA
        .CODE
MAIN    PROC    FAR
        MOV     AX,@DATA    ;Load DS with assigned
        MOV     DS,AX       ; data segment address

        MOV     AX,4C00H    ;Use software interrupt
        INT     21H         ; to terminate program
MAIN    ENDP
        END     MAIN
```

Figure 17-23   Skeleton Code with Code Added for O/S Support

Now all we need is a program to write. The program presented here is a simple mathematical calculation using data from the data segment. Specifically, we will be calculating the following algebraic expression where A, B, C, and RESULT are defined to be 16-bit words in the data segment.

$$RESULT = (A \div 8) + B - C$$

Let's begin by defining what the data segment is going to look like. Each of the variables, A, B, C, and RESULT, need to have a word-sized location reserved in memory for them. Since the first three will be used as inputs to the expression, they will also need to be initialized.

For the sake of this example, let's initialize them to 104_{10}, 100_{10}, and 52_{10} respectively. Since RESULT is where the calculated result will be stored, we may leave that location undefined. Figure 17-24 presents the four lines of directives used to define this memory.

```
A       DW      104
B       DW      100
C       DW      52
RESULT  DW      ?
```

Figure 17-24 Data Defining Directives for Example Code

This code will be inserted between the .DATA and .CODE directives of the code in Figure 17-23.

The next step is to write the code to compute the expression. Begin by assuming the computation will occur in the accumulator register, AX. The process will go something like this.

- Load AX with value stored at the memory location identified by A.
- Divide AX by eight using the arithmetic right shift instruction.
- After dividing AX, add the value stored at the memory location identified by B.
- After adding B to AX, subtract the value stored at the memory location identified by C.
- Lastly, store the result contained in AX to the memory location RESULT.

Converting this step-by-step sequence into assembly language results in the code presented in Figure 17-25.

```
MOV   AX,A          ;Load A from memory
SAR   AX,3          ;Divide A by 8
ADD   AX,B          ;Add B to (A/8)
SUB   AX,C          ;Subtract C from (A/8)+B
MOV   RESULT,AX     ;Store (A/8)+B-C to RESULT
```

Figure 17-25 Step-by-Step Example Operation Converted to Code

The last step is to insert this code after the two lines of code that load the data segment register but before the two lines of code that perform the program termination in Figure 17-23. Figure 17-26 presents the final program.

```
        .MODEL  SMALL
        .STACK  100H
        .DATA
A       DW      104
B       DW      100
C       DW      52
RESULT  DW      ?
        .CODE
MAIN    PROC    FAR
        MOV     AX,@DATA    ;Load DS with assigned
        MOV     DS,AX       ; data segment address
        MOV     AX,A        ;Load A from memory
        SAR     AX,3        ;Divide A by 8
        ADD     AX,B        ;Add B to (A/8)
        SUB     AX,C        ;Subtract C from (A/8)+B
        MOV     RESULT,AX   ;Store A/8+B-C to RESULT
        MOV     AX,4C00H    ;Use software interrupt
        INT     21H         ; to terminate program
MAIN    ENDP
        END     MAIN
```

Figure 17-26 Final Code for Example Assembly Language Program

17.7 Additional 80x86 Programming Resources

This chapter falls short of teaching 80x86 assembly language. It is meant to serve only as an introduction. There are a number of resources available both in print and on the web to learn more about programming the 80x86 in assembly language including:

- Abel, Peter, *IBM PC Assembly Language and Programming*, 5th ed., Prentice-Hall, 2001.
- Hyde, Randall, *The Art of Assembly Language*, No Starch Press, 2003. (Available on-line at http://webster.cs.ucr.edu/AoA/DOS/)
- *Intel(R) 186 Processor – Documentation*, Intel Corp., on-line, http://developer.intel.com/design/intarch/intel186/docs_186.htm.

17.8 What's Next?

Over the past seventeen chapters, I have tried to cover three main areas: representation and manipulation of numbers using digital logic, combinational logic and memory circuit design, and basic computer architecture. The intent of this book was never to make the reader a designer of hardware. Instead, the presentation of hardware was meant to provide the reader with well-established tools for logic design along with an understanding of the internals of the computer. The tools can be applied to software as well as hardware. The understanding of hardware can also be applied to software design allowing for improved performance of software applications.

This, however, is merely a beginning. What's the next step for you the reader? The answer to that question depends on what your interests are. At this point, you should have the foundation necessary to begin a deeper study of topics such as advanced computer architecture, embedded systems design, network design, compiler design, or microprocessor design. The possibilities are endless.

Problems

1. What character/symbol is used to indicate the start of a comment in assembly language for the assembler we used in class?

2. Which of the following four strings would make valid assembly language labels? Explain why the invalid ones are not allowed.

   ABC123   123ABC
   JUMP HERE   LOOP

3. Assume that the register BX contains 5680_{16} when the instruction **SAR BL,3** is executed. What would the new value of BL be?

4. Assuming that CX contains 0055_{16} when the instruction **DEC CH** is executed, what will CX contain and how will the flags CF, PF, SF, and ZF be set afterwards?

5. Below is a summary description of the 80x86 shift arithmetic left (SAL) instruction:

   Usage: SAL dest,count
   Modifies flags: CF OF PF SF ZF (AF undefined)
   Operation: Shifts the destination left by "count" bits with zeroes shifted in on right. The Carry Flag contains the last bit shifted out.

Assuming that AX contains 2345_{16} when the instruction SAL AH,2 is executed, what will AX contain and how will the flags CF, PF, SF, and ZF be set afterwards?

6. For each of the assembly language commands below, what is the binary value for the active low signals ^MRDC, ^MWTC, ^IORC, and ^IOWC.

		^MRDC	^MWTC	^IORC	^IOWC
mov	ah,[5674h]				
in	bh,1234h				
mov	[ax],bx				
out	4af5h,bh				

7. Assume the register BX contains the value 2000h and the table to the right represents the contents of a short portion of memory. Indicate what value AL contains after each of the following MOV instructions.

```
mov    al, ds:[bx]
mov    al, ds:[bx+1]
mov    ax, bx
mov    ax, 2003
```

Address	Value
DS:2000	17h
DS:2001	28h
DS:2002	39h
DS:2003	4Ah
DS:2004	5Bh
DS:2005	6Ch

8. Of the following jump instructions, indicate which ones will jump to the address LOOP, which ones will simply execute the next address (i.e., not jump), and which ones you don't have enough information to tell.

```
Instruction         Current Flag Settings
   je   loop        sf=0, zf=1, cf=0
   jl   loop        sf=1, zf=0
   jng  loop        sf=0, zf=1, of=0
   jne  loop        sf=0, zf=1, of=1
   jnb  loop        sf=1, zf=0, cf=0
   jmp  loop        sf=0, zf=0, of=0
   jge  loop        zf=0, sf=0, of=1
```

9. Modify the code in Figure 17-26 to calculate the expression $((4 \times A) + B - C) \div 32$ where $A = 41_{10}$, $B = 142_{10}$, and $C = 18_{10}$.

INDEX

A

accumulator register, 361
accuracy, 5
active-low signals, 151, 247
ADC. *See* analog-to-digital converter
adders, 141
    full, 144
    half, 141
address decoder, 243
address decoding, 250
address latch, 333
address lines, 245
addressing
    immediate, 392
    pointer, 392
    register, 391
addressing modes, 391
AF. *See* auxiliary carry flag
aliasing, 31
ALU. *See* arithmetic logic unit
analog, 3, 26
analog-to-digital converter, 6, 259
AND gate, 72, 73, 74, 90, 109, 114, 153
AND rules, 97, 98
application layer, 303
arithmetic logic unit, 360
arithmetic overflow, 67
arrays, 383
assembler, 375
assembler directive, 378
assembly language, 338, 339, 344
    comment field, 378
    instruction field, 377
    label field, 376

    operand field, 377
Associative Law, 95
auxiliary carry flag, 364
AX. *See* accumulator register

B

base address, 367
base pointer, 362
base register, 361
Basic Input/Output System, 245, 248, 261
BCD. *See* Binary Coded Decimal
BCD addition, 64
BEDO. *See* Burst EDO
binary addition, 43, 141
Binary Coded Decimal, 36
binary conversion, 23, 67
binary pulse, 9
binary signals, 8
binary subtraction, 45
binary system, 7
BIOS. *See* Basic Input/Output System
bit, 20, 17
bitwise operations, 166
    AND, 167
    OR, 171
    XOR, 171
BIU. *See* bus interface unit
boolean algebra, 89
    laws of, 95
    simplification, 101
BP. *See* base pointer
buffer, 329
Burst EDO, 266
bus, 244, 325
bus contention, 246

bus interface unit, 365
BX. *See* base register
byte, 20

C

cache
    block, 286, 290
    direct mapping, 290, 295
    fully associative mapping, 290, 295
    hit, 289
    L1, 285
    L2, 285
    line, 286
    mapping function, 290
    miss, 289
    set associative mapping, 290, 297
    size, 290
    split, 286
    tag, 286
    write back policy, 300
    write policy, 290, 299
    write through policy, 299
cache replacement algorithm, 290, 295
    First In First Out, 296
    Least Frequently Used, 296
    Least Recently Used, 296, 298
    Random, 296
capacitor, 262
carry flag, 364
CAV. *See* constant angular velocity
central processing unit, 332
CF. *See* carry flag
checksum, 175
    1's complement, 177

2's complement, 177
chip select, 242, 246, 256
clock, 210, 220
code segment, 369
collisions, 310
combinational logic, 80, 92
Commutative Law, 95
compiler, 375
conditional branching, 327, 388
configuration registers, 333
constant angular velocity, 281
constants, 383
control lines, 245
counter, 213
counter register, 362
CPU. *See* central processing unit
CRC. *See* cyclic redundancy check
crosstalk, 305, 308
CS. *See* code segment
CX. *See* counter register
cyclic redundancy check, 179
cylinder, 281

D

data buffer, 333
data lines, 244
data register, 362
data segment, 369
datagrams, 310
datalink layer, 304, 306, 308
datasum, 175
DDR SDRAM. *See* Double Data Rate SDRAM
decode cycle, 346, 370
decoders, 154
DeMorgan's Theorem, 104, 110, 119

Index 403

demultiplexers, 157
destination index, 363
DF. *See* direction flag
DI. *See* destination index
digital signal processing, 7
direct memory access, 356
direction flag, 363
directive. *See* assembler directive
Distributive Law, 96
divide-by-two circuit, 212
DMA. *See* direct memory access
don't cares, 137
Double Data Rate SDRAM, 267
double word, 20
DRAM. *See* Dynamic RAM
DS. *See* data segment
DSP. *See* digital signal processing
duty cycle, 13
DX. *See* data register
dynamic RAM, 262

E

EDO. *See* Extended Data-Out
encoding, 39
endian, big/little, 345
ES. *See* extra segment
Ethernet frame, 308
    CRC, 309
    data, 309
    destination address, 309
    filler bytes, 309
    length, 309
    preamble, 308
    source address, 309
    start delimiter, 309

EU. *See* execution unit
exclusive-OR gate, 74, 142
execute cycle, 346, 370
execution unit, 360
Extended Data-Out, 266
extra segment, 369

F

falling edge, 9, 203
Fast Page Mode, 265
fetch cycle, 346, 370
flags, 327, 360
floating-point, 58
formatting, 283
FPM. *See* Fast Page Mode
frame, 306
frequency, 12
frequency modulation, 272

G

Gray code, 39

H

Hamming Code, 188
header, 306
hexadecimal, 35
hexadecimal addition, 61
http, 313

I

IC. *See* integrated circuits
ICANN. *See* Internet Corporation for Assigned Names and Numbers
IEEE Std-754, 58
IEEE Std-802.3, 321, 304, 308
IEEE. *See* Institute of Electrical and Electronics Engineers
IF. *See* interrupt flag

Institute of Electrical and
   Electronics Engineers, 321
instruction pointer, 344, 362
instruction queue, 370
integrated circuits, 159
Intel assembly
   ADC, 386
   ADD, 386
   AND, 386
   CALL, 389
   clearing bits, 390
   CMP, 389
   DEC, 386
   DIV, 386
   IN, 385
   INC, 386
   INT, 391
   IRET, 391
   JMP, 387
   Jxx, 388
   LOOP, 389
   MOV, 385, 386
   MUL, 386
   NEG, 386
   NOP, 391
   NOT, 386
   OR, 386
   OUT, 385
   PULL, 390
   PUSH, 390
   RET, 389
   SAL, 387
   SAR, 387
   setting bits, 390
   SHL/SHR, 387
   SUB, 386
   XOR, 386
Intel directives
   .CODE, 380, 394
   .DATA, 380, 394
   .MODEL, 380
   .STACK, 380
   DB, DW, DD, DQ, 382
   DUP, 383
   END, 382, 394
   EQU, 383
   PROC, 381, 394
   SEGMENT, 378
Internet Corporation for
   Assigned Names and
   Numbers, 321
internet protocol, 307, 310
interrupt driven I/O, 354
interrupt flag, 363
interrupt service routine, 354
interrupts, 391, 394
intersector gap, 280
intertrack gap, 279
inverter, 72, 91, 205
I/O channels/processors, 356
I/O ports, 333, 371
IP. *See* instruction pointer or
   internet protocol
IP address, 169, 254
IP header
   address fields, 313
   fragment offset, 312
   header checksum, 312
   identification, 311
   length, 310
   options, 313
   padding, 313
   time to live, 312
   total length, 311
   type of service, 311
   version, 310
ISR. *See* interrupt service
   routine

K

Karnaugh map, 126
Karnaugh map rules, 131

L

latches
    D latch, 209, 223, 242, 262
    edge-triggered, 210
    S-R latch, 209
    transparent latches, 211
leakage current, 263
least significant bit, 20, 34, 165
LED. *See* light emitting diode
LIFO, 330
light emitting diode, 13, 147, 162
linker, 375
logic gates, 71
low level formatting, 283
LSB. *See* least significant bit

M

MAC address, 309, 321
machine code, 338
maximum, 55
Mealy machine, 237
memory
    address, 242
    asynchronous, 266
    cell, 203
    hierarchy, 269
    magnetic core, 241
    map, 248, 259, 352
    model, 380
    processor, 332
    space, 249
    synchronous, 267
    volatile, 245
minimum, 55

modified frequency modulation, 273
Moore machine, 237
most significant bit, 20
MP3, 7
MSB. *See* most significant bit
multiplexer, 156

N

NAND gate, 120, 160, 205, 256
NAND-NAND Logic, 119
negative-going pulse, 10
network interface card, 309
network layer, 304, 310, 313
next state truth table, 231
nibble, 20, 34
NIC. *See* network interface card
noise, 6
non-periodic pulse trains, 10
NOT gate. *See* inverter
NOT rule, 96
Nyquist Theorem, 33

O

object file, 375
OF. *See* overflow flag
offset address, 367
one's complement, 46
one's complement checksum/datasum, 176, 312, 319
Open Systems Interconnection Model, 303, 307
OR gate, 73, 74, 90, 109, 114
OR rules, 96
O/S level formatting, 283
OSI model. *See* Open Systems Interconnection Model
output truth table, 231

overflow flag, 364

P

packet, 306
Packetyzer, 321
parallel port, 214
parity, 174, 190, 193
parity flag, 364
partitioning, 283
pattern detection, 234
period, 11
periodic pulse trains, 11
PF. *See* parity flag
physical address, 368
physical layer, 304
pipelining, 347
platter, 270
polling, 353
POS. *See* product-of-sums
positive-going pulse, 10
powers of 2, multiplication and division by, 65
preamble, 306
precedence, 92
prefix, 15
presentation layer, 303
principle of locality, 285
processor status register, 327
product-of-sums, 114
program counter, 344
protocol, 306
protocol analyzer, 321
protocol stack, 307
pull-up resistors, 163
pulses, 9, 11

Q

queuing time, 275

R

RAM. *See* Random Access Memory
RAM cache, 285
random access memory, 260
read enable, 242
read only memory, 261
read-write head, 270
refresh circuitry, 263
register, 300, 326, 360
registered ports, 313
request for comments, 320
return address, 389
RFC. *See* request for comments
rising edge, 9, 203
ROM. *See* Read Only Memory
rotational latency, 275, 276
roundoff error, 31
run length limited, 273

S

sampling, 5, 6, 31
SDRAM. *See* Synchronous DRAM
sectors, 279
seek time, 275
segment, 369
    addressing, 366, 367
    registers, 366
Self-Monitoring Analysis and Reporting Technology, 278
sequential access, 278
session layer, 303
seven-segment display, 147
SF. *See* sign flag
SI. *See* source index
sign bit, 50
sign flag, 364
signed magnitude, 51, 56

SMART. *See* Self-Monitoring Analysis and Reporting Technology
SOP. *See* sum-of-products
source index, 363
SP. *See* stack pointer
SRAM. *See* static RAM
SS. *See* stack segment
stack, 330
    pointer, 362
    segment, 369
state, 217
state diagram, 218
    errors, 222
    reset condition, 221, 226
    transitions, 218, 222, 226
state machine, 217, 222
static RAM, 262
strings, 383
substrate, 270
sum-of-products, 109, 125, 129, 153
switch circuit, 163
Synchronous DRAM, 267

T

TCP. *See* transmission control protocol
TCP header
    acknowledgement, 315
    checksum field, 315
    control bits, 315
    data offset, 315
    destination port, 314
    option field, 316
    sequence number, 314
    source port, 314
    urgent pointer field, 316
    window field, 315

TCP ports, 313
TF. *See* trap flag
thrashing, 295
timing diagram, 79
track, 279
trailer, 306, 307
transfer time, 275, 276
transistors, 7
transmission control protocol, 307, 313
transport layer, 303, 310, 313
trap flag, 363
tristate output, 247
truth table, 75, 83, 110, 112, 115, 118, 126
two's complement, 47

U

undefined values, 204
unsigned binary, 17, 55

W

Winchester head, 272, 279
word, 20
write enable, 242

X

XOR compare, 173
XOR gate. *See* exclusive-OR
XOR subtraction, 182

Z

ZBR. *See* zone bit recording
zero flag, 364
ZF. *See* zero flag
zone bit recording, 282

ABOUT THE AUTHOR

David Tarnoff is an assistant professor in the Computer and Information Sciences Department at East Tennessee State University where he teaches computer hardware, embedded system design, and web technologies. He holds a bachelors and masters of science in electrical engineering from Virginia Tech. In 1999, David started Intermation, Inc., a business that develops software for remote data collection and automation. His research interests include embedded system design and the application of web technologies to teaching and research. David lives in Tennessee with his wife and their son.

NOTE TO THE READER

This textbook was developed after years of teaching computer organization to students of computer science. It incorporates the feedback from hundreds of students and dozens of faculty members and industry professionals. The success of this textbook is a direct result of its users. Therefore, it is important that there always be a direct link between the author and the readers. Please send any feedback you have regarding errors, updates to the material, or suggestions for new material to tarnoff@etsu.edu.

In addition, one of the purposes of this book is to put the concepts of computer organization into the hands of anyone who wants to learn about the topic. As a result, electronic versions of this book should be freely downloadable from the Internet. If you cannot find a version for download, please e-mail the author at tarnoff@etsu.edu, and you will be directed to the proper resources.

Thank you for supporting this work.